Arkansas Pensioners

1818-1900

Records of Some Arkansas Residents
Who Applied to The Federal Government
for Benefits Arising from Service
in Federal Military Organizations
(Revolutionary War, War of 1812, Indian
and Mexican Wars)

Compiled
by
Dorothy E. Payne

Please direct all correspondence and orders to:

www.southernhistoricalpress.com
or
SOUTHERN HISTORICAL PRESS, Inc.
PO BOX 1267
375 West Broad Street
Greenville, SC   29601
southernhistoricalpress@gmail.com

ISBN #0-89308-537-5

```
******************************************

            DEDICATED

               IN

           MEMORY OF

         PAUL McELHANON

         31 DECEMBER 1905
           2 JUNE 1982

******************************************
```

100°   99°   98°   97°   96°

38°

Arkansas R.

M

S   S   O   U   R

Negracka or Red Fork

Strong Saline

R.

37°

Saline Cr.

Neosho or Grand

Nembetonon or Grand Saline

T   E   R   R   I   T   O   R

Clermos Band

36°

O   S   A   G

Verdigris R.

Cav Sal.

Arkansa River

North Fork of Canadian R.

Little North Fork

35°

Canadian River

Dryden R.

Falls

South Fork of Canadian R.

Cavant

34°

C   H   O   C   T   A   W

False Washita River

Blue Water River

Pawnee Villages

O

Bayou R.

33°

Rio Roxo or Red River

S   P   A   N   I   S   H

Poso Lacre Cr.

T

S

P

A

N

I

S

H

T

I

S

H

32°

23°   22°   21° West Longitude   20° from Washington   19°

Drawn a

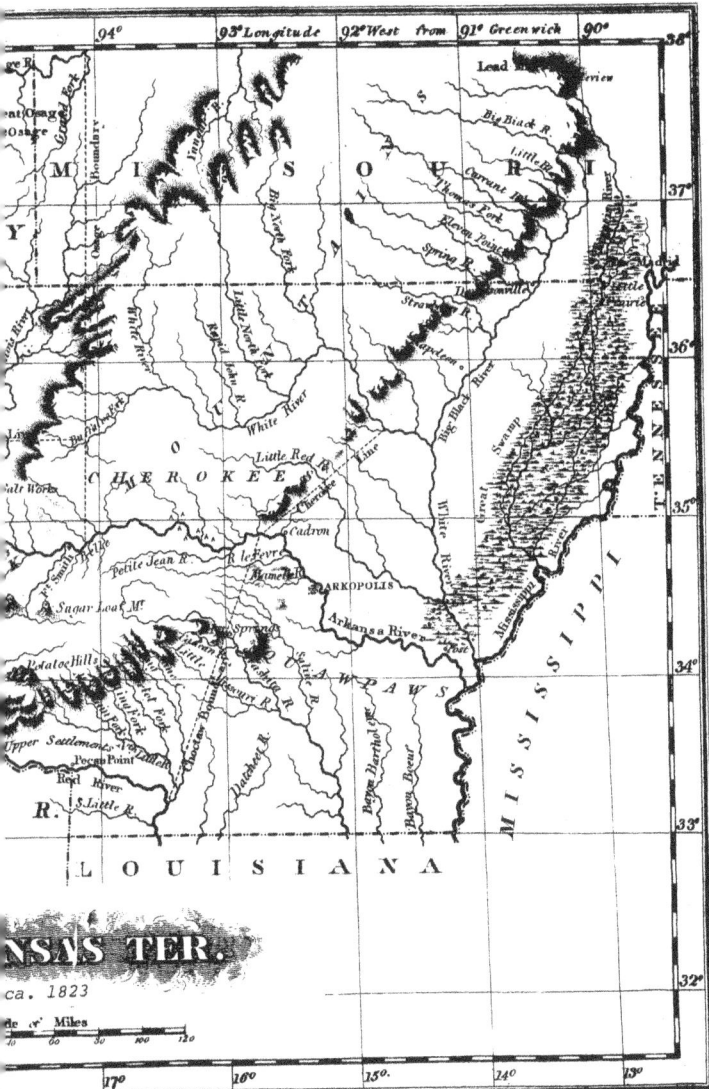

MISSOURI

CHEROKEE

QUAPAWS

LOUISIANA

MISSISSIPPI

TENNE.

94°   93° Longitude   92° West   from   91° Greenwich   90°

38°
37°
36°
35°
34°
33°
32°

Lead

Big Black R.
Little R.
Thomas Fork
Currant
Eleven Point
Spring R.
Strawberry
Little North Fork
Big North Fork
White River
Buffalo R.
Little Red R.
Line
Cherokee
Cadron
White River
Big Black River
Great Swamp River
St. Louis
Little Rock

ARKOPOLIS
Arkansa River
Post

Petite Jean R.
R. le Fevre
Mamele
Hot Springs
Little
Poteau R.

Potatoe Hills
Sugar Loaf Mt.
Kiamesha R.
Boggy
Upper Settlements
False Washita
Pecan Point
Red River
S. Little R.
Bayou Bartholomew
Bayou Bœuf

R.

ARKANSAS TER.

ca. 1823

Miles

17°   16°   15°   14°   13°

Published by F. Lucas Jr.

B.T. Welch & Co.

PREFACE

The Ledgers of Payments, Military Service Records, Military
Pension Applications and the Original Muster Rolls, that I have
used to compile this volume are all stored in the National Archives.

The pension applications are arranged by war then alphabetically
by soldier's name. Copies may be obtained by mail by writing
to: Reference Services Branch, General Services Administration,
Washington, D.C. 20408, for NATF form 26.

The War of 1812, Indian Wars and Mexican War Pension Applications
are well defined, however, the Old War Pension Applications
are not as easily understood. Essentially, the Old War Applications
were claims for benefits because of death or disability, during
the above named wars. Many of those claims have now been placed
in the respective files, and are cross indexed.

Some soldiers, who served in some of the Indian Wars and the
Mexican War, also served in the American Civil War. That service
often resulted in benefits, thereby resulting in another cross
filing of said application. I have not included any Civil War
Records in this book, as the object has been to try to close
a gap left between the time that Arkansas became a state and
the 1850 census.

In applying for copies of applications, it is important to include
the REMARKS information, as that is usually the indication that
a cross filing has occurred, and is sometimes an indication
that the information is not yet available.

Beginning on page 157, the muster rolls of the Arkansas Volunteers
who served in the Indian Wars of 1836, have been abstracted
and alphabetized. The soldiers were payed for travel from place
of residence to the rendezvous, so the residence has been included
in this volume. These names are not included in the index at
the back of this book.

On page 170 the complete muster rolls of those soldiers who
served in the 1st Regiment of Arkansas Mounted Volunteers, commanded
by Colonel Archibald Yell and Colonel John Seldon Roane, the
muster rolls of the Battalion of Arkansas Volunteers commanded
by Lt. Colonel William Gray, and the rolls of the companies
of Captain Gaston Meares and Captain Stephen Enyart during the
Mexican War are included. I have taken the information from
the original muster rolls, which are not available by mail. The
service records that are obtainable by mail, are compiled information
taken from these muster rolls and other sources. The names in
this section are not included in the index at the back of the
book.

The County Court Records and the Federal Census Records that
are included, may or may not be of value to the researcher,
however, in most instances there is enough coincidence to suggest
some investigation.

All of the sources used in this book are original, therefore
the spelling, etc. are subject to question. The mistakes, that
are found in this volume, are human error.

AARON,THOMAS-War of 1812 pension Application W.O.#26727 W.C.#29104; B.L.W.#13829-160-12. Married Susanna V. Smith 19 March 1818 at Cairnesville, Franklin County, Georgia. Service in Captain Farrar's Company of 8th U.S. Infantry from 1 June 1813 to 4 March 1815. Soldier died 2 May 1864 at Spring Hill, Arkansas. Application of Susanna Aaron, aged 75, of Boughton, Nevada County, Arkansas dated 10 June 1878. Original discharge of Thomas Aaron, dated 4 March 1815 and signed by Captain Farrar, enclosed in this application.

AARON,WILLIAM-Revolutionary War Pension Application #W10287, B.L.W. #67675-160-55. Application dated 9 October 1832 Franklin County, Georgia, William Aaron aged 79. Enlisted in the 10th Regtiment of the Virginia Line in January 1777 in Amherst County, Virginia. He was stricken with measles after a march to New Jersey. After his recovery, he joined Headquarters at Germantown, Pennsylvania, but suffered a relapse of measles. Marriage certificate of William Aaron and Rebecca Rudd, dated 3 November 1829 at Cairnesville, Franklin County, Georgia, included in this application. William Aaron died in the Fall of 1841.

ADAIR,JAMES-War of 1812 pension application W.O.#30023, W.C.#15156 B.L.W. #97099-40-50 and #94917-120-55. Service in Captain Norton's Company of South Carolina Militia from 1 February 1815 to 24 March 1815. Married Sarah Sharp 10 March 1828 in Pickens County, South Carolina. Soldier died in De Kalb County, Alabama 8 August 1850. Application of Sarah Adair dated 6 July 1878 Sharp County, Arkansas she stated that her husband was born in 1795 in Pickens County, South Carolina, that she moved to Sharp County in 1866. Her age stated as 77 years old. Affidavit by John K. Adair, relationship not stated. Sarah Adair died 5 November 1884 in Sharp County, Arkansas.
1850 Federal Census, De Kalb County, Alabama, page 328; James Adair 55 S.C., Sarah 48 N.C., Margaret 19 S.C., James 15 S.C., Charlotte 11 Tenn., Julia A. 9 Ala., Perlina 6 Ala., Mary M. 3 Ala.

ADAMS,ENOCH-Old war pension application dated June 1880 Arkansas. Service in Captain Watt's Alabama Volunteers, Creek War. Inv. App. #20132, no certificate number. (not abstracted, the lack of certificate number indicates that no pension was granted)

ADAMS,FRANCIS-Revolutionary War Pension Application #W5198. He was born 24 November 1763, place not stated. He was living in the Waxhaw Settlement, which later became Lancaster District, South Carolina, when he entered service, about July 1778. He served under Captains Henry Coffee, Marshall Jones and James Montgomery, in the South Carolina Troops. He served at the Battles of Rocky Mount, Black River, Hanging Rock, Wright's Bluff, Four Holes, Grandy's Fort and the Siege of Charleston. He was discharged in November 1781. Francis Adams was married to Mrs. Mary Ryan, who was the daughter of William Farrell, in Lancaster District, South Carolina on 27 November 1817. He is referred to as Captain Francis Adams in the marriage certificate. He applied for pension 18 December 1832 in the 2nd District, Henry County, Georgia. By 1843, he had moved to Macon, Noxubee County, Mississippi, where he died 12 September 1846. Widow's application dated 22 July 1853, Union County, Arkansas, Mary Adams, age 68, stated that she had moved to Union County, Arkansas about the year 1850.

ADCOCK,WILLIAM-War of 1812 pension application W.O.#31588, W.C.#5963. B.L.W.#65637-40-50 and #12344-120-55. Service in Captain Reynold's Company of Tennessee Militia from 4 October 1813 to 4 January 1814. Married Jane Wadley 20 May 1819 in Rutherford County, Tennessee. Application dated 24 March 1855 Maury County, Tennessee, William Adcock aged 63, entered service at age 18 and was born in Granville County, North Carolina. Soldier died

12 February 1865 in Clark County, Arkansas, widow died 16 June
1884 in Point Cedar, Arkansas. L.S. Adcock, son, living in Clark
County, Arkansas.
Clark County, Ark. Probate Court Record Book G page 196, settlement
of estate of William Adcock:Jane Adcock administrator; dated
23 November 1868. Clark County marriage records; Roby Adcock
and Martha Hadley, Book D page 160, dated 29 Apr 1860; Tenard
Adcock and Sarah Ashbrook, Book D page 36, dated 29 Oct 1857;
William F. Adcock and Mary Malin Book D page 34, dated 18 Oct
1857.

AKINS,WILLIAM-Revolutionary War Pension Application #W5600,
dated 5 November 1832, Morgan County, Georgia. William Akins
was born in Cecil County, Maryland in 1756. When he first entered
service he was living in Mecklinburgh County, North Carolina. He
married Elizabeth McCorkle 4 March 1784 in Mecklinburgh County
and stated that he lived "upwards of 30 years in York District,
South Carolina and 13 years in Morgan County, Georgia." Application
for transfer of pension to Benton County, Alabama dated 10 March
1840 to be near his son, not named however John L. Akins gives
affirmation to his statements. William Akins died in Benton
County, Alabama 25 May 1842, widow Elizabeth applied for pension
in Cherokee County, Alabama in May 1844.

AKINS,WILLIAM-War of 1812 pension application W.O.#6575, W.C.#3755.
B.L.W.#74661-40-50 and #86507-120-55. Service in Captain Turner's
Company of South Carolina Militia from 26 November 1814 to 3
March 1815. Married Vilet Chastain 7 August 1811 in Greenville,
Greenville County, South Carolina. William Akins settled in
Bradley County, Arkansas in 1845 and died there 2 March 1866. Widow
applied for pension in Bradley County in 1871. Copy of family
record enclosed in this application, to wit; "William Akins
was born 17 Dec 1790, Vilet Akins, wife of William Akins was
born 14 Sept 1798, Benjamin Akins, son of William Akins and
Vilet Akins, was born 27 Jan 1815, Fatima Akins was born 21
Dec 1818".
1850 Fed. Census, Bradley County, Ark. page 103 William Aiken
age 60 bn Ga., Violet age 53 bn S.C., James age 25 bn Ala.,
William age 20 bn Ala., Henry age 18 bn Ala., Jasper age 16
bn Ala., Mary age 8 bn Ala., Elenor Tidwell age 19 bn Ala.;
page 94 Benjamin Aiken age 34 bn S.C., Gincy P.(?) age 39 bn
Ga., Amanda Dean age 4/12 bn Ark., Peter Tidwell age 76 bn S.C.,
Polly Tidwell age 66 bn Ga.

ALBARTY/ALBERTY,FREDERICK-Revolutionary War Pension Application
#W3749. B.L.W.#26841-160-55. Application dated 12 August 1819,
Surry County, North Carolina, Frederick Alberty aged 78, stated
that he held the rank of Ensign in a company commanded by Captain
Joseph Philips of the 4th North Carolina Regiment commanded
by Colonel Thomas Polk. He served at the Battles of Germantown
and Brandywine. Application dated 16 August 1820, Frederick
Alberty stated that his family consisted of his wife and four
children, vis; Frederick age 14, James age 12, Andrew age 10,
David age 7. Marriage bond for Frederick Alberty and Elizabeth
Rafer filed in Surry County, North Carolina 29 March 1788. Register
of births of children of Elizabeth and Frederick Alberty contained
in this application, to wit; "Jesse Alberty born 27 Dec 1788;
Nancy Alberty born 28 Feb 1791; Juda Alberty born 30 June 1793;
John Alberty born 18 July 1795; Franky Alberty born 30 Sept
1797; Polly Alberty born 7 Dec 1801; Frederick Alberty born
12 Mar 1804; James Alberty born 14 May 1807; Andrew Alberty
born 3 Dec 1809; David Alberty born 3 Sept 1812. One statement
made that Frederick Alberty had been married twice before and
had other children, one of whom was named Moses. Frederick Alberty
died in Surry Co., N.C. 29 August 1827.

ALBERTY,JOHN-War of 1812 pension application W.O.#11309 W.C.#28522.

B.L.W.#65698-40-50 and #65769-120-55. Service in Captain Jack
Witcher's Company in General Adkerson's Brigade of North Carolina
Militia. Enlisted at Surry County, North Carolina 28 November
1814, discharged at Norfolk, Virginia 22 February 1815. Family
data contained in this application all suspect, possibly due
to lack of literacy.; John Alberty and Mary Wright were married
10 September 1814 at Hickory Log in Cherokee County, Georgia
in the custom of the Cherokee Indians, she being Cherokee. They
had six children including Moses, who would have been sixty
had he been living in 1875. Son, John W., age 51 in 1875, daughter
Franky Thornton, age 57 in 1875. Also mention of son Jack (John?).
Mention of Henry Alberty, brother of soldier John Alberty, who
has a son named Samuel. Mention of Sarah Jane Alberty born 23
February 1833, relationship not specified. Mary Wright was the
daughter of Jack Wright and the sister of Rebecca Bryan. In
his application dated 14 February 1851, John Alberty stated
that his age was 58. In 1875 Mary Alberty stated that her age
was 84. Statement made that John Alberty had written to his
parents, who were residing in Surry County, North Carolina,
about his marriage to Mary Wright.
1850 Federal Census-Vineyard Township, Washington County, Arkansas;
page 423-Samuel Alberty, 44 bn N.C., Sarah, 34 bn Ten., Henry,20
bn Ark, John, 17 bn Ark, Levi, 16 bn Ark, Eliza, 14 bn Ark,
Andrew, 6 bn Ark, Samuel, 4 bn Ark, Mary, 2 bn Ark, Andrew Agnew,
67 bn N.C.; page 425-George Alberty, 39 bn Geo., Eveline, 24
bn Ten., Emerellus, 5 bn Ark., Luella, 2 bn Ark., Henry Alberty,
20 bn Ark.; page 426-Daniel Alberty, 39 bn N.C., Nancy, 13 bn
Ga., George, 10 bn Ark., John H. Alberty, 78 bn N.C., Rebecca,
68 bn N.C., Mary, 24 bn N.C.
Washington County, Ark., Direct Deed Index, Vol. A; Book F page
479 dated 4 Aug 1849, George Alberty to D.W. Hannals.; Book
H page 312, Andrew Agnew to James Thompson; Book J page 311,
John Alberty to John Newman dated 17 Jun 1854; Book D page 57
dated 5 Sept 1840, George Bilton to George Alberty.

ALEXANDER,ALFRED S.-Old war pension application; Inv. Cert. #3302
File #24890. Service in Captain Allen's Company of Tennessee
Volunteers, Mexican War. (not abstracted.)

ALLEN,JAMES-Old war pension application Inv. Cert. #7750 File
24889, filed 1853, Arkansas. Service in Taylor's Arkansas
Cavalry, Mexican War. (not abstracted)

ALLEN,JOSIAH-Old war pension application dated 1885 Arkansas. Pension
granted to Andrew Lafayette Allen. O.W. Minors App. #22845 Cert.
#4174 File #12067. (not abstracted)

ALLEN,WILLIAM-War of 1812 pension application S.O.#29010 S.C.#21070.
B.L.W.#26315-160-12. Service in Captain Charles Humphrey's Company
of 41st U.S. Infantry from 18 December 1813 to 31 May 1815. He
enlisted near Mount Holley State of New Jersey and was discharged
in New York. He was born in 1770 in New Jersey, married to Sarah
Williams 15 April 1838 in Caldwell County, Kentucky. She died
in 1871, place not stated. Application dated 22 March 1873,
Pine Bluff, Jefferson County, Arkansas, William Allen stated
that he was 103 years old. His original discharge certificate
is in this brief. Only child mentioned, Georgia Montena. William
Allen died 1 October 1879, National Military Home, Ohio.

ALTON,SYLVESTER-Old war pension survivors application #23154
Cert.#3012 File #2901 Mexican Widows #3730. Sylvester Alton
served in Company D 1st United States Dragoons in the Mexican
War. This is a voluminous application file, much of it pertaining
to a special investigation by Federal Pension Agents. Sylvester
Alton married Alice White 10 September 1846 at Ft. Smith, Arkansas.
She was a sixteen year old Cherokee girl and stated that she
did not know if there was an official record of that marriage.

Sylvester and Alice had 9 children, only one of whom was living in 1889. Six of the children had died before the Civil War and two of them had died after the war. During the Civil War, Sylvester had "fled to the North" when the Rebels were near. After the Rebels had been run out of Indian Territory, Sylvester returned and took Alice and their two children to Kansas. After the war was over, they then returned to Ft. Gibson, Indian Territory. Sylvester then applied for and was granted a pension on his service in the Mexican War. Sylvester died 13 March 1886 and Alice was granted a Widow's Pension. On 8 November 1888, the Commissioner of Pensions in Washington, D.C. received a letter, written by "John Curran" which stated that Alice Alton was receiving her pension under a fraudulent declaration. The ensuing investigation revealed that the letter had been written by "John Crane",(apparently an alias) postmaser at Harris, Indian Territory, in an apparent retaliation against a member of Alice Alton's family. After "John Crane" had made an attempt to break into the home of Alice Alton, her son-in-law, Eugene L. Bracken took her into his home for safety. Much of the investigation centered around a man named August Kensing, who had been in the employe of "John Crane". When Kensing had become ill and unable to work, he had been "thrown out". Alice had taken the man, Kensing, into her home until he had regained his strength. She and her son-in-law then hired Kensing to erect a brick wall around the graves of Sylvester Alton and the deceased children. After the completion of his work, Kensing had moved on. Alice's pension was restored until 7 June 1891, when she remarried. The marriage record enclosed and granted "under the intermarriage law of the Cherokee Nation, to Lester Schneider, a white man and Mrs. Alice Alton, a Cherokee Indian Woman". Lester Schneider was born in France, served in the Mexican-American war and in the American Civil War in Company E, 2nd Regiment of Indian Home Guards. He was an "adopted citizen of the Cherokee Nation". He had previously been married to Maria___?, whom he had divorced in May 1891. Lester Schneider died 1 January 1894 and was buried at the U.S. National Cemetery at Ft. Gibson, Indian Territory, in Sec 3 number 2451. Alice then applied for pension on his Civil War service record, but was rejected and advised to reapply on his service in the Mexican War. A partial Bible record is enclosed in this application, to wit, "Sylvester Alton was born 14 August 1820; Alice Alton was born 31 December 1830; Cornelia Alton was born 4 August __?(torn page); Benjamin F. Alton was born 24 April 1852; Mary Alton was born 6 September 1861". In 1889, Rachel Brown age 19, stated that she was a niece of Alice Alton, and apparently lived with her.

ANDERSON,JAMES B.-War of 1812 pension application S.O.#19516 S.C.#13100, W.O.#14399, W.C.#30910. Service in Captain Alexander Hill's Company of Tennessee Militia from 13 November 1814 to 13 May 1815. B.L.W.#1911-80-50 and #39587-80-55. Married Mary Cypert 9 July 1812 in Warren County, Tennessee. In 1850, they resided in Wayne County, Tennessee, but moved to Izard County, Arkansas about that same year. In 1871 soldier was in Stone County, Arkansas and died there 16 July 1875. Widow, Mary applied for pension in 1878 at Mountain View, Stone County, Arkansas. Complete family record enclosed in this application, to wit;"James B. Anderson was born 16 August 1792, Mary Anderson was born 1792, we was married 9 July 1812, Betsey Anderson was bornd the 10th day of June 1813, Bartlett Anderson was bornd 26 October 1814, Matilda Anderson was bornd 14 August 1816, Robert Anderson was bornd 19 September 1818, William Anderson was bornd 14 January 1820, Ebeline Anderson was bornd 30 January 1822, Abigail Anderson was bornd 19 November 1824, George Anderson was bornd 25 March 1826, Passans Anderson was bornd 18 October 1827, James Anderson was bornd 5 October 1829, Mary Anderson was bornd 23 May 1832, John Anderson was bornd 4 July 1833, Martin V. Anderson was bornd 2 May 1841" Martin Anderson is identified as the nephew of James Anderson. In 1879, the whereabouts of the children

of James and Mary was listed as follows; Betsey, Matilda and Passans dead, Bartlett living in Texas, Robert in Mississippi, William and John in Izard County, Arkansas, Ebeline Gower in Missouri, Abigail Martin in Stone County, Arkansas, James in Boone County, Arkansas, and Mary Gower in Stone County, Arkansas. Federal Census Record-1850 Wayne County, Tenn. page #325 family #833; James B. Anderson 58 Virginia; Mary 58 Tenn.; James 22 Tenn.; Mary 17 Tenn.; John 13 Tenn.; Martin 7 Tenn.; Nancy 18.; Tenn.; Robert Cypert 95 N.C. pensioner.
Revolutionary War Pension Application of Robert Seypeart/Scypeart, #S39066; He was born 5 September 1755. Enlisted at Chatham Court House, Chatham County, North Carolina on 15 May 1776. Served as Sergeant in Captain James Emmett's Company, Colonel Jethro Sumner's Regiment of North Carolina Militia. He was at the Battles of Germantown, Brandywine and Monmouth. Discharged 31 October 1778. Pension application dated 26 December 1820, Wayne County, Tennessee, at which time his family consisted of; wife, Isabelle, age 57; daughter, Abigail, age 21; and son, Robert, age 18.

ANDERSON,PICKNEY-Old war pension application, Inv. Cert. #4221 File #24453. Service in 12th U.S. Infantry, Mexican War. Filed 1846 in Arkansas. (not abstracted)

ANGEL,LAWRENCE/ANGELL,LAURENCE-Revolutionary War Pension Application #S31519, dated 12 November 1832 in Johnson County, Indiana, claimant age 72. Entered service in July 1776 in Major Shepherd's Company of Colonel Joseph William's Regiment in Surry County, North Carolina. Marched over the mountains and crossed the Holston River to and against the Cherokee Indians at a place known as "The Over Hill Tovens"(?) In 1778, he served under the command of Colonel Hampton, at which time he marched from Surry County, North Carolina to Charleston, South Carolina to repel a threatened attack by the British. In August 1780 entered service in a Regiment of Mounted Riflemen, whereupon he was appointed Issuing Commissary, and was at Kings Mountain. In May of 1781, he served under command of Colonel Melmada, in an effort to prevent the British, who had taken possession of Charleston, South Carolina, from spreading "over the country". He served in 1781, in Wilmington, North Carolina, "to dislodge a detachment left by Lord Cornwallis". Lawrence Angel was born in Surry County, North Carolina in 1760, where he lived until 1812 when he resided in Kentucky and Tennessee, from there to Minerva Township, Johnson County, Indiana. In 1834, his pension was transferred from Indiana to Independence County, Territory of Arkansas. He died in Jefferson County, Missouri 25 November 1836. Sons James and Jesse received the balance of the account. James and Polly Angel of Independence County, Arkansas give affirmation of claimant.

ARMSTRONG,SOLOMON-War of 1812 pension application S.O.#16683 S.C.#17027. B.L.W.#38777-40-50 and #81157-120-55. Service in Captain Atkinson's Company of Kentucky Militia from 24 August 1813 to 9 November 1813. Married Anne Doss in 1810 in Cumberland County, Kentucky. He enlisted in service in Adair County, Kentucky. In April 1855 he was in Smith County, Texas and on 13 May 1871, he was living at the farm of his son (not named) in Benton County, Arkansas, at which time he stated that he was age 84. He died 26 July 1879 in Benton County and Elijah Armstrong applied for burial expenses.
Benton County, Arkansas; Will Book C, page 409: "I, Elijah Armstrong of Rogers in the County of Benton State of Arkansas; I hereby constitute Mary Jane Armstrong to be Executrix; after payment of just debts, I give to each of my children, J.C.Armstrong, Sarah Armstrong, Solomon Armstrong, B.A.Armstrong, Anna Armstrong, Bessie Armstrong, Nancy J. Armstrong, Josephine Heylands & Horner (?) Armstrong (compiler's note; this list is scrambled by the Court recorder, some names could be repeats) the sum of one dollar; for the payment of the aforesaid legacies I give and

devise to my said executrix all the personal estate owned by me at my decease" signed 26 December 1905; recorded 19 August 1906.
1850 Federal Census, Benton County, Arkansas, page 84; Elijah Armstrong, 25 Mo.; Darcus, 27 Ill.; Amanda, 7 Ark.; William, 5, Ark.

ASH,WILLIAM-War of 1812 Pension application W.O.#34686, W.C.#25670. B.L.W.#23527-40-50 (canceled, and contained in this file) #17443-80-50, and #26616-80-55. Soldier's discharge certificate in file. Service in Captain John B. Dempsey's Company of Tennessee Militia from 24 September 1813 to 22 December 1813. He entered service in Bedford County, Tennessee, and served at the Battle Of Horseshoe Bend, in the Creek Indian Nation. He also commanded a company of Georgia Militia in the Seminole Indian War in 1836. William Ash was born in Wilkes County, Georgia ca 1791, the son of William Ash. Married Martha Strange, 15 January 1825 in Franklin County, Georgia at the home of Seth Strange. He applied for Bounty Land in 1850 and 1855 in Franklin County, Georgia. After he received his warrants, he went to Montgomery County, Arkansas, where he signed a Power of Attorney, giving power to John Seth Ash, of Montgomery County, Arkansas, to sell his property in Franklin County, Georgia. He signed that Power of Attorney on 15 June 1859, and he died in Montgomery County on 30 November 1859, at the home of A.B.Anderson. Martha Ash applied for pension in Gwinnett County, Georgia on 16 June 1879, at which time, affidavits were given by John S. and Margaret Ash, of Norcross, Georgia, who stated that they had been with William Ash when he died.
Revolutionary War Pension Application of William Ash: #W5646. He enlisted into service in Camden or York District, South Carolina in 1776. He served under Captain Bratton, Colonel Neal and Colonel Lacey in the South Carolina Troops. He was in the "Snow Campaign", the Battles of Congaree, Friday's Fort, Ashley, Rocky Mount, Sumter's Defeat and Biggin's Church. He married in York District, South Carolina Jane Fleming on 8 April 1783. They moved to Wilkes County, Georgia, then to Franklin County, Georgia, where he died 15 October 1831. Jane Ash applied for pension in Franklin County, Georgia. She removed the Family Record from her Bible to send with her pension application. "The children of William and Jane Ash: John Ash born 30 November 1783; Alexander F. Ash born 5 March 1785; James Ash born 24 October 1786; Doby Ash born 18 April 1789; William Ash, Jr. born 26 January 1791; Jannet Ash born 21 January 1793; Robert Rutherford Ash born 31 May 1795; Mary Hunter Ash born 6 March 1798; Elisabeth Ash born 26 December 1800; Elijah McWhorter Ash born 20 November 1802; Isabella P. Ash born 29 October 1804; Rachel A. Ash born 29 October 1804".

ATKINSON,THOMAS-War of 1812 pension application S.O.#26822, S.C.#17616. B.L.W#71315-40-50 and 74172-120-55. Service in Captain Nathan Davis' Company of Tennessee Militia. Enlisted 18 December 1813 at Giles County, Tennessee and was discharged 18 December 1813 at Huntsville, Alabama. He was engaged in the Battle of the Horseshoe in the Big Bend of the Tallapoosa River in Alabama. Married Betsey P. Samuel 15 August 1822 in Caswell County, North Carolina. Residing in Dallas County, Arkansas circa 1852, and in 1872 his application for pension was filed by Carter Atkinson, J.P. for Dallas County.
Federal Census Record-1850 Dallas County, Arkansas page #21 Saline Township; Thomas Atkinson 59 N.C.; Elizabeth 45 N.C.; Henry 27 N.C.; Frances A. 24 N.C.; Thomas 19 Tenn.; Harris B. 16 Tenn.; Josiah S. 15 Ky; Mary 13 Ky; John 11 Ky; Edward 8 Ky; James K.P. 5 Ky; Carter Atkinson 61 N.C. Ann P. Samuels (?) 66 N.C.

AULD,MICHAEL-War of 1812 pension application W.O.#11715 W.C.#6801.

B.L.W.#25881-160-55. Service in Captain Andrew Ramsey's Company of Missouri Rangers. Married Elizabeth Harkleroad 1 February 1814 at Cape Girardeau, Missouri. Application by widow Elizabeth in Phillips County, Arkansas,in 1857, she stated that her husband had died in Cape Girardeau, Missouri in May 1815 or 1816, however a Bounty Land Application was made in Missouri in 1854, in his name. Affidavits by: Elizabeth Barr, daughter of Elizabeth and Michael Auld; Hiram, John and Frank Harkleroad, brothers of Elizabeth Auld; and Daniel Harkleroad, father of Elizabeth Auld.

BADER,MICHAEL-Old war pension application dated 1848 Arkansas. O.W. Widow's Cert. #1121 File #29629. O.W. Minor's Cert. #1126 File #12238. Widow Johanna Bader; minors Louretta J. and Mary E. Bader. Service in 8th U.S. Infantry, Mexican War. Michael Bader died in the hospital at Fort Smith, Arkansas on 19 December 1848. His widow, Johanna Bader, whom he married 1 March 1843 in Germany, applied for a pension on his military service in Crawford County, Arkansas on 16 November 1849. She had two children; Louretta Jane Bader, born 13 August 1845 in Germany, and Mary Eunice Bader, born 17 December 1847 in New York City. Johanna married in 1850, a man named Kuhne, who deserted her and her children. She applied for a divorce, which was denied, however, she being German, she failed to understand the decision and was of the impression that she had been divorced. She reapplied for her pension, but was denied. On December 11, 1851, the probate Court of Sebastian County granted guardianship of her two daughters to John Pearson. He applied for pension on their behalf. As late as 1860, Johanna was alive and still not receiving pension. In April 1879, Louretta J. Bader, now Finton, and Mary E. Bader, now Miller, applied for arrears in the pension stating that their guardian was dead, and that all of the papers had been burned in the "late war". Mary Bader Miller stated that she had been married 13 December 1865 and Louretta had been married on 16 February 1860, both of them were living in Dayton, Sebastian County, Arkansas.
1850 Federal Census, Ft. Smith Township, Crawford County, Arkansas; page 292: William Irvine, 70 Ireland; Mary, 55 Ireland; Elizabeth McCaffry, 70 Ireland; Johanna Bader, 35 Germany; Louretta, 5 Germany; Eunice, 3 Ark.

BAGGETT,SILAS-War of 1812 pension application W.O.#45342, W.C.-#35492. B.L.W.#37918-80-50 and #28838-80-55. Service in Captain Butt's Company of Georgia Militia from 26 September 1814 to 2 March 1815. He served as substitute for John Henry. Apparently married three times; 1st to Nicie Williams, 2nd to __? Williams, 3rd to Mary Ann Mitchell 21 July 1861 in Jefferson County, Arkansas. Resided 1851 in Bradley County, Arkansas; in 1855 in Jefferson County, Arkansas. He died on 4 February 1872 in Cleveland County, Arkansas. Widow, Mary Ann, died 12 February 1912 in Cleveland County. (not abstracted)

BAGLEY,ASHER-Revolutionary War Pension Application #S46367. Bounty Land Warrant #8140, issued 5 April 1793. Service in Captain Aaron Ogden's Regiment of the New Jersey Line. Made application for pension 9 July 1828 in Pulaski County, Territory of Arkansas. Soldier died in Pulaski County 16 November 1840, survived by widow Catherine and children, not named.

BAKER,ESAIAS-War of 1812 pension application W.O.#32653, W.C.#28179. B.L.W.#32580-80-50 and #19541-80-55. Service in Captain Bird S. Hurt's Company, Tennessee Militia from 13 November 1814 to 13 May 1815. Resided in Searcy County, Arkansas before 1851; married Provy Baker in Searcy County on 10 January 1854. Soldier died on 23 March 1868 in Searcy County, widow to Marion County before 1878. (not abstracted)

BALDRIDGE,FRANCIS-War of 1812 pension application W.O.#10958,

W.C.#6289. B.L.W.#40268-80-50 and #46508-80-55. Service in Captain
Thomas Williamson's Company of Tennessee Militia from 10 December
1812 to 20 April 1813 and from 24 September 1813 to 10 December
1813. Two original discharge certificates contained in this
file, one of which was signed by Colonel William Pillow, the
other signed by Major General Andrew Jackson. He volunteered
into service in Davidson County, Tennessee and served in the
Creek Indian Wars. Married Frances Deckie in Rutherford County,
Tennessee on 21 November 1811. They raised a family of 12 children.
Soldier died 11 October 1847 in Clinton County, Illinois. Frances
Baldridge applied for Bounty Land in Bond County, Illinois on
1 November 1851, and on 12 September 1856 she applied for Bounty
Land in Benton County, Arkansas. Affidavit from David C. Baldridge,
of Bond County, Illinois, nephew of Francis Baldridge. Her pension
application, dated 15 June 1874, Benton County, Arkansas contains
the following family record, "Francis Baldridge was born August
3rd 1785; Frances Baldridge was born September 20th 1792; James
H. Baldridge was born August 25th 1812; Merinda Caroline Baldridge
was born February the 6th 1817; Catherine Minerva Baldridge
was born February 10th 18__? (the balance of this entry can't
be made out it is so badly defaced; Mary Logue Baldridge was
born March 25th 18__? (can't make out balance); Francis Marion
Baldridge was born September 25th 1822."

BALLEW,JOSEPH-Revolutionary War Pension Application #S31541,
dated 16 October 1832 in Shelby County, Tennessee. Joseph Ballew
was born 17 March 1757 or 1758 in Buckingham County, Virginia. He
stated that his father then moved to Amherst County, Virginia
and from there to Morganton, Burke County, North Carolina. Joseph
Ballew entered service in Burke County, North Carolina in Captain
Thomas Kenedy's Company and was engaged in a skirmish with Tories
and British at Ramsauer's Mill. Next service under Captain John
McFarlin and Lieutenant George Walker at Davidson's Fort, on
the Catawba River, and at King's Mountain. He served under Captain
Harry Highland in several skirmishes with Cherokee Indians. After
the war he remained in Burke County for several years, then
moved to Knox County, Kentucky for about 7 years then moved
to Alabama for two years, then moved to Shelby County, Tennessee.
Application, dated 3 May 1845, to have his pension transferred
to White County, Arkansas where he has moved "to reside with
his children, some of whom have settled in said county." Affidavit
dated 2 October 1832 Hardiman County, Kentucky signed by Captain
William Walker, stated that he had served in the war with Joseph
Ballew. Application for increase in pension because of old war
wounds described as being "all in front".

BALLEW,RICHARD-Revolutionary War Pension Application #S15305,
(possibly related to Joseph) Entered service in 1779 in Burke
County, North Carolina. He was born in Buckingham County, Virginia
in 1763. Mentions brother named Peter.

BALLEW,STEPHEN Senior-Revolutionary War Pension Application
#S16835.(possibly related to Joseph) Entered service in Burke
County, North Carolina, as a substitute for his father, Robert
Ballew. Stephen Ballew was born ca 1762 in Amherst County,
Virginia.

BARNES,JAMES-War of 1812 pension application W.O.#36857 W.C.#
27217. B.L.W.#33339-80-50 and #40775-80-55. Service in Captain
Reynold's Company of 39th U.S. Infantry. Married Mary Huddleston
25 January 1816 in Maury County, Tennessee; Marriage license
enclosed. James Barnes was born in Chatham County, North Carolina,
enlisted in service when he was age 22, at Maury County, Tennessee,
on 1 January 1814. He was "covering Sergeant to Robert Summerville
when he fell at the Battle of Horseshoe". James Barnes was discharged
at Nashville, Tennessee on 1 January 1815. In her application
widow stated that they had lived in Maury, Harden and Shelby

Counties, Tennessee and in Saline and Dallas Counties, Arkansas. Widow died in Dallas County about 1889. Affidavits in 1879 by F.W. Barnes age 58 and Catherine Alston age 61 stating that they are children of James and Mary Barnes.

BARRON,THOMAS-War of 1812 pension application S.O.#24797, S.C.#17218.-B.L.W.#47682-80-50 and #13324-80-55. Service in Captain William Ganaway's Company of Kentucky Militia from 15 November 1814 to 15 May 1815. Married to Elizabeth Curnell 20 February 1820 in Arkansas. Removed to McLennon County, Texas before 1852. (not abstracted)

BAUGHMAN,JOHN-War of 1812 pension application W.O.#10216, W.C.#5497. B.L.W.#35439-80-50 and #36625-80-55. Service in Captain Wilson Maple's Company of Tennessee Militia from 13 November 1814 to 18 May 1815. Married to Dorathy Moier on 22 January 1805 in Botetourt County, Virginia. Bounty Land application dated 1851 in Carroll County, Arkansas. Soldier died in Carroll County in January of 1857, Dorathy Baughman applied for pension in Marble Creek, Iron County, Missouri in 1872.

BECK,VIVEN-War of 1812 pension application S.O.#12457, S.C.#18839. B.L.W.#21658-160-12. Service in Captain T. Post's Company, 12th U.S.Infantry and in Captain White Young's Company, 8th U.S.Infantry from 4 June 1812 to 4 June 1817. Discharge certificate contained in file. Married to Sarah McDonald in Clark County, Arkansas in September 1831. He applied for pension in 1871 in Mt. Ida, Montgomery County, Arkansas. (not abstracted)

BECKWITH,LAURENCE-Old War Survivor's Cert. #3270 File #24910 Old War Wid. Rej. #24990 Mexican Wid. #2720. Service in Company G Mounted Regiment of Arkansas Volunteers, Mexican War. He enrolled 1 July 1846 at Washington, Arkansas. He was wounded at the Battle of Buena Vista, and mustered out of service in Mexico on 20 June 1847. Laurence Beckwith married Jenetha Hill 28 February 1857 in Sevier County, Arkansas. He died 29 November 1874 at Brownstown, Sevier County. In 1885 widow, Jenetha, residing in Picayune, Howard County, Arkansas.

BEEBE,SAMUEL-War of 1812 pension application S.O.#8960 S.C.#22782. B.L.W.#11337-160-55. Service in Captain E. Egliston's Company of New York Militia from 20 December 1813 to 5 January 1814. Married Lucy Ann Rogers in January 1817 in Warsaw, New York. Resided in De Witt County, Illinois in 1855; in Miami County, Kansas in 1871 and in 1878 he was in Conway County, Arkansas. He died in Conway County before 1886. (not abstracted)

BELL,WILLIAM-War of 1812 pension application W.O.#39667 W.C.#32129. Enlisted in service in Raliegh, North Carolina in Captain John R. Clark's Company of North Carolina Militia on 18 July 1813 discharged 13 August 1813. Married Mary Perry 5 August 1832 in Franklin County, North Carolina. Enclosed in this brief is a letter that William Bell wrote to his parents while in service. Addressed to Zadok Bell of Raliegh, Wake County, North Carolina, vis, "Dear parents; I and my brothers are well". William Bell was born ca 1793 and died 25 April 1860 in Jefferson County, Arkansas. Mary Bell was born ca 1810. She applied for pension in Dorsey County, Arkansas (which part had previously been part of Jefferson County) stating that she had moved to Arkansas in 1847. Family Bible from the American Bible Society, printed by D. Fanshaw in New York 1829, contains statement "Robert B. Bell was born 23 June 1833" apparently the oldest child of Mary and William. Bounty Land application dated 19 May 1855 Jefferson County, Arkansas witnessed by Edward and John P. Bell. Relationship not shown.

BELOTE,EDMUND-War of 1812 pension application W.O.#42641,

W.C.#33285. B.L.W.#22043-160-12. He enlisted into service while
residing in Samson County, North Carolina, in the 10th Regiment
of U.S.Infantry on 17 May 1814. He was at Colonel Wellborn's
Headquarters at Wilkesborough, under command of Lieutenant James
Hall, until about the first of March 1815. They began a march
to Canada at that time, but after about 60 or 70 miles, were
informed that peace had been made. They began a series of marches
through North Carolina, from Raliegh to Augusta, Georgia, then
to the Chattahoochie River, where they built Fort Gaine. They
were then marched into Alabama, where he stated that they built
flat bottomed boats, while at Fort Mitchell, which they used
to float down the Chattahoochie River to the mouth of the Flint
River. They built Fort Scott, and while working on that fort,
Edmund Belote had a hand badly mashed between logs. They had
a skirmish with the Creek Indians, and then built Fort Hughes
on the Flint River. He was discharged on 16 May 1819, after
5 years service. His original discharge certificate is contained
in this file. He married Elizabeth Weaver in Panther Creek,
Georgia in October 1818. They resided in Lumpkin County, Georgia
in 1850, and moved to Faulkner County, Arkansas about the same
year. Isom R. Hall, of Faulkner County, stated "I first met
Edmund Belote in 1810 in North Carolina, I then moved to Hall
County, Georgia in 1836, where I met Edmund Belote and his wife
Elizabeth, I moved to Faulkner County, Arkansas in 1852, where
I again met Edmund and Elizabeth Belote". Soldier died 17 February
1857 in Faulkner County, Arkansas, at the home of his son, John
Belote. Edmund Belote was born 20 March 1791 in either Bertie
or Samson County, North Carolina. Elizabeth Belote died in Faulkner
County on 3 October 1884.

BENSON,BENJAMIN-War of 1812 pension application S.O.#28341,
S.C.#20244. B.L.W.#11860-80-50 and #40054-80-55. Service in
Captain Wilson Maple's Company of Tennessee Militia from 13
November 1814 to 20 May 1815. Resided in Jackson County, Alabama
in 1850. Removed to Jefferson County, Arkansas before 1856,
and was there in 1872.(not abstracted)

BERRY,JOHN-War of 1812 pension application S.O.#26101, S.C.#19119.
B.L.W.#101702-40-50 and #42491-120-55. Service in Captain Reuben
Moore's Company of Virginia Militia from 31 August 1814 to 6
December 1814. Married Soreno Turner 2 August 1826 in Jackson
County, Alabama. Resided 1854 in Marshall County, Mississippi;
1871 in Augusta, Woodruff County, Arkansas. Soldier died 18
May 1872. (not abstracted)

BEVANS/BIVINS,JASON-Old war pension application dated 1874 Arkansas.
O.W.Inv.Cert.#4945, File #24911, O.W. minor's app.Rej.#21474.
Service in Captain Allen Wood's Company C, 12th Regiment, U.S.
Infantry, Mexican War. He became ill in Mexico City in October
1847 and was discharged because he was losing his eyesight. His
original discharge certificate is contained in this file. Jason
Bevins died 14 February 1866, in Madison County, Arkansas. He
was married to Martha Jane Graham Steward 25 December 1859 in
Madison County; their children: James Wilson Bivins born 15
January 1861; Eliza Jane Bivins born 16 March 1866. Widow's
Application dated 28 May 1866, she was age 29. She died 8 November
1868, in Madison County. Her pension application contains affidavit
from Charles, Catherine and Phillip Graham, relationship not
stated. Minor's application dated 4 November 1882, Huntsville,
Madison County, Arkansas, by James T. Withrow, guardian of minors
James W. and Eliza Jane Bevans.(note various spellings of this
name)

BIRD,WILLIAM C.-War of 1812 pension application S.O.#18425,
S.C.#11518. B.L.W.#18562-160-50. Served as Sergeant in Captain
William H. Moore's Company of Tennessee Militia from 10 December
1812 to 17 December 1813. Resided 1851 in Dallas County, Arkansas. In

1871 in Yadkin County, North Carolina. Soldier died 3 February 1876. (not abstracted)

BIVENS,JOHN-War of 1812 pension application W.O.#22744 W.C.#24267. B.L.W.#96818-80-50 and #36989-80-55. Service in Captain B. Collins Company of Tennessee Militia from 13 November 1814 to 13 May 1815. Soldier married first to Patience Spears, who died in St. Paul, Arkansas on 25 January 1857. Married second, Ann Boone on 17 July 1857 in Ozark, Franklin County, Arkansas. Soldier died 26 August 1870 in Madison County, Arkansas. Widow applied for pension 13 May 1878 in Madison County, stating that she was age 65, and that her husband had been born in North Carolina. She also stated that she had previously been married to George Boone, who died in Ozark, Franklin County, Arkansas in 1854.
1850 Federal Census, Madison County, Arkansas; page 259, family #193; John Bivins,Sr. 57 N.C.; Patience 57 N.C.; Turner 21 Tenn., Martha Brooks 17 Tenn: family #194; John Bivins Jr. 23 Tenn; Dolly 18 Mo., Marcus L. 6 Ark.;Huntsville Township, page #308: Jonas Bivins 30 Ala., Sarah 24 Mo., John 7 Mo., Joseph 3 Ark., William 2 Ark.; same page: Margarett Bivins 56 N.C., Elias 22 Tenn., Mary Ann 17 Tenn.

BLACK,WILLIAM-Revolutionary War Pension Application #S31554. He was born 18 July 1755 in Lancaster County, Pennsylvania. He was residing in Cumberland County, Pennsylvania in 1776, when he was commissioned Captain of a company of militia. From November 1776 until April 1777 he served in Colonel Frederick Watt's Regiment, in which capacity he was at the Battle of Sunbury. He served in Colonel David Mitchell's Regiment at the Battle of White Marsh. He spent several tours of duty guarding the frontiers. In his application, he stated that he moved to Washington County, North Carolina in 1784, from there to Knox County, North Carolina in 1804 and then to Madison County, Alabama. He was living in Limestone County, Alabama by 1819 and applied for his pension there on 10 December 1832. He moved to Hempstead County, Territory of Arkansas in 1834, stating that he had a brother and a son living in Arkansas. His parents are not named, however, an affidavit by James Officer of Scott County, Kentucky in which he stated that he was called into service under William Black at the farm of John Black in Cumberland County, Pennsylvania.
Hempstead County, Ark. Will Book B page 47; Will of William Black; Wife not mentioned; children named, William Black, Samuel Black, Alexander Black, Jane Black, Margaret Catlett, James H. Black, Rebecca Amenth(?), Jonathan Black; signed March 1844 recorded 18 May 1844.
1840 Fed. Census Hempstead Co, Ark.; page 169-Mary Black with 1 female 10-15, 1 female 15-20, 1 female 60-70. Jonathan Black with 1 male under 5, 1 male 5-10, 1 Male 30-40, 1 female under 5, 1 female 10-15, 1 female 30-40; page 170-James H. Black with 2 Males under 5, 2 males 5-10, 1 male 40-50, 1 female 10-15, 1 female 20-30, 1 female 30-40; page 174- William Black age 85, with 1 male 30-40.
Benton County, Arkansas Will Book A, page 174, will of Samuel Black, "wife, Elizabeth, oldest son William and other sons Thomas J. and James H. Black. Daughter Emily Black" signed 20 March 1856, recorded 24 April 1856.

BLAKELEY,JOHN-War of 1812 pension application S.O.#3268, S.C.#5199. B.L.W.#16717-160-50. Served in Captain John McNair's Company, Captain Joseph Duncan's Company and in Captain James Stewart's Company of Tennessee Militia from 10 January 1814 to 21 July 1814 and from 20 September 1814 to 3 May 1815. Married to Lavinia Brown 8 June 1817, Knoxville, Tennessee. Resided 1850 in Madison County, Arkansas, in 1871 he was in Fayetteville, Washington County, Arkansas. (not abstracted)

BLEVINS,HUGH ARMSTRONG-War of 1812 pension application W.O.#38550

11

W.C.#28715. B.L.W.#34611-80-50 and #32747-80-55. Service as Sergeant in Captain Alexander Hill's Company of Tennessee Militia from 13 November 1814 to 13 May 1815. He volunteered at McMinnville, Warren County, Tennessee and served at the Battle of New Orleans. He was residing in Arkansas by 1832. Married first to Emily King, who died in Hempstead County, Arkansas ca 1838. Second marriage to Sarah Carpenter 19 January 1840 in Hempstead County, marriage record enclosed in this file. In 1887, widow, Sarah, was residing in Mineral Springs, Howard County, Arkansas and stated that she had lived in Arkansas since her marriage. Hugh Blevins was born in 1796, place not stated, and died 4 January 1859 in Hempstead County.
Hempstead County, Ark.-Will Book C page 102-Will of Hugh A. Blevins Wife Sarah; children named Allen, Armstead W. and John C. Blevins. signed 20 Nov 1858 recorded 12 Jan 1859.
Clark County, Ark. marriage Book E page 58; Armstead W. Blevins and Ellen Deadman-13 Feb 1867.
Federal Census records-1850 Hempstead County, Arkansas page 251; Hugh A. Blevins 56 Tenn.; Sarah 34 Tenn.; Allen 29 Tenn.; Armstead 10 Ark.; John 8 Ark.; Hugh 6 Ark.; Elizabeth 4 Ark.; Mary 2 Ark.; Female age 1 Ark.; Catherine 14 Tenn; Martha 12 Tenn.

BOATRIGHT,WILLIAM-War of 1812 pension application S.O.#1702, S.C.#5535. B.L.W.#34556-80-50 and #27570-80-55. Served as Lieutenant in Captain Jonathan Waddle's Company of Tennessee Militia from 13 November 1814 to 18 May 1815. This file contains an order for Court Martial. Soldier residing 1851 and 1871 in Madison County, Arkansas. He died 8 August 1875. (not abstracted)
1850 Federal Census, Madison County, Arkansas, page 297: William Boatright 63 Va., Nancy 41 Tenn., Tennessee 14 Ark., Martha 12 Ark., Cerilda 6 Ark., Elizabeth Waits(?) 6 Ark., John 4 Ark. Page 308; John Boatright 40 Tenn., Eliza 26 Tenn., Emily 14 Tenn., Fanny 12 Tenn., Henry 10 Ark., Lucinda C. 8 Ark., Hugh C. 2 Ark., Martha 1 Ark.

BONHAM,WILLIAM-War of 1812 pension application S.O.#29520, S.C.-#21341. B.L.W.#48651-80-50 (canceled and contained in this file) #65089-40-50, #92972-40-50 and #28402-80-55. Served in Captain Jacob Short's Company of Illinois Militia from 3 September 1812 to 13 November 1812. Married to Rachel Hand in St. Clair, Illinois. Resided 1852 and 1870 in Fayetteville, Washington County, Arkansas. (not abstracted)

BONNER,WILLIAMSON-War of 1812 pension application W.O.#36778 W.C.#26145. B.L.W.#30224-80-50 and #41601-80-55. Service in Captain Charles Wade's Company of Tennessee Militia from 13 November 1814 to 13 May 1815. Drafted at Gallatin, Tennessee. Married 1st to Marina Redit who died in Shelby County, Tennessee in 1836; 2nd to Carry Bentley who died in Phillips County, Arkansas 4 July 1848; 3rd to Evaline Skinner 29 November 1849 in Phillips County, Arkansas. Bounty land application dated 18 April, Bonner aged 55. Williamson Bonner died in Phillips County, Arkansas 10 August 1870. Original discharge dated 13 May 1815, Nashville, Tennessee and signed by Major General William Carroll, contained in this brief.
1850-Federal Census; Phillips County, Arkansas, Spring Creek Township page 157 family #9: Williamson Bonner 54 Virginia, Eveline 40 La., John C. 25 Tenn., W.S. (male) 23 Tenn., Harriett E. 19 Tenn., Thomas L. 13 Tenn., Florida A. 10 Tenn., Joseph 9 Tenn., B.F. (male) 9 Tenn., Lucinda 6 Tenn., Aurelia A. 4 Ark., Minerva 3 Ark.; page 158, Alfred Bonner 28 Tenn., Elizabeth 24 Ala., Thomas 3 Tenn., Williamson 2 Tenn., Mary 5/12 Ark.

BOREN,JAMES-War of 1812 pension application S.O.#28066, S.C.#20338. B.L.W.#49446-160-55. Service in Captain Owen Evan's Company of Illinois Militia from 28 March 1813 to 13 June 1813. Married

Bertha Hendricks in 1812 in Johnson County, Illinois. They were residing in Madison County, Arkansas in 1850. From 1853 thru 1872 they were in Carroll County, Arkansas. (not abstracted) 1850 Federal Census, Madison County, Arkansas, War Eagle Township, page #295, family #656: James Boren 60 Tenn., Ruthy 35 unknown, Susan 27 Illinois, Sarah 16 Ark., James 12 Ark., John 10 Ark., Stephen 3 Ark.

BOSWELL,WILLIAM-War of 1812 pension application W.O.#29839, W.C.#26956. B.L.W.#83252-40-50 and #61105-120-50. Service in Captain John Miller's Company of Tennessee Militia from 22 February 1814 to 10 May 1814. He volunteered at Fort Deposit, on the Tennessee River and stated that he lost a mare worth sixty five dollars. This file contains certificate "for loss of soldier's horse due to fatigue" dated 9 May 1814 signed by John Miller. He married first Nancy Tompson; second, Anna Copeland on 9 August 1832 in Livingston, Overton County, Tennessee. Jane Bunch, age 61, of Berryville, Carroll County, Arkansas in 1879 stated that she had been an eye witness to the wedding ceremony of William and Anna Boswell. In 1851, they were residing in Newton County, Arkansas, where William Boswell applied for Bounty Land. He was granted patent #83252, "issued in favor of William Boswell, assigned to Aaron Alread, records of Miscellaneous Military Grants, Vols. 222 page 60" recorded by James P. Fancher 19 June 1879, (a must for researchers of this family) Affidavits from Nathaniel and Bradley Bunch and from Frances and Joseph Wright, all of whom have known William and Anna Boswell between 30 and 50 years. William Boswell died in Madison County, Arkansas 22 May 1860. Anna Boswell died 4 October 1902.

BOURLAND,SLATEN-War of 1812 pension application W.O.#36811 W.C.#29639-B.L.W.#53242-40-50 and #82247-120-55. Service in Captain Thomas Stokes' Company of Tennessee Militia from 1 September 1812 to 23 December 1812. Bounty land application in 1855, Slaten Bourland, age 64, stated that he was drafted into service in Hopkins County, Kentucky at Joseph Davis' Mill. He married 1st Polly Reefe 10 October 1815, she died 13 December 1833; 2nd Eliza Burnham 25 March 1834 in Calloway County, Kentucky. Soldier died 27 August 1871 in Franklin County, Arkansas. Soldier resided 1834-1837 in Calloway County, Kentucky; in 1842 he was in Holly Springs, Mississippi, and in 1870 in Franklin Co, Arkansas. Widow's application dated 17 April 1879, Eliza Bourland age 64, residing in Bates County, Missouri. Affidavits by William Burnham (age 55) and James Burnham, brothers of Eliza, residing in Marshall County, Kentucky in 1879. State that Eliza Burnham and Slaten Bourland were married in our father, Frederick Burnham's home in Calloway County, now Marshall County, Kentucky. William Burnham stated that he was born in Mecklenburgh County, North Carolina, moved to Calloway County, Kentucky in 1834 and that his father died there in 1835/6.

BOURN,WHITFIELD-War of 1812 pension application S.O.#19646, S.C.#14019, W.O.#36858, W.C.#26579. B.L.W.#42869-80-50 and #18706-80-55. Service in Captain Thomas Lewis' Company of Kentucky Militia from 29 March 1813 to 28 September 1813. His pension application dated 17 June 1871, Dripping Springs Township, Crawford County, Arkansas, he was age 73 or 74. He was taken prisoner near Fort Meiggs in an engagement resulting in what was called "Dudley's Defeat", and was taken by the enemy to an old fort from which ten Indians took him to Detroit, at which place he was allowed, by exchange or some other way to return to Kentucky. This apparently the reason he never received a discharge. He married first Clarinda Weaver, in Crawford County, Arkansas on 4 September 1831, she died in Crawford County on 21 January 1851. Second marriage to Medaline Price on 30 August 1852 in Crawford County, Arkansas. She had previously been married to Moses Kelley, who died in Crawford County on 26 June 1849. Soldier

died in Crawford County, Arkansas on 1 April 1879 and Medaline Bourn applied for pension 14 June 1879. She gave the following narrative, "Whitfield Bourn lived in Jessamine County, Kentucky until 1825, when he moved to the "Lovely Purchase" and remained there some years. That is now the Indian Country, west of Arkansas. When that was given to the Indians, he removed to Crawford County, Territory of Arkansas". Medaline Bourn came to Arkansas from the State of Missouri in 1846. Affidavits by son, Dudley Bourn, and son-in-law, J.M.Harshaw, also from John S. and Mary Matlock, John Price and Mary Alverson. Medaline Bourn died 15 January 1887 in Crawford County.
1850 Federal Census, Crawford County, Arkansas, page 338; Whitfield Bourn, 52 Ken.; Clarinda, 36 Tenn.; George, 18 Ark.; Mary, 16 Ark.;Margaret, 11 Ark.; Frank, 9 Ark.; Levi, 7 Ark.;

BOWEN,CHARLES-War of 1812 pension application S.O.#7208, S.C.#268. B.L.W.#20885-40-50 and #67826-120-55. Service in Captain Rufus Morgan's Company of Tennessee Militia from 23 September 1813 to 31 December 1813. Soldier's discharge certificate contained in this file. He married Susan Shell 10 December 1810 in Knox County, Tennessee. Resided 1850 thru 1871 in Osceola, Mississippi County, Arkansas. (not abstracted)

BOYD,BRUCE-War of 1812 pension application S.O.#17561, S.C.#17518. B.L.W.#15760-160-50. Service in Captain William Taylor's Company, 18th U.S. Infantry from 11 January 1812 to 12 February. Resided 1851-1871 in Carrollton, Carroll County, Arkansas. Married in December 1859, to Martha Leathers in Carroll County, Arkansas. (this application not abstracted).

BOYD,WILLIAM-Revolutionary War Pension Application #R1094, dated 13 February 1834, Washington County, Territory of Arkansas. Stated that he was born 11 August 1760 in Southampton County, Virginia. He was residing in Roane County, North Carolina, when he enlisted in the North Carolina Militia in 1777. He served in a skirmish with the Tories at the junction of the Rocky and Pee Dee Rivers. His application was rejected. He reapplied in 1837 at which time he signed his name as William Boyd Senior.

BRIANT/BRYANT,JOSEPH-War of 1812 pension application S.O.#22886, S.C.#14171, W.O.#10171, W.C.#22146. B.L.W.#56024-40-50 (canceled and contained in file) and #35549-160-55. He was born 7 May 1795 in South Carolina, was residing in Kingston, Roane County, Tennessee, when he enlisted in service on 30 September 1813. He served in Captain William D. Nelson's Company of Tennessee Militia until 1 January 1814. He married Martha Hart 11 February 1819 in Kingston, Roane County, Tennessee. They moved from Tennessee to Crawford County, Arkansas before 1851, where he applied for bounty land on 27 September 1851. He applied for pension in 1871 in Madison County, Arkansas. He died in Madison County on 28 February 1873 and his widow applied for pension there. She submitted his original pension certificate, which is contained in this file.
1850 Federal Census, Crawford County, Arkansas, page 341: Joseph Bryant, 55 S.C.; Martha, 49 S.C.; Morton Dotson, 21 Tenn.

BRIANT,WILLIAM-War of 1812 pension application S.O.#30611 S.C.#21828 W.O.#43240 W.C.#33632. Service in Captain J.N. Williamson's Company of Tennessee Militia from 20 September 1814 to 20 April 1815. Served at the Battle of Pensacola. Married 21 September 1827 Davidson County, Tennessee to Elisa O'Briant. Soldier's pension application dated 16 September 1876 Camden, Ouachita County, Arkansas. He stated that he has had three children, all daughters, one of whom is Amanda Wilson born 15 January 1839. William Briant was born ca 1797, he died 16 October 1883 in Barham, Ouachita County, Arkansas.

BRIGHT,PURRINGTON-War of 1812 pension application W.O.#37414 W.C.#27097.Service in Captain Bethea's Company of South Carolina Militia from 24 September 1814 to 24 January 1815. Soldier born in Virginia circa 1797. Married Charlotte Esterling 1 February 1817 in Marlborough, South Carolina. Resided in South Carolina until 1834, from there to Kemper County, Mississippi until about 1850, then to Hempstead County, Arkansas. Soldier died in Hempstead County 21 May 1866. Widow residing in Nevada County in 1871 stated that she did not move, rather the new county was formed around her. Godfrey Bright, age 76 in 1879 stated that he had known Charlotte Bright since her marriage (65 years). William L. Bright witness to signature of Purrington Bright in Hempstead County in 1855 (relationship not stated).
Federal Census record-1850 Hempstead County, Ark. page 231 Purrington H. Bright 56 Virginia; Charlotte 50 S. Car.; Amanda 26 S.C.; Garland 15 Miss.; William E. 13 Miss.; Eliza 5 Miss.
Dozier Bright 21 S.C.; Roxy 17 Miss.
Pennington Bright 60 N.C. listed with William Clark.
Benton County, Arkansas Will Book A, page 123, Noncupative will of Alfred Bright, who died Tuesday Evening 29 July 1851, "his wife, Sarah E. Bright, should have all of the property that he possesses" Recorded 5 August 1851.

BROCK,CALEB-War of 1812 pension application S.O.#28844, S.C.#20774 W.O.#15746, W.C.#11498. B.L.W.#34109-80-50 and #26349-80-55. Service in Captain John Frost's Company of North Carolina Militia from 1 February 1814 to 31 July 1814. Caleb Brock was born near Norfolk, Virginia circa 1796, married Mary Frances Jones 22 June 1820 in Rowan County, North Carolina. He died in Des Arc, Prairie County, Arkansas on 10 October 1876. Widow's application 1878; she stated that they had resided since the war: 2 years in Rowan County, North Carolina, 6 years near Middleburg, Tennessee, 25 years in Tippah County, Mississippi, and 23 years in and near Des Arc, Prairie County, Arkansas. Widow, Mary, died 11 February 1883 in Des Arc, Arkansas. Children identified in this application; William H. Brock, born 11 January 1826, residing in Prairie County, Arkansas in 1878 and is the oldest living son; Ann Caroline Bledsoe, born 30 April 1824, residing in Sharon, Madison County, Mississippi in 1878 and is the oldest living child.; James Brock, age 33 in 1878 and residing in Prairie County, Arkansas; Emily Frances Patterson, age 50 in 1878 and residing in Independence County, Arkansas.

BROWN,JAMES-War of 1812 pension application W.O.#13236, W.C.#25320. B.L.W.#26596-80-50 and #44686-80-55. Service in Captain Daniel Newman's Company of Tennessee Militia from 13 November 1814 to 13 May 1815. He was born 8 August 1796 in North Carolina, entered service in Sparta, White County, Tennessee and served at the Battle of New Orleans. He married Mary McDaniel on 4 December 1836 in Lewisburg, Arkansas. Soldier resided 1851 in McLennan County, Texas. In 1855 and 1858, they were in De Witt County, Texas. Soldier died 15 April 1863. Widow in Mission Valley, Victoria County, Texas in 1878. She died 25 September 1903.

BROWN,STEPHEN-War of 1812 pension application S.O.#22878, S.C.#15119. B.L.W.#32245-80-50 and #39086-80-55. Service in Captain Robert Moore's Company of Tennessee Militia from 28 September 1814 to 3 May 1815. He married Polly Cranford 31 January 1816 in Wilson County, Tennessee. Resided 1851 in Searcy County, Arkansas, 1855 thru 1871 in Izard County, Arkansas. (not abstracted)
1850 Federal Census, Sevier County, Arkansas, page 175: Stephen Brown, 58 Virginia; Mary, 50 N.C.; Andrew, 12 Tenn.; Lesel(?), 10 Tenn.; Elizabeth, 14 Tenn.; William Green, 21 Tenn.

BROWN,WILLIAM-Revolutionary War Pension Application #S31563, dated 19 May 1834 in Lincoln County, Missouri. Stated that he

was born in Bedford County, Virginia in 1756. He enlisted in service in 1776 in what is now the town of Jonesboro, Tennessee, in Captain James Robinson's Company. He served at the Battle of Lookout Mountain under command of Captain Isaac Butler in Colonel Joseph Martin's Regiment. Stated that when Captain Butler was killed, he (William Brown) and his brother Joseph Brown were standing to either side of the said, Captain Butler. Refers to Joseph as his twin brother, who served with him throughout the Revolution. He stated that they served under Colonel John Sevier, who arrived at King's Mountain and Yorktown at the close of both battles. Made reference to Mrs. Mary Thurman as witness to his service. Stated that "I have lived since the war in North Carolina, now Tennessee, and came to Lincoln County, Missouri about 20 years ago and left this county the 10th of May 1832 and went to Arkansas Territory to reside with a son and have lately returned to Lincoln County to reside with Levi Brown another son. Affidavit from Joseph Brown, twin brother, also a resident of Lincoln County, Missouri. William Brown's pension reapplied in Pike County, Arkansas 23 April 1839.
Affidavit by Mary Thurman, Pike County, Missouri 19 June 1832 "I was born in the year 1760, my father Jonas Little, removed to Jonesborough then in North Carolina now Tennessee. My brothers George, John and Benjamin Little served in the Revolutionary War with William and Joseph Brown. Colonel Jonathan Tipton was my uncle." She stated that she thought that William and Joseph Brown may have served under Captain Robert Sevier rather than Captain John Sevier.
Affidavit by Martha Coker, Pike County, Arkansas 2 May 1839 "William Brown's father, John Brown, has been dead some 30 years".

BROWN,ZEDEKIAH-War of 1812 pension application W.O.#9846, W.C.#5143. B.L.W.#27667-80-50 and #26055-80-55. Service in Captain Ford's Company of Virginia Militia from 29 August 1814 to 28 February 1815. Soldier's discharge certificate contained in this file. He married Judith Duncan 5 November 1812 in Buckingham County, Virginia. Soldier died 16 August either 1848/ 1849/1850. Widow applied for bounty land in 1851, in Buckingham County, Virginia; second bounty land application in Fulton County, Kentucky in 1855; pension application in 1872 in Des Arc, Prairie County, Arkansas; pension application in 1886, in Hickory Plains, Prairie County, Arkansas.

BROWNE,JONATHAN-War of 1812 pension application S.O.#24851, S.C.#19136, W.O.#9021, W.C.#6383. B.L.W.#28308-80-50 and #33266--80-55. Service in Captain George Bowen's Company, Ensign William Hannah's Detachment of South Carolina Regiment of Artillery commanded by Colonel Reuben Nash, from 3 February 1814 to 25 July 1814. He enlisted at Varennes, Pendleton District, South Carolina, and was discharged "somewhere in the Creek Nation". When first search failed to reveal his service records, Jonathan Browne sent a letter to Commissioner of Pensions in which he stated "Check the muster rolls of William Hanna, and there you will find my name the first one on the list of privates, these muster rolls I made myself". He married Malinda Greenlee(f) in Pendleton District, South Carolina in April 1811, Mary Clements and Elizabeth Winters, residents of Attalla County, Mississippi, in October 1874, stated that they were wedding guests at the marriage of Malinda Greenlief and Jonathan Browne "and partook of the fine supper prepared on the occasion". Bounty land application in 1850 in Bradley County, Arkansas. Bounty land application in 1855 made in Union Parish, Louisiana. Soldier died in Jackson Parish, Louisiana on 18 January 1872. Affidavit of Pennal Quarrells of Jackson Parish, Louisana, "I first became acquainted with Jonathan and Malinda Browne in 1819, and I was intimately acquainted with their oldest child, Elijah Browne, who died in 1866 at the age of 51 years".

BRUCE,WINSTON-War of 1812 pension application S.O.#28622, S.C.#20531, W.O.#41526, W.C.#32392. B.L.W.#16587-160-50. Service in Captain R. Desha's Company, 24th Regiment of U.S. Infantry from 17 July 1812 to 31 December 1813. Married first Rebecca Webb; second Eliza ___? 24 January 1866 in Union County, Arkansas. Bounty land application in 1851 in Union County, Arkansas. Soldier died 12 October 1873 in Round Rock, Williamson County, Texas. (not abstracted)

BRYAN,TARANCE-War of 1812 pension application S.O.#29430, S.C.-#21285. B.L.W.#52835-80-50 and #48677-80-55. Service in Captain John Water's Company of South Carolina (?) Militia from 21 November 1814 to 6 May 1815, also allegedly served as substitute for Robert McCrary. Soldier's discharge certificate contained in this file. He married Elizabeth Patterson in Hall County, Georgia. His bounty land application in 1853 filed in Paulding County, Georgia, his pension application made in 1873 in Polk County, Arkansas. He died 26 February 1885 in Cove, Polk County, Arkansas. (not abstracted) Possibly related to this pensioner: Thomas Bryan, War of 1812 pension application S.O.#18458, S.C.#11588, W.O.#31779, W.C.#23496. B.L.W.#37228-80-50 and #29917-80-55. Service in Captain Jack Water's Company of Georgia(?) Militia from 21 November 1814 to 6 May 1815. Married first Mary Dooley; second Thomasin Grogan 8 August 1847 in Walker County, Georgia. (not abstracted)

BUCHANAN,ANDREW-War of 1812 pension application W.O.#20261 W.C.#22141. B.L.W.#37371-40-50 and #88399-120-55. Service in Captain Cavanagh's Company of Tennessee Militia from 24 September 1813 to 10 December 1813. Married Sinai Neal 27 November 1828 in Warren County, Kentucky. Bounty land application dated 14 March 1851, Washington County, Arkansas. Andrew Buchanan stated that he was age 59. Soldier died 12 April 1857 in Prairie Grove, Washington County, Arkansas. Widow, Sinai age 80, applied for pension in 1878 in Washington County, her signature witnessed by James and Lucy Neal.
Washington County Will Book A&B -page 48; mem. of will of Andrew Buchanan signed 29 Mar 1852 probated 1 May 1897; Executor Sinai Buchanan: Legacy to servants Isaac and Rebecca, legacy to Cane Hill Collegiate Institute and C.P. Church. (notation of Cir. Ct. Recorder, "see Vol. X page 213")
Washington County Will Book A&B page 34- mem. will of James Buchanan, signed 27 Sept 1843 probated 27 Dec 1848; "To wife Elizabeth; the farm whereon I now live, at her death said farm to my son Andrew Buchanan".
Washington County Deeds; Andrew Buchanan to John Moore dated 14 Feb 1835, Book A page 78; Andrew Buchanan to Isaac Marrs dated 13 Dec 1837, Book A page 424; Andrew Buchanan to Church dated 21 Sept 1838, Book B page 237; Andrew Buchanan to Wm. and J.P. Neal dated 23 Nov 1844 Book E page 114.

BUCHANAN,JOHN-War of 1812 pension application S.O.#25211, S.C.#15608 W.O.#21815 W.C.#25693. B.L.W.#28170-80-55 and #16318-80-55. Service in Captain T.H.Clark's Company of Virginia Militia from 2 August 1814 to 22 February 1815. Married 1st; 10 December 1819 in Prince Edward County, Virginia to Margaret (Peggy) Brightwell. Affidavit by Albert B. Buchanan dated 29 March 1879, age 44, stated that he was the son of John and Margaret Buchanan, and that his mother died 13 December 1842 in Lauderdale County, Tennessee. Soldier married 2nd to Nancy Clapton about the year 1848 in Lauderdale County, Tennessee. Soldier died 10 December 1877 in Sharpe County, Arkansas. Widow died about 1895.

BULL,ROBERT-War of 1812 pension application W.O.#41374, W.C.#33628. B.L.W.# 46344-40-50 and #100504-40-50, supplement. Service in Captain John Reed's Company of Georgia Militia from 21 November 1814 to 8 March 1815. He enlisted in Jasper County, Georgia. E.T.

Brady, of Hopkins County, Texas in 1882, stated "I was well acquainted with Robert Bull in Pike County, Georgia and lived within 1/2 mile of him 35 years ago. He was oft in my shop". He married first Susannah Sullivan 18 March 1811, she died 24 June 1851 "in the State of Arkansas". Nancy Holiday, daughter of Robert and Susan Bull, was residing in Williamson County, Texas in the year 1882. She stated that her father was born in North Carolina and that he had died 13 August 1861 in Ashley County, Arkansas. Robert Bull married second, Malinda Finkley/Finklea on 26 July 1853 in Drew County, Arkansas at the home of Elizabeth Scarborough. Malinda was the widow of Thomas Finklea, who died in September 1852. The following contained in "Version of The Psalms of David", printed in Edinburgh in the year 1768, in which it is recorded, "Robert Bull, son of Ambrose Bull and his wife Elizabeth, was born the 23rd day of April in the year of Our Lord 1788". Widow's pension application dated 24 February 1882, Hopkins County, Texas. She died 29 November 1895 in Winnsboro, Wood County, Texas at the home of her son, T.G. Finklea.
Ambrose Bull, Revolutionary War Pension Application #R1418, widow's application dated 13 August 1838, Pike County, Georgia. Ambrose Bull volunteered in Craven County, North Carolina in Captain Roach's Company of Militia. Elizabeth stated that she was married to Ambrose Bull in Craven County, North Carolina in 1777, and that he died in Craven County in March 1789. She was born in January 1753. Her application for pension was rejected because of his length of service.
1850 Federal Census, Ouachita Township, Bradley County, Arkansas, page 97: William L. Bull, 33 Ga.; Mary A., 36 Ge.; Susan, 11 Ga.; William R., 7 Ala.; Henry, 6 Miss.; Mary, 5 Miss.; James, 4 Miss.;

BUNCH,NATHANIEL-War of 1812 pension application W.O.#10382, W.C.#5995. B.L.W.#26602-80-50 and #43708-80-55. Service in Captain Abel Willis' Company, 2nd Regiment of Tennessee Militia from 4 October 1813 to 2 March 1814. Original discharge certificate, dated 10 February 1814, signed by Captain Abel Willis and Major Charles Sevier, contained in this file. Nathaniel Bunch served in Andrew Jackson's Regiment in the Battle with Creek Indians. He was married to Sarah Ray 15 November 1810 in Overton County, Tennessee. In 1850, he was a resident of Newton County, Arkansas, his bounty land application was made out by Bradley Bunch, J.P. of Carroll County, Arkansas. In 1856, his bounty land application contains an affidavit by David Collier of Carroll County, who stated that he had been a neighbor of Nathaniel Bunch in Overton County, Tennessee during the war of 1812 and since that time they have lived close neighbors a good portion of the time. Nathaniel Bunch died 16 February 1859 in Newton County, Arkansas. In 1873, Sarah Bunch applied for pension with following proof, "I, James Fancher, Clerk of the County Court within and for the County of Carroll, State of Arkansas, do hereby certify that this is a true and exact copy of the Family Record of Nathaniel Bunch which was this day presented to me, contained in The Holy Bible, Old and New Testament, published in the year 1832, leather bound, and that the records have every appearance of being genuine. Family Record, "Marriages; Nathaniel Bunch married to Sarah Ray November 15th 1810; Births; Nathaniel Bunch was borned April 23rd 1793, John Bunch was borned December the 1st 1812, Anna Bunch was bornd March 27th 1814, Charles Bunch was bornd October the 29th 1815, Calvin Bunch was bornd March the 4th 1817, Bradley Bunch was bornd December the 9th 1818, Obedience Bunch was bornd March the 12th 1820, Nathaniel Bunch was bornd June the 14th 1824, Nancy Bunch was bornd January the 24th 1826, Larkin Bunch was bornd October the 24th 1827". Affiants stated that Anna Bunch married Samuel Allred/Alread, Obedience Bunch married ___? Selby and that Nancy Bunch married ___? Whitely.

BURFORD,EDWARD W.-War of 1812 pension application S.O.#22893,

S.C.#22533. B.L.W.#13062-40-50 and #30904-120-55. Service in Captain Jacob Reed's Company of South Carolina Militia from 1 February 1815 to 24 March 1814. Married Rebecca ___? in Anderson District, South Carolina. Resided 1850 thru 1871 in Cass and Bartow Counties, Georgia. Soldier died 9 July 1883 in Arkansas. (not abstracted)

BURKS,GEORGE F.-War of 1812 pension application S.O.#21443, S.C.#18848,W.O.#36087 W.C.#25285. B.L.W.#71380-40-50 and #77157--120-55. Service in Captain Anthony W. Woodson's Company of Virginia Militia from 4 April 1814 to 29 July 1814. Soldier's application dated 4 July 1871, Shelby County, Tennessee, stated that he was born in Prince Edward County, Virginia, and that he volunteered at Prince Edward Court House. He was discharged at Norfolk, Virginia. He married Harriet B. Key 5 March 1817 in Charlotte County, Virginia. George Burks died 19 June 1872 in Shelby County, Tennessee. Widow, age 78, applied for pension 26 April 1879 in White County, Arkansas. She stated that since the war they had lived; Prince Edward County, Virginia until 1817; Lunenburg County, Virginia from 1818 to 1825; Limestone County, Alabama from 1825 to 1836; De Soto County, Mississippi from 1836 to 1839; Shelby County, Tennessee from 1839 to the death of soldier. Affidavit by James M. Key and Eliza Key of White County, Arkansas. Relationship not stated. Widow died in 1884 in White County, Arkansas.
Federal Census records-1850 Shelby County, Tenn. page 205 Mary Burks 39 Tenn.; Nancy 19 Tenn.; Sarah 15 Tenn.; William 11 Tenn.; Mary 8 Tenn.; Delila 2 Tenn.; Susan 3 Tenn.; Ceasar 7/12 Tenn. Page 207 George F. Burks 57 Virginia listed with Ann Sims(?).

BURKS,WILLIAM-War of 1812 pension application W.O.#33421 W.C.#20003 B.L.W.#55700-80-50 and #50149-80-55. Service in Captain G.C.Brandon's Company of Mississippi Militia from 17 September 1812 to 17 March 1813 and in Captain Francis Wood's Company of Mississippi Militia from 7 January 1815 to 31 March 1815. Soldier born ca 1792 in Lincoln County, Georgia. Married Permelia Walthall 28 February 1816 in Jasper County, Georgia (marriage certificate enclosed). Soldier died 5 February 1863 in Chickasaw County, Mississippi. Widow died 27 August 1887 in Johnson County, Arkansas.

BURROUGH/BURROWS,WILLIAM JUNIOR-War of 1812 pension application S.O.#34729, S.C.#25647, W.O.#45282, W.C.#35428. B.L.W.#114719-160-55. Service in Captain Steven Griffith's Company of Mississippi Militia. His father, William Burrough Senior, served in the same company with him. He enlisted near Huntsville, Alabama on 2 November 1813, discharged 2 December 1813. He married Nancy E. Dyer 24 March 1840 in Crawford County, Arkansas. William J., Benjamin and Elmina Orrick, residents of Crawford County all attended the wedding of William and Nancy Burrough. Jesse Renfroe stated that he lived within 5 miles of William Burrough and had known him for fifty years. William Burrough, born ca 1796, died 29 June 1892 near Mountainsburg, Crawford County, Arkansas, and is buried "in what is known as the Peter's Graveyard". Widow, Nancy, died about 1899 in Crawford Co.

BURT,HEWITT-War of 1812 pension application S.O.#28891 S.C.#20867 W.O.#40044. B.L.W.#46619-40-50 and #79779-120-55. Service in Captain Peter B. Rogers' Company of South Carolina Militia from 10 December 1813 to 15 March 1814. Married Mary Baird 3 May 1814 in Abbeville, South Carolina. Application dated 26 April 1873, Hewitt Burt age 82, resident of Ozan Township. He died 4 February 1880 in Hempstead County, Arkansas. Widow, age 85, applied for pension 26 June 1880.
Federal Census record-1850 Hempstead County, Ark. page 210 Hewitt Burt 58 Virginia; Mary 54 S.Car.; Hewitt E. 27 Ark.; William T. 20 Ark.; George W. 15 Ark.; Andrew 9 Ark.; Susan 22 Ark.

BURTON,NOEL-War of 1812 pension application S.O.#19659, S.C.#12660 W.O.#35283, W.C.#24255. B.L.W.#54543-40-55 and #45443-120-55. Noel Burton was born 21 August 1793 in North Carolina. He died 3 July 1875 in Clay County, Arkansas. He enlisted in service at Hillsboro, Caswell County, North Carolina in Captain James Holder's Company of North Carolina Militia from 28 November 1814 to 22 February 1815. Married first to Nancy Dobbins 15 August 1816 in Caswell County, North Carolina. She died in McNairy County, Tennessee. He married second, Charlotte Clemons 13 May 1849 in McNairy County, Tennessee. Soldiers discharge certificate contained in this brief.

BUSBY,ROBERT-War of 1812 pension application S.O.#27967, S.C.#19631 W.O.#36053, W.C.#25838. B.L.W.#13038-80-50 (duplicate contained in this brief) and #20286-80-55. Soldiers bounty land application dated 25 November 1850, Lafayette County, Mississippi, stated that he entered service in Camden, South Carolina in Captain Chapman Levy's Company of South Carolina Militia from 1 October 1814 to 4 March 1815. In 1855 he was residing in Pontotoc County, Mississippi, and in 1872 in Locksburg, Sevier County, Arkansas. Soldier died 9 November 1876 in Sevier County, Arkansas. He married first, Celia Lowery who died in 1869. He married second, Mary Hall 27 November 1870 in Camden, Sevier County, Arkansas (marriage record enclosed in brief). Widows application dated 12 April 1879, stated that she was age 54, born in Jackson County, Alabama, from whence she moved to Clark County, Arkansas and from there to Sevier County. She died in Sevier County 9 August 1899.

BUXTON,JOHN O'KELLY-War of 1812 pension application S.O.#15078, S.C.#10887, W.O.#34479, W.C.#26422. B.L.W.#20555-80-50 and #38322-80-55. Service in Captain Willis Well's Company of Virginia Militia. He volunteered at Smithfield, Virginia on 4 March 1813, discharged at Norfolk on 14 August 1813. He married Frances Jenno(?) in March 1823 in Sparta, White County, Tennessee. He applied for bounty land in 1850 in Morgan County, Tennessee. Application for bounty land in 1855, made in Bollinger County, Missouri, and his pension application, dated 26 April 1871 was made in Benton County, Arkansas. John Buxton died in Benton County, Arkansas on 14 February 1874. Frances Buxton was residing in Floyd County, Indiana, when she applied for pension 21 January 1879. She stated that her husband had been staying with friends, when he had become ill and died. The friends had refused to send word to her or her family of his illness, "because they said that we were Black Republicans". She submitted a page from the Bible of her husband, which is difficult to read. There is a reference to Sary Buxton, who is identified as the first wife. "William H. Buxton, son of John and Sary Buxton was born October 30th 1814, John O.K. Buxton, son of J.and S. Buxton November 11th 1816, Mary Ann Buxton was born in Feb. 20 1818, Elizer/Eliner(?) Catherine was born March 12th 1822, Mills Wells Buxton was born Sept. 1825(?), Mary Jane Buxton, daughter of John and Franky Buxton, was born July 24th 1826(?)" Also contained in this file is a letter written by Thomas R. Buxton, grandson of John Buxton, to his Uncle Wills W. Buxton. Thomas makes reference to brother, James who lives in Henry County, Missouri; a sister who lives in Texas; a brother named George; a brother who is blind, who went to school in St.Louis to learn the broom trade and later became a preacher. This letter was written from Caverna, McDonald County, Missouri.

BYRD/BIRD,WILLIAM-War of 1812 pension application W.O.#28017, W.C.#27539. B.L.W.#13056-160-50. Entered service at "The Red Banks" in Henderson County, Kentucky in January 1812 in Captain James Hunter's Company, 17th Regiment, U.S.Infantry, and was transferred to Captain Appling's Company of U.S.Rifles. He was discharged in June 1813. He married Charlotte Williams in 1819 in Hopkins County, Kentucky, at the home of her father, Henry Williams. Charlotte had a sister named Frances (married name, Reynolds). William and Charlotte Byrd remained in Kentucky until about 1849, when they moved to Arkansas. He applied for Bounty Land in 1851, while a resident of Wild Haus, Izard County, Arkansas. In that application he stated that his age was 55. He died in Izard County on 12 March 1856. Charlotte Byrd applied for pension in Izard County. Affidavits from: William R. Bryd, who stated that he had lived with William Byrd before his death, and from Charles Crowley of Graves County, Kentucky, who stated that he had been close friends and neighbors of William Byrd since childhood.

CABANISS,ELIJAH-War of 1812 pension application W.O.#36916 W.C.-#27420. B.L.W.#40983-80-50 and #33049-80-55. Entered service in Jones County, Georgia in Captain James Safford's Company of Georgia Militia from 21 November 1814 to 6 May 1815. He was born ca 1795, place not stated. Married first Joicy Cola in Clark County, Alabama. She died in Union County, Arkansas in 1845. He married second Harriet A. Bussey 14 December 1845 in Union County (marriage record enclosed in brief). Soldier died in Union County 2 December 1870, and Harriet, age 57, applied for pension in 1879. Affidavit by John Hearin, age 67 in 1879, who stated that he had known Harriet all of her life. Affidavit by Jesse M. Cabaness, age 70 in 1879, who stated that he had known Elijah Cabaness all his life and had known Harriet 18 years.

CAIN,JOHN-War of 1812 pension application S.O.#29537, S.C.#21309. B.L.W.#34706-40-50 and #85029-120-55. Service in Captain Richard Lewis' Company of Indiana Militia from 18 May 1813 to 18 July 1813. Married Hannah McCauley in May 1814 in Wayne County, Indiana. Resided 1851 in Green County, Wisconsin; 1855 in Fayette County, Iowa and in 1874 in Bentonville, Benton County, Arkansas. (not abstracted)

CALLAHAN,DENNIS-War of 1812 pension application S.O.#13792, S.C.#19875. B.L.W.#34752-80-50 and #41483-80-55. Service in the Virginia Militia in Captain Hugh Stewart's Company, Captain Briscoe Baldwin's Company and Captain John Dickinson's Company. Married Sarah E. Jewell 3 June 1824 in Columbia, Boone County, Missouri. He applied for bounty land in 1851 in Benton County, Arkansas. He submitted his original discharge certificate, which is contained in this file. He died in Benton County on 25 January 1879. (not abstracted)

CALLAHAN,SEBASTIAN or BESTON-War of 1812 pension application W.O.#29125, W.C.#34385. B.L.W.#76217-40-50 and #72486-120-55. Service in Captain John Dickinson"s Company of Virginia Militia from 6 February 1815 to 21 May 1815. Married to Hannah Sharp (or Dorchester), to Cynthia Stevenson and finally on 16 February 1854 in Benton County, Arkansas to Jane S. Daniels. He applied for bounty land in Warren County, Missouri in 1850. Soldier died in Benton County, Arkansas on 6 September 1862. (not abstracted) Benton County, Arkansas, Will Book A, page 215; "I, Beston Callahan, of the County of Benton State of Arkansas, bequeath to my daughter, Josephine Callahan and to my son, Ohier Callahan, all my estate, both real and personal except the note executed to me by my son, Benjamin S. Callahan, in February 1854. If either of my said children, Josephine or Ohier, should die, their part of the estate should go to the other. I wish my two old Negros, Garrison and Charity, to be taken care of. Although, my wife, Jane, has refused to live with me, I have divided my personal estate with her, which she may keep; I appoint my friend, George Callahan, executor of my estate and guardian of my two children, Josephine and Ohier" signed 8 November 1861. Codicil; September 1st 1862; "In consequence of the removal of George Callahan

21

from the State, I do hereby appoint William M. Cooper, executor of my last will and testament and William A. Lampkin as guardian of my children". Recorded 12 September 1862.

CALLEN,CHARLES-War of 1812 pension application W.O.#22799, W.C.-#22158. B.L.W.#54408-40-50 and #65145-120-55. Service in Captain Bowman's Company of Tennessee Militia from 23 September 1813 to 22 December 1813. Married first to Margaret Ingram, second to Sethy Bryan 3 April 1856 in Washington County, Arkansas. Resided 1851 and 1855 in Newton County, Missouri, soldier died 8 September 1870 in Lawrence County, Missouri. Widow removed to Moravia, Appanoose County, Iowa by 1878. (not abstracted)

CAMP,GEORGE-War of 1812 pension application W.O.#33501, W.C.#27764. B.L.W.#25280-160-50. Service in Captain Jesse Laftwick's Company, Captain Edward S. Hall's Company and in Captain John Galt's Company in the Virginia Militia. His commission to Ensign in the 101st Regiment, 7th Brigade and 1st Division of the Virginia Militia, signed by Governor of Virginia, William H. Cabell is in this file. First wife not identified, however, statement by Henry C. Camp dated 30 September 1853, of Benton County, Tennessee "George Camp was my father, and my mother, George Camp's first wife, died in Benton County, Tennessee". Married second Thursea Burns 5 November 1836 in Benton County, Tennessee. George and Thursea had two children mentioned in this application; Harris K. and Elizabeth Camp. Soldier died 5 August 1840 in Benton County, Tennessee. Widow residing in Madison County, Arkansas in 1878. Her age stated as 72.
Federal Census record-1850 Benton County, Tenn. page 284 Thursday Camp female 44 Alabama; Emily 21 Tenn.; Wyly(?) 18 Tenn.; Harris 12 Tenn.; Elizabeth 10 Tenn.

CAMPBELL,JOHN-War of 1812 pension application W.O.#22568, W.C.#7020. B.L.W.#17501-160-50. He was born in Washington County, Virginia ca 1776. Married Mary E. Cowan 23 May 1822 in Knox County, Tennessee. He applied for bounty land in Washington County, Arkansas in 1851. He died 20 November 1858 at his home in Cane Hill, Washington County, Arkansas. His widow removed to Salem, Franklin County, Tennessee before 1876, where she applied for pension. Her application was referred to the Committee on Revolutionary Pensions and War of 1812 Pensions. The 44th Congress of the United States passed H.R.#1985 on 7 February 1876, granting pension to Mary E. Campbell, said Bill introduced by Mr. John M. Bright. On 29 October 1877, Congress passed H.R.#384, also granting pension to Mary E. Campbell. From the War Department, Adjutant General's Office, Washington, D.C. 29 June 1876 the records show the following "John Campbell was appointed Ensign and 2nd Lieutenant, 4th Regt. U.S.Infantry from Virginia 10 July 1799; promoted 1st Lieutenant same Regt. 4 March 1799 (?), transferred to the 2nd Infantry 17 April 1802, promoted Captain 2nd Infantry 30 September 1803; promoted Major 6th Infantry 6 July 1812 and Lieutenant Colonel 28th Infantry 31 January 1814; and was disbanded in June 1815, under the Congressional Act of 3 March 1815, reducing and reorganizing the Army. He is reported present at Detroit 4 September 1797; at Loftus Height 29 October 1798; on the Ohio River 23 March 1801; at Columbian Springs in December 1802; recruiting in Tennessee in February, May, June, July and August 1803, and January, June, October, and November 1804; at Fort Massac (Massacre?) December 1804 and February, March, June and July 1805; at Fort Adams November 1805 and January to June 1806; at Natchitoches June to October 1806; at New Orleans December 1806 and February 1807; at Fort Adams July 1807; at Columbian Springs, commanding company from August 1807 to 18 June 1811; tried by General Court Martial 28 September; unmilitary and oppressive conduct; suspended from all command two months, when released from arrest and returned to duty; at Washington, Mississippi Territory June and October 1811; at Baton Rouge February 1812;

at Fort Stoddart July 1812; tried by General Court Martial at Pass Christian November or December 1812; conduct unbecoming an officer and a gentleman and abuse of trust; guilty of 2nd charge and sentenced to be reprimanded in general orders; at Fort George June, July, August and September 1813; sick at French Mills November and December 1813; on furlough March and April 1814; ordered to Olympia Springs September 1814; present at Olympia Springs, Kentucky from February 16 to April 30, 1815; out of service in June 1815. The 6th Infantry appears to have participated in the attack on and capture of Fort George 27 May 1813". Some of the affiants in this application refer to John Campbell as General Campbell, however his records show his rank as Lieutenant Colonel at the time of his discharge. In 1876, Honorable J.W.Throckmorton, of the U.S. House of Represent- atives testified "I am personally well acquainted with Lt. Col. Campbell and Mrs. Mary Campbell, and lived with him as a part of his family, his widow is now over 80 years old; the remnant of her property was destroyed by fire during the late Civil War".

CAMPBELL,THOMAS-War of 1812 pension application S.O.#11753, S.C.#7458, W.O.#38282, W.C.#28312. Thomas Campbell volunteered into service at Walnut Point, near Northumberland Court House (now called Heathville) in Northumberland County, Virginia in October 1814 in Captain Joseph Desheal's Company, Third Regiment Commanded by Colonel Downen. His First Lieutenant was Griffin Lampkin and Second Lieutenant was Willis Huddleston. They were driven out of Walnut Point by the British, and they retreated to Northumberland Court House. After several weeks of scrimmage, they retreated to "Spry's Hill". In December 1814, they were ordered to Chappell Church on the Rappahannock River in Lancaster County, Virginia. After the war they were dismissed and sent to their homes. He married Rebecca Clutter in Mason County, Kentucky on 11 August 1825. Thomas Campbell died at his home in Sand Creek Township, Decatur County, Indiana on 26 May 1879; his widow applied for and was granted pension in 1879 in Jennings County, Indiana. She removed the family record from her Bible and sent them to the Commissioner of Pensions, said record contained in this file. On 22 January 1883, Mrs. Eliza Smith, resident of O'Kean, Randolph County, Arkansas, applied for arrears in pension of Thomas and Rebecca Campbell, stating "that she, the aforesaid, Eliza Smith, Mary M. Taylor, Amanda Smith and Sarah J. West are the issue and only surviving issue of the said marriage of Thomas Campbell and Rebecca Clutter." Family Record, to wit,- "MARRIAGES; Thomas Campel (sic) to Rebecca Clutter on the 11th August AD 1825; BIRTHS; Thomas Campbell was born in June 26th day 1798(?); Rebecca Campbell was born on the 29th day of July AD 1800; James Campbell was born 29th December AD 1826; Elizabeth Campbell was born on the 9th day May AD 1828; Mary M. Campbell was born September 28th AD 1830; Caty Ann Campbell was born April the 18th AD 1832; Amanda Campbell was born 17th December AD 1833; Sarah Jane Campbell was born March 2nd AD 1836; Eliza Campbell was born March 28th AD 1838; Melvina Campbell was born March 4th AD 1840; Isaac B. Campbell was born July 20th 1842. DEATHS; Melvina Campbell departed this life on ___?; James Campbell on the 13th of April AD 1838; Caty Ann Campbell on the 17th of March 1839; Martha Campbell on the 29th of May AD 1845; Isaac B. Campbell on the first of June AD 1845; Elizabeth Campbell died July 15th Ad 1848; Thomas Campbell died May the 26th Ad 1879".

CANNON,JOHN-War of 1812 pension application S.O.#22487, S.C.#15807. B.L.W.#32830-160-55. Service in Captain William Cannon's Company of South Carolina Militia from 20 January 1814 to 28 July 1814. He was mustered into service in Abbeville District, South Carolina and discharged at Powelton, Georgia. He served in the Creek Indian War, Battle of Horseshoe Bend and the Battle of New Orleans.

Married Jemima Cantrell in 1824 in Gainesville, Georgia. Resided
1851 and 1855 in Tarrant County, Texas and in 1871 in Washington
County, Arkansas (P.O. Maquire's Store). In 1851 he stated his
age as 67.

CARNETT,WILLIAM-War of 1812 pension application W.O.#42136,
W.C.#33793. B.L.W.#5171-160-12. Service in Captain Joseph Clay's
Company and Captain Brittain's Company, 10th U.S.Infantry and
in Captain Turner's Company, 7th U.S.Infantry. Served from 23
April 1813 to 11 May 1816. Original discharge certificate contained
in file. He married Mary Eddleman either 16 July or 20 August
1816 in Wilkes County, North Carolina. Soldier died 5 August
1837 in Benton County, Arkansas. Widow residing in Scott County,
Arkansas by 1882, she died there in 1893. (not abstracted)

CARTER,BERNARD-War of 1812 pension application W.O.#5864, W.C.#2016.
B.L.W.#11020-80-50 and #46814-80-55. Service in Captain Ezekiel
Bass' Company of Tennessee Militia from 20 September 1814 to
20 March 1815. He married Rosa Benthall on 28 March 1811 in
Wilson County, Tennessee. Soldied died 24 April 1853 in Wilson
County, Tennessee. Widow resided in Arkadelphia, Clark County,
Arkansas 1855 thru 1871. (not abstracted)

CARUTHERS,JOHN-Revolutionary War Pension Application #S32163
dated 1 July 1833, Independence County, Territory of Arkansas. He
was born 12 July 1746 in Baltimore County, Maryland. He was
residing in District 96, South Carolina in 1776, when he enlisted
in Captain John Carter's Company of Rangers, Major Andrew Pickens
Detachment. The Colonel, who commanded the Regiment, a Mr. __?
Williams, later deserted and joined the British. His Regiment
was attacked by the British on "Cracker's Neck" and were defeated.
After the defeat, Caruthers returned to his home, which he stated
was in Rutherford County, North Carolina. He joined Colonel
Melmada's Regiment in General Greene's Brigade, and participated
in the Battle of Eutaw Springs, for which he received a discharge.
He served in Captain William Whiteside,s Company in a march
against the Cherokees. About three weeks before the Battle of
King's Mountain, he was taken prisoner while on Nob Creek in
Rutherford County, North Carolina. He was held as prisoner at
King's Mountain until the British defeat at that battle, when
he was rescued. After his release, he joined a volunteer company
and spent the remainder of the war doing battle against the
Tories "by whom he was surrounded in every direction, and that
he had made himself so obnoxious to them, that his only safety
was in the American Army". Benjamin Hardin, participant at King's
Mountain, stated that he had been witness to the rescue of John
Caruthers at that battle. John Caruthers stated that he also
served in the war of 1812 in Captain Jacob Short's Company of
Rangers. After the war he lived in Rutherford, North Carolina
for about 2 years, then to Tennessee for 4 or 5 years, then
to Kentucky for 6 years, he lived in Illinois about 18 years
then to Arkansas Territory. In 1839 he was residing in Clark
County, Arkansas with his grandson, not named, and stated that
was his only living relative in that area.
Clark County,Ark. Deed Book A page 76- John Caruthers to James
Miles, Dec 13, 1821- N E Section 35 Town South 8 Range West
23.
Independence County, Arkansas Marriage Records, page 35, Samuel
Caruthers Senior and Matilda Crow 6 June 1836.

CASSIDY,JEREMIAH-War of 1812 pension application S.O.#6635,
S.C.#6952. B.L.W.#40488-40-50 and #34128-120-55. Service in
Captain Robert Berry's Company of Kentucky Militia from 15 August
1814 to 19 November 1814. He married Isabella Poe 1 October
1807 in Nicholas County, Kentucky. Removed to Washington County,
Arkansas before 1851, where he was still residing in 1871. (not
abstracted)

CASWELL,ISHAM-War of 1812 pension application S.O.#29548 S.C.#21331 W.O.#29845 W.C.#26129. B.L.W.#23513-160-50. Drafted in to service in Eatonton, Putnam County, Georgia 23 August 1813 in Captain David Rosser's Company of Georgia Militia. He was discharged 6 March 1814 and enrolled again 15 December 1814 to 15 March 1815. Bounty land application dated 7 January 1853 at Franklin, Heard County, Georgia. He married in Columbia County, Arkansas on 2 November 1869 to Elizabeth Seward. Soldier died 30 October 1876 in Columbia County and is buried at Barges Chapel about 9 miles S.W. of Magnolia. Widow died in Columbia County on 21 April 1907.

CHAPMAN,DOUGLASS-Old war pension application.O.W. Inv. Cert. #400910 File #48750, Special Act. O.W.Wid. App.#R2525 Ind. Wid. App.#2420. Service in Captain Wheeler's Company, 3rd Regiment U.S. Infantry; Seminole Indian War. He was born in 1816 in Toronto, Canada; enlisted 22 February 1837 at Syracuse, New York. Discharged 24 February 1840 in Fort Smith, Arkansas. Married 10 December 1846 to Cynthia Whitby in Memphis, Shelby County, Tennessee. Marriage Record #1 License number 113. Douglass and Cynthia had at least three children, not named in this application. Soldier's pension application rejected; however, on 9 June 1888, Honorable Thomas C. McRea, of Arkansas, introduced a bill in the Congress of the United States to place the name of Douglass Chapman of Malvern, Hot Springs County, Arkansas on the Federal Pension Roll,"That he receive such pension as is provided by the laws of the United States for persons engaged in the military service of the United States in the War of 1812." Soldier died 19 March 1892 in Hot Springs County, Arkansas, and his widow, age 69, applied for pension on his service. Among the affiants to her application were; Charles G. Whitby, age 65 and George Whitby, age 66 both residents of Goliad, Texas, and both witnesses to her marriage to Douglass Chapman.

CHAPMAN,WILSON-Old war pension application O.W. Wid. App. #13109, transferred to Mexican War, Mex.War.Wid. App.#313. Widow Sarah. Service in Captain Engard's Company of Arkansas Volunteers. (not abstracted)

CHEATHAM,WILLIAM-Revolutionary War Pension Application #S31607, dated 1833 in Cumberland County, Kentucky. He was born 28 August 1762 in Chesterfield County, Virginia. He enlisted in service in 1778 in Captain Henry Cheatham's Company. In 1779 he served in Captain Creed Haskins' Company under Major Boice. In 1779 he served in Captain Barnet Marchom's Company in Colonel Bowling's Regiment. He fought in the Battles of Petersburg and Sunbury. In 1781 he was detailed to purchase cattle for the Siege of Yorktown. Application for transfer of pension dated 7 March 1837, Hempstead County, Arkansas, stating that he had moved to Arkansas to be near three of his children.
Hempstead County, Arkansas Will Book B pages 31 thru 35- will of William Cheatham signed 22 Aug 1836 recorded 8 July 1844; "I William Cheatham, of the County of Cumberland State of Kentucky- _____" Wife Salley (?), children; Richardson, Owen, Martha, Henry, Christopher, Granville K. and Matthew V. Cheatham, also Elizabeth Bowman and Virginia Miller.

CHITWOOD,DANIEL-War of 1812 pension application S.O.#25243 S.C.#-15607.B.L.W.#26353-80-50 and #38626-80-55. Service in Captain Anderson's Company and in Captain Samuel Lane's Company of Georgia Militia from 21 November 1814 to 6 May 1815. Married Mary McCrackin 2 October 1817 in Cass County, Georgia. Residing in Cass County in 1855. In 1871 he was in Franklin County, Arkansas and in 1879 he was in Crawford County, Arkansas. Soldier died before 23 January 1884. (not abstracted)

CHITWOOD,RICHARD-War of 1812 pension application W.O.#20311

W.C.#26407. Married Didamer Elliot 17 March 1829 in Habersham County, Georgia. Service in Captain Samuel Lane's Company of Georgia Militia. Soldier died 8 January 1857 in Habersham County, Georgia.(not abstracted)

CHRISP,WILLIAM-War of 1812 pension application W.O.#38653, W.C.#29738. B.L.W.#90767-40-50 and #79184-120-55. Service in Captain Allen Wilson's Company of Virginia Militia from 26 August 1814 to 26 November 1814. Original discharge certificate contained in file. Married Mary Jeffers Elder 21 April 1821 in Rutherford County, Tennessee. Residing in Gibson County, Tennessee 1851 until soldier's death there on 19 February 1863. Widow to White County, Arkansas before 1879. (not abstracted)

CLARK,BENJAMIN-Revolutionary War Pension Application #S31611, dated 3 October 1832, Hempstead County, Territory of Arkansas. Benjamin Clark, Senior was born in January 1758 in Dobbs, North Carolina. When he was about 2 years old his parents moved to Duplin, North Carolina, where he was residing up to and during the Revolution. He enlisted in service in 1775 or 1776 and served under several different commanders. He served at the Battle of Cape Fear River. After the war he moved to Sampson County, North Carolina for 3 or 4 years, from there to Edgefield County, South Carolina for 9 or 10 years, from there to Logan County, Kentucky for about 18 months, then to Sumner and Wilson Counties in Tennessee for about 20 years. He then moved to Arkansas County in the then Missouri Territory and settled in a place that was later part of Hempstead County, Territory of Arkansas. Mention of son Gilbert Clark, who lived in Sevier County, Territory of Arkansas.

CLEM,MASON-War of 1812 pension application W.O.#44752, W.C.#35199. B.L.W.#79086-40-50 (canceled and contained in file) #49314-80-50 and #39130-80-55. Mason Clem was born ca 1792 in North Carolina, and was drafted into service in Captain William Johnson's Company of Mississippi Militia from 29 September 1814 to 25 April 1815. He was residing in Madison County, Alabama. Married Phoebe Seaton 1 January 1814 in Madison County, Alabama. He applied for Bounty Land in 1852, while residing in Henderson County, Tennessee. He applied for Bounty Land in 1855 while residing in Hot Springs County, Arkansas. He died 7 May 1859 in Rockport, Arkansas. Phoebe Clem remained in Hot Springs, residing with several of her children, then she moved to Pecan Gap, Delta County, Texas, to live with her son, Jack Clem. She applied for pension in Delta County, Texas on 3 September 1888, stated that her age was 91. Her friends and neighbors referred to her as "Grandma Clem". Mrs. Abigail Gibbs, of Hot Springs County, Arkansas in 1888, stated "I will be eighty years old the 9th day of October 1888, I have lived in Hot Springs County, Arkansas forty years. I formerly lived in Hardin County, Tennessee. I knew Mason and Phoebe Clem, maiden name Seaton, in Hardin County. After I and my husband moved to this County, Mason and Phoebe Clem moved to this County. They had sixteen children in all". The 3rd Auditor report shows that a David Clem served in the war of 1812 with Mason Clem.

CLINE,WILLIAM MADISON-War of 1812 pension application W.O.#39786, W.C.#31981. B.L.W.#25106-80-50 and #43612-80-55. Service in Captain Francis Berry's Company, Colonel Samuel Bunch's Regiment of Tennessee Militia from 6 January 1814 to 17 May 1815. William Cline was born in Virginia, ca 1794, and was residing in Jefferson County, Tennessee, when drafted into service. He was married first to Mary Cluck, who died in Jefferson County, Tennessee. He married second; Permelia Grayson 24 December 1837 in Monroe County, Tennessee. They moved to Madison County, Arkansas between 1851 and 1856, where he died 24 March 1858. Permelia Cline moved to Tennessee Valley, Bell County, Texas before 1880, where she had two children living; William A. Cline born 10 September

1847 and Nancy J. Whitely born 26 September 1856. They stated that they had an older sister, "living in the State of Arkansas, when last heard from".

CLINKENBEARD,JONATHAN-War of 1812 pension application W.O.#13264, W.C.#22368. B.L.W.#24607-160-50. Service in Captain William Garrett's Company of Maryland Militia from 20 August 1812 to 20 August 1813. Married Sarah Smart 9 April 1816 in Frankford, Franklin County, Kentucky. Soldier died 28 August 1836 in Pope County, Arkansas. Widow in Holt County, Missouri in 1853; and in Otoe County, Nebraska in 1878. (not abstracted)

CLOWER,JONATHAN-Revolutionary War Pension Application #W22802. He was born 3 December 1763 in Berks County, Pennsylvania, but was residing in Hillsborough, Orange County, North Carolina in May 1781, when he enlisted in Captain Dunahoe's Company , Colonel Dixon's Regiment of North Carolina Militia. He was transferred to Colonel Henry Lee's Regiment and served at the Battle of Eutaw Springs and the Battle of Dorchester. He returned to Pennsylvania after the war and was married in Middletown, Dauphin County, Pennsylvania to Mary Shuler on 25 October 1791. Jonathan Clower was allowed pension on his application executed 14 August 1832 in Bibb County, Alabama. He died in Shelby County, Alabama on 18 September 1836. His widow applied for pension 8 November 1844 in Shelby County, Alabama. In making application, she removed the pages from her Bible, which are contained in this file, apparently all in the handwriting of Jonathan Clower; "Jonathan Clower was born in the year of our Lord December 3, 1763; Mary Clower was born in the year of October 1774 (?); names of their children: Elizabeth Clower was born July the 16, 1792, Catherine Clower was born November the 27, 1794; Miriam Clower was born March the 23, 1797; Mary Clower was born March the 4, 1799; Rebecca Clower was born May the 7, 1801; Nancy Clower was born March the 1, 1803; Delilah Clower was born April the 26, 1805; Lurana Bush Clower was born the 10 day of May 1807; Malinda Clower was born July the 16, 1809; Jonathan S. Clower was born the 10 day of July 1811; James Lawrence Butts Clower was born August the 24, 1813; Marriages; Jonathan Clower and Mary Shuler was married October the 25, 1791 in the State of Pennsylvania, Doffin (sic) County, Middletown Parton Township in John P____? house by Jonathan McCluer Esq. of said County. Jonathan Clower, his book, February the 20, 1826". In 1851, the pension of Mary Clower, was transferred to Little Rock, Pulaski County, Arkansas. There is mention in this application to Daniel Clower, possibly a brother of Jonathan. Daniel also enlisted in service in Orange County, North Carolina. His pension application number is #S37865. In 1819 he was a resident of Giles County, Tenn, and in 1831 he was in Gwinnett County, Georgia.

COBB,WILLIAM-Old War pension application O.W.Wid. Cert #887 File #12771. Service in Captain William Hutt's Company of Alabama Militia, Seminole Indian War of 1837. He was a resident of Monroe County, Alabama, when drafted into service. He became ill and died 12 February 1837, while in service. Widow's application dated 26 March 1839, Conecuh County, Alabama. Her maiden name was Nancy Campbell, and she had married William Cobb in December 1824 in Monroe County, Alabama, at which time she had been about eighteen years old. They had children; Elizabeth Cobb, Christian Cobb, Samuel Cobb, Joseph Cobb, Fanny Cobb and Daniel Cobb. She was inscribed on Alabama pension rolls on 16 December 1840, and was on Arkansas pension rolls 13 February 1842. In 1855, she was residing in Union County, Arkansas.

COBLER,FREDERICK-Revolutionary War Pension Application #S1654. He was born 14 August 1758 in Culpepper County, Virginia. He was residing in Guilford County, North Carolina when he enlisted in service in March 1776. He served in Captain Dalton's Company,

Colonel James Martin's North Carolina Regiment. In 1781 he served in Captain John May's Company. After the war he lived in Guilford and Rockingham Counties, North Carolina until 1806 when he moved to Davidson County, Tennessee. He died there 21 September 1840. In the 1840 census he was listed with John Corbett and his age was 82.

COBLER,JOHN L.-War of 1812 pension application S.O.#13811 S.C.#8931 W.O.#34820 W.C.#29545. B.L.W.#6553-160-50 (canceled). Served as Private in Captain Joel Parrish's Company of Tennessee Militia from 14 March 1814 to 16 May 1814, and as Lieutenant in Captain Richard Tate's Company of Tennessee Militia from 2 September 1814 to 27 April 1815. Married Polly Ann Zachary 14 July 1834 in Davidson County, Tennessee.(she was born ca 1812.) He was born ca 1791. They remained in Tennessee until about 1866 when they moved to Kentucky, and then to Randolph County, Arkansas in 1870. Soldier died in Randolph County, 26 November 1878 and his widow died there 12 March 1883. Daughter, Rachel, stated that John L. Cobler was the son of Frederick Cobler of the American Revolution. Other children named in this application; Frederick H., born ca 1837, and William born ca 1846. Statement made that John and Polly Ann Cobler had 10 children.

COCHRAN,HARPER-War of 1812 pension application S.O.#26686, S.C.#18253. B.L.W.#23965-80-50 and #16592-80-55. Service in Captain Joab Norton's Company and in Captain Putnam Case's Company of Ohio Militia. He srved two tours of duty; 2 June 1812 to 19 September 1812 and from 4 May 1813 to 28 May 1813. Married Lydia Collins in Scott County, Indiana on 3 April 1817. Resided 1850 and 1855 in Scott County, Indiana. Resided in Harrison, Boone County, Arkansas in 1872. (not abstracted)

COCHRANE,RICHARD E.-Old war pension application O.W.Wid. Cert. #799 File #26657. Service as 1st Lieutenant in the 4th Regiment of U.S. Infantry in the Mexican War. He was killed in the Battle of Resaca-de-la-Palma, Texas on 9 May 1846, with surviving widow Sally Cochrane and children not named. Widow's application dated 14 June 1853, Little Rock, Pulaski County, Arkansas. "She resides irregularly in Little Rock since 1851", previous to that time she resided in Kentucky and with friends in the U.S. Army. On 4 March 1861, her pension was transferred to Philadelphia, Pennsylvania, but was soon stopped because she refused to take the loyalty oath required of pensioners who were residents of Confederate States. She stated that she had refused to take the oath because she had property in Little Rock, and was afraid the Confederate Government might confiscate said property. She finally took the oath of loyalty in Little Rock on 20 June 1865, which apparently did not restore her pension. On 9 November 1868, in Washington, D.C. she reaffirmed her loyalty to the United States Government. Mrs. Sally Cochrane died 7 April 1910 at the home of her son-in-law, Thomas B. Lee, who stated that "my wife is her only child".

COFFEE,MELVIN-Old war pension application. O.W.Wid. Cert. #1563 File #29190 O.W. Minor's Cert. #1298 File #11926. He served in Company C Texas Mounted Volunteers under command of Captain Daniel Montague in the Mexican War. He had enlisted in Fannin County, Texas, and died of disease 21 August 1846,"on the Rio Grande". His widow, Louisa Jane, stated that she had married Melvin Coffee in Johnson County, Arkansas on 18 January 1844. They had Malvina Penelope Coffee, born 6 November 1844 and James G. Coffee, born 25 December 1845. Louisa Jane Coffee then married James C. Baskins on 9 November 1847 in Johnson County. He was appointed guardian to the two children at the October 1848 Session of the Johnson County Probate Court. Application for pension dated 31 October 1850, Horsehead Township, Johnson County, Arkansas.

COLE,HIRAM-War of 1812 pension application S.O.#26924, S.C.#18127. B.L.W.#24150-80-50 and #25263-80-55. Service in Captain William Martin's Company of Tennessee Militia from 28 September 1814 to 1 May 1815. Married Mary Simons on 7 September 1819 in Williamson County, Tennessee. Resided 1851 thru 1872 in Yell County, Arkansas. Soldier died 2 May 1880. (not abstracted)

COLE,THOMAS-War of 1812 pension application S.O.#7752, S.C.#11785. B.L.W.#26374-160-12. Service in Captain John A. Roger's Company, 24th Regiment U.S. Infantry from 12 August 1812 to 5 January 1817. Original discharge certificate contained in this file. Married Nancy Adams in August 1812 in Carter County, Tennessee. In 1817 they lived in Newport, Campbell County, Kentucky. In 1871, he applied for pension in Phillip's Bayou, Phillip's County, Arkansas. (not abstracted)

COLLINS,ELI-Revolutionary War Pension Application #S31615, dated 10 December 1832, Limestone County, Alabama. Stated that he was born 26 March 1759 in Sussex County, Delaware. He entered service in June 1776 in Martin County, North Carolina. He joined a company of North Carolina Militia under command of Captain Little, marched to Wilmington, North Carolina, where they were joined with the army of General Ashe. In June 1780 he was residing in Orange County, when he again joined a company of militia under command of Colonel Moore. He stated that they were marched to Cross Creek on Cape Fear River, from there to South Carolina where they were joined up with Gates army shortly before Gates was defeated. He was under the command of Captain James Kell at the Battle of Lindsey's Mill. After the war he remained in Orange County, North Carolina until 1804, then to Wilkes County, Georgia. In 1818 he moved to Limestone County, Alabama. Application dated 24 May 1837, Hempstead County, Arkansas for transfer of pension to Arkansas because "his son with whom he has lived for many years and on whom he looks for protection in a great measure removed to this state and urged him to accompany him". 1840 Federal Census-Hempstead County, Ark. William R. Collins with 1 male 5-10, 3 males 10-15, 2 males 15-20, 3 males 20-30, 6 males 50-60, 1 male 80-90, 1 female 5-10, 1 female 20-30, 1 female 40-50. pensioner Eli Collins age 83.

COLLINS,ISAAC C.-War of 1812 pension application S.O.#28979, S.C.#20998. B.L.W.#24008-80-50 and #29272-80-55. Service in Captain Jesse Bean's Company of Tennessee Militia from 8 September 1814 to 27 April 1815. Married Fannie Bean 1 November 1817 in Fayetteville, Tennessee. They resided 1851 thru 1856 in Johnson County, Arkansas. Applied for pension in 1873 in Ozark, Franklin County, Ark. (not abstracted)

COLLINS,MATTHEW-Old war pension application O.W.Wid. Cert. #1965 File #10634. He enlisted into service on board a boat on the Tennessee River, on 19 March 1848 in Captain John W. Grant's Company, Lieutenant J.B. Collins, Commander, 5th Regiment of Tennessee Volunteers, Mexican War. He became ill and died of disease while in service. Widow, Louisa, applied for pension 7 September 1848, Bradley County, Tennessee. She stated that her maiden name was Gillihan and that she was married 27 February 1840. Louisa and Matthew Collins had children: Robert J. Collins born 22 November 1840; Malisa M. Collins born 8 April 1842 and Margaret C. Collins born 1845. Affidavit of Blewford and Elizabeth Gillihan of Bradley County, Tennessee. Application dated 13 January 1869, Prairie County, Arkansas, Louisa Collins, age 49, stated that she had been a resident of Brownsville in Prairie County since 15 January 1854.

CONNER,JONATHAN-Old war pension application dated 1888, Arkansas. Service in 1836. Inv.#R24054, Indian War Survivor certificate #1138 Ind. Wid.Orig. #8534. Jonathan Conner's application dated

11 August 1892, Brentwood, Washington County, Arkansas, stated that he entered service 12 May 1836 in a Company of Dragoon, under command of Captain Frank Coleman in the Frontier Disturbance with the Sabine Indians. He was discharged in Harrison County, Kentucky in November 1836. After his death, his widow applied for pension, in which application she submitted the following records from his Bible; "Jonathan H. Conner was born 15 June 1806; Jonathan H. Conner died 24 Jan 1898; Jonathan H. Conner was married to Mahaley P. Louderbach 15 Dec 1835, who was born in Harrison Co., Kentucky 13 March 1813; Mahaley P. Conner died 26 July 1852 in Farmington, Iowa; Jonathan H. Conner was married to Miss Mary Burris 30 March 1854 in Athens, Missouri." Mary Conner had a sister named Harriett Miller, residing in Wright County, Minn.

CONWAY,WILLIAM-Revolutionary War Pension Application #S31623. He was born 2 November 1761 near the Broad River in South Carolina. He entered service in 1778 or 1779 in Colonel John Anderson's Regiment of South Carolina Militia. This was a regiment of Mounted Rangers who served at the Battle of Cowpens. He stated that he was married in South Carolina and had three children born there.In 1787 he moved to Washington County, Georgia for three years, then moved to Abbeville, South Carolina. About the year 1800 he moved west of the Mississippi River, where he remained until 1810 when he moved to Hempstead County, Territory of Arkansas. Hempstead County, Ark-Guardianship Record page 68-69; William Conway appointed guardian of Eliza and Jeremiah Conway and Isaac Simmons. 27 May 1831.
Marriage Record Book BB page 149; James Conway and Mary Jane Bradley 23 Mar 1829.
Record Book BB page 79 dated 17 May 1819; Henry W. Conway "of the town of St. Louis, power of attorney to Alexander Gray of the same town".

COOK,BENJAMIN-Revolutionary War Pension Application #S31622, dated 15 September 1828, Monroe County, Alabama. He was born about 1760, place not stated. He entered into service in 1782, while a resident of Bullock County, Georgia. He served in Captain William McIntosh's Company in Major John Habersham's Regiment. He was stationed in Savannah throughout his service and was engaged in recapturing three vessels which had been captured by the British. His original discharge, dated 10 December 1783, signed by John Habersham is enclosed in this application. On 24 February 1845 he filed an application to have his pension transferred to Union County, Arkansas because "all of his children having moved and settled in Union County, Arkansas and he being desirous to reside near them the remainder of his life" He died 27 February 1846. The only family data contained in this pension is statement by a descendent "Benjamin Cook married Nancy Dixon; Their son George Washington Cook married Elizabeth Mendenhall.

COONEY,THOMAS-Old War Pension; O.W. Minors Certificate #1573 File # 6940. Application dated 1850 Arkansas. Dependents Briget and Joanna; minors. Service in Company F 12th U.S. Infantry, Mexican War. He enlisted at Little Rock, Arkansas on 24 September 1847. He died of disease in Guernevaca(?), Mexico sometime in May 1848. His wife, Elizabeth, was deceased by 19 October 1850. Peter W. Walsh was guardian of Brigett Cooney age 11 in 1850 and Joanna Cooney age 5 in 1850, described as orphans of Thomas and Elizabeth Cooney, deceased. They were all residing in Little Rock in 1850. In January 1851, John E. Knight, stated that "Elizabeth Cooney, one of the children of Thomas Cooney, died at my house in the City of Little Rock, on the 3rd day of October 1849, aged about 4 years". In April 1851, the two childern have separate guardians, and one child is living in Little Rock, while the other is a resident of Ft. Smith. In July 1853, the commissioner of pensions applied for arrears in this pension stating "John Collins, the

guardian of Briget Cooney, and a resident of Little Rock; while
Charles Clifford, guardian of Joanna Cooney has removed to Michigan
since taking out guardianship papers".

COOPER,BENJAMIN-War of 1812 pension application W.O.#20285 W.C.-
#27815. B.L.W.#18555-80-50 and #39421-80-55. Drafted in to service
at Campbell County, Tennessee, in Captain Wilson Maple's Company
of Tennessee Militia on 13 November 1814; discharged 9 April
1815. Bounty land application in 1851 filed in White County,
Tennessee, Benjamin Cooper age 66. Bounty land application 1855
filed in Carroll County, Arkansas. Benjamin Cooper married Nancy
Jennings 15 March 1835 in Rhea County, Tenn. Soldier died 15
February 1856 in White County, Tennessee. Widow (age 80) applied
for pension 29 April 1878 in Carroll County, Arkansas. Benjamin
Jennings (bn ca 1819) stated that he was the son of Nancy Cooper
and her first husband, Jackson Jennings, who died about 1822.
Statement by Jonathan Williams, of Carroll County in 1893, "Nancy
Cooper recently died at my house".

CORBETT,JESSE-War of 1812 pension application S.O.#22945 S.C.#15609.
B.L.W.#81694-40-50 and #45409-120-55. Service in Captain John
Dempsey's Company of Tennessee Militia from 24 September 1813
to 23 December 1813. Application dated 28 July 1871, Hot Springs
County, Arkansas, Jesse Corbett age 87. Married to Sarah Holland
10 January 1815 in Bedford County, Tenn. (not abstracted)

CORBETT,JOHN R.-War of 1812 pension application W.O.#26803,
W.C.#18605. B.L.W.#78584-40-50 and #54123-120-55. Service in
Captain James Marshall's Company, Savannah Volunteer Guards,
of Georgia Militia from 22 January 1815 to 23 February 1815. He
was born in Savannah, Georgia ca 1795. Married first to Eliza
Franklin, who died in Savannah, Georgia in 1826. Married second
to Mary A.H. Watts 23 September 1828 in Bibb County, Georgia. His
bounty land application in 1855 was executed in Choctaw County,
Mississippi, where they resided 33 years. Soldier died at his
home in Greensboro, Mississippi on 11 June 1875. Mary A.H. Corbett
applied for pension 29 May 1878 in New London, Union County,
Arkansas. Affidavit from William S. (age 76) and Martha A. Norman
(age 71) residents of Union County in 1878, "we were present
at the wedding of Mary Watts and John Corbett in Bibb County,
Georgia in 1828, we have been friends for 58 years".

CORNISH,WILLIAM;JUNIOR-War of 1812 pension application S.O.#29539
S.C.#21349, W.O.#44468, W.C.#34767. B.L.W.#26586-160-50. Service
in Captain T.J. Van Dyke's Company and Captain Doherty's Company
of 7th U.S. Infantry from 1 June 1809 to 31 August 1814. He
was born 15 December 1796 in Halifax County, Virginia. He stated
that his father, William Cornish, Senior, and brother Thomas
Cornish served in the same regiment with him. In 1874 his signature
is William Cornish followed by the statement "once Junior now
Senior". He stated that he was mustered out of service at old
Fort Pickney on the Mississippi River, where Memphis now stands. He
married Sarah M. Hogg 16 April 1823 at Sparta, Conecuh County,
Alabama. In 1874, William Hogg, of Union County, Arkansas, stated
that he had known William Cornish since 1809. The family Bible
was destroyed when William Cornish Senior's house was destroyed
by fire in North Carolina. Elisha Waldrop stated that "my son,
Knox K. Waldrop, married the granddaughter of William and Sarah
Cornish. Bounty land application in 1851 filed in Union County,
Arkansas. In 1874 they were living in Walnut Hills, Lafayette
County, Arkansas. Soldier died 8 April 1887 at Arkadelphia,
Clark County. In her pension application in 1887, widow stated
that they had lived in Covington County, Alabama, Jackson County,
Florida, Livingston County, Alabama and in Columbia, Lafayette
and Hempstead Counties, Arkansas. Widow died 14 December 1887,
Clark County, Arkansas.

CORNISH,WILLIAM SENIOR-War of 1812- no pension application. Bounty Land Warrant #9456-160-50. Service in Captain Van Dyke's Company of 7th U.S. Infantry from 13 May 1809 to 31 January 1814. Resided 1851 and 1852 in Union County, Arkansas.
1850 Federal Census Record, Union County, Arkansas, family #10: John H. Cornish 48, sheriff, bn Geo.; Jane D. 38 N.C.; Wm. H. Cornish 23 Ala.; John L. 21 Ala.; Rufus K. 15 Ark.; Issabella 12 Ark.; Wesley W. 8 Ark.; Jackson 6 Ark.; Family #23 W. Cornish 81, birth place not stated; Family #283: William Cornish 51 Virginia, Sarah 46 Geo.; Thomas J. 23 Tenn.; Nancy L. 16 Ark.; Jas./Jos (?) H. 14 Ark.; Lydia 12 Ark.; Geo. W. 8 Ark.; Sarah 6 Ark.

COUGHRAM,GEORGE-Revolutionary War Pension Application #R1816 and #R2362. Rejected because he did not serve six months. Entered service when he was 16 or 17 years old, and a resident of Bedford County, Virginia, in the year 1781. He joined a company of militia under the command of Captain Thomas McReynolds in a Regiment commanded by Colonel Trigg. Their regiment rendezvoused on the Big Falling River in Virginia, from whence they marched to Yorktown. He was a participant in the Siege of Yorktown and the surrender of Cornwallis. This application dated April 1838 in Sevier County, Arkansas. His application dated October 1853 in Scott County, Arkansas, for bounty land was also rejected, at which time he stated that he was aged 91.

COULSON,WILLIAM C.-Old war pension application dated 1880, Arkansas. Service in Captain Coffee's Company, Alabama Mounted Volunteers, 1837-1838. O.W.Sur.#R22328 Certificate #504844, O.W. Widow Rej. #25735. (not abstracted)

CRABTREE,ANDERSON-War of 1812 pension application W.O.#6660 W.C.#9386. B.L.W.#39146-80-50 and #41622-80-55. Served in Captain Miles Vernon's Company of Tennessee Militia and as a substitute for Robert Porter in Captain Hawkins Company. He married 29 June 1813 in Bledsoe County, Tennessee, Elizabeth Denton. Application for bounty land in 1851 made in Prairie County, Arkansas. Soldier died 9 August 1852 in Prairie County. Widow applied for bounty land in 1855 from Weakley County, Tennessee. In 1871 she was residing in White County, Arkansas. In April 1875, in White County, Arkansas, her pension application contains the following narrative: "I, Elizabeth Crabtree, was 75 years old the 8th day of March last, I was 13 years 3 mos and 21 days when I was married, my first child, Benjamin F. Crabtree was born 1 year 5 mos and 11 days after my marriage, he died in Hempstead County, Ark in 1864; my second child Hiram Crabtree was born 2 years 5 mos and 8 days after the first child, Hiram died in Weakley County, Tenn, the same week that he and my husband returned from the war,(compiler's note-Hiram served in Capt Hawkin's Co with his father Anderson) my third child was born 2 years 4 mos and 15 days after my second child and was named James E. Crabtree and now lives in Weakley County, Tenn.,my fourth child was born 2 years 3 mos and 11 days after my third child and was named Samuel Crabtree, he also lives in Weakley County, Tenn., my 5th child was born 2 years 3 mos after my 4th child and was named Nancy E. Crabtree, she died when eleven years old, my sixth child was born 2 years 9 mos after my 5th child and was named John W. Crabtree and now lives in White County, Ark. my 7th child was born 2 years 1 mo and 17 days after my 6th child and was named Mary A.M. Crabtree and died in Weakley County, Tenn. in May 1857, my 8th child was born 2 years 7 mos after my 7th child and was named Jonathan L. Crabtree and lives in Saline County, Ark. my 9th child was born 2 years 2 mos and 18 days after my 8th child and was named Elizabeth Crabtree and lives in White County, Ark. my 10th child was born 2 years 3 mos 9 days after my 9th child and was named David P. Crabtree, died in Monroe County, Ark. my 11th child was born 2 years 3 mos 3 days after my 10th child and was named Sarah E. Crabtree and died in White County, Ark. in Oct 1861, my 12th and youngest child was born 2 years 11 mos and 16 days after my 11th child and was named William Anderson Crabtree and is now living in White County, Ark.- I know these things by having them firmly fixed in my mind". In 1879, Sam J. Crabtree of White County was identified as a grandson. Benjamin Crabtree, son of Anderson and Sarah, served in Captain Farris' Company of Georgia Militia in the Cherokee Indian War in 1838.

CRAINE/or Crane,THOMAS-War of 1812 pension application S.O.#24925 S.C.#18859 W.O.#20273 W.C.#20257. B.L.W.#45722-160-55. Service in Captain John Crane's Company of Tennessee Militia from 20 December 1813 to 23 February 1814. He was married twice, first wife not identified. He married Sarah Harper 3 September 1829 at Bolivar, Hardiman County, Tennessee. They lived in Hardiman County until about 1831, when they moved to N.W. Arkansas in Boone and Washington Counties. During the Civil War Thomas Crane was forced to serve as a wagonmaster by the Confederates. He had younger sons at home who "lay in the bush" to avoid conscription into the Confederate army. He had two sons who were residing in Illinois during the war and who were serving in the Union Army. They were; Jasper Craine in Co D 31st Regt of Vols and William T. Craine of Co. F 81st Regt. Ill. Vols. Both of them were killed in the war. His daughters, Clarice Brown, formerly Spiller, and Nancy (both of whom are referred to as half sisters to the two boys who were killed) were residents of Jackson County, Illinois in 1875. They reported the "Rebel" service of their father which caused his pension to be revoked. A special investigation was started, but failed to restore the pension before Thomas' death. He died 9 November 1875 in Boone County, Arkansas. His widow was then granted pension. In her application the family Bible record has been quoted. "Thomas Crain was born 21 July 1796, his wife Sarah Crain was born 6 June 1813, Thomas Crain married Sarah Harper 3 Sept 1829 in Hardeman County, Tenn., Maryann Elizabeth Crain was born 13 Nov 1830, Orpha Caroline Crain was born 9 Dec 1833, Jasper B. Crain was born 6 June 1835, William T. Crain was born 16 June 1844". In 1855 this family was living in Carroll County, Arkansas, and in 1871 thru 1875 they were in Boone County. Widow died about 1894.

CRAWFORD,C.A.-Old war pension application dated 1892, Ark. Service in Captain Patrick's Company, Colonel William's Regiment of Alabama Volunteers. O.W. Widow Cert.#17908 File #29875; Special Congressional Act, June 25, 1892; 52nd Congress, H Bill 3838; "Be it enacted by the Senate and House of Representatives of the United States of America, in Congress assembled, that the Secretary of the Interior is hereby authorized and directed to at once place on the pension roll the name of Elizabeth R. Crawford, widow of C.A. Crawford, soldier in McMillan's Regiment, Captain George Patrick's Company, Alabama Volunteers in the Creek War, 1836, and that she is hereby allowed a pension of twelve dollars per month". She was a resident of Hot Springs, Arkansas. (compiler's note- This application is almost totally destroyed, apparently by fire)

CROSSLIN,EDWIN-War of 1812 pension application S.O.#27346 S.C.#20785 W.O.#31296 W.C.#26398. B.L.W.#114513-160-55. Service in Captain William Pearson's Company of Virginia Militia from 27 May 1814 to 26 November 1814. His entire service was performed at Norfolk, Virginia. He was born ca 1798 in Virginia, married Susan Daughtry, time and place not stated. He was in Richmond County, North Carolina ca 1828 and moved to Wilcox County, Alabama about 1838. His wife Susan died in Wilcox Co. in 1841. He married second Elizabeth Hall 19 February 1843 in Marengo County, Alabama, who had previously been married to Leonard Hall (he died 7 Oct 1842 in Marengo Co.) Elizabeth was born ca 1807 in Richmond County, North Carolina, where she resided until 1831 when she moved to Marengo County,

Alabama. After their marriage Edwin and Elizabeth remained in Marengo County until 1844 when they moved to Monroe County, Mississippi. In December 1869 they moved to Clark County, Arkansas. Edwin Crosslin died 7 August 1875 in Dobyville, Clark County, Arkansas. Widow was still in Clark County in 1878.

CROW,BENJAMIN-Revolutionary War Pension Application #R20353. Rejected for lack of proof. Application dated 17 August 1829, Antoine Township, Clark County, Arkansas Territory. Apparently he served three years in the 8th Regiment of the Virginia Line. Born ca 1783 in Augusta County, Virginia.
Clark County Marriage records; Book A page 81, James H. Crow and Emily Wells-7 June 1832; Book C page 94, William Crow and Elizabeth Smart-12 Oct 1848.

CROWNOVER,DANIEL-Revolutionary War Pension Application S32189, dated 28 October 1838, Union District, South Carolina. He was born 13 June 1763 in New Jersey, but had lived in Union District, South Carolina, "45 years and upwards". Entered service on 1 March 1779, as a substitute for his brother, Benjamin Crownover. He served at the Battle of Stono in regiments commanded by Colonel Wofford and Colonel John Thomas. On 7 August 1781, he enlisted in Virginia Regiments commanded by Colonel Morgan and Colonel Merriweather, and served at the Battle of York. Application for transfer of pension to Pope County, Arkansas dated 20 March 1840, "because his children were moving to Arkansas". Contains certificate of administration of the estate of Daniel Crownover Senior, granted to Daniel Crownover Junior, Yell County, Arkansas 31 August 1844; Daniel Crownover Senior died intestate 29 July 1844.

CRUMP,JOHN G.-War of 1812 pension application S.O.#26450 S.C.#17422. B.L.W.#24404-160-50. Service in Captain William Green's Company and Captain J.L.Jenning's Company of Virginia Militia from 27 February 1814 to 20 June 1814 and from 11 August 1814 to 20 February 1815. Married Eliza G. Watkins 30 April 1827 in Jefferson County, Tennessee. Resided 1852 in Harlan County, Kentucky, and in 1872 in Elmwood, Boone County, Arkansas. (not abstracted)

CRYER,MORGAN-Revolutionary War Pension Application #S31635 dated 15 October 1832, Lafayette County, Arkansas Territory. Morgan Cryer Senior, born 2 February 1756 in South Carolina. Entered service in 1778 in Captain Samuel Taylor's Company, Colonel Thomas Sumter's South Carolina Regiment. He was wounded in the ankle in a battle with the Cherokee Indians and was confined at Ninety-Six, South Carolina. After the war he remained in South Carolina until he was about thirty years old. He was in Opelousas, Louisana a short while before moving to Missouri Territory, which part later became a part of the Arkansas Territory.

CRYER,THOMAS-War of 1812 pension application W.C.#26762. Entered service in New Orleans, Louisana on 23 December 1814 in Captain Thomas Beckman's Company of Louisana Militia. Married 10 February 1825 Ailcy Franklin, in St. Tammany Parish, Louisana. He had a brother named William, who also served in the war of 1812. Another man named Honor Cryer served in Capt. Beckman's Company and may have been related. Thomas Cryer died in 1855 in Tyler County, Texas. (not abstracted)

CULLOM,GREEN-Old war pension application dated 1890, Arkansas. Service in Captain Adam's Company in the Black Hawk War. Inv. Application #25859 Indian War Sur. #2764 Cert. #528. (not abstracted)

CURTIS,JOHN D.-War of 1812 pension application S.O.#30433, S.C.-#25433. B.L.W.#114506-160-55. Service in Captain George Winter's Company of Tennessee Militia from 17 November 1814 to 12 May 1815. Married first to Anne Clemmons 10 August 1818 in Jackson

County, Tennessee. Second to Sallie ___? in May 1837, Lauderdale County, Tennessee. Residing in Washington County, Arkansas in 1859. (not abstracted)

DANIELS,ISAAC-War of 1812 pension application W.O.#35343 W.C.#28361. B.L.W.#32724-80-50 and #8941-80-55. Service in Captain Steele's Company of Tennessee Militia from 28 September 1814 to 27 April 1815. Married Mary Blackwood 2 July 1856 in Wayne County, Tennessee. He died in Wayne County 6 August 1860. Widow applied for pension in Pope County, Arkansas in 1879. She died there 2 May 1886. This application contains records of a special investigation. One statement is made that Isaac Daniels was born in Newbern, North Carolina about 1786, son of Joseph Daniel. He was apparently married three times. 1st not identified, 2nd wife Vica Weatherford who died in 1852. He married third Mary Blackford. The childern of Isaac and Mary identified as Jasper M. Daniels, Amanda Turner and Margaret Oates. Mary Daniels application from Galla Rock Township, Pope County, Arkansas, she stated that she was age 56 in 1879, and that she had moved to Pope County in 1862.

DANIELS,JOHN F.-Old War pension application dated 1882, Ark. Service in 2nd Mississippi Volunteers. O.W. Mother's Application #21186. (mother named Levica, no certificate number, which indicates that pension was not granted) (not abstracted.)

DANLEY,BENJAMIN F.-Old war pension application dated 1848, Arkansas. Service as Sergeant in Company B (Danley's Company) of Arkansas Mounted Volunteers, Mexican War. Inv. Cert. #3774 File #24998. Widow's file #472. He was born ca 1824 in Missouri, volunteered into service in Hempstead County, Arkansas on 30 June 1846. He suffered an attack of typhoid fever and received a medical discharge 11 April 1847 in Monterey, Mexico. His certificate of disability and his discharge are in this file. He married Amanda M. Boyle 15 March 1853 in Pulaski County, Arkansas. She had previously been married to John M. Boyle who died 12 August 1848. Her maiden name was Amanda Waddy. Benjamin Danley died 31 May 1877 in Little Rock, and widow applied for pension there 9 February 1887, her age 64. She died 28 January 1911.

DANLEY,CHRISTOPHER C.-Old War pension application dated 1848, Arkansas. Service as Captain of Co. B, Arkansas Mounted Volunteers. Mexican War. Inv. Cert. #4060, File #25007. (not abstracted)

DANLEY,JOSHUA M.-Old war pension application dated 1848, Arkansas. Service in Danley's Company of Arkansas Mounted Volunteers, Mexican War. Inv. Cert. #3499 File #25008. (not abstracted)

DARMODY,JAMES-Old war pension application dated 1850, Arkansas. Inv Cert. #4803 File #24517. (not abstracted)

DAVIS,HIRAM H.-Old war pension application dated 1857, Arkansas. Service in 3rd U.S. Dragoons, Mexican War. Inv. Cert. #13586. (not abstracted)

DAVIS,JOHN-War of 1812 pension application W.O.#29269 W.C.#23157. B.L.W.#17716-80-50 and #38797-80-55. Service in Captain Jonathan Ousley's Company of Kentucky Militia from 10 November 1814 to 10 May 1815. Married Catherine Elkins 26 October 1826 in Johnson County, Indiana. Residing in Washington County, Arkansas (P.O. West Fork) by 1841. Soldier died in Washington County 22 March 1860. Family Bible published in Philadelphia, Penn in 1826 containing following records: "Catherine Elkins was born in Green County, Kentucky 1 May 1808; John Davis was born 19 March 1790; their children; Robert F. Davis was born 28 August 1828 and died 10 August 1863; E.A. Davis was born 3 January 1831; Andrew J. Davis was born 12 April 1834 and died 12 September 1864; Sarah J. Davis was born 9 August 1837 and died 8 May 1866; John M.V. Davis was born 15 March 1839 and died 22 October 1864; Martha E. Davis was born 3 March 1843; Thomas J. Davis was born 12 March 1845; Nathaniel E. Davis was born 10 June 1849; George Davis was born 25 November 1851." Several execellent letters in this pension file by the widow, recalling tales from her husbands experiences in the war.

DAVIS,JOHN-War of 1812 pension application W.O.#12914 W.C.#8922. B.L.W.#51233-80-50 and #45358-80-55. Service in Captain John Doak's Company of Tennessee Militia from 20 December 1813 to 10 February 1814 and from 28 September 1814 to 27 April 1815. He served at the Battle of New Orleans. Married Nancy F. Owen 30 April 1846 in Boonesville, Lincoln County, Tennessee. A copy of their marriage record is enclosed in this file. Soldier died on 24 August 1846 in Lincoln County, widow removed to Greene County, Arkansas, where she applied for pension on 28 March 1878, at age 64. Because of confusion over a second John Davis in the Tennessee Miltia rolls, widow stated that her husband was the one commonly known as "Buckeye John" Davis.

DAVIS,JOHN-War of 1812 pension application W.O.#6672, W.C.#5214. B.L.W.#26118-80-50 and #43590-80-55. Service in Captain James McNeil's Company, Colonel William Jenning's Regiment of Kentucky Militia from 1 September 1812 to 8 April 1813. He married Mary (Polly) Knox 28 September 1814 in Knox County, Kentucky. They remained in Knox County until his death on 12 November 1860. Mary Davis moved to Washington County, Arkansas before 1871. Affidavits from; Harris H. Davis and Amanda Davis, both of Washington County, Arkansas and from John H. Davis, Assistant Assessor of the Third District, State of Kentucky, described as grandson of Mary Davis.

DAVIS,WILLIAM-War of 1812 pension application W.O.#25809, W.C.-#24808. B.L.W.#25926-80-50 and #14541-80-55. Served as Sergeant in Captain Edward Buchannan's Company of Tennessee Militia. Married first ___Berryhill, second Melinda _____ in September 1844 or 1845 in Walker County, Georgia. Soldier died in Walker County, Georgia on 29 November 1869. Widow to Hartford, Sebastian County, Arkansas before 1870. (not abstracted)

DEANS,REUBEN-War of 1812 pension application S.O.#4108, S.C.#3746, W.O.#25815, W.C.#15897. B.L.W.#18549-80-50 and #20842-80-55. Service in Captain James Shelton's Company of Virginia Militia from 29 October 1813 to 10 March 1814. Soldier's original discharge contained in this file. Married Elizabeth Hubbard 15 August 1865 in Benton County, Arkansas. Resided 1851 in Claiborne County, Tennessee. To Sugar Creek, Benton County, Arkansas before 1855. Soldier died in Benton County on 17 March 1878. Widow died 1 November 1897. (not abstracted)

DENTON,JONAS-War of 1812 pension application W.O.#39246, W.C.#34901. B.L.W.#50821-160-55. Service in Lieutenant Elijah Deaver's Company North Carolina Militia from 16 February 1815 to 13 March 1815. Married Charity Middleton 18 June 1815 in Haywood County, North Carolina. She was born 22 July 1798, Jonas Denton was born sometime in 1793. Resided 1852 in Duck Town, Polk County, Tennessee. Soldier died 26 November 1863 in Harrison County, Missouri. Charity Denton applied for pension in Barry County, Missouri on 24 February 1880, and had moved to Mason Valley, Benton County, Arkansas by 1884. Affidavits from Matthew Scoggins and Lucy Chastain of Barry County, Mo. in 1880 and Matthew Scoggins and Charity Scoggins of Benton County, Arkansas in 1888.

DELL,VALENTINE alias Valentine Tell- Old war pension application O.W. Widows rejected application #26198 Indian War Widow Appl. #9373. Service in 7th U.S. Infantry. Soldier died 5 October 1885 in Fort Smith, Arkansas. Widow named Adelia A. (not abstracted.

DERAINE,CHARLES W./alias John W. Rich- Old war pension application. Dated 1879, Arkansas. Widow Dalina L. O.W. Inv. Cert. #182782 File #46486 O.W.Wid. Rej app. #25427 Mex. Wid. App. #13530. Service in Captain Gabriel Armstrong's Company, Colonel Jack Hayes' Regiment of Texas Rangers, Mexican War. Soldier's pension application, dated 25 April 1879, Woodruff County, Arkansas contains the following narrative "I was born 14 February 1825 in Mecklinburg County, North Carolina near Santsberry (Salisberry ?) and lived there about 4 years then moved to Selma, Alabama until 1838, and moved to Texas on Buffalo Bayou, then to Houston until 1841. I was living with my Stepfather. I moved to St. Louis until about 1847, then I went to San Antonio, Texas. I joined a company of volunteers for service on the Texas Frontiers. My adopted brother, John W. Rich, declined going to Mexico if he could help it and got me to go in his place, by consent of Captain Gabe Armstrong. I was appointed 3rd sergeant of Capt. Armstrong's Company, and I always answered the roll call to the name of John Rich. John Rich later joined a company commanded by Captain Conner. John Rich had his discharge and I had mine, which we both sold to a merchant in San Antonio. John Rich died in Houston in 1858. My half brother, William D.F. Rich served in Captain Armstrong's Company with me. I am a ship's carpenter by trade and a member of the Ship's Carpenters Association in St. Louis, Missouri. My father died about 4 months before I was born. Isaac Rich and my mother were married when I was about 2 years old." When Charles Deraine was in service and on a march along the Rio Grande, south of Loredo, his horse bolted, throwing the soldier onto the pommel, and causing injury. He was given a medical discharge, and remained in Texas for about a year, then moved to St. Louis until 1859 when he moved to Arkansas. He returned to St. Louis in 1862 and married there 13 August 1868 to Mrs. Delina Louvenia Erwin, marriage record enclosed in application. She was the widow of Captain William D. Erwin, who was killed in Tipton County, Tennessee on 8 April 1868. Also contained in this file is the divorce decree of Juliana Deraine and Charles Deraine dated 23 Nov 1867 in St. Louis, "she to have custody of the child, Virginia Marian" In 1870, Charles Deraine returned to Woodruff County, Arkansas. He died 24 October 1894 in Augusta, Arkansas. His widow applied for pension 31 August 1896 in Jackson County, Missouri, she stated that her husband's full name was Charles William Henry De Raine. She was taken care of by her son Henry C. Deraine and her daughter Annie E. Deraine.

DILLARD,JOSEPH A.-Old war pension application. Widow Elizabeth J. Service in Company E 4th Tenn. Volunteers. O.W. Inv. Cert. #8676 File #45787 dated 1857 in Tenn. O.W. Wid Cert. #8007 File #29974 dated 1902 Arkansas. Mex. Wid #16659. Soldier's application dated 14 Nov 1855, Smith County, Tennessee, he was 26 years old. He entered service in Carthage, Smith County, Tennessee, in Captain John D. Goodall's Company, on 10 October 1847. He became seriously ill after landing at Vera Cruz and was discharged in January 1848. Joseph Dillard married Elizabeth Jane Hanks (she was born 8 December 1835, place not stated) in Izard County, Arkansas on 3 March 1853, at the home of William Gillehan. Joseph was born in Smith County, Tennessee, his father named Alexander Dillard, and he had a brother named William A. Dillard born ca 1831. In 1898, Joseph Dillard stated that he had the following children living; Melinia born 2 June 1856; Alford A. born 18 July 1861; James H. born 22 September 1863; Jennie M. born 15 September 1870; Ida M. born 23 March 1873. He died 6 March 1902 and is buried in Flat Rock Graveyard in Izard County, Arkansas. His widow applied for pension 12 May 1902, in Izard County and submitted his original pension certificate, which is contained in this file. An affidavit from William Aikins of Independence Co, who stated that he had been a close friend of Joseph Dillard for 54 years. Elizabeth Dillard died 23 February 1908 in Izard County, Arkansas.

DIXON,JOHN C.-Old war pension application. Service in Company B, 1st Arkansas Volunteer Infantry. Widow, Sarah P. Dixon. O.W.Inv. Certificate #409084, File #48794, O.W. Wid appl.#25432, Mexican War Wid.Cert.#4971. (not abstracted)

DIXON/DICKSON,THOMAS-War of 1812 pension application W.O.#31806, W.C.#33859. Service in Captain Henegar's Company 39th Regiment of U.S. Infantry. B.L.W.#10519-160-50. Thomas Dixon was born 20 December 1792, son of Joseph Dixon, who served in the same Regiment. Married Penninah Cameron (Cannon?), 20 July 1814, in Jackson County, Tennessee. They remained in Jackson County, until February 1829, when they moved to Carroll County, Territory of Arkansas. In 1850 and 1851, they lived in Tishomingo County, Mississippi. He died 10 June 1859 in Madison County, Arkansas, and she applied for pension there 29 May 1878. She stated that her home had burned sometime between the death of her husband and the date of her application.
1850 Federal Census, Tishomingo County, Mississippi, page 102, family #220: Thomas Dixon 57 N.C.; Peninah 45 N.C.; Joseph 20 Tenn.; Abram 16 Ala.; Joanna 12 Ala.; Alisha 8 Tenn.; James 4 Tenn.

DONNELSON,WILLIAM-War of 1812 pension application W.O.#44817, W.C.#35135. B.L.W.#18615-80-50 and #13244-80-55. Served in Captain Peacock's Company of Kentucky Militia from 10 November 1814 to 10 May 1815. Married Elizabeth Asbury, in March 1832, in Covington, Fountain County, Indiana. Bounty Land Application in 1851 made in Jefferson County, Iowa; Bounty Land Application in 1855 made in Appanoose County, Iowa. Soldier died 20 November 1859 in Jefferson County, Iowa. Elizabeth Donnelson died 27 December 1894 in Bentonville, Arkansas, this file gives no information regarding her removal to Arkansas, only that she died there.

DOOLEY,SAMUEL-War of 1812 pension application S.O.#12829, S.C.#8034, W.O.#33758, W.C.#29183. B.L.W.#22097-80-50 and #27061-80-55. He entered service in Fayette County, Ohio on 16 February 1814 in Captain W. Kilgore's Company of Ohio Militia. He was age 15 when he entered service. He helped build Fort Gratiot, on Lake Huron, and was discharged in Detroit, Michigan on 16 August 1814. He stated that he had received a discharge but that it had been destroyed when his house burned in the year 1833. He married Linney Allen, on 6 May 1821, in Shelby County, Kentucky. Also in this file is the marriage record of "Samuel Dooley, of Boone County, and Polly Hayes of Marion County, dated 29 July 1839, Marion County, Indiana". In December 1850, he applied for Bounty Land in Boone County, Indiana, his age 51, and he signed his name "Samuel Dooley, Jr." He applied for Bounty Land in 1855 in Scott County, Minnesota, his pension application in 1871 also in Scott County, Minn. He died 7 September 1872, at the home of William H.H. and Julia A. Dooley in Holt County, Missouri. Polley Dooley moved to Springdale, Washington County, Arkansas, between 1880 and 1887. She was living with her son, Isaac Dooley, when she applied for pension. Affidavits: John A. Dooley, age 56, resident of Madison County, Iowa, son of Samuel Dooley, stated that he attended the wedding of his father and Polly Hayes; Mary Jane Peters, age 51, and T.J. Peters, age 53, residents of Holt County, Missouri, daughter and son-in-law of Samuel Dooley; Betsey O'Fallon, age 54, resident of Holt County, Missouri, daughter of Samuel Dooley.

DOSHER/DOZIER,PETER-Revolutionary War Pension Application #W22951. B.L.W.#75004-160-55. Soldier's application dated 25 September 1833, Clark County, Illinois. He was born 2 November 1762 in Pennsylvania, and while still a child his father moved to Culpepper County, Virginia. He was drafted into service in the Spring of 1781, as a Militia Man in Shenandoah County, Virginia, where

he had lived about a year. His company rendezvoused at the foot
of the Blue Ridge, where Captain Thomas Marshall was placed
in command. After he had served this tour of duty, he served
a tour as a substitute for George Wolf of Shenandoah County. He
stated that after the war he lived in Tennessee for thirty years
before moving to Clark County, Illinois, where he had lived
about 18 months in 1833. He died in Clark County, Illinois on
6 August 1838 at the home of his son, Daniel Dozier. His widow
applied for pension in Marion County, Arkansas in 1857, her
age was 87. She stated that her maiden name was Alley Pritchett
or Pritchard, and that she was married to Peter Dosher 20 June
1790 in Knox (Blount) County, Tennessee. In 1856, Daniel Dosher
submitted the following affidavit from Clark County, Ill. "I
Daniel Dosher, age 62, was born in Knox County, Tennessee on
17 July 1794, my mother has often told me that my sister, Nancy
Dosher was 15 months older than myself, and that my sister Margaret,
the oldest of that family, was 15 months older than Nancy. My
parents said that they were married by publication in the Church. In
the year 1817, I removed from Knox County, Tennessee to Warren
County, and my father and mother, with the balance of the family
removed to Warren County about 1820. I was married to Judith
Maxey 20 August 1813, Margaret and Nancy were married in the
same county that I was, that is Knox County, Tennessee, several
years before I was. My children, while I was in California in
1849, defaced and destroyed the family record that I had made.
Margaret Dosher married Jacob Tarwater and Nancy Dosher married
Walter Maxey. Nancy is now a widow and lives in Arkansas, and
Margaret lives in the south part of this state (Illinois). I
came to Clark County, Illinois in 1830 and my father moved here
about a year ago and remained here until his death". Affidavit
by Adam Dosher, age 74 in 1833, White County, Illinois, who
stated that he well remembered the military service of Peter
Dosher. Also enclosed in this file is the marriage record of
Walter Maxey and Nancy Dozier, dated 8 March 1809, Knox County,
Tennessee.

DOUGAN,THOMAS-War of 1812 pension application W.O.#6682, W.C.#4277.
B.L.W.#30082-80-50 and #49386-80-55. Service in Captain G. Caperton's
Company of Tennessee Militia from 10 December 1812 to 20 April
1813 and from 26 September 1813 to 10 December 1813. He served
at the Battle of Talledega. This application contains two original
discharges, one of which was signed by General Andrew Jackson. Family
in Jefferson (now Grant) County, Arkansas by 1851. Statement
by John Worthen, Grant County, Arkansas, in 1872 that "I have
known Thomas and Hester Dougan since the year 1812". The complete
family record is also enclosed, to wit; " Thomas Dougan was
born 17 August 1781, Hester Kimbrow was born 11 May 1792. They
were married 30 March 1809 in Franklin County, Tenn., Rachel
Dougan was born 10 March 1810, Betsy Dougan was born 8 February
1812, William Dougan was born 16 February 1814, George Dougan
was born 19 January 1816, Phinice Dougan was born 9 March 1818,
Joseph Dougan was born 6 August 1820, Saley M. Dougan was born
19 October 1822, Thomas Dougan was born 24 February 1826, Pulina
Dougan was born 25 June 1831, Thomas Dougan died 11 January
1858, Rachel Dougan died 1 November 1829, William Dougan died
8 March 1842, Thomas Dougan died 21 March 1863." Revolutionary
War applicants possibly related to Thomas Dougan: James Dougan;
application #S3306, dated 4 March 1834, Franklin County, Tenn.,
stated that he was born in Lancaster County, Pa on 6 Jan 1754.
Enlisted in service in 1776 in Guilford County, North Carolina.
Remained in N.C until 1791, then to Tenn. for 3 years, then
to Logan County, Kentucky until 1806, when he moved to Franklin
County, Tenn. His brother Robert Dougan gives affirmation of
his statements. Also; John Dougan, Rev. war pension application
#W9836, He was born 9 Jan 1763 in Lancaster Co., Penn. Enlisted
into service in Lancaster County, N.C. He married in Dec. 1784
in Randolph Co., N.C. Martha Collier. Application filed in Wayne

County, Indiana.

DOUGHERTY,HUGH-Old war pension application Certificate #2113 File #25029. He was enrolled in Captain Thomas' Company of the 2nd Regiment of U.S.Infantry in Philadelphia, Pennsylvania in February 1834. In 1835 in the Cherokee Nation he was struck by a falling tree. He was inscribed on Arkansas pension rolls 14 February 1837. Apparently returned to Phila. later.

DOUGHERTY,PATRICK-Old war pension application Cert. #2308 File #12783. Service in Captain Stuart's Company of 7th Regiment U.S. Infantry. Inscribed on Arkansas pension rolls 6 February 1839 at Fort Smith. Application to have pension transferred to Philadelphia, Pennsylvania dated 4 March 1840.

DOUGHERTY,WILLIAM-Old war pension application Cert. #3485 File #25024. Service in Captain H. Wilson's Company of the 4th Regiment U.S. Infantry. Inscribed on Arkansas pension rolls 3 March 1839. Certificate of disability stating that "William Dougherty was shot through the body with a rifle ball, at the Battle of Okeechobee, Florida, on the 25th of December 1837". He was enlisted 11 March 1831 at New Orleans and was discharged 2 March 1839 at Fort Gibson. His pension was transferred to Washington, D.C. from there to Norfolk, Virginia. He apparently disappeared from Norfolk ca 1845.

DOWNUM,JAMES-War of 1812 pension application W.O.#10506, W.C.#6215. B.L.W.#32109-160-55. Service in Captain A. Raine's Company of Tennessee Militia, from 20 September 1814 to 20 April 1815. Married Hannah Banker, 16 March 1808, in Mecklinburg County, North Carolina. Soldier died 26 February 1854 in Benton County, Arkansas. The following children are identified; Easter Downum was born 24 July 1810, John Downum was born 22 November 1812. Elizabeth Downum was born 24 March 1815. In 1855 James L. Downum and Richard Downum of Benton County, give affidavits, relationship not stated. In 1873 William W. Downum served as witness, relationship not stated. Revolutionary War Pension application of Speakman Downum, #W128; Dated 26 December 1840, Winchester, Franklin County, Tennessee, "application of Mrs. Esther Downum, from the State of North Carolina, County of Wayne, age seventy three years." Speakman Downum was enlisted by Abraham Sheppard, Jr. into the 10th Regiment of North Carolina, commanded by Abraham Sheppard, Sr. He married Esther Straley, 5 August 1782, in Wayne County, North Carolina. He died in Mecklinburg County, N.C. on 18 September 1800. Esther Downum applied for pension in 1840, and submitted her family record with her application, "William Downum son of Speakman Downum and Esther Downum his wife was born the 11th day of May in year 1783; James Downum son of Speakman and Esther Downum his wife was born the 6th day of September 1785; Speakman Downum son of Speakman and Esther Downum his wife was born the 21st day of September 1787; Elizabeth Downum daughter of Speakman and Esther Downum his wife was born the 12th day of March in the year 1790; Esther Downum daughter of Speakman and Esther Downum his wife was born the first day of July in the year of our Lord 1792; Lydia Downum the daughter of Speakman and Esther Downum was born June 6th in the year of our Lord 1795;Speakman Downum son of Speakman and Esther Downum was born November __? in the year of our Lord 1796; Mary Downum was born March the 5th (?) in the year 180_?
1850 Federal Census, Franklin County, Tennessee, page 16, family #209: Mary Downum 40 Va.; Mary 25 Tenn.; Elijah 19 Tenn.; Tilday 16 Tenn.; Sidney 13 Tenn.: page 17, families #216 and #217: James Downum 65 S.C.(?); Hannah 60 N.C.; Sarah 35 N.C.; Margaret 21 Tenn.; Mary 18 Tenn.; George D. 12 Tenn.; John 11 Tenn.; James L. Downum 30 Tenn.; Lucinda 21 Tenn.; Celia 2 Tenn.; Easther E. 7/12 Tenn.

DRAKE,JAMES-War of 1812 Pension Application W.O.#22625, W.C.#19741.
B.L.W.#56729-40-50 and #51055-120-55. He served in Captain Thomas
Craig's Company of Illinois Militia from 5 September 1812 to
2 December 1812. His Bounty Land Application, dated 14 October
1851, Washington County, Arkansas, his age 55, he stated that
he was mustered into service at Saline Lake, Gallitan County,
Illinois, in the War with the Paola Indians. James Drake died
15 June 1857, in Washington County, Arkansas. Married Margaret
Fields in the year 1815 in Gallatin County, Illinois. Margaret
Drake applied for pension on 11 May 1878, in Washington County,
her age 79, she stated, "James Drake was born in 1795, in the
State of Virginia. We remained in Gallitan County, Illinois
about 8 years after we were married, then moved to Washington
County, Arkansas, where we have remained." Mrs. Margaret Drake
died at her home, on the 21st day of March 1879, her son, Wesley
Drake, was the administrator of her estate.
1850 Federal Census, Washington County, Arkansas, Vineyard Township,
page 422, family #38: James Drake 55 Va.; Marget 52 N.C.; Jackson
17 Ark.; Malissa 14 Ark.; Sarah 8 Ark.; Elizabeth Graham 33
Ill.; Malinda Graham 12 Ark.; Sarah Graham 10 Ark.;
Illinois Township, page 428, family #7: Wesley Drake 31 Ill.;
Martha 20 Ark.; Jacob Kellum 14 Ark.; Isaac Kellum 12 Ark.

DRANE,JAMES-War of 1812 Pension Application W.O.#9038, W.C.#6420.
B.L.W.#51293-80-50 and #46920-80-55. He served in Captain S.Williams'
Company of Kentucky Militia from 14 August 1812 to 14 February
1813. Married Roxanna Sherrel in December 1800 or 1802. Soldier
died 5 August 1829 in Obion County, Tennessee. Mrs. Roxanna
Drane, (name also spelled Ruanna Drain) applied for Bounty Land
on 13 April 1853, her age 70, and she was a resident of Washington
County, Arkansas. (P.O. Maguire's Store) She stated that her
husband had volunteered into service in Montgomery County, Kentucky.
She stated that she had left Montgomery County, Kentucky, some
25 years ago. Affidavits from Jonathan Newman and George W. Drain,
residents of Washington County, in 1857. In her pension application,
Roxanna Drane stated, "I was married in the presence of the
following witnesses, to wit; Robert Drane, Jonathan Hathaway,
Catherine Hathaway, Phillip Hathaway, Nancy Hathaway, and Mary
Hathaway, all of whom I believe to be dead unless it may be
Robert Drane, and I know nothing of his residence, or that he
is yet alive. I had two children to said James Drane, before
the close of the War of 1812, and ten afterward, to wit; Mary
and James before said war and Washington, Elizabeth, Robert,
Wesley, John, Rebecca, David, Margaret, Rebecca Junior and Sarah. I
have no family record from which to give the ages of my children
correctly, and further my daughter, Mary, is still living and
is now the wife of Benjamin Hood." Mary Hood stated, "I, Mary
Hood, of the County of Washington, State of Arkansas, swear
that I am the daughter of James and Ruanna Drane, I am sixty
years old, being born in the year 1811."
1850 Federal Census, Washington County, Arkansas, White River
Township, page 352, family #18: George W. Drane 27 Tenn.; Elizabeth
Ark.; Richard 2/12 Ark.: family #22: Benjamin Hood 43 Tenn.;
Mary 40 Tenn.; James 18 Tenn.; David 15 Tenn.; Affa 13 Ala.;
John 9 Ala.; Martha 7 Mo.; Wesley 4 Ark.; Sarah 11/12 Ark.

DRANE/DUANE,JOHN-Old war pension application dated 1851 Arkansas.
Service in Company C 12th Regiment U.S. Infantry-Mexican War. O.W.
Wid. Cert. #1283 File # 266. He enlisted 24 May 1847, and died
of disease in Mexico City on 9 November 1847. Widow, Susan,
applied for pension in Huntsville, Madison County, Arkansas
on 28 January 1850, stated that she and John Drane were married
in De Kalb County, Alabama on 21 July 1840. They had; Emeline
Drain age 9 years and 8 mos in 1850, James Drain age 8 yrs,
William B. Drain age 6 yrs, John W. Drain age 4. The name Drane
is spelled 4 ways in this application. The widow's certificate
is enclosed. Susan died 20 September 1915 in Huntsville, Arkansas, at

the home of her son, T.W. Drain. Affidavit by George W. Drane, who witnessed the wedding, enclosed, no relationship stated.

DUNLAP,ADAM-War of 1812 pension application W.O.#2267, W.O.#20001, W.C.#14013. B.L.W.#93873-40-50 and #52723-120-55. He entered service in Rutherford County, Tennessee on 28 January 1814 in Captain Robert Carson's Company of Tennessee Militia. He was discharged on 3 March 1814. He married Mary Reed in September 1810, in Blount County, Tennessee. He died 8 September 1838 in Bedford County, Tennessee. Mary Dunlap applied for Bounty Land on 19 August 1853 in Bedford County, Tennessee, at which time she stated that "I am the daughter of John Reed, who served in the American Revolution, and his wife Sarah Reed. I was born about the time the American Revolution ended". On 20 April 1871, she applied for pension, her age 100, and she was residing in Pea Ridge, Benton County, Arkansas.
Revolutionary War Pension Application of John Reed, #R8674: dated 15 June 1832, Bedford County, Tennessee, John Reed, age 68. He was born in Randolph County, North Carolina, and stated that he was between the age of 16 and 17 when he volunteered into Captain John Knight's Company of Minute Men. He served at least two years in and around Randolph and Guilford Counties. After the war, he remained in Randolph County, about 12 years, then moved to Washington County, Virginia, then to Blount, Franklin and Rutherford Counties, Tennesse, before settling in Bedford County. He had lived in Bedford County 10 years in 1832, and gave the name of Adam Dunlap, as witness to his veracity. John Reed married Sarah (Sally) Bolen, 31 July 1783. She was the daughter of David Bolen. John Reed died 17 November 1839, and Sarah Reed died in 1845, both in Bedford County, Tennessee. Affidavit dated 28 March 1854: "It is hereby certified that satisfactory proof has been exhibited before the Court of the Tenth Judicial Circuit of the County of Henderson in the State of Tennessee, by the affidavits of William Horton and William Adcock, residents of Henderson County in the State of Tennessee, who are persons entitled to credit, that John Reed, a Revolutionary Pensioner died in the County of Bedford State of Tennessee, leaving a widow, Sally (Sarah) who died in the county and state aforesaid, in the year AD one thousand eight hundred and forty five and that William Reed, Jesse Reed, Elizabeth Price and Polly Dunlap are the only surviving children of said John Reed, who was a Revolutionary Soldier."
1850 Federal Census, Bedford County, Tennessee, page 122, family #23: Mary Dunlap 62 N.C.; Daniel 25 Tenn.; Frances 19 Tenn.

DUNN,FRANCIS-War of 1812 pension application S.O.#12375, S.C.#11287. B.L.W.#24366-40-50 and #76927-120-55. Served in Captain Hamilton's Company of Tennessee Militia from 12 October 1813 to 2 February 1814. Married Etalita Counts 14 December 1850 in Madison County, Arkansas. Resided 1851 in Franklin County, Arkansas. In 1855 and 1871 in Sebastian County, Arkansas. (not abstracted)

DUNN,SAMUEL,Alias, Samuel Lake-Old War Pension Application, dated 1882, Arkansas. Served in Captain Thistle's Company in 1836. O.W.Inv.R#23250, no certificate number.

DUNN,WILLIAM J.-Old War pension application dated 1877, Arkansas. Served in Captain William Winter's Company, Colonel Chisolm's Regiment of Alabama Volunteers, from 1 March 1836 to 30 May 1836. He was mustered into service in Selma, Alabama, served in the Seminole Indian War. Old War Widow's Cert. #485906, File #48958, Indian War Widow #4989. He was born in Jones County, Georgia. He married Mary W. Burken, 24 March 1843, at Champanola, Arkansas. The Congress of the United States, approved a special act pension for William J. Dunn, on 24 May 1890. He died 12 February 1893 at Raiford, Calhoun County, Arkansas, and Congress approved a special act pension for Mary Dunn.

DYER,JAMES-War of 1812 pension application W.O.#42022, W.C.#35489.
B.L.W.#8050-160-12. Served in Captain William O. Butler's Company,
44th Regiment U.S.Infantry from 7 April 1814 to 6 April 1815. This
application file contains three of the original land warrants
(a must for anyone researching this man), an original discharge
signed by Captain Butler and several very interesting letters
written by his widow, children, grandchildren and friends, recalling
his stories of the war. One such letter, written by James M.
Montgomery, of Lafayette County, Arkansas in 1891, recalls that
James Dyer had been discharged at New Orleans, after the battle. He,
James Dyer, left that city on foot at the same time the carrier
of the U.S. Mail left on horseback, and that he had reached
his home ahead of said mail. James Dyer told Mrs. Kate Strange,
of Lafayette County, Arkansas, "on one occasion, General Andrew
Jackson was lying asleep, wrapped in his blanket, in a rain,
some of us took a large piece of hickory bark and laid over
him, to protect him from the rain. After that, Jackson was called
Old Hickory by his men". James Dyer Married Tellitha Garriot
15 January 1820 in Hempstead County, Arkansas. He died 3 December
1864 in Hempstead County. Tellitha Dyer applied for pension
on 27 March 1882, in Franklin County, Texas (P.O. Sulphur Bluff)
at which time she submitted the Family Record from her Bible,
to wit, "James Dyer was born November 17, 1792; Talitha Dyer
was born May 8th 1807; William Dyer was born June 20th 1823;
Joseph G. Dyer was born July 18th 1825; Emeline Dyer was born
July 25th 1827; James G. Dyer was born November 20th 1829; Catherine
H. Dyer was born March 20th 1831; Mary A. Dyer was born April
23rd 1833; Eliza F.C.Dyer was born January 17th 1838; Robert
H. Dyer was born March 17th 1840; Abram W. Dyer was born August
11th 1842; Richard B. Dyer was born October 18th 1845; George
W. Dyer was born December 18th 1847; Elizabeth Jane Dyer was
born December 18th 1847; ___?(possibly Martha) was born March
1st 1850; Emaline Fletcher departed this life February 20th
1847; Richard B. Dyer departed this life January 29th 1847;
James Dyer departed this life December 3rd 1864."
1850 Federal Census, Hempstead County, Arkansas, Spring Hill
Township, page 271, family #29: James Dyer 57 Ky; Talitha 43
Ky; James G. 21 Ark; Catherine 18 Ark; Mary M. 16 Ark; Robert
12 Ark; Eliza 14 Ark; Abram 10 Ark; George W. and Elizabeth
3 Ark; Martha 2/12 Ark; Catherine Garret 65 Va.

EAGAN/EGAN,CORNELIUS-Old War pension application dated 1858,
Arkansas. Served in C3, U.S.Cavalry, 1st U.S.Mounted Rifles
and Companies B&G, 5th Regiment, U.S.Infantry 1844-49 and 1855-58.
Inv.App.#R13956, Cert.#79894, File #45909, Mex.Wid.O.#12873.
(not abstracted)

EARNEST,JOSEPH-War of 1812 pension application W.O.#24196,
W.C.#21551. B.L.W.#40224-40-50 and #71784-120-55. Service in
Captain William Berryman's Company, Colonel Nicholas Miller's
Regiment of Kentucky Militia from 1 September 1812 to 25 December
1812. In 1850, Joseph Earnest stated that he was age 59, and
that he had volunteered at Bowling Green, Kentucky. He also
applied for bounty land on the service of his son Andrew Earnest,
who had served in the Indian War in 1832, stating that Andrew
had died 1 April 1835, age 26. Joseph Earnest was married twice;
1st wife not identified; 2nd- Nancy Woodside 8 September 1836
in Perry County, Illinois. Soldier died 13 January 1855 in Perry
County, Illinois. Widow resided 1855 thru 1878 in Springtown,
Benton County, Arkansas. Her application dated 23 May 1878. at
which time she was age 79, and stated that both she and her
husband had been previously married, but their respective spouses
had died in 1834.

EASTER,JOSEPH-War of 1812 pension application S.O.#28149 S.C.#20158
W.O.#22863, W.C.#17874. B.L.W.#58003-160-55. Enlisted in service
in Jefferson County, Tennessee in Captain William Walker's Company

39th Regiment of U.S. Infantry from 20 November 1814 to 30 April 1815. Married first to Mary Smith who died 10 February 1834. Married second; Lucretia Evans, 10 May 1836, in Roane County, Tennessee. Family in Carroll County, Arkansas by 1855, and in Boone County by 1872. Soldier died 5 April 1876 in Boone County, Arkansas. Widow died 4 January 1909 in Carrollton, Boone County. Statement by Solomon Easter, citizen of Pope County, Arkansas, 15 July 1879, "I am about 70 years old and a brother of Joseph Easter, I have known Lucretia since she was a mere child and I was in their home in 1843, and their oldest child William was a few days old". Joseph Easter born ca 1792.
1850 Federal Census, Carroll County, Arkansas, Crooked Creek Township, page 164, family #574: Joseph Easter 57 N.C.; Lucretia 37 Tenn.; John 23 Tenn.; Joseph 19 Tenn.; James 16 Tenn.; Malinda 12 Tenn.; Sarah A. 10 Tenn.; William 7 Tenn.; Eliza 3.; Solomon 2/12 Tenn.; Thomas Dean 21 Tenn.

EASTER,PETER-War of 1812 pension application S.O.#12842, S.C.#11383 W.O.#16265, W.C.#13986. B.L.W.#69316-40-50 (canceled), #54142-80-50 and #27988-80-55. Service in Captain William Walker's Company 39th Regiment of U.S. Infantry from 20 November 1814 to 30 April 1815. Married Margaret Tate 4 October 1822 in Roane County, Tennessee, in the home of Margaret Tate's brother-in-law, George Painter. In his application he stated that he served in the same regiment with his brother. Soldier died 14 February 1876 in Roane County, Tennessee. Widow died 7 December 1885. Soldier stated that he believed his birthday was 5 January 1795. He was discharged because he had two fingers cut off.

EDERINGTON,ROBERT-War of 1812 pension application W.O.#35714, W.C.#26767. B.L.W.#62120-40-50 and #81805-120-55. He entered service in Green County, Kentucky on 22 August 1813 in Captain Warner Elmore's Company of Kentucky Militia, discharged on 10 November 1813. Married to Martha Hudspeth on, 10 August 1820, at Cotton Gin, Monroe County, Mississippi. He applied for Bounty Land 5 January 1852, his age 55, and his residence in Bradley County, Arkansas. He died 22 October 1857 in Bradley County. Martha Ederington moved to Bell County, Texas where she applied for pension on 7 August 1879. Affidavits from Lillis Cox and Amelia Ederington both of Clay, Bradley County, Arkansas in 1879.
1850 Federal Census, Bradley County, Arkansas, Clay Township, page 96, family #108: Robert Edrington 55 Ky.; Martha 47 Tenn.; Martha H. 14 Miss.; Henry C. 11 Miss.; Sarah J. 8 Miss.; __? Headspath (male) 72 N.C.

EDWARDS,LAMECH-War of 1812 pension application W.O.#10731, W.C.#8534. B.L.W.#37251-80-50 and #13398-80-55. Served in Captain John Hodge's Company of South Carolina Militia. Married first, Nancy Woods, second to Mary Adams on 15 March 1849 in Choctaw County, Mississippi. Soldier died 20 December 1864 in Choctaw County, Miss. (not abstracted)

ELLISON,BURCH-War of 1812 pension application W.O.#33760, W.C.#31055. B.L.W.#10915-160-50. Service in Captain A. Gray's Company 24th Regiment of U.S. Infantry from 8 June 1812 to 8 December 1813. Married Margaret Flinn, in 1817, in Rutherford County, North Carolina. Bounty Land application dated 4 January 1851 in Walker County, Georgia. Soldier died 16 August 1856 in Hamilton County, Tennessee. Widow's application dated 11 November 1878 in Petit Jean, Yell County, Arkansas, she was age 75. Stated that they had lived since the war; in Bedford County, North Carolina, in Bedford County, Tennessee, Rhea County, Tennessee and in Georgia. Stated that her husband was born in Montgomery County, Maryland and that he entered service when he was 32 years old, that his occupation was boot and shoe maker. Widow died 22 February 1888 in Yell County, Arkansas. Children mentioned in this file: Rufus C. Ellison, age 49 in 1879; John J. Ellison, age 55 in 1879.

1850 Federal Census, Walker County, Georgia, page 452, family #18: Burch Ellison 70 shoemaker Md.; Margaret 48 N.C.; Rufus 20 Tenn.; Harriet 17 Tenn.; Rebecca 15 Tenn.; Hugh 10 Tenn.: family #16: David H. Ellison 28 Tenn.; Sarah 22 Tenn. (married within the year).

EMPSON,JAMES A.-Old war pension application dated 1850, Arkansas. Service in Company A, Arkansas Mounted Volunteers-Mexican War. O.W. Wid. Cert. #1415 File #28129 O.W. Minor's Cert #1064 File #5072. Guardian's application dated 12 February 1850, Pope County, Arkansas, William Hamilton, guardian of James A. Empson age 3, only child of James Empson. James Empson and Mary Hamilton were married 19 September 1844 in Pope County, Arkansas, at the home of William Hamilton. James Empson entered service in John Seldon Roane's Company of Arkansas Mounted Volunteers. He became ill at Greenwood, Louisana, and died there on 30 July 1846. His widow, Mary Ann, married John Lewallen 1 October 1848, Pope County, Arkansas; Marriage Record Book A page 120. Pope County Probate Court appointed William Hamilton guardian of minor, James A. Empson, on 25 October 1848. Interior Department records included in this file.

ENDSLEY,JOHN-War of 1812 pension application S.O.#29138, S.C.#21023 W.O.#38227, W.C.#28935. B.L.W.#17415-160-50. Service in Captain Nathaniel Martin's Company from 1 February 1814 to 10 August 1814 and in Captain James Word's Company 6 November 1814 to 16 March 1815 South Carolina Militia. He volunteered in Laurens District, South Carolina. He married first to Ellender Miller, who died in Campbell County, Georgia in 1856. Second Mary E. Wheat 29 November 1857 at Carroll County, Georgia. Their marriage record enclosed in this file. Soldier's bounty land application dated 24 January 1851 in Coweta County, Georgia, his application for pension dated 19 August 1873 in Atlanta, Cass County, Texas. Soldier died 12 October 1873 in Miller County, Arkansas. In her application widow stated that she and John had lived in Campbell County, Georgia twelve years, Cass County, Texas 1 year and in Miller County, Arkansas, nine years. She stated that she had only one child under the age of sixteen in 1882; Ida Endsley, bn May 1869, however, her stepdaughter Susann Endsley age 68, described as an idiot, is in her care. Mary Endsley died 23 September 1918 in Miller County.
1850 Federal Census, Coweta County, Georgia, page 308, family #360: John Endsley 50 S.C.; Elender 48 S.C.; Susan 27 Ala.; Tinsy 24 Ga.; Abram L. 15 Ga.; Peasant M. 11 Ga.; Almeda 6 Ga.; Nar__? (male) 11 Ga.
Possibly related to his pensioner: John Endsley, Revolutionary War Pension Application #R3349. He apparently served two tours of duty in the year 1781, in Captain Isaac White's Company of North Carolina Regiment. He married Deborah __? on 15 September 1791, in Lincoln County, North Carolina. He died 29 August 1827. Deborah Endsley applied for pension in Blount County, Tennessee, on 3 May 1847. She had no proof of her husband's service, nor did she have proof of her marriage, so her application was rejected. She submitted the family record, which contained the names and birthdates of her children; "James Endsley was born June the 18th day 1792; Sarah Endsley was born December the 17th day 1794; Mary Endsley was born January the 7th day 1797; John Endsley was born January the 9th day 1800; Jane Endsley was born September the 26th day 1802; Martha Endsley was born March the 29th 1805; Elizabeth Endsley was born January the 7th 1808; William Endsley was born November the 13th 1812; Deborah Endsley was born January the 22nd day 1817."

ERWIN,JOSEPH-War of 1812 pension application S.O.#8351, S.C.#5120 W.O.#34702, W.C.#30443. B.L.W.#30103-80-50 and #33609-80-55. Served as Sergeant in Captain Josiah Renshaw's Company of Tennessee Militia from 10 December 1812 to 30 April 1813 and from 26 September

1813 to 24 December 1813. He was in the Creek Indian War and served at the Battle of Talledega. He married Rebecca Davis 22 January 1818 in Giles County, Tennessee. In 1850, they were residing in Henry County, Tennessee and by 1855 they had moved to Carroll County, Arkansas. Soldier died in Carroll County 1 December 1878. In her pension application, widow Rebecca included the complete family record, to wit; "Rebecca Davis was born 14 October 1800, Joseph Erwin and Rebecca Davis was married 22 January 1818, Joseph Erwin Jun the 2nd was born the 3rd day of February 1794, Franklin Bainbridge Porter Erwin was born October 30th, 1818, Elizabeth Catherine Erwin was born 16th day of November 1820, Thomas Johnson Erwin was born 15th day of November 1822, Joseph La Fayette Erwin was born November 18, 1825, Harriet Adalade Erwin was born 22nd April 1828, Rebecca Anastatia Erwin was born 6th August 1830, John D. Erwin was born February 1, 1833, Nancy Abigail Erwin was born April 10th 1835, Mary Helen Paralee Erwin was born December 2nd 1837, Michael Pike Erwin, twin, was born December 2nd 1837, Henrietta Tennessee Erwin was born December 15th 1842". In 1878, Samuel S. and Jacob Meek, of Carroll County, Arkansas stated that they had been friends of Joseph and Rebecca Erwin for 50 years.
1850 Federal Census, Henry County, Tennessee, page 277, family #85: Joseph Erwin 56 N.C.; Rebecca 52 N.C.; Adeline 21 Tenn.; Anastasia 19 Tenn.; John 17 Tenn.; Nancy A. 15 Tenn.; Michael 13 Tenn.; Mary 13 Tenn.; Henrietta 8 Tenn.

ERWIN,MATTHEW-War of 1812 pension application W.O.#24208, W.C.#23802. B.L.W.#43300-40-50 and #85931-120-55. Served in Captain William Lauderdale's Company of Tennessee Militia from 26 September 1813 to 28 December 1813. Married to Irene Stephenson, 13 January 1826, at Hartsville, Sumner County, Tennessee. Soldier resided 1851 and 1855 in McNairy County, Tennessee and died 28 November 1860 in Laurence County, Missouri. The administrator of his estate, Wilson Erwin. Widow resided 1878 in Fair Play, Polk County, Missouri and in 1887 she was in Clarkesville, Johnson County, Arkansas, with her daughter Hettisue Sears and son-in-law Henry Sears. Henry Sears had taken guardianship papers on Irene Erwin. Mrs. Matilda McMahan of Oxford, Mississippi, born 17 February 1816 in Smith County, Tennessee, maiden name Erwin, half sister of Irene Erwin.

EVANS,THOMAS JEFFERSON-War of 1812 pension application S.O.#30111 S.C.#21639, W.O.#43144, W.C.#34687. B.L.W.#63877-40-50 and #77588--120-55. Served in Captain John Porter's Company of Tennessee Militia. Survivors application dated 6 March 1875, Thomas Evans age 86, a resident of Kentucky Township, White County, Arkansas. Stated that he had served at the Battle of Talledega. He stated that his first wife's name was Nancy Watts, whom he married 10 August 1807 in Franklin County, Georgia. In 1880 he was residing in Crockett County, Tennessee, where he applied for a new certificate, stating that he had lost the original. The duplicate is contained in this file. Soldier died at Spring Hill, Texas on 12 July 1883. Widow's application dated 27 October 1883 Rose Bud, White County, Arkansas. Thomas Evans had been married three times: first to Nancy Watts, their children John and Jeff Evans were in Tennessee in 1880's.: second marriage to Mary (Polly) Howell who had a son, William Evans of Spring Hill, Texas: Third marriage to Mary Jane Ruffin, widow of William Ruffin who died in Haywood County, Tennessee in 1848. Mary Jane Ruffin and Thomas Evans were married 1 June 1858 in Haywood County, Tennessee, they had a daughter named Anna and a daughter M.W. Owens age 36, in 1883, of White County, Arkansas, who stated that her father had left his home in White County, Arkansas, to go to his older children in Crockett County, Tennessee on 15 December 1879. G.Jefferson Evans, age 74 in 1887, stated that he was the son of Thomas Evans and his first wife Nancy, and that she died when he was about three or four years old.

EZELL,TIMOTHY-War of 1812 pension application S.O.#28501, S.C.#20402. B.L.W.#20800-80-50 and #43617-80-55. Service in Captain Obadiah Waller's Company of Tennessee Militia from 13 November 1814 to 13 May 1815. He served at the Battle of New Orleans. Married Elizabeth Crosthwaite 2 January 1813 in Lincoln County, Tennessee. Timothy Ezell born ca 1792, place not stated, died 29 June 1883 in Independence County, Arkansas. Resided 1851 thru 1883 in Barren Fork, Independence County, Arkansas. Affidavits by Thomas Huddleston and John W. Shaver of Evening Shade, Sharpe County, Arkansas.
1850 Federal Census record, Independence County, Arkansas, family #501; Timothy Ezell 58 S.C.; Elizabeth 55 Tenn., Mary L. 31 Tenn., Asa 28 Tenn.: family #506; Micajah Ezell 37 Tenn., Emily 26 S.C., William J. 12 Tenn., Elizabeth 10 Tenn., Nancy 9 Tenn., Mary 5 Tenn., Sarah 1 Ark.

EZELL,TIMOTHY-Revolutionary War Pension Application #S38686, dated 17 June 1818, Giles County, Tennessee. In 1820 he was residing in Lincoln County, Tennessee, "that part which formerly was Giles County". Service in Colonel Archibald Lytle's North Carolina Regiment.

FAIRCHILD,JOHN-War of 1812 Pension Application S.O.#28993, S.C.#21152. B.L.W.#33307-80-50. Served in Captain William Spencer's Company of Mississippi Militia from 10 April 1814 to 7 October 1814 and from 8 February 1815 to 7 March 1815. Married to Sarah Ann Morrison, 30 May 1819 in Claiborne County, Mississippi. He applied for Bounty Land in 1851 in Hempstead County, Arkansas. His pension application in 1873, was executed in Nevada County, Arkansas. (not abstracted)
1850 Federal Census, Hempstead County, Arkansas, Missouri Township, page 241, family #3: John L. Fairchild 54 merchant S. Car.; Sarah A. 63 Ky.; John L. 19 Miss.; Joseph M. 17 Miss.; Benjamin W. 14 Miss.; William P. 8 Ark.

FALKNER,GEORGE-Old war pension application. O.W. Wid. Cert. #1668 File #7245. Service in Captain Edward Hunter's Company G of Arkansas Mounted Volunteers commanded by Colonel John Seldon Roane. George Falkner became ill and died in San Antonio, Texas on 25 October 1846. Widow's application dated 21 March 1851, Hempstead County, Arkansas, Sarah Falkner age 27 and daughter Mary E. Falkner born ca 1845. Sevier County, Ark, Madison Township, "Record Book of Marriages" page 33; George Falkner of Hempstead County, and Sarah Marburry, dated 31 July 1842.

FANCHER,JAMES-War of 1812 pension application W.O.#21494, W.C.#15229. B.L.W.#54490-40-50 and #61837-120-55. Service in Captain John Miller's Company of Tennessee Militia from 22 February 1814 to 10 May 1814. This file contains U.S. Government grant of land to James Fancher, dated 3 March 1855, Fayetteville, Arkansas (a must for anyone researching this family). This family moved from Tennessee to Arkansas ca 1838. Complete Family Bible record in this application, to wit; " Marriage records; James Fancher, the son of Richard Fancher, was married the 8th day of January 1816 (Rock Springs, Overton Co,Tenn) to Elizabeth Carlock; Bynum Fancher was married the 17th of August 1817 to Celia Matlock; Thomas W. Fancher was married on the 7th day of June A.D. 1857 (female not named); J.P. Fancher, the son of James Fancher was married to Sue E. Crump July 2nd 1869. Births: Asenath Fancher, the daughter of James, was borned Dec 5th 1818; Claborn Fancher, the son of James, was borned February the 4th 1821; Arminty Fancher, the daughter of James, was borned 14th day of Feb 1823; Martha Jane Fancher was bornd Aug the 10th 1825; Hampton Binum Fancher was born the 9th of January 1828; Sarah Marada Fancher, the daughter of James, was born August 26th 1830; Thomas Washington Fancher was born the 24th of January 1833; Margaret Catherine

Fancher was born the 6th day of August 1835; Henrietta Fancher, the daughter of James, was born the 23rd day of January 1838; Jas.P., the son of James and Elizabeth Fancher, was born Oct. 13th 1842; James Fancher, the son of Richard Fancher, was born January 24th 1799; Deaths: Richard Fancher died the 21st day of May 1829, Sarah Fancher died the 5th day of Oct 1839, James Fancher died June 8th 1866, George M. Dallas Fancher deceased Sept 9th 1847, age 10 months, Arminta Coker deceased the 16th of March 1847, age 25 yrs." In 1878, Theophilis McMillan of Carroll Co stated that he had known James Fancher since 1812, and Dr. A.A. Baker stated that he came from Tennessee to Arkansas with the Fanchers.

FANCHER,ALEXANDER-War of 1812 pension application W.O.#42494 no certificate number. Widow Jane. Service in Captain Miller's Company of Tenn. Militia.(not abstracted)

FARR,DAVID-War of 1812 Pension Application W.O.#17578, W.C.#11740. B.L.W.#32634-80-50 and #47803-80-55. He served in Captain John Hodge's Company of South Carolina Militia from 20 January 1814 to 13 July 1814. He married first, Mary Ann Strother in Greenville District, South Carolina. She died in Tuscaloosa County, Alabama in 1821. He married Elizabeth Betterton, 3 December 1823 in Tuscumbia, Alabama. She was the widow of Thomas Betterton, who died in Tuscaloosa County, Alabama, on 8 August 1822. David Farr applied for Bounty Land on 17 May 1851, Montgomery County, Arkansas, his age 60, his original discharge certificate attached to that application. He died 12 October 1853, at his brother's home in Cherokee County, Georgia. Elizabeth Farr applied for Bounty Land and pension on his military service, stating that they had lived in Tuscaloosa County, Alabama, until 1841, when they moved to Montgomery County, Arkansas. After her husband's death, she lived in Montgomery County, Arkansas and in Ellis County, Texas. Affidavit from William and Thomas Farr, residents of Montgomery County, "David Farr died in Cherokee County, Georgia in 1853, and we were present at the time of his death."
1850 Federal Census, Montgomery County, Arkansas, Caddo Township, page 402, family #20: Thomas Farr 31 Ala.; Sarah T. 25 Ala.; Thomas T. Ark.; John 4 Ark.; Carolina 2 Ark.; Melissa 3/12 Ark.; Martin Lagrone 14 Tex. family #21: James Farr 32 Ala.; Mary L. 30 Ga.; David W. 8 Ark.; Mary Ann 5 Ark.; Thomas N. 3 Ark. Elizabeth T. 7/12 Ark.; Mary Ann Weldon 14 Ala. family #22: David Farr 58 Pa. (?); Elizabeth 47 N.C.; family #23: William Farr 25 Ala.; Jane 17 Ala.; Pauline 3/12 Ark.; William Cannon (?) 18 Ga.

FARRAR/FARROW,JOHN HOWARD-War of 1812 Pension Application W.O.#37298, W.C.#27636. B.L.W.#2033-160-12. Served as Sergeant in Captain George Strother's Company, 10th Regiment, U.S.Infantry from 18 March 1814 to 8 April 1815. His original discharge certificate is contained in this file. His description at the time of his enlistment; about 21 years old, born in Granville County, North Carolina. He married Elizabeth R. Harris, 17 November 1817 in Warren County, North Carolina. They remained in North Carolina, until about 1830, when they moved to Tennessee, Lincoln and Bedford Counties. John Farrar, went to Benton County, Arkansas, where he died 4 October 1865.

FEARS,EBENEZER-Old war pension application dated 1848, Arkansas. O.W. Wid. Cert. #582 File #13152. (not abstracted)

FENLEY,JOHN-War of 1812 pension application S.O.#21814, S.C.#15120 W.O.#19457, W.C.#8528. B.L.W.#18788-80-50 and #43710-80-55. Service in Captain Joshua Hagerty's Company and Captain John Willson's Company of Georgia Militia. Enlisted into service in Jasper County, Georgia. Married first to Charlotte Bordin who died in Arkansas about the year 1840. Married second to Martha Huggins 14 September 1850 in Pulaski County, Arkansas. She had previously

been married to Benjamin Huggins, who died in 1843, in Madison County, Alabama. Her maiden name was Martha Cobb. John Fenley died, 3 August 1873, in Saline County, Arkansas. Marriage record of John and Martha Fenley contained in this brief. Also contains two original discharges. Widow residing in Saline County, Arkansas in 1878, age 74.
1850 Federal Census, Pulaski County, Arkansas, page 321, family #102: John Finley 58 Ala.; Martha 45 Ala.; William Huggins 15 Ala.; Jane Finley 14 Ark.; __?Finley (male) 10 Ark.; Mary E. Finley 8 Ark.; Scott Huggins 3 Ala.; Andrew Huggins 25 Ala.; Eliz Huggins 25 Ala.; Laveza Huggins 12 Ala.;

FERGESON,JOSEPH R.-War of 1812 Pension Application S.O.#10869, S.C.#9141. B.L.W.#39827-80-50 and #33756-80-55. He served in Captain B. Ford's Company of Virginia Militia. Married Jane Ayres, 25 December 1822 in Buckingham County, Virginia. Bounty Land Application in 1852 and 1855 executed in Calloway County, Kentucky. He applied for pension in 1871 in Danville, Yell County, Arkansas. (not abstracted)

FERGUSON,JAMES-Revolutionary War Pension Application #S31675, dated 21 May 1833, Lawrence County, Territory of Arkansas. He was born 30 May 1752 in Orange County, Virginia. Entered service in late 1778 or early 1779 in Orange County under command of Captain James Burton in a Regiment of Virginia State Guards under command of Colonel Francis Taylor. He escorted General Burgoyne and other prisoners from Albemarle to Winchester, Virginia. He remained in service for two years, guarding prisoners. He served in General Wayne's Regiment at the taking of Cornwallis. After the war he moved to North Carolina, where he remained 5 years, and from there to South Carolina. He lived in Tennessee 28 years and then moved to Arkansas Territory, where he had lived one year in 1833.
Lawrence County, Arkansas; Probate Book B, page 235; "James Ferguson, late of said County, has died without having made any last will and testament; and Mary Ann Ferguson and Thomas McCarroll of said County, having duly qualified according to law as administratrix and administrator to said James Ferguson, deceased____ they to perform all and singular the duties of administratrix and administrator according to law" "Recorded the 19th day of September AD 1834 and of the American Independence the 59th Year".

FERRELL,WILLIAM-War of 1812 Pension Application S.O.#20301, S.C.#15723. B.L.W.#13206-160-50. He served in Captain Henry Hamilton's Company of Tennessee Militia from 13 November 1814 to 13 May 1815. Married Lucy Guinn, 22 May 1822, in Bedford County, Tennessee. Resided 1851 thru 1882 in Fulton County, Arkansas. Soldier died 1 November 1884 in Bloomer, Sebastian County, Arkansas. This file contains a certificate of service and a certificate of discharge in the Tennessee Mounted Volunteers, from 31 October to 10 May in 1838. (Seminole War). (not abstracted)

FINE,WILLIAM-War of 1812 pension application W.O.#1248, W.C.#7029. B.L.W.#84068-40-50 and #39837-120-55. Service in Captain Joseph Acklin's Company of Mississippi Militia from 13 November 1813 to 22 December 1813. He volunteered into service in Madison County, Alabama. Married 2 April 1807 in Jefferson County, Tennessee to Catherine Scivley. In 1873, Rebecca Davis, of Bedford County, Tennessee, stated that Catherine Fine was her sister and that Catherine and William were married in her father's home. Soldier died 4 September 1864 in Washington County, Arkansas.
Washington County, Ark., Will Book A page 263- will of William Fine; probated 16 Sept 1865- To wife Catherine, entire estate during her lifetime, at her death to be equally divided among children.
Washington County, Ark. deed records; William Fine to Seth Mills

dated 29 Sept 1838 Book C page 56; Alfred Fine to William Fine,Sr.
dated 8 July 1843 Book D page 516; Snallen(?) Fine to C.G. Gilbreath
dated 23 Apr 1844 Book E page 54; William Fine to James Gillilland
dated 4 Mar 1847 Book E page 543 & 546; William Fine to Sewalen
Fine dated 29 Nov 1847 Book F page 66; William Fine to Bluford
Fine dated 19 May 1848 Book F page 235; William Fine to Dedrick
Yons dated 10 Mar 1849 Book F page 379; William Fine to James
Gillilland dated 10 Mar 1849 Book F page 380; William Fine to
Alfred Fine dated 30 Dec 1853 Book H page 101.
1850 Federal Census record, Washington County, Arkansas, Prairie
Township, family #231; Spencer Fine 43 Tenn., Jane 32 Tenn.,
William 16 Ark., Caladonia 14 Ark., Sophronia 12 Ark., Malonia
(?) 10 Ark., Martha 8 Ark., Cuniller (? F) 6 Ark., Elizabeth
4 Ark Savannah 3 Ark., James 3/12 Ark.; West Fork Township,
family #81, William Fine 69 Va., Catherine 59 Tenn. family #9;
Jonathan Fine 35 Ala., Rachel 27 Ky., Peter 11 Ark., Alfred
9 Ark., Walter 7 Ark., John 6 Ark., Milly 4 Ark., Thomas 3 Ark.,
Isaac 1 Ark.

FISHER,ANDERSON-War of 1812 Pension Application S.O.#29640,
S.C.#21382. B.L.W.#40859-160-55. He served in Captain Henry
L. Douglas' Company of Tennessee Militia from 10 December 1812
to 20 April 1813 and from 24 September 1813 to 27 December 1813.
Married Lina/Sina Johnson, 10 December 1811, in Wilson County,
Tennessee. Resided 1855 in Fayette County, Tennessee. Applied
for pension in 1874, in Beebe Station, White County, Arkansas. (not
abstracted)

FITZHUGH,EARIEL/Earl-War of 1812 pension application S.O.#25697,
S.C.#16367, W.O.#41579, W.C.#32180. B.L.W.#18676-160-50. Service
in Captain Thomas Williamson's Company of Tennessee Militia
from 10 December 1812 to 22 December 1813. This file contains
an original discharge signed by General Andrew Jackson, and
an affidavit by John Oliver who served with Fitzhugh. Eariel
Fitzhugh married first Margaret (Peggy) Lawrence, about 1815
in Davidson County, Tennessee. They had at least two children,
namely Jackson and Franklin Fitzhugh, who were deceased at time
of this application. Margaret died in Dyer County, Tennessee
in 1839. Eariel married second Mary Ann Huff in Dyer County, Tenn
9 June 1840. The family migrated to Hot Springs County, Arkansas
in the year 1848, where they continued to reside until Eariel's
death there on 23 April 1881. This file contains copy of the
complete record from the family Bible, to wit; (1)Ezekiel Harrison,
the son of Eariel & Mary Ann Fitzhugh, was born the 31st day
of Jun 1841 (2) Claiborne Chitwood, the son of Eariel and Mary
Ann Fitzhugh, was born the 16th day of Dec 1842. (3) Franey
Morilda Fitzhugh was born on the 11th day of Mar 1844. James
Earl Fitzhugh, the son of Earl and Mary Ann Fitzhugh, departed
this life on 18 August 1846. (4) James Earl, the son of Earl
and Mary Ann Fitzhugh, was born the 20th of Feb 1846 (5) Mary
Jane, the daughter of Earl and Mary Ann Fitzhugh, was born the
22 July 1847 (6) William Eariel Fitzhugh was born the 4th day
of Jan 1849 (7) John White Fitzhugh, the son of Eariel and Mary
Ann Fitzhugh, was born November 23, 1850 (8) Benjamin Sterlin
Fitzhugh was born August 4th 1852 (9) George Washington Fitzhugh
was born the 8th day of February 1854.

FLIPPEN,THOMAS H.-War of 1812 pension application W.O.#27440,
W.C.#18760. B.L.W.#73937-120-50, canceled and contained in this
file, #50473-40-50 and #86422-120-55. Served as Sergeant in
Captain Hugh Brown's Company of Kentucky Mounted Volunteers. He
married Elizabeth Baugh on 29 November 1816 in Barren County,
Kentucky. On 4 August 1851, Thomas Flippen age 58, applied for
Bounty Land in Marion County, Arkansas. He stated that he had
entered service in Vincennes, Indiana Territory. He submitted
his original discharge certificate, which was dated 30 October
1812, signed by Captain Hugh Brown and Colonel Samuel Caldwell. This

certificate is contained in this file. Thomas Flippen died 24 March 1856 in Marion County. Elizabeth Flippen applied for pension on 7 June 1878, she was age 79, and a resident of White River Township, Marion County, Arkansas. Nancy Burgen and Elizabeth Paynter, of Marion County, Arkansas, "do solemnly swear that we were present at the wedding of Thomas Flippen and Elizabeth Baugh in Barren County, Kentucky, near Glascow, on the 29th day of November 1816, and that we have lived near her most of the time since (being sisters to Elizabeth Baugh, now Flippen)." Elizabeth Flippen stated "my husband's troops, commanded by General Hopkins, went to the relief of Fort Harrison, besieged by Indians, and from there they attempted to go to the Peoria (?) Towns, but after marching several days across the prairies, failed to find the towns(?). One evening, when a high wind was blowing, the Indians fired the prairie. The soldiers cut the grass with their knives and set fire to the grass behind them, then marched onto the burned grass to save themselves from the roaring sea of fire that was approaching them. Many of their horses were stampeded. When they returned to Fort Harrison, they were nearly starved as they had been out eleven days, and had left the fort with only three days rations".
1850 Federal Census, Marion County, Arkansas, page 310, family #21: William Flippen 33 Ky.; Agness 34 Ky.; Elizabeth 9 Ark.; Ellen Jane 6 Ark.; Thomas Henry 4 Ark.; Letitia 8/12 Ark. page 320, family #320: Thomas H.P.Flippen 31 Ky.; Harriet 26 Tenn.; Agnes Cordelia 2 Ark.

FORD,LEWIS-Revolutionary War Pension Application #W24223 dated 16 October 1837. He was residing in Amelia County, Virginia, when he enlisted in service in Captain Edward Walker's Company in Colonel Vivian Brookins' Regiment. He later served as a captain in Colonel Holt Richardson's Regiment. This file contains his commission to Captain dated 25 March 1779. Lewis Ford married Anne Lankester 10 February 1788 in Davidson County, Tennessee. They had seven children. Lewis Ford died 10 February 1833 in Smith County, Tennessee, where he had resided 30 years. Anne Ford died 7 August 1853 in Independence County, Arkansas, leaving surviving children; Nancy L. Lancaster, Elizabeth Cottrell and Lucy Hylton. The administrator of her estate was Elijah Hylton. The pages from the Lankester Family Bible were submitted as a part of this application, to wit; "Mary Lankester was born February 27th 1755; John Lankester was born January 2nd 1757; Judith Lankester was born May 27th 1759; William Lankester was born July 18, 1762; Martha Lankester was born November 2, 1765; Richard Lankester was born June 29, 1768; Anney Lankester was born May 2, 1771; Elizabeth Lankester was born March 1, 1774; Thomas Lankester was born February 15, 1778; Susann Lankester was born December 11, 1780; Robert Lankester was born July 9, 1784."

FORD,NIMROD-War of 1812 pension application W.O.#38457, W.C.#31041. B.L.W.#21589-80-50 and #32991-80-55. Service in Captain John Hampton's Company of Tennessee Militia from 5 January 1814 to 14 July 1814. Married Ann Tucker Williams 28 September 1831 in Shelby County, Tennessee. Residing in Independence County, Arkansas by 1851. Statement that Nimrod Ford "was killed by a clan of Bush Whackers in Independence County, Arkansas on the 18th day of October 1864". In 1879, Robert Williams, of Independence County, stated that "Nimrod Ford and Ann Williams were married in my father's home." Family Bible quoted by Mary E. Sherril of Sharp County, Arkansas, the oldest child of Nimrod and Ann Ford, to wit: "Nimrod Ford and Ann T. Williams was married 28 September 1831, Nimrod Ford was born 20 February 1798 (in Maryland), Ann T. Ford was born March 1, 1807, Mary E. Ford was born October 15, 1832, Thomas B. Ford was born February 20, 1834, James (?) M. Ford was born May 25, 1835, Benjamin F. Ford was born September 20, 1837." Nimrod Ford was buried "in the graveyard at Don Smith's in Independence County."

1850 Federal Census, Independence County, Arkansas, Union Township, page 347, family #488: Nimrod Ford 53 Md.; Ann 44 Va.; Jenny M. 16 Tenn.; Benjamin F. 14 Tenn.; Mary Atkinson 35 ?; __?female 8 Ark.

FOSTER,THOMAS-War of 1812 pension application W.O.#5358, W.C.#25069. B.L.W.#95405-40-50 and #23436-120-55. He volunteered into service at Shelbyville, Bedford County, Tennessee on 24 September 1813 in Captain John B. Dempsey's Company of Tennessee Militia. He married Elizabeth Presgrove in Murry County, Tennessee on 9 December 1813. They had moved to Benton County, Arkansas before 1851. He died in Benton County on 10 December 1863. Elizabeth Foster applied for pension in 1871, she was a resident of Pea Ridge, Benton County, Arkansas. George R. Foster, of Benton County, presented the Family Bible (printed in 1828) for record of proof, however, pension agent rejected this as proof because "not sworn to-no record of marriage!" The record, to wit, "Thomas Foster was born February 21, 1795; Elizabeth Foster was born April 13, 1797; Mary Foster was born October the 17th 1814; Nancy Foster was born November the 23rd 1816; George Rily Foster was born September 24th 1818; John Wethersby Foster was born July the 14th 1820; Susan Foster was born March 30th 1822; Robert Carroll Foster was born December 11th 1832 (?); Loving Foster was born October 2nd 1825; Elizabeth Foster was born November 6th 1827; Sarah Foster was born May 13th 1829; William Foster was born September 23rd 1830; David Henry Foster was born October 15th 1832; Martha Adeline Foster was born __? 1836". Nancy Foster was dead by 1879, Mary Foster married __? Jones and Martha Adeline Foster Patrick was residing in Benton County.
1850 Federal Census, Benton County, Arkansas, Osage Township, page 75, family #407: Thomas Foster 55 N.C.; Elizabeth 54 Ky.; Thomas 20 Tenn.; David 18 Tenn.; Martha A. 14 Tenn.; Margaret 10 Tenn.

FOX,JACOB-War of 1812 pension application W.O.#8465, W.C.#18472. B.L.W.#54754-80-50 and #44487-80-55. He volunteered into service in Smith County, Tennessee in Captain Bethuel Allen's Company of Tennessee Militia on 28 September 1814. He served in the Battle of New Orleans, and was discharged on 27 April 1815. His original discharge, signed by Brigadier General John Coffee, is enclosed in this file. Jacob Fox married Nancy Garner 23 October 1817 in Warren County, Tennessee. He died 1 May 1849 in Independence, Jackson County, Missouri. Nancy Fox applied for Bounty Land in 1851 in Platt County, Missouri. She moved to Berryville, Carroll County, Arkansas between 1872 and 1878.
1850 Federal Census, Platte County, Missouri, Platte City, page 306, family #36: Nancy Fox (age illegible) N.C.; Margaret 23 Tenn.; Eliza 17 Ind.; Thomas 12 Ind.; Jane 10 Mo.; Catherine Stoy (?) 9 Tenn.; Cornelius 9 Mo.; Ann 6 Mo.: family #37: John J. Fox 22 waggonmaker Ind.; Mary 18 Mo.

FRANKLIN,THOMAS-War of 1812 pension application S.O.#17035, S.C.#7822, W.O.#35715, W.C.#24251. B.L.W.#21199-160-12. Service in Captain George Gray's Company and Captain John O'Fallon's Company of 1st U.S. Rifles. Enlisted at Huntsville, Alabama 7 July 1813, discharged at Port Osage, Missouri on 7 July 1818. His original discharge, which he sent to Washington D.C. in 1819, is contained in this file. He was granted 160 acres of land in Chariton District, Missouri. He married first, Darkie Moore and second to Charity Barnes, 24 March 1828, in Wayne County, Tennessee. In 1871 they were residing in Sub Rosa, Franklin County, Arkansas where he died 4 December 1873. Widow moved to Hazel Dell, Comanche County, Texas by 1879. Children mentioned in this application; Sarah Franklin age 30 in 1879; L.O. Franklin age 39 in 1879. Widow's description of soldier at the time of his enlistment; about 14 years old born in Tennessee, light hair and eyes.

FREEMAN,ALEXANDER-War of 1812 pension application W.O.#37300 W.C.#27090. B.L.W.#33554-80-50 and #40832-80-55. Drafted at Rutherford County, Tennessee, into Captain Maben's Company of Tennessee Militia from 20 June 1814 to 27 January 1815. He was born 18 October 1789 in North Carolina, and died 29 November 1859 in Izard County, Arkansas. He married Anna Dial 18 January 1816 in Bedford County, Tennessee, at the home of Jeremiah Dial. They resided in Coffee County, Tennessee in 1851; in 1855 they were in Bedford County, Tennessee, and in October 1856 they moved to Izard County, Arkansas. Anna Freeman, born ca 1798, was residing in Izard County, Arkansas in 1879. Revolutionary War Pension Application of Jeremiah Dial; #W914, stated that he was born in 1758, in Ireland. He came to America with his father in 1772, landing at Charleston, South Carolina, where he was living when he enlisted in service in Captain Levi Kersey's Company. He was married 13 December 1788 to Ann or Nancy McDonald. He settled in Bedford County, Tennessee about 1809, where he died 22 September 1834. 1850 Federal Census, Coffee County, Tennessee, Eleventh Civil District, page 61, family #1166: Alexander Freeman 60 miller, bn S.C.; Ann 51 Ky.; Rucker 20 Tenn.; Daniel 15 Tenn.; Sarah 12 Miss.; Letha 11 Miss.; Matthew 7 Miss.; Caroline Lingo 33 Tenn.; Frances Lingo 12 Tenn.; Alexander Lingo 9 Tenn.; Zachariah Lingo 6 Tenn.

FREEMAN,GEORGE W.-War of 1812 pension application W.O.#24265 W.C.#29277. B.L.W.#20130-160-12. Volunteered into service at Milledgeville, Georgia in Captain Birch's Company, 7th U.S.Infantry on 5 July 1813, discharged 4 July 1818. He was born 14 February 1798 in Georgia. He was a carpenter by trade. Married 25 September 1828 in Cherokee Nation, Georgia to Jane Vickory. They moved to Washington County, Territory of Arkansas "on the Cherokee Line" in 1832. Jane Freeman, age 64 in 1878 and daughter Lou Freeman age 44 in 1887. Soldier died 28 April 1858 in Washington County, Arkansas, widow died there 9 February 1900. Affidavit by Samuel Alberty, age 73 in 1879, that he had been close personal friends with George and Jane Freeman both in Georgia and Arkansas.

FROSHOUR,HENRY-War of 1812 pension applicatio W.O.#14898, W.C.#14295. B.L.W.#18823-160-50. Volunteered at Blount County, Tennessee in Captain John Trimble's Company of Tennessee Militia. He also served in Captain Samuel Bunch's Company and Captain Tedford's Company. He served 354 days between 1 December 1812 and 17 February 1815. He was a blacksmith and a mechanic. He married Jane R. Finly 10 May 1821 in Shelby County, Alabama. After the war they moved to Murray County, Georgia for 10 years and from there to Arkansas. They resided 1852 thru 22 August 1869, when he died, in Evansville, Washington County, Arkansas. His age at time of death was 79 years 11 mos and 13 days. Widow, born ca 1798, died in Washington County 1 July 1881. Family data: daughter, Mary J., born 1829; Thomas N. Finly, brother of Jane, born ca 1803.
Washington County, Ark., Will Book A&B page 81- Will of Henry Froshour, "To my beloved wife, Jane Froshour and my son Dempre, I bequeath , during this lifetime, all of my estate. I bequeath to my daughter, Mary J. Hoffman, one hundred dollars. The note I hold against John M. Blevins paying one hundred twenty-five dollars to keep A. Ray and her heirs (sic) . To John M. Blevins my blacksmith tools. John M. Blevins and Jane Froshour nominated as executors. Signed 11 Aug 1869, recorded 23 Oct 1869.
Washington County, Arkansas: Letters of Administration Book B-2 1869-1885 page 2; letter of administration granted to Jane Froshour and John M. Blevins on estate of Henry Froshour dated 23 Oct 1869.
Washington Co. deed records; Henry Froshour to J.J. Harrell dated June 8 & 9 1839; pages 148,149,152.
1850 Federal Census, Washington County, Arkansas, Vineyard Township, page 424, family #56: Henry Freshour 61 gunsmith Penn.; Jane

53 N.C.; Dempsey 28 Geo.; Mary 21 Geo.; Nancy 19 Tenn.; Martha 16 Ark.; Barbary 12 Ark.

GAGE,JAMES-Revolutionary War Pension Application #S32262, dated 22 September 1837, Madison County, Arkansas. He was born 9 September 1754 in Woodbury Township, about 15 miles from the town of New York, in what is now the State of New York. He entered service at the plantation of John Withers in Rutherford County, North Carolina 1 June 1776. Captain Robert Porter was in command of the company. They built a fort to furnish security of the local residents against the Indians. He again entered service 1 November 1778 under command of Captain Thomas against the Tories, while living on Fair Forest Creek in South Carolina. He reentered the service in South Carolina at the home of his father-in-law, William Ross (with whom he lived), 25 November 1778. He was again living in Rutherford County, North Carolina, where he had moved with his family, when he reentered service in 1780. He was discharged 1 January 1781. He stated that he lived in Rutherford County, North Carolina about 30 years, from there he moved to Tennessee, from there to Alabama, back to Tennessee, thence to Washington County, Territory of Arkansas and finally to Madison County, Arkansas. Affidavit by Alexander Ross, age 66 in 1837, Madison County, "that William Ross (father-in-law) mentioned by James Gage is my father."
1850 Federal Census, Madison County, Arkansas, page 273: John Gage 43 Tenn.; Lydia 35 Mo.; Rhoda 16 Ark.; Sarah 14 Ark.; William 13 Ark.; Eliza Jane 11 Ark.; John 9 Ark.; James 7 Ark.; Susan 5 Ark.; Margaret 2 Ark.; William 67 N.C.; Rhoda 64 Ky.; Lucinda 22 Tenn.

GAGE,WILLIAM-War of 1812 pension application S.O.#27605, S.C.#19943. W.O.#42128, W.C.#34371. B.L.W.#42819-80-50 canceled, #20841-80-50 and #42819-80-50 duplicate. Service in Captain John Cowen's Company of Tennessee Militia from 28 September 1814 to 29 March 1815. Married first to Clara___.? Statement by Stephen Gage, age 65 in 1883, "William Gage is my father, I came to Arkansas Territory with him in 1829, and settled in Madison County. My mother, Clara Gage died in Madison County in June 1838". William Gage married second Elizabeth Blair (nee Cates/Kates) in Washington County, Arkansas on 27 August 1840. She was the widow of Elam Blair, who died in 1833 in Scott County. Elam had a brother named Hiram. After the death of Elam, Elizabeth had returned to her father's home in Washington County. Affidavit by Sarah Evans, aged 68 "I first became acquainted with William Gage in the year 1829, at this time my father, James Cannon, was moving from Tennessee to Arkansas, as well as myself and the other members of his family. We camped one night at Memphis, Tennessee and met with William Gage and several others of the Gage family. We traveled together the next day and that night camped at Black Fish Lake in Arkansas. My father and family went on and settled in Washington County. Isaac Kates, the father of Elizabeth Gage (then Kates) lived about 5 or 6 miles from us on what was called Little Illinois Creek. William and Elizabeth Gage stopped at our house on their return to Madison County after their marriage, because Richland Creek was too high for them to cross. William Gage had with him a very fine horse, which became sick and died while they were at our house. My daughter, Martha, was born not long after they departed." William Gage died 16 July 1879 in Sub Rosa, Franklin County, Arkansas. Widows application dated 26 November 1881, Franklin County, she was aged 66.
1850 Federal Census, Franklin County, Arkansas, Mill Creek Township, page 143, family #553: William Gage 57 N.C.; Elizabeth 34 Tenn.; James 15 Ark.; John 13 Ark.; Sarah 10 Ark.; George 8 Ark.; Eliza 6 Ark.; Marion 4 Ark.; Susan 2 Ark.; Tennessee 1/12 Ark.; Martha Blare 16 Ark.; Lucinda Blare 13 Ark.

GARLAND,PATRICK-War of 1812 pension application W.O.#11146, W.C.#15855. B.L.W.#5847-80-50 and #9230-80-55. He entered service in Wilkes County, Georgia on 21 November 1814 in Captain Hermon Mercer's Company, Colonel David S. Boothe's Regiment of Georgia Militia. He was discharged 20 May 1815. He was married 25 July 1813 to Elizabeth Hawkins in Wilkes County, Georgia. They moved about the year 1819 from Wilkes County to Putnam County, then to Monroe County in 1830 and to Stewart County ca 1834. He died there on 1 April 1856. Elizabeth Garland moved to La Fayette County, Mississippi in 1870 and to Marion County, Arkansas in 1871. Affidavits from: Martha P. Howe, age 46 in 1878, of Marion County, Arkansas, daughter of Elizabeth Garland; John L. Hawkins, age 70 in 1878, of Macon, Bibb County, Georgia, brother of Elizabeth Garland and from B.P.Garland, of Pike County, Georgia in 1878, brother of Patrick Garland.
1850 Federal Census Record, Stewart County, Georgia, Lumpkin District, page 101, family #860: Patrick Garlane 63 N.C.; Elizabeth 54 Va.; Martha 17 Geo.; Nancy 14 Geo.; Samuel 10 Geo.

GARRETT,ABRAHAM-War of 1812 pension application S.O.#14188, S.C.#9235, W.O.#43078, W.C.#34934. B.L.W.#31843-80-50 and #5620-80-55. He was born ca 1798, the son of Nicholas Garrett. He volunteered into service in Greenville District, South Carolina on 6 November 1814 in Captain Charles B. Garrison's Company of South Carolina Militia. He was discharged on 12 March 1815. Abraham Garrett married Frances Austin in Greenville District, South Carolina about the year 1818 or 1819. In 1851, he applied for Bounty Land while residing in Jackson County, Georgia. Frances Garrett died in Jackson County ca 1858. Soldier's application for pension was made in 1871 in Jackson County, and on 18 May 1876 he married Mary Ann Harris in Gwinnett County, Georgia. She was the widow of Clark M. Harris, whom she had married in the year 1861. Clark Harris had left the State of Georgia, apparently in the company of his son William M. and possibly others, to go to the State of Arkansas. He had never returned, and one of his sons had reported the death of Clark Harris in the year 1874. Abraham Garrett died in Gwinnett County, Georgia on 19 November 1882. Mary Ann Garrett then moved to Conway County, Arkansas. She then became the apparent victim of a fraud, perpetrated by several people to gain access to her pension. This file contains several documents of this investigation.
1850 Federal Census, Jackson County, Georgia, Subdivision #45, page #32: Abraham Garrett 52 S.C.; Frances 51 S.C.; Malinda 31 S.C.; John 28 S.C.; Josiah 20 Geo.; Martha 18 Geo.; Betsey 13 Geo.; Sarah J. 8 Geo.

GARRISON,ALLEN-War of 1812 pension application S.O.#17044, S.C.#11049, W.O.#28919, W.C.#26773. B.L.W.#26489-80-50 and #41414-80-55. Served as musician in Captain Thomas Anderson's Company of Georgia Volunteers from 21 November 1814 to 6 May 1815. He enlisted in Franklin County, Georgia and was discharged at Fort Hawkins. Married Frances Pool 6 July 1820 in Hall County, Georgia. Resided 1850 in Pope County, Arkansas, 1855 in Yell County, Arkansas. Soldier died 23 July 1876 in Logan County. In her pension application, widow stated that they had lived in Hall County, Georgia 5 years, Montgomery County, Tennessee 1 year, Stewart County, Tennessee 17 years and in March 1848 they had moved to Pope County, Arkansas. In 1878, she had at least two children living; Rebecca Griffin age 58 and Henry Garrison age 56, described as her two oldest children. Frances Garrison died 30 August 1879 in Bolesville, Johnson County, Arkansas.
1850 Federal Census, Pope County, Arkansas, page 284, family #608: Allen Garrison 55 Tenn.; Frances 50 Tenn.; Zebulon 20 Tenn.; Allen 18 Tenn.; Frances 15 Tenn.; Robert 12 Tenn.; George 10 Tenn.; Malinda 3/12 Ark.

GARVIN,THOMAS-Revolutionary War Pension Application #R3932,

dated 12 December 1832, Washington County, Territory of Arkansas, Thomas Garvin, resident of Cane Hill. He was born in February 1765, apparently in Lancaster County, Pennsylvania. He was residing in Augusta County, Virginia, when he served under Henry King, Commissary for Prisoners, at Charlottsville Barracks in Virginia in 1780. He served as waggoner, in which service he remained until October 1781. He served as a ranger on the Kentucky Frontier in June 1787. He stated that he resided in Augusta and Greenbriar Counties, Virginia from 1788 till 1805, at which time he moved to Christian County, Kentucky, where he remained until 1817, when he moved to Washington County, Missouri, thence in 1825, Washington County, Territory of Arkansas. This pension application was rejected, however, the heirs reapplied in 1855, vis, from Johnson County, Texas; Susan D. Billingsley, Eliza G. Harris, Sarah R. Daverson and Mary M. Reed (Rud ?).
Washington County, Territory of Arkansas; Will Record Vol A and B- 1833-1886 page 3: Will of Thomas Garvin, names wife Elizabeth, son Joseph, provides support of Rebecca Ann and Susanna D. (relationship not specified), Grandson Asher H. Garvin to share equally. Son Benjamin Garvin and Samuel Hudson nominated executors. Signed 10 Sept 1834, Cane Hill, Ark. Proved 3 Nov 1834.

GATLIN,AARON P.-War of 1812 pension application S.O.#29108, S.C.#21749. Service in Captain Henry Newlin's Company, Colonel Philip Pipkin's Regiment of Tennessee Militia, from 20 June 1814 to 27 January 1815. He was drafted in Williamson County, Tennessee. Married 8 February 1815 in Hickman County, Tennessee to Mary May. In 1850 he resided in Humphrey's County, Tennessee. He died 11 September 1872 in Danville, Yell County, Arkansas, at the home of his son, Jesse Gatlin.
1850 Federal Census, Humphrey's County, Tennessee, page 150: A.P.Gatlin 63 Or 65 N.C.; Mary 53 N.C.; Elizabeth 15 Tenn.; Hannah 14 Tenn.; Hannah May 97 N.C.

GIBSON,ABIRAM-War of 1812 pension application S.O.#26313, S.C.#18548. B.L.W.#41065-80-55. Service in Captain Joseph Bacon's Company of Tennessee Militia from 13 November 1814 to 26 May 1815. Married Mary Ballard in December 1809 in Grainger County, Tennessee. Soldier's bounty land application dated 18 May 1855, name spelled A. Byram Gibson, age 64 and a resident of Perry County, Tennessee. His original discharge certificate is filed with that application, dated 11 October 1815, signed by Captain Robert D. Eaton, and the name is spelled Biram Gibson. His pension application dated 23 December 1871 from Millcreek Township, Izard County, Arkansas. He died sometime in the year 1885 in Izard County, Arkansas.

GILES,JAMES-War of 1812 pension application W.O.#12360, W.C.#21566. B.L.W.#49426-80-55 and #44464-80-50. Service in Captain William Walker's Company of Georgia Militia from 12 October 1814 to 16 March 1815. Stated that he was drafted in Morgan County, Georgia. He married Martha Christopher, 6 January 1814, in Fayette County, Georgia. He was born ca 1784, place not stated, and died 5 January 1852 in Bowie County, Texas. Martha Giles, born ca 1792, applied for pension in Texarkana, Miller County, Arkansas. She stated that they had lived in Green, Morgan, Walden and Baldwin Counties, Georgia and in Clark and Miller Counties, Arkansas, as well as Bowie County, Texas.

GILLEHAN,CLEMONS/CLEMENT-War of 1812 pension application W.O.#33202 W.C.#25410. B.L.W.#7658-40-50 and #77692-120-55. Service in Captain Henry Yeakey's Company of Kentucky Militia from 1 September 1812 to 25 December 1812. He volunteered in Barron County, Kentucky. Married Nancy Shours, 6 March 1823 in Smith County, Tennessee. Soldier died 9 February 1860 in Smith County, Tennessee. Widow moved to Izard County, Arkansas after soldier's death, where she applied for pension in 1879. She stated that her husband was born in Kentucky and entered service when he was about 28

years old. She was 75 in 1879, and stated that her oldest child
was born 21 May 1824 (not named). Clemen Gilehan, born 16 November
1839 in Smith County, Tennessee, stated that he was the 9th
child of Clemen and Nancy Gilehan. Affidavit by Squire Wood,
age 63 of White River Township, Izard County, Arkansas, "I
have known Clemen Gilehan and his wife Nancy, 56 years, my brother
William Wood, born 15 August 1825, was 3 months younger than
their oldest child". William Dillard stated that as a child
of 7 in Smith County, Tennessee, "Nancy and Clemen Gilehan lived
next to my father, and that I always showed up at Aunt Nancy's
barn at milking time with my tin cup in hand". Revolutionary
war pension application #W8850-Gillihan, Clammans, Clemans or
Clement-dated 1 Feb 1840, Washington County, Kentucky, Nancy
Gillihan, age 77 and a resident on the waters of the Beech Fork. She
stated that her husband had enlisted "on the Cheat River, in
the Monogahela Country, within or near the territory that is
now in dispute between the states of Virginia and Pennsylvania."
She was married to Clemmans Gillihan on 26 August 1790, at the
house of Hardin Thomas, then living on Hardin's Creek in what
is now Marion County, Kentucky, but then Nelson County before
the separation of Kentucky and Virginia. Marriage bond of Nancy
Hardin and Clemons Gillihan, signed by her father, Mark Hardin,
enclosed in this file. Clemmons Gillihan enlisted in Jan or
Feb 1777 in Captain Benjamin Biggs Company in the 7th Regiment
of the Virginia Line and continued throughout the war. He was
granted pension in 1828. He died 30 July 1830 in Washington
County, Kentucky. Affidavits by Mordecai and Martin Hardin of
Wash. Co., Ky. Martin, age 84 stated that he became acquainted
with Clemment Gillihan in the year 1774, that he knew him well
while he was a soldier. They stated that Clement Gillihan had
moved to Kentucky about the year 1789 and had settled near Martin
Hardin.

GLISSON,THOMAS-War of 1812 pension application W.O.#40062,
W.C.#34444. B.L.W.#53833-160-55. He served in Captain William
Whitsett's Company of Kentucky Militia from 17 August 1813 to
16 November 1813. He volunteered in Russellville, Kentucky. He
married first Sarah Reynolds and second, Lavinia Blackstock
on 20 March 1835 in Wilson County, Tennessee. In her pension
application, dated 29 June 1880 in Scott County, Arkansas, Lavinia
Glisson described her husband as being about 5 ft 10, light
hair, blue eyes, fair complected. She stated that he had been
raised in Logan County, Kentucky. She stated "We left Wilson
County, Tennessee in the Fall of 1835, to come to the State
of Arkansas and finally settled in 1839 within a half a mile
of the line between Scott and Sebastian Counties. In 1855 we
moved just across the line into Sebastian, half a mile from
the County line, about one mile from the place we lived on in
Scott County. He (Thomas Glisson) was born 10th of February
1795, and died 23 November 1863, he wrote his own name, I have
no papers with his signature, all were destroyed by the ravages
of the late war. The list of our children; Melissy Glisson born
June 9th 1839; Ameretta(?) Glisson born September 9th 1842;
Commodore Perry Glisson born June 17th 1846 (dead); Adolphus
Burton Blisson born October 15th 1848; Finis (?) Caloway Glisson
born April 3rd 1851; Ethaline Glisson born July 6th 1853; Jesse
Tilford Glisson born October 23rd 1855; Henry Elby Glisson born
August 15th 1858; Harvey Henderson Glisson born January 4th
1861." Lavinia Glisson died in Boone County, Arkansas on 16
April 1887. Affidavit by J.A.Flinn, of Boone County, "my mother
lives within about a mile from where Mrs. Glisson died, she
died at my brother's house, W.C.Flinn. She and her son, Harvey
Glisson, lived together, Harvey was a single man about twenty
five. They only owned a team and a wagon. As soon as his mother
died, Harvey sold the team and wagon. I sold him the burial
outfit and Harvey paid the bill. Before he moved on, Harvey
placed $12.00 in my hand to purchase a tombstone for his mother,

the following was to be inscribed on the stone, Lavinia Glisson
born Feb 17, 1816 died April 16, 1887."
1850 Federal Census, Scott County, Arkansas, Tomlinson Township,
page 146, family #284: Thomas Glison 54 N.C.; Lavinia 34 N.C.;
Melvina(?) 11 Ark.; Ametta (?) 8 Ark.; Adolphus B. 2 Ark.

GOAD/GOOD,REUBEN,-War of 1812 pension application S.O.#14192
S.C.#9366.B.L.W.#48667-80-50 and #26247-80-55. Service in Captain
Newland's and Captain Campbell's Companies of Tennessee Militia
from 10 December 1812 to 20 April 1813 and from 28 January 1814
to 16 May 1814. Soldier's discharge in this brief. Married Nancy
A. Davis, 26 January 1834 in Columbia, Tennessee. Resided in
1850 in Maury County, Tennessee, and in Madison County, Arkansas
in 1855. Soldier died before October 1891 in Madison County,
Arkansas. (not abstracted)

GOLDIN,WILLIAM-Old war pension application dated 1849, Arkansas.
Service in Company D Arkansas Mounted Volunteers-Mexican War.
O.W.Wid.Cert. #4699, File #23121. Affidavit of Second Lieutenant
Richard Searcy, Captain of Company D, Ark. Mtd. Vols., "William
Goldin enlisted in June 1846 at Pulaski County, and was mustered
into service at Washington, Arkansas. On the march to Mexico,
he became sick at San Antonio, Texas and died at that place."
William Goldin married Mariah, who was the daughter of Sarah
McIntosh, 1 August 1838 in Independence County, Arkansas. She
applied for pension 20 February 1849 in Big Rock Township, Pulaski
County, Arkansas. The name is also spelled Gouldin in this file.

GORDON,JOHN-War of 1812 pension index; O.W.Inv.Cert.#5053,
O.W.Inv.file #424, W.O.#35618, W.C.#29360. B.L.W.#8396-80-50.Served
in Captain Ingram's Company of South Carolina Militia from 20
January 1814 to 24 July 1814. In his pension application, dated
1 March 1847 he stated that he had entered service as a volunteer
against the Creek Indians, in Greenville County, South Carolina
in Captain Joshua Ingraham's Company, Colonel Reuben Nash's
Regiment. They were marched to Fort Hawkins and then to Fort
Mitchell, on the Chattahoochie River, where John Gordon contracted
the measles. He was barely over the attack, when they were
marched to Fort Bainbridge. The march through the swampy land
caused complications of the measles and undermined his health. They
were sent to Fort Jackson, where they captured some 400 Indians. His
original discharge is attached to this application. He moved
from Greenville County, South Carolina to Polk County, Tennessee
in 1833. His Bible remained in South Carolina, but he stated
that he thought that he was born in the year 1777. In 1847,
he stated that he had a family of nine, "most of them females,
his sons having grown up and left him." He was married to Jane
Shamlin, 1 August 1853 in McMinn County, Tennessee. She was
the widow of William Shamlin, who had died 16 September 1851
in Polk County. John Gordon died in McMinn County on 1 October
1859. Jane Gordon applied for pension in Benton County, Arkansas
in 1879. She was living with her son, John Shamlin. Mary Weeks,
of Benton County, Arkansas stated that, "John Gordon's first
wife, Martha, died in 1848, and his second wife, Elizabeth,
died in 1853, in Polk County, Tennessee." Jane Gordon died 18
March 1900, in Benton County.

GOTCHER,JESSE-War of 1812 pension application S.O.#23635, S.C.#15047.
B.L.W.#23805-80-50 and #17830-80-55. Service in Captain Thomas
Delany's Company of Tennessee Militia from 20 September 1814
to 10 April 1815. Married Annie Payne, 22 March 1822 in Franklin
County, Tennessee. Resided: 1850 in Coffee County, Tennessee;
1855 in Lawrence County, Missouri; 1871 in Benton County, Arkansas.
Soldier died before 21 September 1886. (not abstracted)
1850 Federal Census, Coffee County, Tennessee, Eleventh Civil
District, page 61, family 854: Jesse Gotcher 54 Geo.; Ann 44
Geo.; James 21 Tenn.; Jesse 18 Tenn.; Nathaniel 15 Tenn.

Benton County, Arkansas, Will Book B, page 89. "I, Jesse Gotcher, of Benton County, State of Arkansas, bequeath to my wife, Annie Gotcher, all of my estate, this to include the real estate lying south of Spring and Osage Creeks. At her death, entire estate to my son Nathaniel P. Gotcher." signed 8 June 1868, recorded 3 May 1881.

GRAHAM,BRYANT B.-Old war pension application. Service in Kentucky Volunteers-Mexican War. Widow Betsey Ann. O.W. Wid. App. #787. No certificate number. (not abstracted)

GRAHAM,GEORGE-Old war pension application dated 1849, Arkansas. Widow Sarah Ledyard. O.W. Wid. Cert. #1084 File #28452 O.W. Minors Cert.#1084 File #7591. Service in the 6th Regiment of U.S. Infantry, Mexian War. He was killed at the Battle of Churubusco, Mexico in 1847. The marriage record of George Graham and Sarah Palmer dated 28 December 1845, Crawford County, Arkansas, and the marriage record of John B. Ledyard and Sarah Graham dated 12 January 1848, Crawford County, enclosed in this file. On 5 October 1849, Mrs. Sarah Ledyard petitioned the Court of Crawford County, to be appointed guardian of her son, George Henry Graham, born 1 January 1847. She applied for pension, on behalf of her son, on 21 November 1849 at Ft. Smith.

GRAVES,PHILIP-Revolutionary War Pension Application #R4211, dated 2 July 1828, Hempstead County, Territory of Arkansas. He was born in 1762 in St. Mary's County, Maryland. He was residing in St. Mary's County in 1781, when he enlisted in Captain Francis Miller's Company in Colonel Jeremiah Jordan's Regiment of Maryland Militia. He lived in Nelson County, Kentucky; Lincoln County, Missouri and from there to Hempstead County, Territory of Arkansas.

GRAY,JACOB-Revolutionary War Pension Application #S31709, dated 30 January 1834, Pulaski County, Territory of Arkansas. He was born 31 August 1762 in Granville County, North Carolina. He was taken by his parents to Mecklenburgh, North Carolina when he was 2 years old. He entered service there in 1780 in Captain John Foster's and in Captain Robert Davis' Companies of North Carolina Rangers. He also served in Colonel Henry Hampton's Regiment of South Carolina State Troops. He was transferred to Captain Jacob Barnett's Company in Colonel Wade Hampton's Regiment. They were ordered to take the port at Orangeburgh, which they did by firing three rounds on the British with a brass field piece. After the Battle of Eutaw Springs, his enlistment had expired, so he returned home to North Carolina in the spring of 1782. His brother, Shared, who lived in South Carolina, had been drafted and found it inconvenient to serve at that time, so Jacob served as substitute for him in Captain Benjamin Hale's Company. He stated that after the war he lived for awhile in Kershaw and Lancaster Districts, South Carolina, before moving to Williamson County, Tennessee. In 1834, he stated that he had lived in Pulaski County, Territory of Arkansas for 13 years. As references he gives the names: The Honorable Benjamin Johnson, Colonel Samuel M. Rutherford, The Honorable Ambrose H. Sevier, all of Washington City and General Andrew Jackson, President of the United States, whom he knew in Tennessee and New Orleans. Also referred to "my brother Shared Gray, of this county."

GRAY,JOHN-War of 1812 pension application W.O.#21063, W.C.#24854. B.L.W.#97528-40-50 and #76409-120-55. Service in Captain Charles Johnson's Company of Tennessee Militia from 28 January 1814 to 10 May 1814. Married Mary G. McBride, 9 October 1819 in Williamson County, Tennessee. Soldier died 15 April 1870 in Evansville, Washington County, Arkansas. Widows application dated 1879, contains Family Bible record, to wit; "John V. Gray was born 19 January 1794 in Halifax County, Virginia, Mary G. McBride was born January 19th 1800, John Gray and Mary G. McBride were married October 9th 1819, near Franklin, Williamson County, Tennessee. Their children: Anne Tennessee, bn October 29, 1820, and died March 7, 1857; George Washington, bn October 17, 1822 and died October 1825; James Alexander, bn July 3, 1825 and died October 1826; William Franklin, bn March 5, 1830 and died May 5, 1877; Thomas Jefferson, bn November 15, 1833 and died October 24, 1864; Mary Elizabeth, bn April 9, 1835, living; John Carnes, bn August 19, 1839 and died December 1, 1877; Wyllard Starr, bn October 16, 1842 and died October 24, 1864". Affidavit by Sanford F. Gray, age 78 in 1879, Washington County "I am personally well acquainted with John and Mary Gray. (relationship not stated) Widow stated that they had lived in Tennessee and Indiana before moving to Washington County, Arkansas in 1827.

GRAY,SHARED-Revolutionary War Pension Application #S31707, dated 30 January 1834, Pulaski County, Territory of Arkansas. He was born 11 June 1758 in Granville County, North Carolina. Entered service in Mecklenburgh, North Carolina in 1777 or 1778 in Captain William Hagan's Company in Colonel Adam Alexander's Regiment. He served in a march on the Cherokee Indians at "Valley Towns". In 1780 and 1781, he served in several different organizations of Rangers. Stated that about the close of the war, he was living in Kershaw District, South Carolina for about four years, before returning to Mecklenburgh, North Carolina. In the year 1815 he moved to Bedford County, Tennessee, and stated that he was in Williamson County, Tennessee, until about 1820, when he moved to Pulaski County, Territory of Arkansas. As references he named; The Honorable Benjamin Johnson, The Honorable Ambrose H. Sevier, Colonel Samuel M. Rutherford, Richard C. Byrd, The Honorable William S. Fulton and "my brother Jacob, of this County".

GREER,JOSHUA-War of 1812 pension application S.O.#23647, S.C.#15528. B.L.W.#7464-80-50 and #20539-80-55. Service in Captain John Dalton's Company of Tennessee Militia from 13 November 1814 to 13 May 1815. Married Mary T. Burge, 5 November 1812 in Warren County, Tennessee. Resided: 1850 thru 1855 in Warren County, Tennessee, 1871 in Fulton County, Arkansas, and in 1878 in Izard County, Arkansas. (not abstracted)
1850 Federal Census, Warren County, Tennessee, page 101, family #1380: Joshua Greer 57 cabinetmaker N.C.; Mary 55 N.C.; John Greer 19 cabinetmaker Tenn.; Malvina 21 Tenn.

GREGG,SAMUEL-Revolutionary War Pension Application #S16840, dated 29 September 1833, Lawrence County, Alabama, Samuel Gregg, Senior, age 75. He was born and raised in Augusta County, Virginia. He first served as a volunteer under Captain Edward Irvine against the Indians on the Greenbriar River in Virginia. He mentioned a brother who was killed by Indians. Later he was called into service to guard the prisoners taken at "Cowpens". In 1781 he was serving under Captain Thomas Smith, he stated that he was marched out of Virginia, crossed the Dan River, and to the Battle of Guilford Court House. His tour of duty had ended, so he returned to Virginia where he reentered the army and served at the Siege of Yorktown and was present at Cornwallis' surrender. After the war he moved to East Tennessee, and from there to Alabama, where he had resided 23 years in 1832. His pension was transferred to Washington County, Arkansas in 1838, where he had removed to be with his children. On 8 July 1850 in Washington County, Arkansas, Henry and Samuel Gregg applied for arrears in pension of Samuel Gregg, Sr, stating that they were sons of Samuel Gregg,Sr. Other children named; Ellis Gregg, Lydia Bigham (wife of William Bigham), and Jane White (wife of Robert White). Samuel Gregg died 12 January 1841 in Washington County, Arkansas, at the home of his son Henry.

GREGG,HENRY-War of 1812 pension application S.O.#14199, S.C.#12731. B.L.W.#25914-160-50. He enrolled in Captain Fleming Hodge's

Alabama Troops, attached to the Tennessee Militia. He enlisted
on 18 October 1813, at Limestone County, Alabama. He was stationed
at Fort Montgomery, and was discharged on 19 February 1814. He
also served in Captain Hugh Carris' Company of Tennessee Militia
from 28 September 1814 to 27 March 1815. He married Mary Murrell,
1 October 1815, in Limestone County, Alabama. He applied for
Bounty Land in Washington County, Arkansas. Affidavit from Richard
Murrell of Weakley County, Tennessee in 1852, "I know that Henry
Gregg volunteered into the service and I volunteered with him
at the times and places stated." Henry Gregg applied for pension
in 1871, also in Washington County, his age 79.
Washington County, Ark. Will record- Vols. A & B page 128; Will
of Henry Gregg-"To my daughter, Delaney Cardwell, all of my
household and kitchen furniture, and the interest on the note
I hold on my son Lafayette Gregg. To Andrew S. Gregg sr and
Henry C. Cardwell, all the remainder of my estate, they to collect
all sums due me and distribute same to my grandchildren" signed
29 March 1877, recorded 13 April 1877.
1850 Federal Census, Washington County, Arkansas, Prairie Township,
page 391, family #41: Henry Gregg 57 Tenn.; Mary 55 Tenn.; Lafayette
22 Ala.; Family #117: Samuel Gregg 50 Tenn.; Adolphus 25 Ala.;
Marget 22 Tenn.; Andrew 21 Ala.; Samuel 19 Ala.; Sarah 14 Ala.;
John 10 Ala.; Livonia 9 Ala.; Constantine 9 Ala. White River
Township, page 355, family #57: James Gregg 52 Tenn.; Mary 47
Tenn.; Adaline 17 Tenn.; Nathan 14 Ala.; Mary 12 Ark.

GRESHAM/GRISHAM,THOMAS P.-War of 1812 pension application W.O.#38356,
W.C.#32560. B.L.W.#36929-80-50 and #18898-80-55. He was mustered
into service at Gates' Court House, North Carolina, on 21 September
1814 in Captain John J. Inge's Company of North Carolina Militia.
They were marched to Norfolk, Virginia, where he received his
discharge on 5 February 1815. Marriage bond of Thomas Gressom
and Mary Hester in August 1819, Granville County, North Carolina,
signed by Thomas and Wheeler Gressom. Thomas Grisham applied
for Bounty Land in Calhoun County, Arkansas on 2 August 1851. On
17 October 1857, Thomas Gresham was in Calhoun County, in his
field sowing wheat, when he died. Mary Gresham applied for pension
in 1879, she stated that he was born in Granville County, North
Carolina, and that he had been a hatter. She stated that they
had lived in Tipton County, Tennessee before moving to Calhoun
County. Affidavit by William H. Grisham, citizen of Panola County,
Texas, "I am the son of Thomas and Mary Grisham, I was born
in Granville County, North Carolina on the 12th day of August
1820."

GRIFFITH,HENRY W.-War of 1812 pension application W.O.#34871
W.C.#23163. B.L.W.#38039-80-50 and #42189-80-55. Service in
Captain Coleman's Company of South Carolina Militia from 10
December 1812 to 15 March 1814. Married first to Elizabeth Brooks,
second to Nancy Mariah Williams, 6 November 1821, in Jones County,
Georgia at the home of Stafford Williams, father of Nancy. Henry
Griffith died 25 July 1837 in Upson County, Georgia. Widow's
application dated 8 February 1879 in Magnolia, Columbia County,
Arkansas, she was aged 76. She stated that they remained in
Jones County, Georgia for about 8 years after the war, then
to Upson County, for about 9 years, where her husband died. She
then moved to Troup County, Georgia where she lived about 8
years before moving to Arkansas. Statement, in January 1879,
by Henry Griffith age 56 and John D. Prater age 66 that they
had known Nancy Griffith since before her marriage to Henry
W. Griffith.
Butts County, Georgia Deed Book A, page 59: Henry W. Griffith
of Jones County and Wilson & Lovejoy of Monroe County; Lot 70,
4th District of Monroe. Witnessed by Thomas Coker and John Lovejoy.
dated 6 September 1825.

GRIMMIT,WILLIAM-War of 1812 pension application S.O.#14890,

S.C.#9358. B.L.W.#37931-80-50 and #48175-80-55. Served in Captain Cuthbert Hudson's Company of Tennessee Militia from 28 September 1814 to 12 May 1815. Resided 1851 and 1858 in Saline County, Arkansas. (not abstracted)

GROSS,JACOB S.-War of 1812 pension application W.O.#39065, W.C.#29792. B.L.W.#61480-160-55. Service in Captain James Irwin's Company of Pennsylvania Militia, which he entered at Pittsburg, Pennsylvania. This file contains affidavits from James Chambers, Joseph Long and George McCombs, all of Allegheny County, Pennsylvania, who served with Jacob Gross in the war. Jacob Gross married Mary Morrison 29 December 1814, in Pittsburg, Allegheny County, Pennsylvania, at the home of her father, John Morrison. William and Catherine Witty, sister and brother-in-law of Mary attended the wedding. Jacob and Mary Gross moved to Van Buren, Crawford County, Arkansas ca 1845. Jacob died there 11 June 1853, and Mary died there before 23 May 1884.
1850 Federal Census, Crawford County, Arkansas, City of Van Buren, page 357, family #64: Jacob Gross, hotel keeper, 52 Penn.; Mary 48 Penn.; George, deputy sheriff, 32 Penn.; Lockey(?) 27 Mo.; Morrison 10 Mo.; Andrew 8 Mo.; Mary J. 6 Ark.; George P. 3 Ark.;

HALL,JAMES-Revolutionary War Pension Application #W25741; B.L.W-#87048-160-55. James Hall was born 10 May 1751 in Loudon County, Virginia. He stated that in May 1776, while living about six miles from Fish Dam Ford on the Broad River in Ninety-Six, South Carolina, he enlisted in Captain Thomas Branum's Company, Colonel John Thomas' Regiment of South Carolina Troops. He enlisted a second time in the Fall of 1777 in Captain David Dixon's Company, Colonel Samuel Jack's Regiment of Georgia Troops and stated that he was in the Florida Expedition. In the winter of 1779/80, he served in Captain William Fair's Company. He was in Captain George Avery's Company at the Battle of Eutaw Springs, when he was wounded in the right wrist, destroying the joint. He applied for and was granted pension 18 May 1834 in Harlan County, Kentucky. He died in Harlan County, 27 July 1837. Widow's application dated 14 May 1857, Benton County, Arkansas, she was age 78. She stated that her maiden name was Elizabeth Sousby (Sisby?), and that she and James Hall were married in Buncombe County, North Carolina ca 1798. Children mentioned is her application: Hannah, born February 1800; Anthony, born 29 March 1802; Elizabeth bn ?; Allen, born 1809; Dorothy, age 12 in 1824; Sarah, age 10 in 1824; Esther, age 9 in 1824; Mary, age 7 in 1824; Martha, age 5 in 1824; Sampson born December 1821 and died in infancy.

HAMILTON,JOSEPH P.-War of 1812 pension application S.O.#20501, S.C.#14826. Service in Captain John Howell's Company of Tennessee Militia. (not abstracted)

HAMILTON,THOMAS-War of 1812 pension application W.O.#28737 W.C.#24683. Service in Captain Robert Moore's Company of the Second Regiment of Tennessee Volunteers commanded by Colonel Thomas Williamson, Colonel George Elliott and Colonel George Smith. He volunteered at Sumner County, Tennessee on 1 September 1814 and was discharged in April 1815. Thomas Hamilton married Mary Blair 14 July 1823 in Sumner County, Tenn. He stated that his discharge had been burned when his house burned in Jefferson County, Arkansas on 6 March 1833. Soldier's application dated 7 November 1850, Scott County, Arkansas, Thomas Hamilton age 56. He died in Scott County, 19 December 1857. Mary Hamilton applied for pension in 1879, in Scott County, she stated that she was 72 years old, and had had the following children; James Hamilton was born 15 April 1826; Elizabeth Hamilton was born 3 March 1829; Malinda Hamilton was born 24 March 1831; Mary Hamilton was born 27 February 1833; William Hamilton was born 15 April 1835; Nancy Hamilton was born 10 May 1837; Thomas Hamilton

was born 15 May 1840; Sarah Hamilton was born 27 April 1843; Robert Hamilton was born 27 April 1846; Martha Jane Hamilton was born 22 December 1849; Zerrilda Hamilton was born 11 February 1852.
1850 Federal Census, Scott County, Arkansas, Hickman Township, page 127: Thomas Hamilton 54 Tenn.; Mary 58 Ky.; Polly 19 Ark.; William S. 15 Ark.; Thomas 13 Ill(?); Nancy 11 Ill.; Sarah 9 Ill.; Martha 7 Ark.; Thurilda 5 Ill.; Robert 10 Ill.

HANNA,REUBEN-War of 1812 pension application S.O.#25556, S.C.#15679, W.O.#10584, W.C.#6197. B.L.W.#14764-80-50 and #23173-80-55. He served in Captain James Thompson's Company of South Carolina Militia from 23 January 1814 to 4 August 1814. In his Bounty Land Application, dated 1 December 1850, Itawamba County, Mississippi, he stated that he served in the Creek Nation at Fort Bainbridge and Fort Mitchell on the Chattahoochie River, that he was at Fort Bainbridge when General Jackson fought the Battle of Horseshoe. His original discharge is attached to that application. He applied for pension in Sebastian County, Arkansas on 25 November 1871, his age 78. Mary Hanna applied for pension on 14 December 1873, in Sebastian County, she stated that her husband had died 11 November 1873. She removed the family record page from her Bible, sent them with her application. That page is contained in this file, however, the names and dates are badly faded, especially the birthdates. "Marriage Records: Reuben Hanna & Mary Hanna was married November the 16th AD 1814; James M. Herring and Elmina C. Hanna was married April the 25th 1837; Milton M. Hanna and Amanda Bennett was married April 15th 1838; Isic Kennada (?) and Eli__? Hanna was married November the 6th 1838; Joseph Mangum and Arta E. Hanna was married March 28, 1843; Elbert W. Hancock and Muranda Hancock was married March 26, 1838; Stephen E. Herring and Martha M. Hanna was married September 18, 1845; Andrew Jackson Hanna was borned in the year of our Lord on the 6th day of August 1833." Affidavits from Jack Hanna, son of Reuben and Mary Hanna, and Martha Doss, who stated that she was the fourth child of Reuben and Mary Hanna. 1850 Federal Census, Itawamba County, Mississippi, page 314, family #176: Milton M. Hanna 31 S.C.; Amanda 29 Ala.; James W. 11 Ala.; Reuben 5 Ala.; Hiram G. 3 Miss.; Jerusha 1 Miss.; Frances Bennett 5 Ala.

HARDIN,BENJAMIN-Revolutionary War Pension Application #S32293, dated 7 January 1833, Independence County, Territory of Arkansas. He was born 15 March 1764 in Mecklenburgh County, North Carolina. He joined a volunteer horse company in Rowan County, North Carolina on 14 June 1780, under command of his father, Captain Benjamin Hardin, Senior. Their Major was Phillip Rutherford and their Colonel was Matthew Locke. At the time of his enlistment, Benjamin Hardin was residing in Rutherford, North Carolina. They first marched to Lincoln County, North Carolina, where they attacked and defeated British Colonel John Moore and his Regiment of Tories. He was later with his father's company under command of Colonel George Davidson, when they reinforced General McDowell at the Old Cherokee Ford on the Broad River, and later served at King's Mountain. After King's Mountain, he returned home and joined a body of troops under command of Colonel John Sevier and Colonel Arthur Campbell against the Cherokee Indians. After the war, he lived on the Holston River in North Carolina until 1785, when he moved to Tennessee until about 1793. He moved to Kentucky until about 1815 when he moved to Missouri, thence to Arkansas Territory. Affidavit by John Caruthers that he had been acquainted with Benjamin Hardin during the Battle of King's Mountain and several other battles.
Washington County, Ark. Deed records-Rodney Earheart to Benjamin Hardin dated 2 Dec 1839 Book C page 243.
Clark County, Ark. Marriage Records; Benjamin Hardin and Mary Sorrels- Book A page 88 dated Sept 7, 1832; James Hardin and

Nancy Ellen Cooke-Book A page 58 dated Sept 9, 1831; Joseph Hardin and Sally Cornelius-Book A page 45 dated Nov 16, 1831. Independence County, Arkansas Marriage Records; Euel Hardin and Matilda Webb, 3 December 1836, page 3; John L. Craig and Margaret Hardin, 12 May 1835, page 32; Nancy Hardin and Rev. Josephus Cornwall of Mo., 13 Nov. 1828, page 6.

HARDIN,THOMAS-Old war pension application dated 1850, Arkansas. Inv.App.#14876, Inv.Cert.#363530, File #48601, Mex.Sur.O.#25352, Mex.Sur.Cert.#20547, Mex.Wid.O.#18145, Mex.Wid.Cert.#14219. Service in Company H, 5th Regiment of Tennessee Volunteers, Mexican War. He was born 1 January 1826 in McMinn County, Tennessee. He married Susan Davis in October of 1848, at Lookout Valley, Hamilton County, Tennessee. She was born near Huntsville, Alabama on 7 March 1832. He applied for pension in Sebastian County, Arkansas. Stated that he had lived in Moralton and Ozark, Arkansas and in Tuscumbia and Stevenson, Alabama. He died 5 August 1905 in Chattanooga, Tennessee.

HARDING,JOHN-War of 1812 pension application S.O.#29656, S.C.#21431 W.O.#38235, W.C.#31634. Service in Captain Benjamin A. Muzzy's Company of New York Militia. In his application dated 15 April 1871, Washington County, Arkansas, he stated that his age was 74, and he was born in New York City. He served in the service known as "The Sea Fencibles" stationed in Block House No. 3 on Long Island on the Narrow's near New York. He married Jane Gilbert, in June 1867, in Jasper County, Missouri. He died 29 December 1875 in Illinois Township, Washington County. His widow applied for pension 18 March 1880, stated that she was 75 years old. She had previously been married to Obed Gilbert, who died 28 May 1863, age 63, in Umstead County, Minn. John J. Harding, age 56 in 1880, son of John Harding, stated that my mother, Ophelia Harding died 5 May 1857.

HARP,SOLOMON-War of 1812 pension application W.O.#13899, W.C.#12914. B.L.W.#24055-80-50 and #31806-80-55. Service in Captain Daniel Newman's Company of Tennessee Militia from 13 November 1814 to 13 March 1815. Married Nancy Wright, 15 June 1843 in Carroll County, Arkansas. In his bounty land application dated 9 April 1855 Newton County, Arkansas, he stated that he was aged 65, and that he was drafted in White County, Tennessee. Soldier died 10 April 1862 in Newton County, Arkansas. In her pension application dated 25 March 1878, Nancy Harp stated that her husband was discharged at New Orleans, but she has no proof because "all of my papers were destroyed during the last war by the Rebels". Seborn Wright stated that he witnessed the marriage of Solomon and Nancy, also the death of Solomon.
1850 Federal Census, Newton County, page 008, family #109: Solomon Harp 61 N.C.; Nancy 34 Tenn.; Jabal 17 Ala.; Sehorn 18 Ala.; Nelson 15 Ala.; Alla 14 Tenn.; D.D.Cavin 11 Ala.; Benjamin 10 Ala.; Martha 8 Ala.;

HARPER,THOMAS H.-Old War pension application dated 1883, Arkansas. Served in Captain Smith's Company of Texas Volunteers, Mexican War.Mex.War.O.#2888, Sur.Cert.#5844, Mex.Wid.O.#15524. (not abstracted)

HARRIS,CHARLES-War of 1812 pension application W.O.#8415, W.C.#3962. B.L.W.#25060-80-50 and #31597-80-55. Served in Captain Michael Gaffney's Company of South Carolina Militia from 1 October 1814 to 7 March 1815. Married Jane Cannon 24 December 1807 in Pendleton County, South Carolina. Soldier died in Greene County, Arkansas on 15 November 1865. Emeline Harris and Hannah Jane Wright stated that Charles Harris had been staying with them, when he became ill, and that they had taken him to the home of another relative, where he died soon after.

HAWKINS,MARTIN L.-War of 1812 pension application W.O.#14929 W.C.#10442. B.L.W.#21693-160-50. Served as Captain in the 17th Regiment of Kentucky Volunteers from 16 April to 17 February 1815. Married Jane Walker 4 July 1823 at Nicholasville, Jessamine County, Kentucky. He died 28 October 1841 in Carroll County, Arkansas. Widow resided 1850-1878 in Fayetteville, Washington County, Arkansas. Widow's bounty land application dated 11 November 1850, Washington County, Arkansas, Jane Hawkins, age 46, she stated that they lived in Kentucky until 1832, when they moved to Arkansas. She had lived with her son-in-law, Edward Freyshlag, since the death of her husband. Affidavits by David Walker and Alfred M. Wilson, of Washington County, who stated that they knew Jane and Martin long before their marriage.
1850 Federal Census, Washington County, Ark. Fayettville Township, page 440; Jane Hawkins 46 Ky, Sarah 17 Ark., Mary 16 Ark., Martin 10 Ark., Flora Ridge 12 Ark.

HAWKINS,WILLIAM-War of 1812 pension application W.O.#33438 W.C.#20683. Service in Captain Francis Berry's Company, Colonel Samuel Bunch's Regiment of Tennessee Drafted Men. William Hawkins' bounty land application dated 1 August 1851, he stated that he was age 80, and that he was drafted at Dandridge, Tennessee. He married Elizabeth Carpenter, 24 April 1816 in Grainger County, Tennessee, a copy of this license is enclosed with widows application. She stated that they lived in Grainger County, Tennessee until the Fall of 1831, when they moved to Vermillion County, Illinois. They moved to Madison County, Territory of Arkansas in the Fall of 1833. William Hawkins died there 8 August 1858.
1850 Federal Census, Madison County, Arkansas, Richland Township, page 265, family #261: William Hawkins 62 Va.; Elizabeth 58 Va.; John 29 Tenn.; Stephen 24 Tenn.; Rhoda 26 Tenn.; Mary 13 Tenn.

HAYS,CAMPBELL-War of 1812 pension application S.O.#26193, S.C.#19605, W.O.#21920, rejected. Served in Captain John Donaldson's Company of Tennessee Militia from 2 September 1814 to 1 September 1815. Resided in Randolph County, Arkansas by 1851. Married Ellen Grubb, 14 December 1863 in Carroll County, Arkansas. Ellen Hays applied for pension on 4 May 1878, however, she never completed the the questionaire, so her pension application was abandoned.

HAYS,WILLIAM N.-Old war pension application dated 1850, Arkansas. Service in Captain Stephen B.Enghart's Company, Arkansas Mounted Volunteers, Mexican War. O.W. Minors Cert. #4198 File #11214. He was married to Alia (Alice ?) on 11 May 1823, she died in 1844. He was mustered into service on 15 June 1847 at Ft. Smith, Arkansas. He died of disease in Mexico on 20 December 1847. On 27 July 1850, Washington County, Arkansas, James Hukill and Madison Sawyers, guardians of the orphans of William Hays, applied for pension on their behalf. Said orphans: Dodson Clayton Hays, born January 29th 1839, Miriam Ann Harrison Hays born October 12th 1841 and Mary Adaline Hays, who was over the age of sixteen in 1854. Malinda House stated that she was the second daughter of William and Alia Hays.

HENDRICKS,DAVID D.-Old war pension application dated 30 November 1849, Franklin County, Arkansas. O.W. Wid.Cert.#1810, File #11277. He served in Captain William G. Preston's Company, 1st Regiment of Arkansas Mounted Volunteers in the Mexican War. He died of disease 4 June 1847, in Mexico. David Hendricks was married to Muhulda Martin on 12 September 1839. They had one child, James R. Polk Hendricks, born 5 June 1844. Muhulda Hendricks married David H. Dean on 20 September 1848. Muhulda died in February 1859 in Franklin County, Arkansas. John Roark was granted guardianship papers on James R.Polk Hendricks, in 1850.

HEWITT,SYLVESTER-Old War Pension Application dated 1877, Arkansas.

Served in 1st Georgia Infantry. O.W.Inv.#20086, M.W.Cert.#8655. (not abstracted)

HICKMAN,CALEB-Old War Pension Application dated 1880 Arkansas. Served in Company I, 5th Regiment of Tennessee Volunteers, Mexican War. O.W.Inv.#22549, Mex.War Cert.#3062, Mex.Wid.#6925. (not abstracted)

HIGGS,THOMAS-Old War Pension Application dated 1886, Arkansas. He served in Captain Coffee's Company of Alabama Volunteers, 1836 and 1837. O.W.Inv.#24073, Mex.Sur.#24585, Ind.W.Sur.#4228, Cert.-#3655, Ind.War.Wid.O.#6980. (not abstracted)

HILL,JOEL-Revolutionary War Pension Application #W23288, dated 10 December 1832 in Limestone County, Alabama. He was born 26 May 1763 in Caroline County, Virginia. He was living in Surry County, North Carolina, when he enlisted in July 1779, in Captain Woolridge and Captain John Morgan's Companies of Colonel Martin Armstrong's Regiment. From 1780 thru 1782, he served in Captain Robert Hill's Company, whom he identified as his brother, in Colonel Paisley's Regiment. He married Anne Watson, 16 October 1791, in Richmond County, Georgia. A copy of the marriage bond included in widow's application. Also enclosed is a copy of the family record, to wit; "Anne Watson was born October or November 10, 1773; Elizabeth Hill was born 26 July 1792; John P. Hill was born 12 November 1794; William Hill was born 14 May 1797; Margaret Hill was born 3 September 1799; Mary Hill was born 23 December 1802." Joel Hill died 6 January 1843 in Bay Township, Jackson County, Arkansas. His widow was granted Bounty Land Warrant #28636 for 160 acres.

HOBBS,JOB-Revolutionary War Pension Application #S32328. B.L.W.-#91042-160-55. He was inscribed on Arkansas pension rolls commencing 4 March 1831. He stated that he was born in Frederick County, Virginia, the son of Vinson and Ruth (nee Thomas) Hobbs. The children of Vinson and Ruth Hobbs are; James, Merry, Hannah, Vinson, Joel, Ezekiel, Ruth, Rachel, William, Absolom, Abner, and Job. Job Hobbs stated that his brother, Ezekiel also served in the Revolution (His pension application #W8940, B.L.W.#26632-160-55, dated 6 October 1834, Washington County, Virginia, was used by pension application board to check statements of Job Hobbs. Ezekiel Hobbs died in Washington County in 1835, his widow applied for pension on his service. She submitted the Marriage bond of Ezekiel Hobbs and Elizabeth Lilly dated 27 July 1803, Washington County, Virginia; Hardy Lilly; surety. In an affidavit by John McCullock, he stated that he and Ezekiel had served together in an expedition to Kentucky in 1778, under command of Captain George Adams and Major Daniel Smith). In Madison County, Arkansas, 8 July 1859, Job Hobbs stated that he was 100 years old on 21 June 1859; that he was residing in Washington County, Virginia when he entered the war. He stated that his father died in Washinton County, Virginia, but he did not remember the date, and his mother died in the same county some time afterward. He stated that he moved to Powell Valley, Virginia about 1780 and that his family moved there about the same time that he did. He served in Captain James Fulkerson's Company, Colonel William Campbell's Regiment, which he had joined in Powell's Valley. He remained in Powell's Valley about 10 years before moving to Madison County, Kentucky, for four years, thence to Knox County, Tennessee for 3 years, to Montgomery County, Tennessee, for 4 years, to Davis County, Kentucky, then to Spencer County, Indiana for 14 years, then to Marion County, Indiana, and from there to Washington County, Arkansas. In 1859, he stated that he had resided in Madison County, Arkansas, for 12 or 13 years. When asked about his brothers and sisters in Virginia; "my oldest brother died somewhere in Kentucky, my oldest sister died in Washington County, Virginia, doesn't know where next oldest sister died, next oldest brother died on Turkey Creek in Tennessee, next oldest brother died on a creek called Big Piney not far from Duck River, Tennessee, one brother was killed by Cherokee Indians in either Tennessee or Kentucky, the last time he saw Ezekiel was in Washington County, Virginia, 40 years ago, and brother Absolom was living in Lee County, Virginia, at that time."

HOGAN,WILLIAM-War of 1812 pension application W.O.#7165, W.C.#2446. B.L.W.#497-40-50, #49845-40-50 (canceled and enclosed in this file) and #93679-120-55. Service in Captain James Gideon's Company of Tennessee Militia from 28 January 1814 to 10 May 1814. He stated that he was drafted in Williamson County, Tennessee. Married Anna Atkinson, 13 May 1813 in Maury County, Tennessee. Soldier died 29 July 1851 in Johnson County, Arkansas. His widow applied for pension in 1871, her pension certificate is enclosed in this file. In making application, she removed the page from her Bible which contained the family record, sent it to the pension board, which has been filed with the application. The record; "William Hogan was born 19 September 1793, Anna Hogan, his wife, 17 October 1794, and was married 13 May 1813, Isaiah Hogan, first son to William and Anna Hogan was born 21 April 1814, Polly Hogan, first daughter, was born 30 April 1817, Becky Hogan, 2nd daughter, was born 1 February 1819, Sarah Saner Hogan, 3rd daughter, was born 21 September 1820, John Hogan, 3rd son, was born 24 February 1822, David Hogan, 2nd son, was born 12 September 1815, Samuel D. Hogan, 5th son, was born 6 February 1825, Edward B. Hogan, 6th son, was born 25 November 1826, Holland W. Hogan, 7th son, was born 23 January 1828, Anderson Hogan, 9th son was born 23 December 1831, Elizabeth Hogan, 4th daughter, was born 13 July 1834, James M. Hogan was born 22 May 1838, William Hogan, 4th ,son was born 1 February 1824, and died 4 April 1825, Jesse Hogan, 8th son, was born 16 November 1830, and died February 1832, John C. Hogan was born 24 February 1822, and died 15 October 1845, David Hogan was born 12 September 1815 and was killed 23 February 1847, Isaiah Hogan was born 21 April 1814 and died 11 January 1847, Mary Jane Hogan, the daughter of Anderson and Bathsheba Hogan was born 4 July 1859".

HOLEMAN,JOHN-War of 1812 pension application W.O.#20080, W.C.#13409. B.L.W.#18739-80-50 and #13903-80-55. He was drafted in Bledsoe County, Tennessee, in Captain Hankin's Company of Tennessee Drafted Men from 10 January 1814 to 13 May 1814. He married Frances Clarke, 17 October 1844 in Carroll County, Arkansas. He died in Carroll County on 23 June 1866. (not abstracted) 1850 Federal Census, Carroll County, Arkansas, Prairie Township, page 146, family 333: John Holeman 61 N.C.; Frances 34 N.C.; Isaac Clark 13 Tenn.; Jackson Holeman 22 Tenn.; John J. 5 Ark.; Peter 10 Ark.

HOLMAN,JOHN-Revolutionary War Pension Application #S31753, dated 12 October 1832, Hempstead County, Territory of Arkansas. John Holman was born 25 December 1736 in Goochland County, Virginia, where he lived until he was about 42 years old. He enlisted in service in 1777 in the Virginia Militia, and was assigned to guarding the prisoners that were taken when General Burgoyne surrendered. After the war, he lived in North Carolina about 2 or 3 years, returned to Virginia for 2 years, from there to Kentucky and from Kentucky he moved "west of the Mississippi" to a place called St. Michael and finally to Hempstead County in 1825.
Hempstead County, Arkansas-the will of John Holman, recorded 11 Feb 1837, "All personal property to my daughter, Judith Thompson"

HORN,HARMON-War of 1812 Pension application S.O.#29567, S.C.#22536. Service in Captain James Burleson's Company of Mississippi Militia. (not abstracted)

HOUSE,WILLIAM H.-War of 1812 pension application W.O.#16315
W.C.#9239. B.L.W.#22669-160-55. Service in Captain Samuel Lane's
Company of Georgia Militia from 21 November 1814 to 6 May 1815,
also served in Creek Indian War, 29 May to 1 September in 1836.
Married first to Mary Potts, who died in Jasper County, Georgia.
Married second to Nancy T. Frankline, 19 April 1827, at Forsyth,
Monroe County, Georgia. A copy of their marriage record is enclosed.
Deposition of Eliza M.E.Deese, dated 31 January 1876, a resident
of Fort Smith, Arkansas, "I am the sister of Nancy House, nee
Frankline. William H. House was my school teacher in the year
1822 in Monroe County, Georgia. Nancy and William were married
in my father's home, William Frankline." Affidavit of Adaline
Gardner, resident of Washington, D.C. in 1878; daughter of William
and Nancy House. In widow's pension application she appointed
Samuel Gardner of Washington, D.C., as her attorney. Soldier
died 11 October 1845 in Tallapoosa County, Alabama, widow removed
to Prescott, Nevada County, Arkansas where she died 15 January
1885.

HUDDLESTON,WILLIAM-War of 1812 pension application S.O.#15762
W.O.#32071, W.C.#23429. B.L.W.#38909-80-50 and #28797-80-55. Service
as musician in Captain Crane's Company of 2nd Tennessee Volunteers
from 28 September 1814 to 28 March 1815. He volunteered at
Springfield, Robertson County, Tennessee. In 1851, he was living
in Pike County, Arkansas. In his bounty land application dated
16 June 1855, he stated that he was age 58, and a resident of
Red River County, Arkansas. He married 25 November 1866, Mary
Corbell, in Pike County. She applied for pension 17 September
1878, stating that her husband died in Pike County, 10 July
1871 and that his first wife _____? Lee had died in Memphis
Tennessee, date not known. (compiler's note-The Pike County
Courthouse burned in 1895, destroying all records to that date)
1850 Federal Census, Pike County, Arkansas, Brewer Township,
page 193, family #92: Lewis Huddleston 45 N.C.; Mariah 27 Ark.;
Benton 7 Ark.; William C. 7 Ark.; S.F. 2 Ark.; David M. 5/12
Ark.; William 54 N.C.; Synthia Holliday 20 Ark.; William M.
Huddleston 17 Ark.; Ann 14 Ark.

HUDSON/HUTSON,EDWARD-Revolutionary War Pension Application #R5328,
dated 29 November 1837, Randolph County, Arkansas. Stated that
"he was 80 years of age on the 25th day of December 1836". He
served in General Francis Marian's Regiment at the Battle of
Eutaw Springs. He lived in Lancaster District, South Carolina
some 8 or 10 years, he was married and had 2 children born there. He
moved to Green County, Tennessee, where he lived 5 years, then
moved to Smith County, Tennessee, where he lived "some three
or four and twenty years" before moving to Randolph County,
Arkansas, ca 1817. His wife was still living in 1837 and they
have had 10 children. He lived with his son-in-law.
Randolph County, Arkansas; Will Record 1, pages 171 and 172,
"Whereas, Edward Hudson, Sr, of the County of Randolph, died
intestate on or about the 4th day of April AD 1845, we do hereby
appoint Edward Hudson, of the County of Randolph, administrator,
with full power and authority, according to law. Edward Hudson,
Abram Breeding and Robert O'Neal are bound to the State of Arkansas
in the sum of seven hundred and forty dollars. That Edward Hudson,
Sr, died, leaving heirs: Mary Ann Hudson, widow of deceased,
Joseph Hudson, Elender Hudson, Henry Hudson, Edward Hudson,
Bashaby Hudson, Polly Ann Bellow and the heirs of John Hudson
and the heirs of Nancy Wallis". Will Record 1, page 307; Whereas
Mary Ann Hudson, of the County of Randolph, died 9 November
1848, without having made a last will and testament, we do hereby
appoint Edward Hudson, administrator, according to law. I, Edward
Hudson, do solemnly swear that Mary Ann Hudson, upon whose estate
I have prayed papers of administration, died leaving as her
heirs; John Hudson's heirs, Nellie White, Joseph Hudson, Henry
Hudson, Nancy Wallace, Bashaby Rice and Polly Bellote (?)".

HUDSON,ELI-War of 1812 pension application S.O.#25711, S.C.#19330 W.O.#12461, W.C.#29362. Service in Captain William Fitzgerald's Company of Virginia Militia. He enlisted in Nottaway County, Virginia in 1814 and was discharged at Norfolk in 1815. His duty was making cartridges for use by the army. He was married 2 September 1819 in Nottaway County, Virginia, to Lucretia P. Jackson. In his pension application in 1871, in Madison County, Arkansas, he stated that he was 78 years old. He died in Madison County, 6 March 1875. In the widow's application in 1879, Henrietta M. Proctor, age 46 and Mary J. Berry, age 44 state "we are daughters of Eli and Lucretia Hudson, and we have a brother Richard W. Hudson, age 58, who lives in Tennessee." Lucretia Hudson died in Madison County, Arkansas, 8 June 1892, at which time daughter Henrietta stated "I am her only surviving child".

HUGHES,GEORGE-Old war pension application dated 1849, Arkansas. Service in Company B, 14th Regiment of U.S. Infantry-Mexican War. Inv. Cert. #4685 File #25170 Mex Wid. Cert. #538 Mex. Sur. #2940. (not abstracted)

HUKILL,JAMES S.-Old war pension application dated 1850, Arkansas. Service in Captain Engart's Company of Arkansas Mounted Volunteers, Mexican War. Inv. Cert. #4993 File #25169 O.W. Minor's App. #26110 O.W. Wid. Pending File.

HULSE,ABRAHAM-War of 1812 pension application W.O.#15423, W.C.#13844. B.L.W.#50505-80-50 and #36446-80-55. Service 1 October 1813 to 8 February 1814. Married Nancy Rector, 15 March 1816, in Sullivan County, Tennessee. Abraham Hulse was elected twice to the Tennessee State Legislature, during his second term he died in Nashville on 4 December 1837. His widow applied for pension 6 April 1878 in Washington County, Arkansas, stating that she had moved to Arkansas from Tennessee in 1869. In her application she included the Family record, to wit; "Abraham Hulse and Nancy Rector was married the 15th day of March in the year 1816; Abraham Hulse was born the 15th day of June 1791; Nancy Hulse was born the 28th day of August 1796; Polly Hulse was born the 26th day of June 1817; John P. Hulse was born the 14th day of March 1819; William A. Hulse was born 17th day of April 1821; James P. Hulse was born the 9th day of May 1823; Enoch S. Hulse was born the 9th day of March 1825, and departed this life the 11th day of November 1831; Abraham Hulse,Sen, departed this life , with the consumptive fever, on the 4th day of December 1837; Abraham G. Hulse was born the 5th day of March 1827; Isaac N. Hulse was born the 21st of December 1829; Elizabeth Hulse was born 24th August 1835; Jacob Hulse was born 2nd day of December 1837".
Independence County, Arkansas Marriage Records; page 48, John Hulsey and Martha Steel 13 July 1837.

HULSE,WILLIAM A.-Old war pension application dated 1850, Arkansas. Service in Captain Engard's Company of Arkansas Mounted Volunteers, Mexican War. Inv. Cert. #5066 File #45797 Mex. Sur. #18355 Mex. Wid. O. #15541 Cert. #12562. This is a voluminous file, with a great deal of going back and forth between Arkansas and Missouri.
William Hulse was born in Sullivan County, Tennessee. He applied for pension on his service in the Mexican War 28 May 1850 in Washington County, Arkansas. He stated that he had entered service 15 June 1847 at Fayetteville, and that he had been discharged in June 1848, after a fall from his horse had severely injured his ankle. On 25 September 1864, William Hulse enlisted in the Missouri State Militia at Jefferson City, Mo. He was assigned to drive a wagon and ox team to haul wood and coal for the U.S. Soldiers. He applied for pension in 1870 in Saline County, Missouri stating that he had left Arkansas in April 1862 "that he was compelled to leave that state because of his Union principals,

he had been robbed by Rebels or bushwhackers, all of his personal property had been taken and his houses had been burned". His first wife, Lucy Billingsley, (she had son J.D.Billingsley of Saline County, Mo.) died 24 December 1872. His second wife Elizabeth died in Dallas County, Missouri, in 1884/5. William A. Hulse married Adelia J. Teed (widow of Arlo Teed) on 11 November 1886 at Springfield, Missouri. He is referred to as the Rev. Mr. Hulse by many of the affiants in this file. He died 12 June 1899 in St. Joseph, Missouri. On 9 November 1897, Adelia Hulse, applied for pension in Springtown, Benton County, Arkansas, on the service of her first husband, Arlo Teed. He had served in the Civil War as Captain of Company G, 18th Regiment of Iowa Volunteer Infantry. The children of Arlo and Adelia Teed: Harry H. bn 22 December 1859; Anna bn 20 January 1861; Ida bn 7 April 1863, died 18 August 1864; Louisa bn 16 October 1867, died 6 January 1882; Frank R. bn 14 December 1868; Homer O. bn 13 March 1874. Arlo Teed married Adelia J. Francisco in Evanston, Illinois. In her application, Adelia stated that "I am unable to furnish a copy of the Church record of Baptism of my children for the reason that no such record is in existence, all such records having been destroyed by the Great Chicago Fire". Adelia Francisco was born 26 November 1836 in Bloomingdale, Passaic County, New Jersey. She had brother Henry and sister Celia (Vreeland). John W. Harvey, who served in the same company that Arlo Teed (18th Iowa) served in stated "on 17 October 1863, our regiment left Springfield, Missouri, in pursuit of General Joe Shelby and followed him until he crossed the Arkansas River near Clarkesville, Arkansas, the regiment then turned up the river and reached Ft. Smith on October 31. In the Spring and Summer, the 18th Iowa was on the Arkadelphia Campaign and Captain Arlo Teed was in command of his own company". Adelia's application for that pension was rejected, and she applied for pension on the Mexican War service of her second husband, William Hulse, which was granted.

HUMBER,CHARLES H.-Old war pension application. Service as Captain in 7th U.S. Regiment of U.S. Infantry-Mexican War. Widow, Laura C. O.W. Wid. Cert. #5436 File #10134. Widow's pension application dated 21 January 1858, Laura C. Humber, age 19, resident of Ft. Smith, Sebastian County, Arkansas. She was married to Charles Humber 5 December 1854, and he died 2 January 1858 in Ft. Smith. The following letter was received by The Congress of the United States, "He served with exemplary fidelity and devotion both in Florida and Mexico, and wherever else his regiment was stationed. He was never absent from duty except when compelled by sickness. In his trunk, after his death, several leaves of absence were found, which he had never used. In the summer of 1857, while stationed at Ft. Smith, he was ordered to Utah. He was suffering from the disease of which he died, and which it is supposed, was contracted in Mexico. His wife felt herself called upon to decide whether to go with her husband to take care of him, or to remain at Ft. Smith, with her infant child, which also was in delicate health. She determined to go and take the child with her. Several days beyond Fort Leavenworth, the attending physician told her that if the child proceeded, it could not possibly live. The only course left open to her was to turn back to Ft. Smith. Captain Humber, himself, was then disabled from either marching on foot or riding horseback. Instead of going back with his wife and child, he pushed on with his command to Fort Laramie. Mrs. Humber made her way to Ft. Smith, carrying the sick infant most of the way on her lap. The day after their arrival at Ft. Smith, the child died, and eight days later, Mrs. Humber gave birth to her second child. When Captain Humber reached Fort Laramie, his health was very bad. When he received news of the death of his child, he obtained a surgeon's certificate and left Fort Laramie on 27 October. One of his traveling companions stated, "on our way down, Captain Humber was very ill, and I was apprehensive that he might die before we reached Fort Kearney. Within one hundred miles of the post, the snow commenced falling fast and we were compelled to stop in the timber on Platte River for two days. On the 8th of November, with a worn out team of starving mules, we resumed our journey, my companion and I walking through the deepest snow, as the tired animals could scarcely draw the carriage with the sick Captain and our provisions. On the 12th of November our team gave out entirely and there was no alternative left but for us to abandon carriage, mules and the other property, and walk the 18 or 20 miles to Fort Kearney. We had not proceeded far, when the Captain threw himself on the snow and said he could go no further, urging us to go on and save ourselves. We got him to his feet and on we trudged, making slow and painful progress through snow which had now drifted deeply in our way. The Captain continued to urge us to leave him, and we continued to carry him through the deepest drifts, until we came to a trading post within three miles of Fort Kearney. This gave us new life and after a tramp of three hours, we reached Fort Kearney." Captain Charles Humber finally reached Ft. Smith, Arkansas, but died a few weeks later. Special report to the 36th Congress of the United States, dated February 28, 1860, "The Committee on pensions, to whom was referred the petition of Laura C. Humber, widow of the late Charles W. Humber, beg leave to report, that it appears from the records of the War Department, the husband of the petitioner entered the United States Army as a cadet in September 1835, was Second Lieutenant in the 7th Infantry July 1, 1840, First Lieutenant September 1845, Brevet Captain, for gallant and meritorious conduct in the Battle of Cerro Gordo 8th April 1847, severly wounded at San Geronimo, 19th August 1847 and died at Ft. Smith, Arkansas on January 2, 1858. The petitioner prays a pension on the grounds that her husband died of disease contracted in the line of duty, in the service of the United States." Congress approved the pension for Laura Humber on 20 February 1861, however, on 12 April 1861, the American Civil War began. She never received any of her pension funds. Laura C. Humber married Frank A. Rector on 20 February 1862, they were divorced later, and Frank Rector died 10 September 1874 near the Red River in the Choctaw Nation. Laura resumed the name Humber, and reapplied for pension on the service of Charles Humber. The Congress of the United States was again petitioned for her pension, and by special legislation, she was granted pension on 28 February 1891.

ISH,JOHN-War of 1812 pension application W.O.#14978, W.C.#13845. B.L.W.#32175-80-50 and #41685-80-55. Service in Captain George W. Gibbs' Company of Tennessee Militia from 10 December 1812 to 20 April 1813, he also served in Captain John H. Anderson's Company. John Ish was born 23 April 1786 in Knox County, Tennessee, (this statement made by his wife ?). After the war he moved to Indiana for a short while, then moved to Missouri before moving to Clark County, Arkansas. He was married to Synthia Edmiston, 20 May 1819 in Clark County, by David Edmiston, Justice of Peace. John and Synthia had eleven children; among which; Columbus E. Ish born 10 January 1821; Phoebe Adeline Ish born 15 October 1826; Jacob K. Ish born 23 April 1831. John Ish died in Washington County, Arkansas 15 October 1857. Widow applied for pension in 1878, age 78.
Washington County, Arkansas; Will Book A&B page 49; Mem. will of John Ish, "I wish my real estate, at my wife's death to be sold, or sooner, at her discretion, and the proceeds equally divided among my children".
1850 Federal Census, Washington County, Arkansas, Vineyard Township, page 420, family #3: John Ish 64 Penn.(?); Cynthia 50 Tenn.; Elizabeth Ann 27 Ark.; Phebe 23 Ark.; David 20 Ark.; Jacob 19 Ark.; Mary 17 Ark.; Sarah 14 Ark.; Frances 11 Ark.; William 8 Ark.
ISLEY,GEORGE-Old War Pension Application, dated 1885, Arkansas.

Served in Company B, 5th Tennessee Volunteers, Mexican War. O.W.Inv. Cert.#6918, File #99, O.W.Wid.R.#25028, Mex.Wid.#4792. (not abstracted)

JACKSON,HENRY-War of 1812 pension application W.O.#18734, W.C.-#16157. He was drafted into service in York District, South Carolina on 1 October 1814 in Captain Robert Caldwell's Company of South Carolina Militia. He was discharged 28 February 1815 in Charleston, South Carolina. He married Elizabeth Graham 31 August 1820 in York District, South Carolina. He applied for bounty land 29 October 1850 in Shelby County, Tennessee. In 1855, he again applied for bounty land in Prairie County, Arkansas, his age 60 years. Widow applied for pension 2 April 1878, she was aged 78, and a resident of Des Arc, Prairie County, Arkansas. Her lawyer, after examination of county records sent the following letter to the Pensions Office in Washington, D.C., "By examination of the records of this office, I find that Henry Jackson purchased with Land Warrant no. 3960, on the 5th of March 1853, the NE 1/4 NE 1/4 sec 18 T 4 NR5W, cert. of purchase no. 847, and on the same day, Andrew Jackson purchased 120 acres in sec 7, same township and range, with warrant no. 32887, certificate of purchase no. 848; the family are under the impression that Andrew Jackson got warrant no.32887 from Henry Jackson. Examine the Record of Warrant no.3282 also no. 3288-perhaps you may be able to get a clue to the officer under whom he served". Affidavit of Robert Graham, age 81, resident of Lafayette County, Mississippi in 1878 "that he was present at the wedding of Henry Jackson and Elizabeth Graham", and from Archie Graham, age 70, resident of York District, South Carolina in 1878, "that he was present at the wedding of Henry Jackson and Elizabeth Graham". 1850 Federal Census, Shelby County, Tennessee, page 192, family #1612: Henry Jackson 54 S.C.; Elizabeth 51 S.C.; Thomas 15 Ala.; Jasper 13 Ala.; Madison 12 Ala.; Loiusa 10 Ala.; Elizabeth 7 Ala.; Lewis 5 Miss.; George W. 20 Ala.

JACOBS,JUSTIN-War of 1812 pension application S.O.#4329, S.C.#3936 W.O.#37378 W.C.#28999. Service in Captain R. Steward's Company, 31st Regiment, U.S. Infantry. Justin Jacobs was married first in July of 1831 in Vermont, she died in the Spring of 1850. He married second, Mary A. Clark, who was the widow of Levy Clark. Levy Clark died 11 May 1863 in Clifton Park, New York. Justin Jacobs died 24 September 1878 in Hamilton, Wisconsin. Widow, Mary, moved to Little Rock, Pulaski County, Arkansas to reside with her son Luman Clark and his wife Sophia. She applied for pension in Arkansas in 1879.

JAMES,HENRY W.-War of 1812 pension application S.O.#23740, S.C.#65121 W.O.#37623 W.C.#27988. Service in Captain Weakley's Company of Tennessee Militia from November 1814 to May 1815. He was born ca 1797, place not stated, and was residing in Robinson County, Tennessee when he enlisted. He was about 17 or 18 years old at that time, and stated that he served at the Battle of New Orleans. He was a minor at the time of his discharge, so his discharge certificate was given to his father, who sold it. His first wife, Martha Brown died June 1861. He resided from the date of his discharge to 1837 in Tennessee, from 1837 to 1849 he resided in Mississippi, and from 1849 to his death on 31 July 1873, he resided in Hempstead County, Arkansas. Henry James married Catherine Evans (nee Barnes) 23 October 1865. She was the widow of Wilson Evans who had died 19 January 1863. Affidavit by Daniel W. James of Yell County, Arkansas, dated 12 April 1851, stated that Henry James left home when he was about 17 to enter the service. 1850 Federal Census record, Hempstead County, Arkansas, Red Land Township, page 249; Henry W. James 53 S.C., Martha 51 N.C., Lewis B. 15 Tenn., Hiram H. 12 Miss., William Askew 20 Tenn., Sarah A 17 Tenn.

JENKINS,WILLIAM-Revolutionary War Pension Application #S31774, dated 14 August 1832, Jackson County, Alabama. He was born on Clear Creek in the State of Maryland in 1762. He was living in York County, South Carolina, in 1780, when he enlisted in service. He volunteered in his uncle's, Captain Thomas Jenkins, Company, in Colonel William Bratton's Regiment. William Jenkins was appointed Sergeant on his first evening in the army. His first engagement was with a group of Tories and a band of British Dragoons near the home of Colonel Bratton. Later, while on a recruiting mission in their home neighborhood, William Jenkins, Thomas Jenkins, John Henry, James Meeks and Ezekiel Candloe were taken prisoner. They were held in jail for five weeks in District Ninety-Six. After their release, they returned to their regiment, at which time, William Jenkins was appointed Lieutenant. He served two 3 month tours, then was promoted to Captain. After the war, he remained in York County, South Carolina, about ten years, then moved to Pendleton District, S.C. for about 20 years. He lived in Rutherford and Franklin Counties about 9 years before moving to Jackson County, Alabama. On 24 January 1838, he was residing in Pike County, Arkansas, and applied to have his pension transferred because of "the removal of my son, to this state, with whom I wish to spend the remainder of my days".
1840 Federal Census, Pike County, Arkansas, page 68: Jesse Jenkins with males, 2 between 10-20, 2 between 20-30, 1 between 30-40, 1 between 80-90, William Jenkins, age 80, pensioner; females; 1 under 5, 1 between 5-10, 2 between 10-15, 1 between 30-40, 1 between 50-60.

JESTER,JOSEPH-Old War Pension Application dated 1849, Arkansas. O.W.Inv.Cert.#4083, File #25180. (not abstracted)

JOHNSON,ISAAC-Old War Pension Application dated 1849, Arkansas. Service in Captain Pike's Company, 1st Arkansas Volunteers, Mexican War. O.W.Inv.Cert.#4575, File #25188, Mex.Wid.#1086. (not abstracted)

JOHNSTON,JAMES-War of 1812 pension application W.O.#33943, W.C.#27151. He served in Captain Samuel G. Hopkins' Tennessee Dragoons and in Captain James Stuart's Company of Tennessee Militia. He entered service in Maryville, Tennessee on 8 October 1812. He was discharged 7 April 1813, his original discharge contained in this file, which gives his description when he entered service; about 30 years old, born in Virginia, 5 ft. 9 inches, blue eyes light hair and by occupation a carpenter. He married Sarah Milburn 9 March 1847 in Bradley County, Tennessee. Soldier's Bounty Land Application dated 22 November 1850 Bradley County, Tenn. He died in Ft. Smith, Arkansas on 29 May 1865. Sarah Johnston applied for pension 5 December 1878 in Greenwood, Sebastian County, Arkansas. Affidavits from Mrs. Elizabeth Redding, age 60, and William J. Johnston, age 53, both residents of Sebastain County in 1878.

JONES,HAMILTON-War of 1812 pension application S.O.#30556, S.C.#21788. B.L.W.#42706-80-50 and #40201-80-55. Service in Captain James Gault's Company of Tennessee Militia. (not abstracted)

JONES,PHILIP-Revolutionary War Pension Application #S32342, dated 5 November 1832, Logan County, Kentucky, at which time he stated that he thought that he was about age 70, the family record having been destroyed. He entered the service at Amelia Court House in Virginia, in Captain Samuel Booker's Company of Colonel Holt Richardson's Regiment. He was marched to Salisbury, North Carolina, from there to Charlottesville, then to Camden, South Carolina. He served at the Battle of Savannah, Eutaw Springs and at Cowpens. After his discharge, he served as a substitute for his brother, Gabriel Jones, who had become ill. During this tour he was at the Siege of York. On 3 April 1838, Philip Jones applied to have his pension transferred to Johnson County, Arkansas because his children had moved to Arkansas and he wished to be with them.

KEENER,TILLMAN-Old War Pension Application by Special Act, dated 1890, Arkansas. He served in Captain White's Company, Alabama Volunteers, Florida War. Widow, Stacey. O.W.Wid.Cert.#7833, File #29800. (not abstracted)

KEITH,RILEY C.-Old War Pension Application dated 1855, Arkansas. He served in Captain Blalock's Company, North Carolina Volunteers, Mexican War. O.W.Inv.App.#20866, Mex.Wid.#5742. (not abstracted)

KENEDAY,JAMES-War of 1812 pension application S.O.#16183, S.C.#9909 W.O.#33603, W.C.#24295. Service in Captain Ezekiel Smith's Company of Georgia Militia. He enlisted in Jones County, Georgia. His Bounty Land Application in 1851, was made from Jefferson County, Arkansas, at which time his age was 63. He married Louisa Swofford in Jefferson Co. on 3 July 1861. (not abstracted)

KERSEY/CASEY,GEORGE-War of 1812 pension application W.O.#33264, W.C.#26602. B.L.W.#10283-80-50 and #48586-80-55. Served in Captain Charles Conway's Company of East Tennessee Mounted Gunmen from 20 September 1814 to 1 May 1815. He volunteered into service in Knoxville, Tennessee. His original discharge, signed by Captain Charles Conway and by Major John Chiles, is contained in this file. George M. Kersey married first, Lucy Brock, who died ca 1826. He then married Elizabeth Gilliam 20 December 1830 in Jackson County, Alabama. He applied for Bounty Land in 1850 in Marion County, Tennessee, in 1858, he applied from Sebastian County, Arkansas. Elizabeth Kersey applied for pension on 19 September 1878, her age 65, she was a resident of Vesta, Franklin County, Arkansas. She stated that her husband died in Sebastian County on 9 September 1863. Affidavits from Harris Gilliam, age 73, and Amy Partain, age 75 of Grundy County, Tennessee in 1879.

KIMBALL,SOLOMON F.-Old war pension application dated 1855, Arkansas. Service in Captain Engart's Company of Arkansas Mounted Volunteers, Mexican War. Inv.Cert.#8458 File #25205 Mex. #9049 Cert. #7596. (not abstracted)

KING,WILLIAM-War of 1812 pension application S.O.#20657, S.C.#19370 W.O.#37207, W.C.#29711. He was drafted at Winchester, Tennessee, into Captain John Robinson's Company of Tennessee Militia. He served at the Battle of Talledega. He was married in Franklin County, Tennessee to Isabelle Mann in September 1817. He married second, Sarah Seaman, at Cape Fain, Stone County, Missouri. She died about 1869 or 1870. He married third Catherine Eubanks, widow of John Eubanks, on 6 January 1873 in Stone County, Missouri. In his application, dated 29 May 1871 in Carroll County, Arkansas, soldier stated that his wife's name was Isabella Mann. William King died in Stone County, Missouri, 29 December 1873. His widow, Catherine, applied for a new pension certificate on 4 June 1889, "because Mrs. Kings house in Little River County, Arkansas was destroyed by fire."

KIRBY/KERBY,CHRISTOPHER-Revolutionary War Pension Application #S32356, dated 19 December 1835, Washington County, Territory of Arkansas. He was born in Hallifax County, Virginia 10 September 1760. He was living in Surry County, North Carolina when he enlisted in service. He stated that he enlisted at a place called "the Old Store" near the Yadkin River. In July 1779, he served in a Company of Light Horse Dragoons commanded by Captain William Underwood in Regiments commanded by Colonel Martin Armstrong and Colonel Joseph Williams. In his first tour his regiment was sent into the State of Virginia in pursuit of a band of

Tories. He was serving in Captain James Shepherd's Company in 1780, at which time he stated, that they were marched up the Catawba River, joining other regiments as they went to the Battle of Cowpens, and from Cowpens they proceeded to King's Mountain. He moved to Green County, Tennessee, after the war, and finally to Washington County, Territory of Arkansas.

KIRBY,JAMES M.-Old War Pension Application, dated 1880, Arkansas. He served in 1837 and 1838.O.W.Inv.App.#23753, Ind.War.Sur.#1541. (not abstracted)

KIRBY,JOSEPH L.-Old War Pension Application, dated 1855, Arkansas. O.W.Inv.#15673, Ind.War Wid #1574. (not abstracted)

KIRK,THOMAS-War of 1812 pension application W.O.#10168, W.C.#6408. B.L.W.#22788-40-50 and #80670-120-55. Served in Captain William Hamilton's Company of Tennessee Militia from 12 October 1813 to 2 February 1814. His original discharge certificate, signed by William Hamilton, Captain of East Tennessee Volunteers, is contained in this file. He married Sarah Bolinger in Claiborne County, Tennessee about the year 1812. Thomas Kirk died in Franklin County, Arkansas on 17 November 1850. Sarah Kirk applied for Bounty Land in 1851 in Franklin County. Because she had no formal record of their marriage, she produced affidavits of friends and neighbors; William Boatright, age 97, of Madison County, stated that he was well acquainted with Thomas Kirk and his wife Sarah, who were residents of Grainger County, Tennessee, and lived near neighbors prior to the War of 1812. Francis Dunn stated that he was acquainted with Thomas Kirk, sometime prior to the year 1810, and also with Sarah Kirk from childhood, he and Thomas Kirk belonged to the same Company in the War of 1812, that sometime prior to the breaking out of the War, Thomas Kirk married Sarah Bolinger, said parties lived on affiants farm in the State of Tennessee, that he knew the parties in the County of Madison, State of Arkansas, William Riley was the name of their oldest child. Henry H. Bolinger, of Madison County, stated "Thomas and Sarah Kirk's oldest son, William Riley, must have been born before 1812, we were raised up boys together in East Tennessee."
1850 Federal Census, Franklin County, Arkansas, White Oak Township, page 115, family #157: Thomas Kirk, basketmaker blind 62 Va.; Sarah 58 S.C.; Henderson 28 Ky.; Barbary 15 Ark.

KIRK,WILLIAM G.-Old War Pension Application. Service in Company I, 2nd Kentucky Volunteer Infantry. O.W.Minors R#26151, Mex.Sur.-Cert.#13105, Mex.Wid.Cert.#9724. (not abstracted)

KLINE,FREDERICK-Old War Pension Application, dated 1889, Arkansas. He served as carriage maker from 1855 to 1860 at Little Rock Arsenal, Ordinance Department. O.W.Inv.Cert.#756209, File #49314. (not abstracted)

KNIGHT,SAMUEL G.-Old war pension application. Widow, Catherine. Service in Captain Cady's Company 6th Regiment of U.S. Infantry, Mexican War. O.W. Wid.Cert.#5181, File #10183. (not abstracted)

LACEY,WILLIAM-War of 1812 pension application S.O.#29625, S.C.#21400 W.O.#40896, W.C.#31488. Served as Sergeant in Captain James Brown's Company and Captain John L. Town's Company of Virginia Militia. He volunteered at Charlotte Court House, Virginia on 10 July 1813. He was stationed throughout his service at Norfolk, Virginia, where he was discharged 15 January 1814. He was married to Sallie Campbell Graham, who died 6 August 1832. They had at least one child, B.T. Lacey bn ca 1816 and was residing in Pettis County, Missouri in 1881. William Lacey married second Julia A. Eldridge on 26 August 1833 in Pulaski, Giles County, Tennessee. He applied for bounty land in 1850 in Union County,

Arkansas. William Lacey died in Union County, Arkansas on 20 November 1880, and his widow applied for pension 21 February 1881, she was 71 years old and a resident of Union County. 1850 Federal Census, Union County, Arkansas, El Dorado Township, page 226, family #28: William S. Lacy 60 Clergyman Va.; Julia A. 41 N.C.; William A. 30 lawyer Mi.; Susan 20 Va.; John P. 22 Mi.; Drury 20 Mi.; Watson E. 10 Tenn.; Sterling 8 Tenn.; Archibald 6 Tenn.; Fanny L. 3 Ark.; John P. 7/12 Ark.

LACK,BENJAMIN J.-Old war pension application dated 1892, Arkansas. Mex. Sur. Cert. #13481 Mex. Wid. O. #13563. (not abstracted)

LAFFERTY,JAMES R.-Old war pension application. Service as Private in Company A, 4th Regiment, Tennessee Volunteers and as Captain in Company B, 4th Arkansas Cavalry, Company E, 1st Regiment, Arkansas Cavalry, and Company H, 1st Arkansas Cavalry. Inv.Cert.#6249 File #25217, Mex.Wid.O.#13332, late war, Inv.O.#556598. (not abstracted)

LAMBERT,MATTHEW-Old War Pension Application. Special Act Pension. Service in Captain Lander's Company, Alabama Volunteers, 1836. O.W.Inv.Cert.#505261, File #49016. (not abstracted)

LANE,LEWIS L.-Old War Pension Application, special act, dated 1892, Arkansas. Served as Sergeant in Captain Roe's Company, 1st Georgia Militia. O.W.Inv.Cert.#786675, File #49184, Ind.Wid.-#4859, Ind.Wid.Cert.#2527. (not abstracted)

LATIMER,WITHERAL-Revolutionary War Pension Application #S31809, dated 15 April 1833, Carroll County, Tennessee. He was born in New London Connecticut, on 18 March 1757. He first entered service as a substitute for his brother, in 1775 in New London in a company commanded by his father, Major Jonathan Latimer, Nathan Hale was the Lieutenant. In his second tour of duty in the year 1776, he served in a company of Connecticut Militia, and was at the Battle of White Plains. In 1777, he was drafted into a company under command of his father, Colonel Jonathan Latimer, and sent as his substitute, Robert Latimer. In 1778, Witheral Latimer was appointed Quartermaster Sergeant in the Regiment of Colonel Jonathan Latimer, at which time he served at the Battle of New London. His commission certificate as Adjutant of the 3rd Regiment of Infantry, State of Connecticut, dated 1 April 1783 and signed by his father, Colonel Jonathan Latimer, is contained in this file. He remained in New London, Conn. until 1790, when he moved to Davidson County, North Carolina, which is now in Tennessee. He spent several years in Sumner, Bedford and Carroll Counties, Tennessee, and on 7 September 1837, he applied to have his pension transferred to Pope County, Arkansas because "all of his children are in Arkansas, and he moved here with the youngest". The widow of Witheral Latimer's brother, Charles, applied for a pension on 5 Jan 1846 in Sumner County, Tenn, but was rejected. That pension application is listed under the name Charles Latimer, Rev. Pension Appl. #R6177. Widow Mary stated that she and Charles were married 7 Dec 1783. She has included her Family Bible record in that application.

LAWRENCE,JAMES-War of 1812 pension application W.O.#11429, W.C.#19743. He entered service at Fort Hawkins, Georgia on 20 November 1814 in Captain John Reed's Company of Georgia Militia. He was discharged at Milledgeville, Georgia in the Spring of 1815. He married Kizziah Wade in Gwinnett County, Georgia on 26 August 1819. They remained in Gwinnett County, until about 1833, when they moved to Chattooga County, Georgia, where James Lawrence applied for Bounty Land on 5 July 1853. They moved to Searcy County, Arkansas shortly thereafter. James Lawrence died in Searcy County (now Stone) on 12 December 1862. Kizziah Lawrence applied for pension on 14 October 1878 in Stone County, Arkansas.

Joseph W. Lee, of Blue Mountain, Stone County, Arkansas, stated that he had in his possession the old Family Bible, formerly belonging to the said James Lawrence, that the following is a copy of the family record in said Family Bible, "James Lawrence was born on the 26th day of October 1796; Kizziah Wade was born on the 9th day of November 1801; James Lawrence and Kizziah Wade was married August 26th 1819; James Lawrence departed this life on the 12th day of December 1862; John W. Lawrence was born the 11th day of April in the year 1821; Asa M. Lawrence was born July the 4th in the year 1823; ___? Lawrence was born June 14th 1825; (there appears to be at least two other listings, page badly mutilated) Mary Lawrence was born August 21st 1831; James F. Lawrence was born March the 3rd 1834; Nancy Elizabeth Lawrence was born November 23rd 1836; Lucinda Lawrence was born September the 21st 1836; Sarah Jane Lawrence was born September the 20th 1842."

LEA,JAMES A.-Old war pension application. Widow, Minerva. Service in Company H, 5th Regiment Tennessee Volunteers and in 3rd Regiment, U.S. Infantry. O.W. Wid.Cert.#770, File #13079, O.W. Minor's Cert. #1724 File #29380. He was married to Minerva Jane Walker 7 November 1845 in Bradley County, Tennessee. They had one child, Emily, born in 1847. James Lea/Lee died at the National Bridge, Mexico, of disease. Minerva and Emily Lea were inscribed on Arkansas pension rolls in May 1853. Minerva married Lorenza De Lano, and they moved to Lorain County, Ohio.

LEAKE,THOMAS S.-War of 1812 pension application W.O.#18796, W.C.#30370. B.L.W.#11256-40-50 and #87055-120-55. Service in Captain Benjamin Lewis' Company of South Carolina Militia. He was drafted in Laurens District, South Carolina and discharged near Buford's Island. He married Sarah Charlotte Dillard 10 November 1825 in Laurens County, S.C. The bridesmaid was Sallie Adair, born 11 January 1808 in Laurens County, S.C. Others attending the wedding were; Sims P. Dillard of Howard County, Arkansas in the year 1878; Lemuel Dillard, Lucinda Finney, Mary Bell and Serena Memford (then Serena Dillard). Soldier's Bounty Land Application dated 21 November 1850, Cass County, Georgia his age 56. In 1855, he applied for bounty land from Hempstead County, Arkansas. Thomas Leake died 27 May 1865 in Gray Rock, Titus County, Texas. His widow returned to Howard County, Arkansas, where she applied for pension on his military service in 1878, age 70.
1850 Federal Census, Cass County, Georgia, page 208, family #1522: John Leak 65 S.C.; Polly 56 S.C.; Barnet 25 S.C.; Whitfield 18 S.C.; Suda 15 S.C.; Elizabeth 13 S.C.: page 174, family #1050: Thomas S. Leak 53 S.C.; Sarah C. 41 S.C.; Thomas 20 S.C.; Lemuel 18 S.C.; Moses H. 16 S.C.; Sarah 14 S.C.; George W. 11 Ga.; Julia 9 Ga.; Western 7 Ga.; Eliza 4 Ga.; Elizabeth 1 Ga. page 139, family #557: Armstead Leak 27 S.C.; Dorcus 60 S.C. page 134, family #487: Armstead Leak 60 S.C.; Mary 50 S.C. Moses 17 S.C.; Nancy 15 S.C.; John S. 12 S.C.; Thomas W. 10 S.C.; Martha 20 S.C.

LEE,RICHARD-Old War Pension Application, dated 1884, Arkansas. Served in C, ___?(word looks like attack) Volunteers. O.W.Inv.#22688, Mex.Wid.O.#14481. (not abstracted)

LEEPER,JAMES-Revolutionary War Pension Application #S31815, dated 9 December 1833 in Washington County, Territory of Arkansas. He was born in September 1761 in Augusta County, Virginia. After the war he lived in Lincoln County, North Carolina and Franklin County, Tennessee. He migrated from Jackson County, North Carolina to Washington County, Territory Of Arkansas. He died 7 January 1842 and is buried near Fayettville.
Washington County, Ark. Wills, Vol. A & B 1833-1886, page 23; Memo of will of James Leeper; signed 27 Dec 1841, probated 21

Jan 1842; provisions made for slaves; executor, son Matthew.
1840 Federal Census, Washington County, Arkansas, page 280: James
Leeper, age 79.
1850 Federal Census, Washington County, Arkansas, Fayetteville
Township, page 440, family #56: Matthew Leaper 45 lawyer N.C.;
Lucy 32 Ky.; Jane 12 Ark.; Laura 9 Ark.; Allice 6 Ark.; Matthew
2 Ark.; Rebecca Washington 64 Va.; Whiting Washington 25 Ky.;
Lucy Smith 57 Va.

LEGG,JOHN M.-Old War Pension Application, dated 1887, Arkansas. He
served in Captain Still's Company, Georgia Infantry in 1838.
O.W.Inv.App.#24442, Ind.War.Sur.#4132. (not abstracted)

LEMMONS,WILLIAM-War of 1812 Pension Application.(This application
is listed in the 1812 index, however, it is an old war pension)
Old War Widow File #12111. B.L.W.#91676-160-55. William Lemmons
volunteered at Fayetteville, Tennessee, on 17 November 1814. He
served as saddler in Captain Ephriam D. Dickson's Company of
Tennessee Militia. He was killed at the Battle of New Orleans,
on 23 December 1814. He was married to Sarah Cox in July or
August, 1802 in Williamson County, Tennessee. She was allowed
half pay pension under the act of 16 April 1816, for the death
of her husband in service. This file contains affidavits from
Aden White and John Cassaday, of Polk County, Arkansas in 1839,
who had known William and Sarah Lemmons prior to the war of
1812. In 1860, Sarah Lemmons was a resident of Polk County,
Arkansas, at which time, Aden White and James Lemmons stated
that they knew William Lemmons was killed in battle, "because
we saw him in the war and he never came back home, and we read
a letter from his captain stating that he had been killed in
battle."

LEONARD,JOHN-Old War Pension Application, dated 1853, Arkansas. He
served in Company K, 7th U.S.Infantry. O.W.Inv.Cert.#7846, File
#24680, Mex.Wid.O.#14096. Company K, 7th U.S.Infantry was organized
and left New York Harbor, June 3rd 1848, enroute for the City
of Mexico, arrived at Vera Cruz, Mexico on June 26, 1848. They
were ordered to New Orleans, Louisana, where they arrived July
4th 1848. The muster roll showed John Leonard present at New
Orleans. He applied for pension 16 March 1853, Chickasaw Nation,
Arkansas, after a wood cutting accident, in which his toes were
cut off. He was married to Clara Bond, at the home of her uncle,
William Bond, in Warrenton County, Missouri, in the year 1856. John
Leonard, applied for a duplicate pension certificate on 28 February
1854 in Sebastian County, Arkansas. Clara Leonard stated that
she was with her husband in Fort Smith, Arkansas, the night
the fort was taken, during the War of the Rebellion. She was
hidden, with her little brother, in the cellar. Clara and John
Leonard were transferred to Washington, D.C. before 1878. He
died there on 23 May 1897.

LEVERTON,JOHN-War of 1812 pension application S.O.#13486, S.C.#11692.
B.L.W.#51811-40-50 and #2239-120-55. Service in Captain Simeon
Perry's Company of Tennessee Militia. He also served in the
Black Hawk War. In his pension application dated 1871 in Washington
County, Arkansas, he stated that he thought that he was born
in 1792, and that he was a native of North Carolina. He married
Sarah Waters in 1817 in Sevier County, Tennessee. In 1851 and
1855 he was in Catoosa and Murray Counties, Georgia. In 1868
he was in Bradley County, Tennessee.
1850 Federal Census, Murray County, Georgia, page 232: Bailey
Leverton 28 Tenn.; Alcy 27 Tenn.; William 8 Ga.; Mary 6 Ga.;
Zachary T. 3 Ga.; John Leverton 58 Tenn.; Sarah 52 Tenn.; George
20 Tenn.; Elizabeth 22 Tenn.; Amanda 18 Tenn.; 15 yr old female
born Tenn.

LEWIS,EVIN-Old War Pension Application, dated 1885, Arkansas. He

served in Captain Elliot's Company, Tennessee Volunteers. O.W.Inv.
#20723, O.W.Wid.Rej.#22782.

LEWIS,STEPHEN-War of 1812 pension application W.O.#29870,
W.C.#20679. Service in Captain John Jones Company, 39th Regiment,
U.S. Infantry from 1 December 1813 to 21 October 1814. Married
first to Minnie Odom, who died in Alabama. Married second to
Louisa Bradley 18 October 1855 in Union Parish, Louisana. Widow's
pension application dated 1878 in Union Co, Arkansas. She stated
that Stephen Lewis was born in North Carolina and was about
16 years old when he entered service.

LEWIS,WILLIAM-War of 1812 pension application W.O.#24612, W.C.#13813.
Service in Captain Reedy's Company of South Carolina Militia
from 1 October 1814 to 4 March 1815. He was born near Salem,
North Carolina, 7 July 1786. He was married to Nancy Thomas
on 15 February 1816 in Chester District, South Carolina. They
remained in Chester District until 1833, when they moved to
Montgomery County, Alabama until 1835. On 15 April 1836, they
moved to Bradley County, Arkansas. William Lewis died 26 July
1847 in Warren, Bradley County, Arkansas. In her pension application,
his widow submitted the following statements from her Bible;
"William Lewis was born the 7th of July 1786; Nancy Lewis was
born in June 1796 and was married the 15th of Feb 1816".
1850 Federal Census, Bradley County, Arkansas, Pennington Township,
page 104, family #231: Nancy Lewis 52 S.C.; Nancy 6 Ark.

LIGET,JOHN-Revolutionary War Pension Application #S31816. He
was born in Augusta County, Virginia in March 1762. He was residing
in Rockbridge County, Virginia, in 1780, when he entered service
in Captain James Gilmore's Company, Colonel Howard's Regiment
of Virginia Militia. He was in that company at the Battle of
Cowpens. He served at the Battle of Guilford Court House in
Captain James Hall's Company, Colonel McDowell's Regiment. He
was wounded in the left hand at the Siege of Yorktown. He was
granted pension on his application, which was executed on 18
September 1832 in Montgomery County, Illinois. In 1836, he applied
to have his pension transferred to Washington County, Arkansas,
where he had moved to be near his children. John Liggett is
listed in the 1840 Federal Census, Washington County, Arkansas,
page 281, his age 77.

LISTENBEE,JAMES A.-War of 1812 Pension Application S.O.#12651,
S.C.#7759, W.O.#12422, W.C.#7395. He served in Captain John
Montgomery's Company of South Carolina Militia. His original
discharge certificate is enclosed in this file. James Listenbee
married Jane Stark Alderson, 9 October 1814, in York County,
South Carolina. They were residing in Oxford, Lafayette County,
Mississippi, in 1851, when James applied for Bounty Land. They
remained in Mississippi until at least 1871, when he applied
for pension. They moved to Marion County, Arkansas, where James
Listenbee died on 26 March 1875. Jane Listenbee applied for
pension on 21 October 1878 in Marion County. In 1878, James
M. Carson, age 79, resident of Yellville, Arkansas, stated that
he had attended the wedding of James and Jane Listenbee. James
Alderson, brother of Jane, was residing in Lafayette County,
Mississippi in the year 1878.
1850 Federal Census, Lafayette County, Mississippi, page 298,
family #1013: James A. Listenbee 58 N.C.; Jane 40 S.C.; Mary
A. 22 S.C.; Creicy J. (?) 20 S.C.; William F. 17 S.C.; John
S. 15 S.C.; Isiah 13 S.C.; Robert 4 Miss.; David C. 8 Miss.;
Benedict A. 4 Miss.

LINDERMAN,ISAAC-Old War Pension Application, dated 1852, Arkansas. He
served in Captain Lawler's Company of Illinois Volunteers, during
the Mexican War. Inv.Cert. #7177, file #25221. (not abstracted)

LINDSEY,RUFUS M.-Mexican War Pension Application dated 1887, Arkansas. Service in Captain English's Company, Arkansas Volunteers. Mex.Sur.App.#22344, Cert.#18849. (not abstracted)

LITTLETON,SAVAGE-Revolutionary War Pension Application #S32378, dated 10 October 1834. He was born 3 March 1750 in Kent County, Delaware. When he was very small, he moved to Johnston (?) (could be Lincoln) County, North Carolina. He entered into service in the State of South Carolina in Captain William Arrington's Company. He served at Sullivan's Island, South Carolina and stated that he spent some time in scouting against Tories "who blew exceedingly troublesome". Savage Littleton was taken prisoner by a troop of British Dragoons, and after being held for awhile was given parole. He broke his parole and rejoined his company. He stated that he had been married in South Carolina and remained in that state for two or three years after the war. He lived in Kentucky 14 years and then returned to South Carolina for 2 years. He then returned to Kentucky for about 7 years then moved to Robinson County, Tennessee, and apparently moved to Arkansas Territory about 1833.

LOCK,FIELDS-Mexican War Pension Application dated 1887, Arkansas. Served in Company F, 3rd Missouri Mounted Volunteers. Widow, Ellen. Mex.Sur.App.#4128, Cert.#9718, Mex.Wid.App.#9883, Cert.#8201. (not abstracted)

LOCKE,MATTHEW-Mexican War Pension Application. Served as Corporal in Company F, 1st Regiment of Mississippi Infantry. Mex.Sur.App.# 9120, Cert.#3126, dated 1887, Arkansas. Mex.Wid.App.#19809, Cert.#15738, dated 1911, Texas. Remarks: XC2660448. (not abstracted)

LONG,FRANKLIN-Mexican War Pension Application dated 1889, Arkansas. Served in Company B, 5th Regiment, Tennessee Infantry. Widow, Anna E. Mex.Sur.App.#21917, Cert.#18478, Mex.Wid.App.#19719, Cert.#15739. Remarks: XC2660450. (not abstracted)

LONG,WILLIAM-Mexican War Pension Application dated 1887, Arkansas. Served in Captain Henry's Company, Tennessee Cavalry. Mex.Sur.App. #9130, Ind.War Sur.#4898. (not abstracted)

LOPP,JOHN F.-Mexican War Pension Application dated 1889, Arkansas. Served in Companies A and H, U.S. Mounted Rifles. Mex.Sur.App.#21743, Cert.#18356. Remarks: Reb.Inv.Cert.#661860, Co.B, 5th Ind. Inf. (not abstracted)

LOVE,JAMES H.-Mexican War Pension Application dated 1887, Arkansas. Served in Company B, 1st Regiment, Arkansas Cavalry. Widow, Mary L. Mex.Sur.App.#4178, Cert.#2237, Mex.Wid.App.#6029, Cert.-#4140. (not abstracted)

LOVETT,AARON-Mexican War Pension Application dated 1887, Arkansas. Served in Company K, 1st Regiment, Pennsylvania Volunteers. Mex.Sur. App.#9141, Cert.#8253. Remarks: O.W.Inv.Rej.#23071. (not abstracted)

LOW,THOMAS B.-Mexican War Pension Application. Served in Company B, 2nd Regiment, Mississippi Volunteers. Mex.Sur.App.#17242, Cert.12900, dated 1887, Missouri, Mex.Wid.App.#9575, dated 1891, Arkansas. (not abstracted)

LUCAS,JOHN-Mexican War Pension Application dated 1887, Arkansas. Served in Company G, 13th Regiment, U.S.Infantry. Widow, Sarah. Mex.Sur.App.#15551, Cert.#11039, Mex.Wid.App.#5801, Cert.#3350. (not abstracted)

LUCKETT,SAMUEL-Mexican War Pension Application dated 1890, Arkansas. Served in Company F, 1st Regiment, Mississippi Volunteers. Mex.Sur. App.#22758, Cert.#19101, Mex.Wid.App.#17869. (not abstracted)

LUMBLEY/LUMLEY,WILLIAM-Revolutionary War Pension Application #S32000, dated 1 April 1822, Warren County, Tennessee, his age 58. He enlisted in service in the year 1780 in Captain Howell Myrick's Company, Colonel Campbell's 1st Regiment of Virginia Line of the Continental Army. He served at the Battle of Guilford Court House, the Battle of Camden, Siege of Ninety-Six, Battle of Eutaw Springs and several other skirmishes until his discharge in 1782. In 1837 he stated that he had moved from Tennessee to Illinois, then to Arkansas, then to Barry County, Missouri and finally to Washington County, Arkansas. His purpose being "to better his station in life". Reference is made to a son, Washington Lumbley, who resided in McMinnville, Warren County, Tennessee in the year 1823. William Lumley died 28 October 1843, and his widow, Mary Lumley, was granted a certificate for arrears in his pension in 1844.

LYON,GILES-Mexican War Pension Application dated 1887, Arkansas. Served in Company F, 2nd Regiment, Tennessee Volunteers. Mex.-Sur.App.#11035, Cert.#10070. (not abstracted)

McALLISTER,WILLIAM CRAWFORD-War of 1812 Pension Application W.O.#6438, W.C.#7235. B.L.W.#90223-120-55. He entered service in Williamson County, Tennessee on 24 January 1814 in Captain Archibald McKinney's Company of Tennessee Militia, and served against the Creek Indians. He was discharged on 10 May 1814. His original discharge certificate enclosed in this file. He was married to Polly Webb, daughter of Meredith Webb, on 31 May 1810, Maury County, Tennessee. A copy of the marriage bond is in this file. William McAllister died in Pope County, Arkansas on 16 September 1852. Polly McAlister applied for pension on 4 August 1871, at which time she was a resident of Dover, Pope County, Arkansas. She submitted an affidavit with the following statements, "I was born the 5th day of December AD 1794, William McAlister was born the 15th day of October AD 1787, we were married about ten miles from Columbia, the County Seat of Maury County, Tennessee, at my father's (Meredith Webb) house, on the 31st day of May AD 1810. We lived in the State of Tennessee from 1810 till 1841, in the year 1841 we came to Pope County, Arkansas. Our oldest son, Crawford McAllister, was born April 29th 1811, our son, Clark was born January 17th 1813, our oldest daughter, Cassy, was born July 12th 1814; Cassy and Clark are now dead. We had 12 children born to us. I received Bounty Land Warrant #90223 for 120 acres, which was assigned to Alexander Wheeler, who located the same, upon the W1/2 SE1/2 & SE 1/4 SW1/4 sec 18 in township 9 of range 20 in the district of lands subject to sale at Clarkesville, Arkansas. A patent issued to him for said lands on the 15th day of August AD 1860." Affidavit dated 1 August 1877, Pope County, Arkansas, "I, Margaret Holledger, do solemnly swear that I was born on the 14th day of June AD 1802, that I am a sister of Polly McAllister, that the place of my birth is Maury County, Tennessee. I was married to P.C. Holledger in the year 1818, in my father's (Meredith Webb) home in Maury County. I and my husband came to Arkansas in the year 1829." Deposition, dated 29 November 1877, "I, Meredith Webb, of Logan County, Arkansas, was born on the 8th day of September 1800. I am the brother of Polly McAllister. I think my sister was married sometime in the Spring, I remember the corn was up and the leaves on the trees were nearly full grown at the time. They were married in the year 1810, which I know because my father moved from Kentucky to Maury County, Tennessee in the year 1809, Polly and William were married the next Spring. It was a clear beautiful Sunday, I do not remember the date. While William McAlister was away at war, my father sent me to stay with my sister, Polly." Crawford McAllister, son of Polly and William McAllister, resident of Van Buren County, Arkansas in 1877, stated, "I was married in the State of Tennessee in the year 1833 and came to the State of Arkansas in the year 1847."

In 1877, Polly Walker, of Pope County, Arkansas, stated, "I was born on the 12th day of January AD 1803 in the State of Tennessee. I lived about 2 and 1/2 miles from Meredith Webb, in Maury County, Tennessee. I have resided in Pope County, Arkansas for forty four years." Affidavit, dated 27 August 1877, Pope County, "I, John R.Horner Scott, was born the 16th day of October AD 1813. I have been a resident of Pope County since the year AD 1829."
1850 Federal Census, Pope County, Arkansas, page 290, family #693: George C. McAlister 26 Tenn.; Mary E. 20 Tenn. page 261, family #304: Elizabeth McAllister 65 S.C.; Andrew 17 Mo.; Marinda 13 Mo.; John McAllister 22 Mo.; page 254, family #206: Joseph McAlister 24 N.C.; Sarah 26 Ala.; James 11/12 Ark.; page 240, family #9: Crawford McAlister 39 Tenn.; Eliza 38 N.C.; Sibaline 15 Tenn.; Mary A. 12 Tenn.; Wilson 10 Tenn.; Andrew 8 Tenn.; Amanda 6 Tenn.; Martha 1 Ark.

McAVOY,MARK-Old war pension application dated 1846 Arkansas. Inv. Cert. #2910, file #25665. Service in 6th Regiment of U.S. Infantry, Mexican War. (not abstracted)

McBRIDE,FRANCIS M.-Mexican War Pension Application dated 1886, Arkansas. Served in Company C, 13th Regiment, U.S.Infantry. Mex. Sur.App.#4433, Cert.#16680, Mex.Wid.App.#20089, Cert.#15965. Remarks: Reb.Inv.Cert.#685057, Co.D, 1st Battalion, Ark.Inf. (not abstracted)

McBROOM,JOHN J.-Mexican War Pension Application dated 1887, Arkansas. Served in Company K, 1st Regiment, Arkansas Cavalry. Mex. Sur.App.#4437, Cert.#14671. (not abstracted)

McCABE,LOVE-Old war pension application dated 1852, Arkansas. Inv. Cert. #7102, file #25664. Service in 3rd Regiment of Tennessee Volunteers, Mexican War. (not abstracted)

McCABE,PATRICK-Mexican War Pension Application dated 1888, Arkansas. Served in Company G, 6th Regiment, U.S.Infantry. Mex.Sur.App.#18828. Remarks: Ind.War.Sur.#170, Cert.#3021. Application #24519, Dependent of #18828. (not abstracted)

McCALL,DANIEL-Mexican War Pension Application dated 1887, Arkansas. Served in Company K, 1st Regiment of Tennessee Volunteers. Mex.Sur. App.#9275, Cert.#3297. (not abstracted)

McCALL,JOHN-Mexican War Pension Application dated 1892, Arkansas. Served in Company K, 1st Regiment, Tennessee Volunteers. Special Act Pension. Mex.Wid.App.#10627, Cert.#13503. (not abstracted)

McCANN,DAVID-Mexican War Pension Application dated 1888, Arkansas. Served in Company C, 2nd Regiment, Illinois Volunteers. Mex.Sur.App. #18828, Cert.#14970. (not abstracted)

McCANN,FRANCIS-War of 1812 pension application W.O. #23016, W.C.#20251. B.L.W. #90988-40-50 and #69177-120-55. He was born ca 1792, enlisted into service in Lancaster County, Pennsylvania in Captain William Hamilton's Company of Pennsylvania Militia. He also served in Captain George Musser's Company. He married Sarah Cramer, 17 August 1817, at Shippenburg, Cumberland County, Penn. Children identified in this application: Lucinda H. (Webb) born ca 1823; Teresa (Collins) born 1828 in Pennsylvania; Emma McCann born ca 1841. They were living in Pulaski County, Arkansas by 1850, and soldier died there on 3 July 1861. Henry D. Parker of Pulaski County, identified as son-in-law, and Charles J. Collins identified as grandson. Sarah McCann died in Pulaski County 14 December 1886.
1850 Federal Census, Pulaski County, Arkansas, page 370, family #811: Francis McCann 56 Ireland; Sarah 50 Pa.; Agnes 19 Ohio;

Sarah 17 Ark.; Catherine 11 Ark.; Emma 8 Ark.; Francis M. 16 Ky.; S.Brissow 24 Tenn.

McCANN,HIRAM-Old war pension application. Service in Company K, 3rd Regiment of Tennessee Volunteers, Mexican War. Widow Martha. O.W. Wid. Cert. #436, File #6810. B.L.W.#64300-160-47. Soldier died 16 June 1848. (not abstracted)

McCANN,JOHN-Mexican War Pension Application dated 1887, Arkansas. Served in Company F, 8th Regiment, U.S.Infantry. Mex.Sur.App.#4466, Cert.#7897. Remarks: Late War Inv.Cert.#84188, Co.A, 9th Ill.-Vol.Inf. (not abstracted)

McCARVER,WILLIAM-Mexican War Pension Application dated 1887, Arkansas. Served in Company B, 5th Regiment, Tennessee Volunteers. Widow, Sarah R. Mex.Wid.App.#1475, Cert.#1550. (not abstracted)

McCAULEY,THOMAS-Mexican War Pension Application dated 1887, Arkansas. Served on U.S.S. "Raritan" and "Etna." Mex.Sur.App.#14771, Cert.#9546. (not abstracted)

McCAUSLIN,WEBSTER-War of 1812 pension application S.O.#24607, S.C.#15225. Service in Captain John Dalton's Company, 2nd Regiment of Tennessee Militia from 13 November 1814 to 13 May 1815. He served as a substitute for Wesley Malone, and was at the Battle of New Orleans. He received B.L.W.#26381-80-50, which he sold to James Logan, and which was stolen in Cleveland, Ohio in May 1855. Webster McCaslin (sic) applied for Bounty Land in Scott County, Arkansas on 24 February 1851, in 1855 he applied in Sebastian County. His pension application was executed in 1871, he was a resident of Booneville, Arkansas.
1850 Federal Census, Scott County, Arkansas, Washburn Township,page 155, family #411: Webster McCaslin 54 N.C.; Nancy 52 Ky.; Andrew 20 Ark.; Boon Township, page 156, family #413: John McCaslin 22 Ark.; Amanda G. 20 Ark.; William 4/12 Ark.

McCLELAN,JESSE C.-Mexican War Pension Application dated 1889, Arkansas. Served in Company I, 5th Regiment, Tennessee Volunteers. Widow, Melissa. Mex.Wid.App.#8234, Cert.#7098. Remarks: See O.W.Inv.#16218, Rej. (not abstracted)

McCLINTICK,ADAM, alias, William Taylor, alias, W.C.Johnson-Mexican War Pension Application dated 1888, Arkansas. Mex.Sur.App.#19563, Cert.#16644. Remarks: Fraudulent Claim. (not abstracted)

McCLUNG,JOHN-Revolutionary War Pension Application #W1446. B.L.W. #38522-160-55. Soldier's application dated 23 October 1827, McMinn County, Tennessee, he stated that his family consisted of himself, his wife age about 40, and five children, all girls except one boy age 9. He stated that he was born in Pennsylvania, but does not know when or where, as both of his parents died when he was a young child. He was taken to Warren County, Georgia, while still a young child, but does not say by whom. He lived in Warren County until he was about 15, at which time he went to South Carolina and enlisted into service in May 1779, in Edgefield County, in Captain Richard Johnston's Company, Colonel Samuel Hammon's Regiment of the Continental Line of South Carolina. He assisted in the siege and capture of Brown's Fort in Augusta, Georgia. He received a discharge for this tour of duty, however, he stated that it had been destroyed when his house burned. He served a three month tour of duty in 1781 in Captain John Carter's Company, and another tour in Captain Robert Day's Company. In 1781 and 1782, he served in several organizations from Warren County, Georgia. He moved to "French Broad", North Carolina in 1806, and in 1809 he moved to Pendleton District, North Carolina. About 1814, he moved to White River in the Territory of Arkansas, and remained there about two years before moving to Morgan County,

Alabama. He lived in Overton, McMinn and Smith Counties, Tennessee. He was married in St. Clair County, Alabama 11 October 1824 to Nancy Lester. In 1827, Joseph McCormick of McMinn County stated "as a child, John McClung lived in the state of Georgia, as a neighbor. All of his relatives with whom I was acquainted were Tories and opposed to the American cause in the Revolution. The declarant, having supported the cause of his Country, produced a disturbance between himself and his relatives, so he ran off from them to the State of South Carolina and enlisted. The next time I saw him was at the Siege of Augusta, in the service of his Country". John McClung died in Sumner County, Tennessee on 24 September 1844. His widow applied for pension 20 February 1856 in Franklin County, Illinois, at which time John and James B. McClung (residents of Jefferson Co., Ill.) stated that they were well acquainted with John and Nancy McClung. In January 1857, she applied to have her pension transferred to the Arkansas agency, stated that she was a resident of Yellville, Arkansas. On 15 September 1870, she was residing in Searcy, White County, Arkansas. In March of 1871, the pension agent of Little Rock wrote "Nancy McClung, claiming to be 105, traveled from her home, some fifty miles, in a wagon driven by her daughter, a woman well advanced in years, for the purpose of securing her pension. It appears that she was told that in order to obtain an increase in her pension, she would have to submit her pension certificate, which she did and it was never returned to her". Further statement "I am of the opinion that she has been swindled, it appears that over 5 parties have had something to do with it some way or other. I have no doubt but some of them have made way with her checks and have withheld them from her."

McCOOL,ELIAS-Old war pension application dated 1850, Arkansas. Inv. Cert. #4880, File #25666. Service in Captain Inglish's Company of Arkansas Volunteers, Mexican War. (not abstracted)

McCORKLE,STEPHEN-War of 1812 pension application. W.O.#33145, W.C.#28543. He enlisted into service when he was 19 years old at Yorkville, South Carolina in Captain William Kendrick's Company of South Carolina Militia. He married first, Jincy Hart, who died in York District, South Carolina, in August of 1824. He married second, Mary Spratt, 9 December 1825 in York District, South Carolina. They remained in York District until 1845, when they moved to De Soto County, Mississippi, where soldier died 25 October 1857. Widow moved to Drew County, Arkansas before 1860. Children identified in this file: W.H. McCorkle, age 55 in 1878 and a resident of York County, South Carolina, son of Stephen and Jincy McCorkle; Joseph McCorkle, age 46 in 1878 and resident of De Soto Co., Mississippi, son of Stephen and Mary McCorkle; Mary J. Gobbert, age 42 in 1879, wife of Fayette Gobbert and resident of Drew County, Arkansas, daughter of Stephen and Mary McCorkle.

McCRARY,JONATHAN-Mexican War Pension Application dated 1887, Arkansas. Served in Company C, 5th Regiment, Tennessee Volunteers. Mex.Sur.App.#4456, Cert.#9381. Remarks: O.W.Inv.Rej.#16230. (not abstracted)

McCREERY,DECIUS-Old war pension application dated 1855, Arkansas. Inv. Cert. #8399, file #25667. Service in Company F, 4th Regiment of Kentucky Volunteers, Mexican War. (not abstracted)

McDOWELL,JOHN L.-War of 1812 pension application S.O.#5001 W.O.#40573, W.C.#31013. B.L.W. #89341-120-55. Soldier's bounty land application dated 15 September 1855, he was age 61 and residing in Owen County, Kentucky. He served in Captain John Wyatt's Company of Kentucky Militia, was in the Battle at Moravian Town, in which his company took prisoners, but General Tecumseh was killed and Colonel Johnson was wounded. In his pension appli-

cation dated 24 March 1871, Fayette County, Kentucky, he stated that he was married to Nancy Vance at the home of James Vance in October 1817. She died in 1867 in Franklin County, Kentucky, and he married Mary Hannah Bertrand, 24 November 1869, in Franklin Co.(marriage record enclosed in this file). John McDowell died 23 December 1878 in Franklin County, Kentucky, and his widow moved to Pine Bluff, Jefferson County, Arkansas. She applied for pension there on 1 October 1880, her age 64. Her son, R.C. Bertrand of Pine Bluff, referred to John McDowell as Captain McDowell. Mary McDowell died in Greely, Arkansas on 6 December 1895.
1850 Federal Census, Owen County, Kentucky, District #1, page 244, family #291: John L.McDowell 56 Ky.; Nancy 54 Ky.; Alexander 17 Ky.; Harvey (?) 14 Ky.; Edward 12 Ky.; family #285: James McDowell 31 Ky.; Ephriam 30 Ky.

McDOWELL,JOSEPH-Mexican War Pension Application dated 1888, Arkansas. Served in Company B, 1st Regiment of Louisiana Volunteers. Widow, Elvira. Mex.Wid.App.#6278, Cert.#4933. (not abstracted)

McELROY,CHAPLEY W.-Indian War Pension Application dated 1893, Arkansas. Service in Captain Caper's Company, Alabama Volunteers, Florida War. Ind.Wid.App.#4351, Cert.#2635. (not abstracted)

McGIMSEY,CHARLES-Mexican War Pension Application dated 1887, Arkansas. Served in Company I, 1st Mississippi Infantry. Mex. Sur.App.#9328, Cert.#3160. (not abstracted)

McGRAW,JAMES-Old War Pension Application dated 1878, Arkansas. Served in Company D, 5th Regiment of Tennessee Infantry, Mexican War. O.W.Inv.App.#25200, Mex.Sur.#18741. (not abstracted)

McGREGOR,GEORGE-Mexican War Pension Application dated 1887, Arkansas. Served in Company G, 2nd Regiment, Mississippi Rifles. Mex.Sur.App.#9330, Cert.#3303. (not abstracted)

McGREW,JAMES-Mexican War Pension Application dated 1888, Arkansas. Served in Company E, 3rd Regiment, Tennessee Volunteers. Mex.Sur. App.#18741, Cert.#15653. (not abstracted)

McGUYRE,NEELEY-Old war pension application O.W. Inv. Cert. #6952 File #25660, O.W. Wid. #R22475. Service as Corporal in Captain Benton's Company, 1st Regiment of Tennessee Volunteers. (1818) (not abstracted).

McINTERF/McINTURF,THOMAS-War of 1812 pension application S.O. #24615, S.C.#20732, W.O.#35919, W.C.#26168. He enlisted into service in Carter County, Tennessee, in Captain Adam Winsell's Company of Tennessee Militia and was discharged at Kingston, Tennessee. He apparently was married twice, first wife not identified. He married 8 December 1849 in McMinn County, Tennessee, to Nancy Pugh (widow of Andrew Pugh, her maiden name was Nancy Hardin). Soldier died 24 July 1871, Booneville, Logan County, Arkansas. Widow applied for pension 15 April 1879 in Booneville, Arkansas. Rebecca Lewis, her daughter, also a resident of Booneville.

McKEE,ANDREW M.-Mexican War Pension Application dated 1887, Arkansas. Served in McAllister's Company, 4th Regiment, Tennessee Volunteers. Widow, Elizabeth. Mex.Sur.App.#9371, Cert.#11798, Mex.Wid.App.#6559, Cert.#4922. (not abstracted)

McKEEHAN,CHARLES C.-Mexican War Pension Application dated 1890, Arkansas. Served in Company H, 5th Regiment, Tenessee Volunteers. Widow, Sarah. Mex.Wid.App.#8801, Cert.#7079. (not abstracted)

McKENZIE,JOSEPH G.-Mexican War Pension Application dated 1887, Arkansas. Served in Company F, 3rd Regiment, U.S.Dragoons. Mex. Sur.App.#15120, Cert.#10823. (not abstracted)

McKISICK,DANIEL-Revolutionary War Pension Application #W26251. "His name appears on a list of applicants for invalid pensions returned by the District Court of North Carolina submitted to the House of Representatives by the Secretary of War on March 2, 1795 and printed in The American State Papers, class 9 page 168". He served as Captain of a Company of Dragoons in Lincoln County, North Carolina. He remained in Lincoln Co., N.C. until 1807 when he moved, with his wife and family, to Bedford County, Tennessee, where he died 19 November 1818. His widow, Jane remained in Bedford County, Tennessee, until May 1836, when she moved to Benton, County, Arkansas. On 14 August 1839, Jane McKisick, aged 80 and a resident of Benton County, applied for pension. In her application she stated that she did not remember the date of her wedding, but was sure that she and Daniel McKisick had been married in Lincoln County, North Carolina either in 1776 or 1777, as her second child was still at the breast at the time of the Battle of Ramsuer's Mill. Daniel McKisick had been an active participant in the Revolution, and as such, had incurred the wrath of the local Tories, to such an extent that they had been making frequent raids on his home, in an effort to catch him. His widow stated that the Tories had robbed her home on several occasions, and had finally taken her wearing apparel, bed clothes and numerous articles needed by herself and her two small children. Her husband felt that for her safety he needed to be home, but also felt the need to fight for his country. The amassing of British Troops and Tories at the site of Ramsuer's Mill, which was located about 8 or 10 miles from the home of Daniel and Jane McKisick, prompted the local Militia to attack. There were no regular officers so the command fell to Captain Falls, who fell in battle. Daniel McKisick was wounded in the left arm. When she was told about the battle and that her husband had been wounded, Jane McKisick rushed to the scene of the battle. The British had been routed, and General Rutherford's Brigade was arriving at the scene. Jane found her wounded husband at the Rhinehart farm near Ramsuer's Mill. While she was caring for him, she could see the soldiers burying the dead. Daniel McKisick's arm had been severally wounded, the bone having been shattered. He was out of battle for several months, however, she stated that after he was able he led an expedition against the Cherokee Indians. In an affidavit by Mary Patton, born 16 September 1763, widow of John Patton, sister of Jane McKisick, "I was living with Jane and Daniel McKisick at the time of the Battle of Ramsuer's Mill, and while Jane proceeded to the battlefield to find her wounded husband, I ran to my father's home, a distance of 4 or 5 miles. Three or four days later, Daniel McKisick and the other wounded were brought to my father's home". In an affidavit by John Robinson, of Benton County, who served in General Ruther-ford's Brigade, he stated that while he could not state that Daniel McKisick was at the Battle of Ramsuer's Mill, he (Robinson) was with General Rutherford, and that they had arrived as the battle had ended. He stated that they had taken prisoner's, among whom was the brother of Colonel Moore, who had commanded the enemy at the battle. Robinson stated that he had become acquainted with the family of Daniel McKisick in Bedford County, Tennessee. John Robinson further stated that he had been "visited with a paralytic affliction of his right side, since which time he has been unable to write". Affidavit by Captain Ezekiel Dickson, age 56 in 1836, who was a close family friend both in Tennessee and in Arkansas.
Benton County, Arkansas, Will Book A, page 71-"I, Jane McKisick, of the County of Benton, State of Arkansas, bequeath my trusty negro man Jack and my trusty negro woman Charlotte and her child to my son James; to the heirs of my deceased son David, 200

dollars; to my son Wilson McKisick 200 dollars; to my son Joseph McKisick my negro girl Violet; to my grandson Daniel McKisick my negro woman Sylvia and her son Henry; to my daughters Margaret Dickson and Mary Dickson beds and furniture. I will and direct that the pension allowed to me by the United States Government, as the widow of Daniel McKisick, decd, who was a Captain in the Army of the Revolution, be divided among my children. I hereby nominate my sons James and Joseph, executors of this will." Signed 27 June 1844, rec.16 Jan 1845.

Benton County, Arkansas, Will Book A pages 95,96,97-"I, James McKisick, of the County of Benton, State of Arkansas, bequeath to my beloved wife, Polly Vance McKisick, the plantation on which we live, including the Davidson Field, livestock and negros. I made considerable advances to my daughter Jane Bell's first husband Mr. Waller(?) and have made advances since she married Mr. Moore; to my daughters Jane Bell and Eliza Ruth equal shares in three town lots in Ozark; to my beloved son Alexander H. McKisick my books, watch and guns; to daughter Polly Vance no further legacy; to daughters Sarah Louisa and Letitia Morton the tract of land on Illinois, including the mouth of Osage Creek; to daughter Madeline Wilson, Negro Woman Jane and Negro boy Jerry; at the death of my wife, son Alexander to receive plantation". Signed 24 Dec 1847 Rec 14 Apr 1848.

Benton County, Arkansas Will Book A page 194, "I, Ezekiel Dickson, bequeath to Joseph Daniel Dickson 100 dollars in the note I hold against Samuel Mays; the remainder of the note to Isabella M.B. Blake and Mary E. Ogden; to Ezekiel I.A. Dickson I give my horse Bolivar, Ezekiel Dickson to give his daughter Nancy Eliza 25 dollars; to Isabella M.S. Dickson I bequeath a red steer; to James M. Dickson I give my hogs and sheep; to Margaret Adeline Dickson I give a spotted cow and calf; to Caledonia Dickson I give a bed, bed clothes and bedstead; to Mary Harris Dickson I give 40 acres of land, it being part of a certain 160 acre tract laying in the Round Prairie; to Robert A. Dickson I give 40 more acres of said tract; to Mary Kelley and Joseph McKisick Dickson, grandchildren, I give the west half of said 160 acre tract" Signed 3 March 1858, rec. 27 Oct 1858.

McKISICK,DANIEL R.-Mexican War Pension Application dated 1887, Arkansas. Served in Company E, 12th Regiment, U.S.Infantry. Widow, Amanda S. Mex.Sur.App.#9393, Cert.#2667, Mex.Wid.App.#17329, Cert.#13599. (not abstracted)

McKIMENS,MICHAEL B.-Mexican War Pension Application dated 1887, Arkansas. Served in Company F, 3rd Regiment, Louisiana Volunteers. Widow, Amanda. Mex.Sur.App.#9389, Cert.#3438, Mex.Wid.App.#13893, Cert.#10748. (not abstracted)

McKNIGHT,THOMAS-Mexican War Pension Application. Served in Grey's Battalion, Arkansas Mounted Volunteers. Rebellion service as Sergeant in Company A, 1st Regiment, Arkansas Volunteers. Late War Inv. Cert.#415111. (not abstracted)

McKNIGHT,WILLIAM-Revolutionary War Pension Application #S32407, dated 7 January 1833, Independence County, Territory of Arkansas. He was born in 1761 in Rowan County, North Carolina. He entered service in Spartanburg County, South Carolina in Captain Major Parson's Company of Volunteer Horse Soldiers, served against the Cherokee Indians, also served at the Battle of Musgrove's Mill and at King's Mountain. He served as a Minute Man throughout the war. He remained in Spartanburg, South Carolina, until 1807, when he moved to Caldwell County, Kentucky. In 1815, he moved to Missouri, which part is now Arkansas. William McKnight died 22 January 1844.

Lawrence County, Arkansas, Probate Record C, pages 248-252, "I, William McKnight, Senior, of the County of Lawrence, State of Arkansas; constitute and appoint my sons James and David

my sole executors; to my sons James and David all land, horses, hogs, sheep, cattle, farming utensils, household and kitchen furniture; the above named land being and lying in the County and State aforesaid, being the north west fractional quarter of section seven, township sixteen, north range three west, containing one hundred and twenty eight acres; also a part of the southwest quarter of section five, township sixteen north range three west containing twenty five acres to my eldest daughter Mary; I will and bequeath five dollars each to my son John, my daughter Minerva, my son Thomas, my daughter Martha, my son William and my son Hugh; I will and bequeath to my daughter Jane sixty dollars." signed 7 February 1842, witnessed by Benjamin Gibson and B.F.Payne. Recorded 3rd day of June 1845.
Independence County, Arkansas Marriage Records: page 93, Minerva McKnight and James Brundrett, 26 October 1841; page 23, William P. Morris and Polly McKnight, alias Polly Perry, 24 July 1825;

McLEAN,ALEXANDER-War of 1812 pension application W.O.#36187 W.C.#27087. He was born 25 December 1794 in Argyle, Washington County, New York. Served in Captain Ichabod Judson's Company. He was married first to Mary Ingram, who died 1 October 1829, leaving an infant son who died 9 October 1829. Alexander McLean had been a clerk in Washington County, New York, for three years, he then became first clerk in the Post Office in Albany, New York. Later he worked in the Custom House, in New York City, for three or four years, but failing health prompted him to move to Arkansas, where he opened a trading post among the Indians. He worked as a clerk for a merchant named Mr.Rogers, in Fort Smith, Arkansas. He became Clerk of Courts for Crawford County, Arkansas, in which capacity he served for nearly a quarter of a century. He served as Clerk of the United States Court for the Western District of Arkansas for eight or nine years prior to his death. He was married to Frances A. McCrackin, 19 December 1842 in Crawford County, Arkansas. He died in Van Buren, Arkansas, on 8 October 1859. His widow applied for pension on 25 April 1879 in Hot Springs County, Arkansas, her age 58, and she was a resident of Watermelon Island. Mary Waring, age 61 and a resident of Watermelon Island, stated that Alexander McLean had shown her his bounty land warrant, and had stated that he planned to keep it for his two sons, ages 4 and 7 in 1857.
1850 Federal Census, Crawford County, Arkansas, City of Van Buren, page 358, family #75: Alexander McLean 56 N.Y.; Frances A. 28 Ky.; Anabella 6 Ark.; Lavinia 2 Ark.; Jane McCrackin 54 Va.

McLEAN,JAMES C.-Mexican War Pension Application dated 1877, Arkansas. Served in Company E, Grey's Battalion, Arkansas Mounted Volunteers. Widow, Mary A. Mex.Sur.App.#17154, Cert.#13140, Mex.Wid.App.#18864, Cert.#14859. (not abstracted)

McLEAN,LAUCHLIN/LOCHLIN-War of 1812 pension application W.O.#11086, W.C.#6876. Service in Captain Isaac Sullivan's Company of North Carolina Militia. He enlisted in Lumberton, North Carolina in July 1812, discharged in October 1812 at Ft. Johnson. He married Sarah McLean (her maiden name) 15 March 1810 in Robeson County, North Carolina. They remained in Robeson County until his death on 15 June 1841. About 1850, Sarah and at least some of her children moved to Georgia and from there she moved to Marion County, Arkansas, "near Clear Creek". On May 1876, she applied for pension from Marion County. Her pension application contains several affidavits from Robeson County, North Carolina, by members of the McLean family, most of the relationships are not identified; Nathaniel McLean of Lumberton, Robeson County, N.C. Attorney; John G. McLean, acting J.P. to Robeson Co., who stated that he was born in Argile in 1800; Alexander McLean, of Robeson Co., apparently a former student of Lochlin; Hugh and Eliza McLean of Robeson Co. who refer to Sarah as "his half aunt". The

statement was made that Lauchlin McLean was buried in the family
graveyard, referred to at one time as Sion Alford Graveyard,
in Robeson, Co. In making application for pension, she removed
the family record page from her Bible to send to the Pension
Agency, and it is contained in this file. The record: "Sarah
McLean was borned May 3rd 1793, Sarah McLean Junior was borned
February 21, 1811, Flora McLean was borned September 5, 1813,
Lucinda McLean was borned March 28, 1816, William McLean was
borned August 21st 1818, Anna W. McLean was borned March 10th
1821, William D. McLean was borned May 15th 1824, Mary McLean
was borned 10 (?) 1826, Giles McLean was borned April 4, 1829,
Elijah McLean was borned May 24th 1832, Lochlin McLean was borned
August 9th 1840, William McLean was borned May 8, 1844, James
F. McLean was borned September the 9th 1859" (compiler's note,
the last two entrys made on the front of that page, indicating
that it may have been someone other that the children of Sarah
and Lochlin). In 1876, Sarah listed her children as Sarah, Lucinda,
Anney, Giles, Mary, James, Lauchlin and Eliza. There is reference
to one child about 10 who died in Robeson County in 1824/25. Lucinda
McLean married Peter J. Trawick (?) 25 November 1838, she had
two children, a daughter born 1840 and a son born 1845. In 1846,
Peter Trawick died, she married 15 April 1847 John Newton. They
had three daughters born 1848, 1850 and 1856. Lucinda was a
resident of Marion County, Arkansas, in 1876.

McMULLEN,DANIEL B-Mexican War Pension Application dated 1887,
Arkansas. Served in Companies I and E, 4th Regiment, Kentucky
Volunteers. Mex.Sur.App.#9429, Cert.#14130. (not abstracted)

McNAIR,JAMES C.-Mexican War Pension Application dated 1887,
Arkansas. Served in Company C, 5th Regiment, Tennessee Volunteers.
Widow, Harriett. Mex.Sur.App.#13907, Cert.#10347, Mex.Wid.App.#18516,
Cert.#14753. (not abstracted)

McNAIR,JOHN-War of 1812 Pension Application W.O.#30367, W.C.#25181.
B.L.W.#33039-80-50, canceled and contained in this file. He
was born ca 1785 in either Knox or Sullivan County, Tennessee. He
served in Captain Samuel Bunch's Company, Colonel John Williams'
Regiment of Tennessee Militia from 15 November 1812 to 25 March
1813 in the war with the Seminoles. Later he and Andrew Cowan,
were sent by Brigadier General James White, to spy on the Creek
Indians. He stated that they found the Indians embodied at four
different places, to wit; Taladega, Tukahatchee, Hilloby and
Tallashatchie, making preparations for an attack on the frontier,
of which they immediately gave notice to Governor Wiley Blount,
of Tennessee and General White. They were ordered to continue
on the frontiers of the Creek Nation, until an army could be
raised and sent against the hostile Indians. They remained,
according to orders, and met the army on their way into the
Creek Nation, above Turkey Town, near the Coosa River, about
1 November 1813. He served as a Captain of a company of volunteers
in the Creek Indian War, under command of Colonel Samuel Bunch,
from 10 January 1814 to 24 May 1814. John McNair married Mary
Ann Sheretz, 12 July 1821 in Knoxville, Knox County, Tennessee. He
died in Union County, Illinois on 28 November 1852. Mary Ann
McNair moved to Searcy County, Arkansas before 1856. She was
residing in Boone County, Arkansas in 1874.

McNAIR,JOHN W.-Mexican War Pension Application dated 1888, Arkansas.
Served in Company C, 5th Regiment, Tennessee Volunteers. Mex.
Sur.App.#18285, Cert.#14015. Remarks: Late War Wid.O.#146547,
Co.C, 57 Ill. Vols. (not abstracted)

McPHERSON,ISAAC-War of 1812 pension application S.O.#26816,
S.C.#18236, W.O.#42563, W.C.#33455. Service in Captain James
McKanney's Company of East Tennessee Mounted Gunmen from 20
January 1814 to 20 May 1814. He volunteered into service at

Kingston, Roane County, Tennessee, and served at the Battle of Horseshoe. The Interior Department records show that he received B.L.W.#29579-80-50, which was located by Isaac McPherson at Des Moines, Iowa on 31 January 1853, and that he received warrant #36602, for 80 acres, which was located at Springfield, Missouri on 3 July 1857. He was married first to Elizabeth Kennedy, in December 1821 in Leesburg, Tennessee. In 1850 they were residing in Washington County, Tennessee and in 1855 they were in Van Buren County, Iowa. Elizabeth McPherson died 28 November 1862 in Jasper County, Missouri. Isaac McPherson married in Washington County, Arkansas, on 11 June 1877, Rosania S. West. She was the widow of Levi West, who died in Washington County on 3 January 1862. John M. McPherson, born 5 February 1872, identified as the son of Isaac and Rosania McPherson. Isaac died on 25 September 1882, in Washington County, Arkansas. Rosania applied for pension on 4 December 1882, in Washington County, her age stated as 59, her sons C.J.West and C.L.West, witnessed her signature. Affidavits from John Brown and John Reynolds of Washington County in 1882.
1850 Federal Census, Washington County, Tennessee, page 103, family #3: Matthew McPherson 23 potter Tenn.; Catherine 19 Va.; William H. 1 Tenn.; Robert Collins 26 Tenn.; Julia Fellers 24 Tenn.; page 148, family #657: Isaac McPherson 54 Tenn.; Elizabeth 48 Tenn.; Eliza Wood 24 Tenn.; William McPherson 20 Tenn.; Margaret 17 Tenn.; Alex 8 Tenn.; James 6 Tenn.; Amanda Wood 2 Tenn.

McWHIRTON,DANIEL Y.-Mexican War Pension application dated 1887, Arkansas. Served in Captain Allen's Company M, 1st Regiment, Tennessee Volunteer Infantry. Widow, Joan P. Mex.Sur.App.#12658, Cert.#5171, Mex.Wid.App.#13110, Cert.#10352. (not abstracted)

MABREY,SEABORN W.-Mexican War Pension Application dated 1892, Arkansas. Served in Captain Curtis' Company, 3rd Regiment, Georgia Volunteers. Widow, Sarah. Mex.Sur.App.#24137, no Cert. Mex.Wid.App. #14565, no Cert.#. (not abstracted)

MACHEN,JOHN-War of 1812 pension application S.O.#29617, S.C.# 21406. B.L.W.#13822-80-50 and #22274-80-55. Served as Sergeant in Captain Joshua Ingram's Company, Colonel Reuben Nash's Regiment of South Carolina Militia, in the war with the Creek Indians. He volunteered at "Touey's Old Field" in Greenville District, South Carolina. On 2 November 1850, John Machen, Senior, applied for Bounty Land in Greenville District, S.C. his age 73. He applied for Bounty Land in 1855 in Pickens District, S.C. His pension application was executed on 14 February 1871, he was a resident of Columbia County, Arkansas, however he requested that correspondence be address to his son, vis, John Machen, Prescott Station, Cairo & Fulton Railroad, Nevada County, Arkansas. In his application he stated that he was married to Leah Renwick in December 1815 in Spartanburgh District, South Carolina, but she had been dead many years. John Machen Senior died in Prescott, Arkansas on 24 April 1883.

MAGNESS,JOHN R.-Mexican War Pension Application. Served in Captain Porter's Company, 1st Regiment, Arkansas Volunteers. Widow, Mary M. Mex.Sur.App.#13217, Cert.#8158, dated 1887, Arkansas; Mex.Wid.App.#12042, Cert.#9401, dated 1894, Oregon. (not abstracted)

MAHAFFEY,WILLIAM-Mexican War Pension Application dated 1887, Arkansas. Served in Company F, 3rd Regiment, Kentucky Volunteers. Mex.Sur.App.#4263, Cert.#2246. Remarks: O.W.Inv.Pending. (not abstracted)

MALONE,MOSES-Old War Pension Application dated 1884, Arkansas. Served in Captain Abraham Grigg's Company in 1838. O.W.Inv.App.#22769, Ind.Wid.#247. (not abstracted)

MANASCO,WILLIS-Old War Pension Application, dated 1891, Arkansas. Served in Alabama Volunteers 1834-36. Ind.War Sur.#3404, Ind.-Wid.O.#9722. (not abstracted)

MANEES,JAMES W.-Mexican War Pension Application dated 1888, Arkansas. Served in Lenow's Company, Tennessee Mounted Volunteers. Mex.Sur.App.#18416, Cert.#15290. (not abstracted)

MANNING,ISAM-Mexican War Pension Application dated 1887, Arkansas. Served in Captain Preston's Company K, Arkansas Mounted Volunteer Infantry. Widow, Samantha E. Mex.Sur.App.#4285, Cert.#13255, Mex.Wid.App.#18632, Cert.#14805. (not abstracted)

MAPLE,BENJAMIN-Mexican War Pension Application. Served in Company H, Ohio Volunteers. Widow, Lucy Ann. Mex.Sur.App.#4303, Cert.#8380, dated 1887 Missouri; Mex.Wid.App.#19615, Cert.#15536, dated 1910 Arkansas. Remarks: Widow died 17 July 1910-Mountain Home, Arkansas. (not abstracted)

MARTIN,CARRAL-Mexican War Pension Application dated 1887, Arkansas. Served in Captain Preston's Company, Arkansas Mounted Volunteers. Widow, Rachel. Mex.Sur.App.#4699, Cert.#52222. (not abstracted)

MARTIN,EZEKIEL-Mexican War Pension Application dated 1892, Arkansas. Served in Company B, 1st Regiment, Arkansas Mounted Volunteer Cavalry. Widow, Nancy. Mex.Sur.App.#10840, Cert.#8579. (not abstracted)

MARTIN,HENRY-Mexican War Pension Application dated 1887, Arkansas. Served in Company K, 1st Regiment, U.S.Artillery. Mex.Sur.App.#4311, Cert.#2664. (not abstracted)

MARTIN,JAMES B.-War of 1812 pension application S.O.#29864, S.C.#21511,W.O.#36252, W.C.#27144. Service in Captain Edward Gingle's Company and in Lieutenant Robert Ottis' Company of North Carolina Militia. Soldier's bounty land application, 1850, Independence County, Arkansas, he stated that he was born in Mecklinburg County, North Carolina; that he had lived in Lincoln and Iredell Counties, North Carolina, had lived in Oglethorpe County, Georgia for 10 years, then to Madison County, Georgia, until 1830, then to Perry County, Missouri until 1848 when he moved to Independence County, Arkansas. He was a blacksmith by trade. Survivor's pension application dated 1 September 1874, Independence County, Arkansas, "ten miles north of Sulphur Rock". He stated that he enlisted in Salisbury, Rowan County, North Carolina on 12 March 1814, "we were marched to Alabama, assisted in the building of Fort Jackson, then marched back to Salisbury, N.C. and mustered out of service". He was age 79, in 1874, and had lived in Arkansas about 25 years. He was married to Sarah Lance 6 June 1879 in Independence County, Arkansas. He died there on 16 March 1879, at his home in Blackriver Township in Independence County. Both Sarah and James had been previously married. Neither spouse identified. Widow, Sarah, applied for pension 27 August 1879.

MARTIN,JOHN-Old War Pension Application, dated 1890, Arkansas. Served in Captain Justin's Company of Alabama Volunteers in 1836. Widow Gatey. O.W.Inv.App.#R25035, Ind.Wid.#1696. (not abstracted)

MARTIN,JOSEPH-Mexican War Pension Application dated 1889, Arkansas. Served in Company H, 1st Regiment, Mississippi Volunteers. Widow, Martha E. Mex.Sur.App.#21626, Cert.#18216, Mex.Wid.App.#13108, Cert.#10042. (not abstracted)

MARTIN,OWEN-War of 1812 pension application W.O.#37813, W.C.#27908. Service in Captain Glover's Company of Kentucky Mounted Volunteers. He was born 11 March 1792 in Halifax County, Virginia. He entered service in Vincinnes, Indiana and served in the Wabash Expedition. He

was married first to Sallie Smith, who died in Illinois in 1836. He married second, Mary Ann Smith, 9 November 1840, in Searcy County, Arkansas. He applied for bounty land from Hot Springs County, Arkansas in 1850. He died in Conway County, Arkansas, on 1 July 1878. Widow, Mary A. applied for pension in Conway County on 30 March 1882, age 60.
1850 Federal Census, Hot Springs County, Arkansas, Hot Springs Township, page 304, family #487: Owen Martin 58 Va.; Mary 26 Ky.; Hannah J. Ark.; Sarah A. 6 Ark.; Nancy L. 4 La.; family #486: John Martin 32 Ill.; Fanny 27 Miss.; Michael 10 In.; Joseph N. 8 Ark.; John F. 7 Ark.; Jesse 6 Ark.; Sarah E. La.; Rebecca 3 Ark.; Polly A. 3/12 Ark.

MASON,SAMUEL–Mexican War Pension Application dated 1888, Arkansas. Served as 1st Corporal in Company A, 1st Regiment, Arkansas Cavalry. Widow, Sarah E. Mex.Wid.App.#7421, Cert.#5963. (not abstracted)

MASSEY,SAMUEL–War of 1812 pension application W.O.#5924, W.C.#16570. Service in Captain John Green's Company of North Carolina Militia. Samuel Massey married Christianna (Roberts) Stevenson 24 March 1813 in Tuscaloosa, Alabama. She was the widow of John H. Stevenson, who had died 1 January 1813, in Rutherford County, Tennessee. Samuel Massey died near Dover, Pope County, Arkansas on 19 January 1863. In her pension application, in Pope County, she submitted the names and birthdates of her children: Her first child was born dead, 29 October 1813; second child Mary P., died 4 October 1815, age 12 mos. 22 days; Lucinda Massey, born 2 February 1816; John C. Massey, born 3 January 1817; Adaline R. Massey, born 23 September 1819; Maneroy C. (?) born 12 April 1821; Twins born dead 4 May 1822; Delilia R. Massey, born 28 November 1823; Hardin P. Massey, born 23 October 1825; Grief J. Massey, born 16 November 1828; Salenia H. Massey, born 15 April 1829; William C. Massey, born 22 November 1832; Julia Ann L. Massey, born 22 April 1834; Malissa F. Massey, born 18 December 1836; Twins born dead 4 March 1838; Martha P. Massey, born 2 January 1845". Christianna stated that her health had been bad after the birth of the last twins, so she had no more children until she was age 52. Several friends confirmed that statement. Lucinda Massey married Enoch Vance, of Saline County, on 4 February 1844. Lucinda died in Ft. Smith on 25 November 1863. On 22 September 1877, Pulaski County, W.M. and Virginia Allison, stated that Virginia was the daughter of Enoch and Lucinda Vance, and that Enoch Vance had served in the 8th Regiment of Missouri Cavalry; also, that he had served as Captain in the 4th Regiment of Arkansas Cavalry. Martha P. Massey married Columbus Rowell, and was living in Chile, South America in 1877.
Pope County, Arkansas Will Book B, page 148, "I, Christianna Massey, of Bayliss Township, in the County of Pope, at the age of 96, bequeath one dollar each to my beloved daughter Virginia Miriam (?), wife of Joel Gurley, my daughter Lucinda, wife of E.H. Vance, my son John C. Massey, my daughter Minerva, wife of Henry Capps, my daughter Delilah, wife of Thomas Potts, my son H.P. Massey, my daughter Salena, wife of Winfield Castner(?), my daughter Julia Ann, wife of Jonathan Davis, my daughter Melissa Frances, wife of James Kilgore, my daughter Martha P.T., wife of Columbus Rowell. The remainder of my estate to my beloved son William Massey, and he to act as executor of this will." Signed 5 Nov 1884, recorded 18 Oct 1886.
Pope County Marriage Records; John C. Massey and Jane McCurry 23 Aug 1859; Book C page 185.

MATCHETT,JOSEPH–Mexican War Pension Application dated 1887, Arkansas. Served in King's Company, 6th Regiment, U.S.Infantry. Mex.Sur.App.#17641, Cert.#13116. Remarks: Late War Wid.O.#753295, Co.D, 156th Ohio Vols. (not abstracted)

MATHENY,WILLIAM G.-Mexican War Pension Application dated 1888, Arkansas. Served in Company K, 14th Regiment, U.S.Infantry. Mex. Sur.App.#4374, Cert.#9825. (not abstracted)

MATHES,JAMES E.-Mexican War Pension Application dated 1888, Arkansas. Served as Corporal in Captain Carter's Company, 1st Regiment, Arkansas Mounted Infantry. Widow, Mary Ann. Mex.Wid. App.#7491, Cert.#6419. (not abstracted)

MATTHEWS,JOHN-Mexican War Pension Application dated 1887, Arkansas. Served in 1st Regiment, Arkansas Cavalry. Mex.Sur.App.#16381, Cert.#11379. (not abstracted)

MATTHEWS,JOSEPH B.-Mexican War Pension Application dated 1887, Arkansas. Served in Company I, 1st Regiment, Georgia Volunteers. Widow, Mary. Mex.Sur.App.#9248, Cert.#3463, Mex.Wid.App.#11012, Cert.#9264. (not abstracted)

MAUPIN,JOHN D.-War of 1812 pension application S.O.#11828, S.C.#8451. Service in Captain Mathew McCowan's Company, 4th Regiment of Virginia Militia from 30 April 1814 to 29 August 1814. He was drafted in Kanawha County, Virginia, and was stationed at Norfolk, his original discharge contained in this file. He married in Virginia, Mary T. Cobbs on 13 March 1817. His Bounty Land Application in 1851 was executed in Marion County, Missouri, in 1855 he was in Shelby County, Missouri, at which time his signature was witnessed by Thomas G. Maupin. He applied for pension on 17 April 1871, he was living with his son, Fleming Maupin in Bentonville, Benton County, Arkansas.

MAXFIELD,ALFRED-Mexican War Pension Application dated 1889, Arkansas. Served in Company A, 4th Regiment, Tennessee Infantry. Widow, Nancy. Mex.Wid.App.#7883, Cert.#9544. (not abstracted)

MAY,LEROY-War of 1812 pension application W.O.#33665, W.C.#21562. Service as Assistant Topographer and as Staff Aide in General Andrew Jackson's Tennessee Militia. He volunteered at Fayetteville, Tennessee, in October 1813, and was discharged at Fort Strother in March 1814. He received a discharge "in General Jackson's own handwriting, which he would not be willing to give up for the 160 acres of land." The marriage record of Leroy May and Mary Richey, dated 23 February 1853, Lamar County, Texas enclosed in this file. His Bounty Land Application was filed on 18 October 1855, at which time he was a resident of Saline Township, Sevier County, Arkansas. On January 30, 1855, Leroy May stated that he would be 71 years old "if I live to see the 28th instant". He stated that Colonel James Patterson of Giles County, Tennessee and William Russell, son of Captain Russell, who lived in Van Buren County, Arkansas, served in the military with him. Leroy May died 9 October 1869 in Mineral Springs, Howard County, Arkansas. Mary May applied for pension 30 November 1878, in Howard County, where she remained until her death, on 2 April 1904.

MAYS,WILLIAM M.-Mexican War Pension Application dated 1887, Arkansas. Served in Company A, 2nd Regiment, Missouri Mounted Volunteers. Widow, Martha Ann. Mex.Sur.App.#13897, Cert.#11290, Mex.Wid.App.#18556, Cert.#15537. Remarks: O.W.Inv.Pending. (not abstracted)

MEADORS,WILLIAM J.-Mexican War Pension Application. Served in Company H, Missouri Mounted Volunteers. Widow, Nancy. Mex.Sur. App.#4544, Cert.#1933, Mex.Wid.App.#12500, Cert.#10628. (not abstracted)

MELLON,THOMAS-Mexican War Pension Application dated 1887, Arkansas. Served in Captain Magruder's Company, Arkansas Volunteers. Widow, Lucy. Mex.Wid.App.#1356, Cert.#2703. (not abstracted)

MENDENHALL,WILLIAM-Mexican War Pension Application dated 1887, Arkansas. Service in Company H, 2nd Regiment of Pennsylvania Volunteers. Widow, Mary J. O.W.Inv.File #24736, Mex.Sur.Cert.#13393, Mex.Wid.App.#14118, Cert.#11286. (not abstracted)

MILAM,JORDAN-Revolutionary War Pension Application #W25709. B.L.W. #82517-160-55. He was born 26 February 1750, place not stated. He first entered service on 1 April 1781, while residing in Henry County, Virginia. He served in Captain David Lanier's Company and in Captain Josiah Shaw's Company, Colonel Abraham Penn's Regiment of Virginia Militia, in which service he was at the Battle of Camden, South Carolina. He enlisted for a second tour and was mustered into service at "Old Pittsylvania Court House" and was marched to "Pittsylvania New Court House". He stated that on their march to the "Old Fields" two of the regimental officers fought a duel and at another time one of their officer's was accidently shot. They continued the march to Jamestown, where they met with the main army under command of General Washington, whereupon, they marched back to Henry County and were discharged. He married Mary Peacock, 2 August 1792 in Abbeville District, South Carolina. (she was born 23 Dec 1773) He applied for and was granted pension 12 September 1832 in Hickman County, Tennessee. In 1851, he moved to Carroll County, Arkansas, where he died 31 December 1851, at the home of Samuel Milam. Widow, Mary, applied for pension in Carroll County on 12 April 1855. Henry and Edward Milam of Marion County, Arkansas, sons of Jordan and Mary Milam.
1850 Federal Census, Hickman County, Tennessee, page 78, family #1116: Jordan Milam 105 Va.; Mary 70 S.C.; page 79, family #1128: Henry Milam 37 Tenn.; Susannah 36 Tenn.; Ann 14 Tenn.; Cordelia 12 Tenn.; Calvin 10 Tenn.; Bartley 6 Ark.; Amanda 4 Tenn.; Mary 4 Tenn.
1850 Carroll County, Arkansas, page 173, family #679: Edward Milam 35 Tenn.; Rebecca 36 Tenn.; Samuel H. 14 Ark.; Mary J. 12 Ark.; Nancy 10 Ark.; Frances 7 Ark.; Susannah 3 Ark.; Josiah 1 Ark.; Elizabeth 4/12 Ark.; family #680: Burris Milam 28 Tenn.; Roda J. 24 Tenn.; Elizabeth 5 Ark.; James B. 4/12 Ark.; William R. Shelton 15 Mo.; family #681: Samuel Milam 38 S.C.; Druciller 27 Tenn.; Elizabeth A. 7 Tenn.; Sarah J. 2 Ark.; Elgathon Ragsdale 67 N.C.; Elizabeth 64 S.C.

MILHOLEN,WILLIAM-Mexican War Pension Application dated 1887, Arkansas. Widow, Micha. Service in Company K, 5th Regiment, Tennessee Volunteers. Mex.Sur.App.#13678, Cert.#7494, Mex.Wid.-App.#17255, Cert.#14328. (not abstracted)

MILLER,DANIEL J.-Mexican War Pension Application dated 1887, Arkansas. Service in Company E, 15th Regiment, U.S.Infantry. Mex. Sur.App.#4607, Cert.#12542. Remarks: Army Wid.#616902; Co.E, 70th Regt.Ind.Inf. (not abstracted)

MILLER,ISAAC-Mexican War Pension Application dated 1887, Arkansas. Service in Company B, 1st Regiment of Illinois Volunteers. Mex. Sur.App.#9515, Cert.#3298. Remarks: O.W.Inv. pending. (not abstracted-

MILLER,JOHN-War of 1812 Pension application S.O.#22989, S.C.#19210, W.O.#37081, W.C.#27311. Service in Captain William Hargraves' Company of Mounted Volunteer Rangers of the Territory of Indiana. He volunteered in Princeton, Gibson County, Indiana in April 1813 and was discharged in October 1813 in Vincennes, Indiana. John Miller married Mary (Polly) Roberts on 17 November 1814, in Gibson County, Indiana. John Conner, of Washington County, Arkansas, stated that he had served in the War of 1812 with John Miller. John Miller also served in the Black Hawk War, in 1831, under command of Captain Franklin Ball, in the Illinois Militia. He was stationed at "Yellow Banks" on the Mississippi River. He applied for Bounty Land on 24 November 1853, at which time he was age 61, and a resident of Bastrop County, Texas. By 1871, they had moved to Fayetteville, Washington County, Arkansas, where he died 18 June 1879. Mary Miller applied for pension on 24 June 1879, in Washington County, where she died, 9 February 1880. George Ellington, of Springdale, applied for burial expenses.

MILLER,JOSEPH A.-Mexican War Pension Application dated 1887, Arkansas. Widow, Louisa. Service in Company D, 2nd Regiment of Illinois Infantry. Mex.Sur.App.#4617, Cert.#9301, Mex.Wid. App.#12238, Cert.#9385. (not abstracted)

MILLER,WILLIAM J.-Mexican War Pension Application dated 1887, Arkansas. Widow, Rebecca. Service in Company H, 3rd Regiment, Missouri Mounted Volunteers. Mex.Sur.App.#22217, Cert.#19461, Mex.Wid.App.#15172. no cert.#. (not abstracted)

MILLINER,DAVID L.-Mexican War Pension Application dated 1887, Arkansas. Service in Company I, 1st Regiment, Arkansas Cavalry. Mex.Sur.App.#4650, Cert.#10007. (not abstracted)

MILLS,JAMES-Mexican War Pension Application dated 1889, Arkansas. Service in Company C, Gray's Battalion, Arkansas Volunteers. Mex. Sur.App.#21919, Cert.#18996. (not abstracted)

MILSTEAD,JAMES M.-Mexican War Pension Application dated 1887, Arkansas. Widow, Sarah E. Mex.Sur.App.#16133, Cert.#9174, Mex. Wid.App.#17294, Cert.#13475. (not abstracted)

MILUM,DUDLEY-Mexican War Pension Application dated 1887, Arkansas. Service in Whitfield's Company, 1st Regiment, Tennessee Infantry. Mex.Sur.App.#4649, Cert.#16377. (not abstracted)

MITCHELL,JAMES-War of 1812 pension application W.O.#23063, W.C. #26962. Service in Captain John Haydon's Company of Kentucky Militia from 28 August 1813 to 7 November 1813. His original discharge certificate, dated 3 November 1813 and signed by Captain John Haydon, enclosed in this file. He was born circa 1793, in Kentucky, and volunteered into service in Harrison County, Kentucky. He married Mary Ann Webber, 1 December 1825, in Columbia, Maury County, Tennessee. After the war, they lived 4 years in Kentucky, 7 years in Maury County, Tennessee, five years in Monroe County, Indiana and finally moved to Washington County, Arkansas about 1847, where James Mitchell died 11 August 1860. Mary Ann Mitchell applied for pension 13 May 1878, at which time she was age 72, and a resident of Cane Hill, Washington County, Arkansas.
1850 Federal Census, Washington County, Arkansas, Cane Hill Township, page 417, family #94: James Mitchell 57 Ky.; Mary 44 Geo.; Nancy 21 Tenn.; James 18 Ark.; William 16 Ark.; Marget 14 Ark.; Alfred 12 Ark.; Roderick 10 Ark.; David 7 Ark.; Mary 4 Ark.; John 1 Ark.; family #95: George Mitchell 23 Ark.; Sarah 18 Ark.; Laura Evans 8 Ark.

MITCHELL,WILLIAM-War of 1812 Pension Application S.O.#13697, S.C.#17003, W.O.#33276, W.C.#29962. He served in Captain Daniel Price's Company, Colonel John Chiles' Regiment of Tennessee Volunteer Cavalry. He volunteered on 6 October 1814 in Knoxville, Tennessee and was discharged on 10 April 1815. He volunteered on 1 September 1836, at Pocahontas, Randolph County, Arkansas, into a company of Arkansas Mounted Gunmen under command of Captain Byrd Simpson in the Seminole Indian War. His first wife, Margaret, died on 4 April 1851. He married Amanda Leathers (nee Robinson) in Randolph County, Arkansas on 9 July 1852. She had been married to William Leathers, on 27 June 1844 in Tennessee.
1850 Federal Census, Randolph County, Arkansas, page 18, family #254: William Mitchell 52 Tenn; Margaret 50 Tenn; Winniford 15 Ark.; Nancy 11 Ark.

MIZE,HARVIE J.-Mexican War Pension Application dated 1887, Arkansas. Widow, Sarah. Service in Company B, 14th Regiment, U.S.Infantry. Mex.Sur.App.4695, Cert.#14065, Mex.Wid.App.#18920, Cert.#14943. Remarks: Rebellion Inv.O.#906529, O.W.Inv.File #180, Co.F, 3rd Tennessee Cavalry. (not abstracted)

MOAD,ALFRED-Mexican War Pension Application dated 1887, Arkansas. Service in Company B, Gilpin's Battalion, Missouri Mounted Volunteers. Mex.Sur.App.#11842, Cert.#12393. (not abstracted)

MOBLEY/MOBBERLEY,CLEMENT-Revolutionary War Pension Application #S31866, dated 7 February 1834 Crawford County, Territory of Arkansas. He was born in Bedford County, Virginia 4 October 1746. When he was first drafted into service he was residing in Camden District, South Carolina, and he paid Captain Robert Hancock 50 pounds to hire a substitute for him. He next was drafted and served under Captain Hancock in a Regiment of South Carolina Militia under command of Colonel John Winn. He finally volunteered into a company of regular soldiers and was stationed at Ninety-Six. After the war he moved to Madison County, Kentucky, and from there to Warren County, Kentucky. He moved to Crawford County, Territory of Arkansas in April 1831. When asked if he has witnesses to his military service his answer was "my brother Isaiah and his wife, Francey Mobley, of this county".

MOBLEY,DAVID-War of 1812 pension application W.O.#18915, W.C.#12726. Service in Captain Thomas Well's Company from 20 September 1814 to 20 April 1815. In April 1858, David Mobley was 63 years old and a resident of Antoine, Pike County, Arkansas. He was married to Barbary Coyer 8 July 1817 in Clark County, Arkansas. He died in Pike County on 5 March 1859. Widow, Barbary, applied for pension 27 April 1878.
1850 Federal Census, Pike County, Arkansas, Missouri Township, page 196: David Mobley 55 N.C.; Barbery 46 S.C.; Mary Ann 18 Ark.; Julia 12 Ark.; Leanna 10 Ark.; Ann M. 4 Ark.; William Mobley 30 Ark.; Margaret 24 Kentucky; Jonathan 6 Ark.; Martin 2 Ark.; Elijah 11/12 Ark.; Sarah McClenon 17 Ark David Mobley Jr. 24 Ark.; Martha 20 Tenn.; W.G. 2 Ark.; David A. 5/12 Ark.

MOBLEY,ISAIAH-Revolutionary War Pension Application #S31864, dated 7 February 1834, Crawford County, Territory of Arkansas. He was born in South Carolina 14 December either 1754 or 1755. He was residing in Fairfield District when he was first drafted into service in a Company of South Carolina Militia under command of Lieutenant Ephriam Lisle in Colonel John Winn's Regiment. He stated that he had not served in any specific engagement, but was involved in several skirmishes with Tories. After the war he moved to Warren County, Kentucky for awhile and then to Crawford County, Territory of Arkansas ca 1830. When asked if he had witnesses to his military service he named "my brother Clement Mobley and his wife, Sibella, of this county."

MOFFIT,JAMES -Old war pension application dated 1849, Arkansas. O.W.Wid. Cert.#870, file #4496. He was married to Euphy Hamilton, 26 September 1826 in Carroll County, Tennessee. They had children: Elijah, born ca 1831, Martha Susan, born ca 1834, Fanny Jane, born ca 1838, Thomas J, born ca 1840, Mahala Ann, born ca 1843, and James Russell, born ca 1846. He served as Captain in Colonel John Seldon Roane's Regiment of Arkansas Mounted Volunteers, Mexican War. He died of illness in San Antonio, Texas on 8 November 1846. Euphy Moffit applied for pension on 22 March 1849, her age 38, in Pope County. Robert Moffit and Thomas Moffit, both residents of Pope County, stated that they had been present at the wedding of James and Euphy. She appointed Robert Hamilton, as her attorney, to secure her pension.
Pope County, Arkansas, Will Book B, page 58: "I, William Hamilton, will that my beloved wife, have the enjoyment of my entire estate,

during her life time. At her death, the west half of the south
west quarter of section fifteen township eight west, in my sons
Hugh L. Hamilton, Thomas H. Hamilton and Oliver H.P.Hamilton
(?). To my daughter, Eupha or her bodily heirs and to the heirs
of my son Alfred Hamilton, one dollar. To my daughter Susan,
feather bed, bedstead and comfortable bed clothing. To my daughter
Susan, feather bed, bedstead and comfortable bed clothing (compiler's note, these two entrys appear to be identical, so I included
them as such). To my grandson, James A. Hamilton one colt. I
make no provision for my son Robert L. Hamilton nor my grandson
William J.Brigum (Brigance?) having heretofore made provision
for them. My son Thomas L. Hamilton to be my executor. Signed,
19 October 1863, rec. 6 August 1867.
Pope County, Arkansas, Will Book B, page 306: "I, Thomas H.Hamilton,
of the City of Russell, County of Pope, State of Arkansas, to
my beloved wife, Martha Ann Hamilton, my entire estate to be
used during her lifetime. At her death, to my daughter Amanda
Elvira Hamilton, lots #4,5,6,7,8,and 9 in block #38 in Russell
Addition to the City of Russellville. I will and bequeath to
James Monroe Hamilton, Effie Gilmore Douthet, Sarah Jane Spillers,
Anderson Simpson Hamilton, Mary Frances Perry, Melissa Dorcus
Williamson, Margaret Ann Maddux, William Thomas Hamilton, Illinois
Catherine Hughey, John Edward Hamilton (all of these being my
children) and William Grant Roberts (being the son of my beloved
wife by a former husband) all of the residue of my estate, share
and share alike. Signed 3 May 1898, rec. 27 May 1903.
1850 Federal Census, Pope County, Arkansas, page 268, family
#395: Euthy Moffitt 39 Tenn.; Francis M. 20 Tenn.; Fanny S. 12
Ark.; Thomas 9 Ark.; Mahala A. 7 Ark.; James R. 4 Ark.; page
246, family #95: Elijah Moffitt 18 Tenn.; Eliza 17 N.C.; page
258, family #263: William Hamilton 62 Tenn.; Fanny 62 Conn.;
William Brigance 11 Ark.; page 288, family #669: Robert Hamilton
39 Tenn.; Malinda 23 Tenn.; Hugh 10 Ark.; Fanny 8 Ark.; Elizabeth
5 Ark.; Eliza M. 1/12 Ark.; page 289, family #670: Thomas H. Hamilton
28 Tenn.; Fanny 26 Tenn.; James 10 Ark.; Euphy 8 Ark.; Sarah
6 Ark.; Simpson 4 Ark.; Mary 2 Ark.; Elizabeth Brigance 18 Tenn.;
page 242, family #28: Hugh L.Hamilton 35 Tenn.; Mary Jane 22
Mo.; Alvin M. 11 Ark.; Susan 6 Ark.; Zachary T. 3 Ark.; page
268, family #396: Alford G. Hamilton 48 Tenn.; Melissa 30 Tenn.;
Henry C. 8 Ark.; Catherine 2 Ark.; Susan Brigance 12 Ark.; John
Brigance 24 Tenn.; page 252, family #161: John Lewallen 24 Tenn.;
Mary A. 22 Ark.; James A. 3 Ark.; Daniel 1 Ark.

MONK,MENAN-Mexican War Pension Application dated 1892, Arkansas.
Widow, Sarah M. Service in Company A, Mississippi Rifles. Mex.-
Wid.App.#10745, Cert.#14245. (not abstracted)

MONTGOMERY,ALEXANDER-War of 1812 pension application S.O.#19295,
S.C.#12160. Service in Captain Bailey Butler's Company of Tennessee
Militia. He married Sally White, 25 April 1826 in Jackson County,
Tennessee. He applied for and was granted pension in Jackson
County, Tennessee, his age 78. His pension was transferred to
the Little Rock Agency in January 1876. He applied for increase
8 March 1882 in Conway County, Arkansas.
1850 Federal Census, Jackson County, Tennessee, District #10,
page 269, family #463: Alexander Montgomery 59 N.C.; Caroline
22 Tenn.; Penelope 20 Tenn.; Lamanda 18 Tenn.; Robert 17 Tenn.;
Esr(?) 15 Tenn.; Thomas 13 Tenn.; Benjamin 11 Tenn.; Nancy 8
Tenn.; family #460: Hamilton Montgomery 23 Tenn.; Mary 19 Tenn.;
Mary 10/12 Tenn.; page 291, family 780: Alexander Montgomery
29 Tenn.; Sally 25 Tenn.; Martha 5 Tenn.; Elizabeth 3 Tenn.;
Mary 1 Tenn.

MONTGOMERY,RICHARD J.-Mexican War Pension Application dated
1887, Arkansas. Served as recruiter, General Service, U.S.Army.
Mex.Sur.App.#13330, Cert.#6383, Mex.Wid.App.#16682, Cert.#14413.
Special Act Pension. (not abstracted)

MOODY,SAMUEL A.-Mexican War Pension Application dated 1887, Arkansas. Served in Company K, 3rd Regiment, Illinois Volunteers. Mex.Wid.App.#1397, no certificate.

MOONEY,GEORGE S.-Mexican War Pension Application dated 1890, Arkansas. Served in Company B, 1st Regiment, Virginia Volunteers. Widow, Martha B. Mex.Sur.App.#23182, Cert.#19440, Mex.Wid.App.#16990, Cert.#13241. (not abstracted)

MOONEY,ISRAEL-Mexican War Pension Application dated 1887, Arkansas. Served as Corporal in Company F, 6th Regiment, U.S.Infantry. Widow, Jane. Mex.Sur.App.#4757, Cert.#7320, Mex.Wid.App.#17226, Cert.-#14429. (not abstracted)

MOORE,ALLEN-War of 1812 pension application W.O.#40587, W.C.#31844. He was born in February of 1776 in Brunswick County, Virginia. He served in Captain William Palmer's Company, 5th Regiment of Virginia Infantry. He moved to Shelby County, Tennessee in 1849 and in January 1851, to Lawrence County, Arkansas. Soldier's first wife, Lydia Naney (?) had at least one child, William E. Allen bn ca 1823. He married second, Mary Wasson 26 April 1860 in Lawrence County. Allen Moore died 12 September 1866 near Powhatan, Lawrence County, Arkansas.

MOORE,JAMES-Old war pension application dated 1856, Arkansas. He served as civilian employee in the U.S. Ordinance Department as Carriage Maker of Quartermaster Dept. U.S. Volunteers. Inv. Cert. #8526 File #24759. (not abstracted)

MOORE,JAMES G.-War of 1812 pension application W.O.#33279, W.C.-#25184. Service in Captains Sharp and Taylor's Companies 46th Regiment of U.S. Infantry and Artillery. He was born in Georgia, and was 16 years old when he enlisted in service. He married 7 October 1828 in Franklin County, Tennessee, Rebecca Webb. Two of their children were ; Reuben Moore bn ca 1830 and Jane Moore bn ca 1834. James Moore died 10 January 1859 in Lawrence County, Arkansas. Widow's pension application dated 21 October 1884, Pocahontas, Randolph County, Arkansas, Rebecca Moore age 74.

MOORE,JAMES T.-Mexican War Pension Application dated 1888, Arkansas. Served in 3rd Regiment, U.S.Infantry. Widow, Sarah. Mex.Wid.App. #5888, Cert.#7013. (not abstracted)

MOORE,JOHN-War of 1812 pension application W.O.#15932, W.C.#11738. Service in Captain John Doak's Company of Cavalry, Tennessee Militia. He enlisted in Lincoln County, Tennessee, and served at the Battle of New Orleans. John Moore married Lucinda Crawford 23 December 1818 near Fayetteville, Bedford County, Tennessee. He died 11 September 1844 in Prairie Grove, Washington County, Arkansas. Affidavit in July 1851 by James Crawford of Washington County, Arkansas, father of Lucinda, he stated that "Lucinda was married to John Moore in my home in Tennessee, and she now has many children and grandchildren". The wedding was witnessed by William D. and Elizabeth Crawford, also of Washington County. Lucinda died in Washington County, Arkansas on 4 October 1882. 1850 Federal Census, Washington County, Arkansas, Mountain Township, page 366, family #32: Lucinda Moore 51 Va.; Marget 24 Tenn.; Mary 19 Ark.; James 17 Ark.; William 9 Ark.; Rhodes A. West 8/12 Ark.; John J. Henderson 15 Ark.; David Henderson 12 Ark.

MOORE,THOMPSON-War of 1812 pension application W.O.#32421, W.C.#25400. Service in Captain George Winston's Company of Tennessee Militia from 19 November 1814 to 2 May 1815. Affidavit from James Jones of Blount County, Alabama, who served in the war with Thompson Moore. He was drafted at Rhea County, Tennessee. Thompson Moore married Mary (Polly) Jones, 22 August 1826, in Blount County, Alabama. (marriage license enclosed in file)

Bounty Land application dated 23 January 1851, Franklin County, Alabama, Thompson Moore age 56. They moved to Yell County, Arkansas in 1861, and he died there on 27 December 1862. The only child mentioned in this file; Laura born circa 1852. Mary Moore applied for pension on 10 July 1878 in Yell County and died about 1890.

MOORE,WILLIAM C.-Mexican War Pension Application dated 1887, Arkansas. Service in Captain Holly's Company, 2nd Regiment, Missouri Mounted Volunteers. Widow, Letitia. Mex.Sur.App.#14666, Cert.#11802, Mex.Wid.App.#16444, Cert.#13145. (not abstracted)

MOORE,WILLIAM EDWIN-Mexican War Pension Application dated 1887, Arkansas. Served in Company K, 1st Regiment, Arkansas Mounted Volunteers. Widow, Naomi H. Mex.Wid.App.#1412, Cert.#265. (not abstracted)

MORGAN,BENJAMIN F.-Mexican War Pension Application dated 1887, Arkansas. Served as Lieutenant in Captain Moseley's Company K, 5th Regiment, Louisiana Volunteers. Widow, Martha L. Mex. Sur.App.#4761, Cert.#7318, Mex.Wid.App.#8335. (not abstracted)

MORGAN,DANIEL T.-Mexican War Pension Application. Served in Company C, 2nd Regiment, Mississippi Volunteers. Widow, Virginia. Mex.Sur.App.#13056, Cert.#8821, dated 1887 Tenn. Mex.Wid.App. #17378, Cert.#14476, dated 1903 Arkansas. (not abstracted)

MORGAN,JAMES-Old War Pension Application, dated 1881, Arkansas. Served in Captain Shepard's Missouri Infantry, Mexican War. O.W. Inv.App.#21722, Mex.Sur.#22582, Mex.Wid.O.#16807. (not abstracted)

MORGAN,JAMES, alias, John C. Calhoun-Mexican War Pension Application dated 1890, Arkansas. Served in Captain Morgan's Company A, Easton's Battalion, Missouri Volunteer Infantry. Widow, Mary J. Calhoun. O.W.Inv.Rej.#21722, Mex.Sur.App.#22582, Cert.#20187, Mex.Wid.App.#16807. (not abstracted)

MORGAN,JOHN-Mexican War Pension Application dated 1888, Arkansas. Served in Captain Inglish's Company I, 1st Regiment, Arkansas Mounted Volunteers. Widow, Nancy J. Mex.Sur.App.#20819, Cert.#18973, Mex.Wid.App.#15816, Cert.#12804. Remarks: O.W.Inv.Cert.#4640, file #25702, O.W.Wid.Rej.#25742. (not abstracted)

MORGAN,JOHN G.-Mexican War Pension Application dated 1887, Arkansas. Served in Company C, 1st Regiment, Georgia Volunteers. Mex.Sur.App. #16269, Cert.#16700. Soldier died 30 March 1914. (not abstracted)

MORGAN,THOMAS-Mexican War Pension Application dated 1890, Arkansas. Served in Captain Porter's Company, Arkansas Volunteer Cavalry. Mex. Sur.App.#22495, Cert.#18874. (not abstracted)

MORLEY,GEORGE-Mexican War Pension Application dated 1887, Arkansas. Served in Company B, 5th Regiment, U.S.Infantry. Widow, Lydia B. Mex.Wid.App.#5455, Cert.#3176. (not abstracted)

MORPHEW,SILAS-Mexican War Pension Application dated 1887, Arkansas. Served in Company E, 1st Battalion, Mississippi Riflemen. Widow, Sophronia A. Mex.Sur.App.#15746, Cert.#15424, Mex.Wid.App.#18379, Cert.#14962. (not abstracted)

MORRIS,JOSEPH W.-Mexican War Pension Application dated 1891, Arkansas. Served in Captain Delay's Company, 1st Regiment, Mississippi Volunteers. Widow, Lavinia, Mex.Sur.Cert.#9656, Mex.Wid.App. #9866. Remarks: O.W.Inv.#5991. (not abstracted)

MORRIS,WILLIAM-Mexican War Pension Application dated 1887, Arkansas. Served in Company F, 2nd Regiment Missouri Mounted Volunteers. Widow, Virginia. Mex.Wid.App.#3950, Cert.#4743. (not abstracted)

MORRISON,GEORGE S.-Mexican War Pension Application dated 1887, Arkansas. Served in Company E, 1st Regiment, Arkansas Cavalry. Widow, Martha. Mex.Wid.App.#1435, Cert.#1941. (not abstracted)

MORROW,ASA G.-Old war pension application dated 1850, Arkansas. Served as Sergeant in Captain William Inglish's Company, Arkansas Mounted Volunteers, Mexican War. He died of disease in San Antonio, Texas on 1 November 1846. His widow, Catherine, age 24, applied for pension in Hot Springs County, Arkansas, on 19 April 1849. The children of James Asa G. and Catherine Morrow; James Asa Morrow born 4 November 1843, and Francis Marion Morrow born 4 June 1846. John C.Douglass, who served as 3rd Lieutenant with James Morrow, stated that Francis M. Morrow, son of James Asa, was about 3 weeks old when the regiment left Saline County, Arkansas, for Mexico, and that James Asa Morrow had obtained permission to spend the nights with his family, while awaiting the march to the war. On 22 July 1850, Catherine Morrow married Isaac W. King. The July term of the Probate Court, appointed Isaac King, guardian of the minor children of James Asa G. Morrow. Catherine King died on 21 March 1856, and Bradford Morris was appointed guardian of the children. He applied for pension on their behalf on 24 December 1859.
O.W. Wid. Cert. #1809, File #29285, O.W. Minors Cert. #1760, File #12518.

MOSER,HENRY-Mexican War Pension Application dated 1887, Arkansas. Served in Company D, 1st Regiment, Arkansas Mounted Infantry. Widow, Emeline Selena. Mex.Sur.App.#9617, Cert.#13639, Mex.Wid.App.#18304, Cert.#14351. Remarks: Rebellion Inv.Cert.#736970, Co.C, 2nd Ark.Vol.Cav. (not abstracted)

MURPHY,ARTHUR-Revolutionary War Pension Application #S31827, dated 21 May 1833, Lawrence County, Territory of Arkansas. He was born in Sussex County, Virginia in the year 1762. He was residing in Bute County, North Carolina when he enlisted into service. After the war he lived in Franklin County, North Carolina, moved to Henderson County, Kentucky, then to Johnson County, Illinois. He moved to Lawrence County, Arkansas Territory about the year 1827.
Lawrence County, Arkansas, Probate Book C, pages 40 and 41; "Arthur Murphy, late of this County is dead without having made any last Will and Testament, and Nathaniel McCarroll of said County, having duly qualified, according to law, as administrator to the said Arthur Murphy, deceased,___ to do and perform all and singular the duties of administrator to said deceased, according to law." Recorded on this the 3rd day of September AD 1835 and of the Independence of the United States of America the 60th year.

MURPHY,BARTHOLOMEW-Revolutionary War Pension Application #R7508, dated October 1832, Perry County, Tennessee. He again applied in April 1842, Poinsett County, Arkansas, where he had moved to be with his children. He was born 9 December 1759 in Anson County, North Carolina. He stated that he had served in the North Carolina Militia and in the Rangers. He stated that he had served as a spy against the Tories. Bartholomew Murphy died in Greenfield Township, Poinsett County, Arkansas on 21 June 1845, survived by widow Anna Murphy.

MURPHY,DENNIS-Mexican War Pension Application dated 1887, Arkansas. Served in Company K, 1st Regiment, Arkansas Cavalry Volunteers. Widow, Elizabeth. Mex.Sur.App.#4847, Cert.#5366, Mex.Wid.App.#12102, Cert.#9253. (not abstracted)

MURPHY,THOMAS-Old War Pension Application. Served in Captain Sim's Company, Alabama Militia, Creek Indian War. Widow, Susan. O.W.Wid.Cert.#7918, file #29885. Applied for pension from Eldorada,

Union County, Arkansas. Committee on pensions report to the Congress of the United States; "The claimant's late husband, Thomas Murphy, was enlisted May 30, 1836, served 3 months as private in Captain Simm's Mounted Company, 23rd Regiment, Alabama Volunteers, Creek Indian War. He was mustered out July 22, 1836." Special Act #34, providing pension for Susan Murphy was passed by the Congress of the United States on February 20, 1893. Thomas Murphy died on 22 February 1866, Susan Murphy died 3 March 1898.

MYRICK,WILLIAM-Mexican War Pension Application. Served as Second Lieutenant in McCullough's Company, Bell's Texas Mounted Rifles. Widow, Nancy Ann. Mex.Sur.App.#16538, Cert.#11671, dated 1887, Texas. Mex.Wid.App.#19513, dated 1910, Arkansas. (not abstracted)

NEAL,BURTON-Mexican War Pension Application dated 1888, Arkansas. Served in Company I, Yell's Arkansas Cavalry. Widow, Sarah. Mex.-Wid.App.#7230, Cert.#5885. (not abstracted)

NEAL,FRANCIS W.-Mexican War Pension Application dated 1888, Arkansas. Served in Company I, Arkansas Volunteer Mounted Infantry. Mex.Sur.App.#18473, Cert.#14137, Mex.Wid.App.#13032, Cert.#14427. Remarks: Rebellion, Co.A, 4th Ark. Cav. and 3rd Ark.Cav. (not abstracted)

NEAL,JAMES, Jr.-War of 1812 pension application W.O.#23094, W.C. #25230. B.L.W. #16563-160-50. Service in Captain Willoughby Barton's Company of Georgia Militia. James Neal Jr. was born near Warrenton, Warren County, Georgia 28 June 1793. He married about the year 1817 to Eliza Bell/Beall, in Warren County, Georgia. They had at least two children, and Eliza died in 1820 in Warren County. James Neal married, 18 December 1824 to Eliza Rawling Davenport in Warren County, Georgia. They remained in Warren County, until 1825, then moved to Florida. In 1851 they were living in Escambia, Florida. They lived in Autauga, Butler and Baldwin Counties, Alabama. In 1858 they moved to Little River County, Arkansas and in 1867 to Crawford County, Arkansas. James Neal died, 30 August 1868, in Crawford County, Arkansas. Eliza R. Neal died in Crawford County on 16 January 1902. In making application for pension she had submitted the Family Bible Record, to wit:
"Eliza Rawling Davenport was born 22 August 1804,(died 16 January 1902), James Neal was born 28 June 1793, died 30 August 1868; married 18 December 1824. Children: James D. Neal was born 4 September 1826, Araminta Neal was born 14 October 1828, Jehu Neal was born 2 January 1831, Sarah Neal was born 2 February 1833, Mary Ann Neal was born 11 October 1834, Louisa Neal was born 8 June 1837, Josaphine Neal was born 13 November 1838, Wade Neal was born 2 May 1842, Samuel Neal was born 27 May 1845." This application file also contains copy of the marriage record of James and Eliza Neal.

NEAL,JAMES P.-Mexican War Pension Application dated 1887, Arkansas. Served in Engart's Company, Arkansas Mounted Volunteers. Mex. Sur.App.#3793, Cert.#11811. (not abstracted)

NEIS,ANTON-Old War Pension Application, dated 1874, Arkansas. Served from 1845 to 1850 in Company I, 6th Regiment of U.S.Infantry. O.W. Inv.App.#16752, Cert.#372662, file #48643. (not abstracted)

NELSON,ENOCH-Revolutionary War Pension Application #R7588, dated 22 October 1834, Miller County, Arkansas Territory, Enoch Nelson age 68 and a resident "of the County west of the Mississippi, now occupied and owned by the Chocktaw Indians, and within a mile and a half of Fort Towson on Red River". He stated that he was born in 1766 in York County, Pennsylvania, near Little York. He was living in Louisville, Kentucky when he was enlisted into service by his father (claimant was underage) and that he and his father served in the same company. He stated that his father commanded a rifle company, and that they served under Colonel George Rogers Clark. After the Revolutionary War, he and his father "came to the Falls of the Ohio with Clark." He stated that Mr. Lewis Ward, who now resides with the Chocktaws, was in service with him.

NELSON,JOHN W.-Mexican War Pension Application dated 1887, Arkansas. Served in Company E, 1st Battalion, Georgia Volunteers. Widow, Eliza A. Mex.Sur.App.#3826, Cert.#1674, Mex.Wid.App.#14316, Cert.#11106. (not abstracted)

NEWMAN,AYERS-Mexican War Pension Application dated 1887, Arkansas. Served in Captain Evan's Company, 4th Regiment, Tennessee Volunteers. Mex.Wid.App.#4623, Cert.#2653. (not abstracted)

NEWMAN,DANIEL A.-Mexican War Pension Application dated 1887, Arkansas. Served in McGee's Independent Company, Alabama Mounted Volunteers. Mex.Sur.App.#3845, Cert.#2935. (not abstracted)

NEWMAN,JACKSON-Mexican War Pension Application dated 1887, Arkansas. Served in Company G, 1st Regiment, North Carolina Volunteers. Widow, Ollie. Mex.Sur.App.#9683, Cert.#3191, Mex.Wid.App.#8616, Cert.#6761. (not abstracted)

NEWMAN,MOSES-Mexican War Pension Application dated 1889, Arkansas. Served in Captain Shepard's Company, St.Louis Battalion, Missouri Volunteers. Mex.Sur.App.#22002, Cert.#19171. (not abstracted)

NICHOLS,DAVID-War of 1812 pension application S.O.#26959, S.C.#18630, W.O.#33824, W.C.#19997. B.L.W.#46769-80-50 and #46587-80-55. He was born ca 1788 in Kentucky. He entered service 18 June 1812 in Franklin County, Tennessee, in Captain John Cowans Company of Tennessee Militia. He served at the Battle of Pensacola and against the Indians at the Black Warrior and Tom Bigbee Rivers. He was married first to Elizabeth Walker, second to Kasiah Brooks on 29 June 1826 in Hardin County, Tennessee. They lived in Hardin County until 1839, when they moved to Carroll County, (which part later became Boone County) Arkansas. David Nichols died 14 February 1874 in Boone County, Arkansas, and his widow applied for pension there. They had two children, only one identified; Cynthia C. Eoff, 49 years old in 1887 and residing in Boone County. Kasiah Nichols died in Boone County on 13 January 1887. 1850 Federal Census, Carroll County, Arkansas, page 165, family #582: David Nicholas 65 N.C.; Kizziah 48 Ga.; Cynthia C. 13 Tenn.; family #591: James Nichols 25 Tenn.; Delila 26 Ala.; William L. 5 Ark.; John B. 4 Ark.; Joseph A. 2 Ark.

NICHOLS,NEWTON-Mexican War Pension Application dated 1888, Arkansas. Served in Texas Volunteers. Widow, Minerva. Mex.Wid.App.#6313, Cert.#5285. (not abstracted)

NICHOLSON,JAMES-Mexican War Pension Application dated 1887, Arkansas. Served in Captain Grant's Company, C Battalion, Georgia Volunteers. Widow, Nancy Spears. Mex.Sur.App.#9697, Cert.#9854, Mex.Wid.App.#11715, Cert.#11817. Remarks: O.W.Inv.Rej.#16767. (not abstracted)

NIMAN,TRUMAN-Mexican War Pension Application dated 1888, Arkansas. Served in Company A, 3rd Regiment, Ohio Volunteers. Widow, Hulda Jane. Mex.Wid.App.#6124, Cert.#4745. (not abstracted)

NOBLETT,DAVID-Old war pension application O.W. Wid. Cert. #761, file #6843. Service in Company E, 12th Regiment of U.S. Infantry, Mexican War. He married Hasky Steward, 15 October 1845, in Benton County, Arkansas. He died of pneumonia in Mexico City, on 12 January 1848. Hasky applied for pension 26 September 1849, she was age 27 and a resident of Benton County. Hasky married Harris Craine on 9 November 1851, and in the year 1854 they were residing in Pope County, Arkansas.

NOLES,GEORGE C.-Mexican War Pension Application dated 1887, Arkansas. Served in Captain Wofford's Company, Georgia Mounted Volunteers. Widow, Susan M. Mex.Wid.App.#5057, Cert.#4419. Remarks: O.W.Inv.Pending. (not abstracted)

NORMAN,ROBERT L.-Mexican War Pension Application dated 1887, Arkansas. Served in Company I, 1st Regiment, Alabama Volunteers. Widow, Catherine. Mex.Wid.App.#1571, Cert.#3510. (not abstracted)

NOWLIN,WILLIAM M.-Mexican War Pension Application dated 1887, Arkansas. Served in Company A, 1st Regiment, Alabama Volunteers. Mex.Sur.App.#3900, Cert.#8772. Remarks: O.W.Inv.Rej.#22358. (not abstracted)

ODOM,WILLIS-Revolutionary War Pension Application #S16993, dated 16 January 1834, Graves County, Kentucky. He was born in Cheraws District, South Carolina in May 1762. He entered service there in April 1778, in Captain James Hick's Company of South Carolina Militia. He served under Captain Evans, on the Pee Dee River, in an assignment to take salt from a Tory named John Mitchell. After he was discharged from that tour of duty, he went to live with his brother in Edgefield District, South Carolina, where he joined a company of Mounted Militia under command of Captain Francis Sinkfield. He remained in this company until March 1780. He then moved with his father from Cheraws District, South Carolina to Bladen County, North Carolina, where he joined a company of Militia, under command of Captain Peter Robinson. After the war he moved back to Edgefield, South Carolina and from there to Lincoln County, Kentucky. Between the years 1788 and 1834 he lived in Lincoln, Washington, Logan, Davis and Graves Counties, Kentucky. In June 1844, he had his pension transferred to Van Buren County, Arkansas where he had moved "to be with my son, Lewis Odom, who lives in Van Buren County, on the middle fork of Little Red River, and to be near my grandchildren". Later that year his pension was transferred to Barry County, Missouri.

OLDFIELD,JAMES B.-Mexican War Pension Application dated 1887, Arkansas. Served in Captain Blanchard's Independent Company, Louisiana Volunteers and in Captain Grice's Company, 5th Regiment, U.S.Infantry. Widow, Martha. Mex.Sur.App.#4928, Cert.#13000, Mex.Wid.App.#13639. (not abstracted)

OLIVER,JAMES M.-Mexican War Pension Application dated 1887, Arkansas. Served in Company C, Indiana Volunteers. Widow, Almira. Mex.Wid.App.#3047, Cert.#726. (not abstracted)

O'NEILL,JOHN-War of 1812 pension application S.O.#28166, S.C.#20289, W.O.#41688, W.C.#32650. He was born 4 July 1794 in Union District, South Carolina. He enlisted in service in Vincennes, Indiana on 15 Februay 1813, in Captain John Milburn's Company of Indiana Militia and was discharged 17 April 1813. He was married to Jane Harvey, 15 September 1815 in New Princeton, Gibson County, Indiana. He applied for pension 21 September 1872 in Bradley County, Arkansas. He died there 27 March 1881, and his widow applied for pension in 1882. Affidavit dated 12 July 1882, Bradley County, Arkansas, to wit, "I, Jasper S. O'Neill, of the aforesaid county and state, do solemnly swear that I am the proper custodian of the old Family Bible containing records of my father and mother, John and Jane O'Neill's family. That I am the ninth child, that I am 50 years of age and that the said record is as follows: "John O'Neill was born 4 July 1794; Jane Harvey was born 22 March 1798; John O'Neill and Jane Harvey was married 19 Sept. 1815". Jane O'Neill stated that after the war they had lived in Gibson County, Indiana, Vandalia, Illinois, Weakley County, Tennesse, Drew County, Arkansas and Marengo County, Texas.

OSBORN,ANDREW J.-Mexican War Pension Application dated 1887, Arkansas. Mex.Wid.App.#3049, Cert.#3881. He married Julia F.G.A., 13 February 1844 at Point Peter, Arkansas. She was born 16 November 1825 in Mississippi. Andrew J. Osborn enlisted into service in July 1846 at Washington, Arkansas, in Captain C.C.Danley's Company B, 1st Regiment, Arkansas Cavalry commanded by Colonel Archibald Yell. He died 11 October 1864 at Ozark, Missouri, and she applied for pension on 26 April 1887, a resident of Tomahawk, Searcy County, Arkansas. In 1892 she was a resident of Yellville, Marion County, Arkansas. She died about 4 November 1896.

OWEN,GEORGE W.-Mexican War Pension Application dated 1890, Arkansas. Widow, Priscilla. Service in Company G, 2nd Regiment, Illinois Volunteers. Mex.Sur.App.#23539, Cert.#20233, Mex.Wid.App.#9542, O.W.R.#23254. (not abstracted)

OWEN,OBADIAH-Mexican War Pension Application dated 1904, Arkansas. Widow, Fanny. Service in Company C, 13th Regiment, U.S.Infantry. Mex.Sur.App.#16441, Cert.#15757, Mex.Wid.App.#17699, Cert.#13916. (not abstracted)

OWENS,BENJAMIN-Revolutionary War Pension Application #R7846, dated 31 July 1838, Conway, Arkansas. He was born 13 May 1765 in North Carolina. He enlisted in service at the age of fifteen, while residing in Fairfield District, South Carolina, in a company of militia commanded by Captain William Robinson. Application rejected because he did not serve six months.

OWENS,GEORGE,Old War Pension Application dated 1883, Arkansas. Served in Captain Simpson's Company, 2nd Illinois Volunteers, Mexican War. O.W.Inv.App.#R23254, Mex.Wid.#9542. (not abstracted)

OWENS,McGEORGE-Old War Pension Application, dated 1846, Arkansas. Served as Sergeant in Captain Blake's Company, 2nd U.S.Dragoons, Mexican War. Inv.Cert.#3013, file #25723. (not abstracted)

OWENS,REUBEN-Old war pension application O.W. Wid. Cert. #1479, File #28581, O.W. Minors Cert. #4005, File #8496. Enlisted at Huntsville, Arkansas on 3 May 1847, in Captain Allen Wood's Company C, 12th Regiment of U.S. Infantry, Mexican War. He died in Mexico City, of disease, on 1 December 1847. He was married to Elvira Moody, 1 February 1845 in Carroll County, Arkansas. They had one child, Melissa Eveline. Elvira Owens married Boran Decalb Moody in Madison County, Arkansas, on 1 February 1848. In October 1853, the Probate Court of Madison appointed Boran Decalb Moody, guardian of Melissa Owens.

PADGETT,NEHEMIAH-Old war pension application, O.W. Cert. #8059, File #5143. Served as 1st Lieutenant in Schurlock's Alabama Volunteers, Seminole Indian War.(not abstracted)

PAGE,FRANCIS NELSON-Old war pension application O.W.Wid.Cert.#3399, File #8500. The Adjutant General's report, "Francis Nelson Page was promoted from the Military Academy, Brevet Second Lieutenant in the 7th Regiment of Infantry, July 1, 1841. Promoted 2nd Lieutenant, October 30, 1841, was Regimental Adjutant from 1845 to 1847. Brevetted 1st Lieutenant, May 9, 1846, for gallant conduct in the defense of Fort Brown, Texas. Promoted 1st Lieutenant, August 22, 1846, appointed Assistant Adjutant General, with the brevet rank of Captain May 13, 1847 (which rank he held at his death). Received the brevet of Major, August 20, 1847, for gallant and meritorious conduct in the Battles of Conteras and Churabusco, Mexico. He was severly wounded at Chapultepec, Mexico on September 13, 1847. He served in Florida from 1856 to April 29, 1858 and was engaged a portion of the time in mustering volunteers into and out of service. He left Florida April 29, 1858, on leave of absence granted for the benefit of his health." He served with General Harvey in Florida, in 1858, when Billy Bowlegs and his tribe were removed. Francis N. Page was married to Susan Du Val, 25 February 1851, in Sebastian County, Arkansas. They had four children; Lucy Nelson Page, born 29 August 1853 at Jefferson Barracks, Missouri; Powhatan Randolph Page, born 8 December 1854 at Jefferson Barracks Missouri; Kate Rector Page born 7 February 1857 at Fort Brooke, Florida; Frank Nelson Page, born 21 February 1852, and dead by 1874. Francis Nelson Page died at his home in Ft. Smith, Sebastian County, Arkansas on 25 March 1860. He was referred to as a grandson of Governor Nelson of Virginia. Because of the American Civil War, Susan Page had difficulty in securing her pension. She had to seek help from friends, to help persuade the pension board to give attention to her application. One such appeal was made to General and Mrs. Grant, that letter in this file.

PALMER,JOHN C.-Mexican War Pension Application dated 1887, Arkansas. Service in Company K, Arkansas Mounted Volunteers. Mex.Sur.App.#5003, Cert.#9445. (not abstracted)

PARISH,DAVID-Mexican War Pension Application dated 1887, Arkansas. Service in Captain West's Company B, Arkansas Regiment Volunteers. Mex.Sur.App.#9770, Cert.#12319. (not abstracted)

PARK,GEORGE-Mexican War Pension Application dated 1887, Arkansas. Served in Company B, Gray's Battalion, Arkansas Volunteers. Mex.Sur. App.#5018, Cert.#14262. (not abstracted)

PARKER,MARIDETH W.-Mexican War Pension Application dated 1888, Arkansas. Service in Company A, Arkansas Mounted Infantry. Mex.Sur. App.#19286, Cert.#17378, Mex.Wid.App.#19105, Cert.#15169. Remarks: Rebellion Inv.Orig.#1134129, Co.H, 3rd Ark.Cav. (not abstracted)

PARKISON,WILLIAM M.C.-Mexican War Pension Application dated 1887, Arkansas. Service in Company G, 2nd Regiment of Tennessee Volunteers. Mex.Sur.App.#11932, Cert.#14319. Remarks: O.W.Inv.File #1315. (not abstracted)

PARKS,JACKSON-Mexican War Pension Application dated 1887, Arkansas. Mex.Sur.App.#5044, Cert.#5903, Mex.Wid.App.#11510, Cert.#8683. Jackson Parks was born near Franklin, in Williamson County, Tennessee ca 1826. He served as 4th Sergeant in Company B, 2nd Regiment, Illinois Infantry. He stated, "At New Orleans, Louisiana, the Regiment was divided, one battalion, under Colonel Collins, going to Vera Cruz, and the other, under Lieutenant Colonel Hicks, going to Tampico. Company B was under command of Lt.Colonel Hicks at Tampico, in Garrison Duty. The Regiment was reunited at Jalopa (?) in the Spring of 1848, and proceeded, with the main army, to the City of Mexico. The 2nd Illinois Regiment remained only a few days in the City of Mexico and were sent to Pueblo, where it remained until the close of the war, on Garrison Duty. After the war, I spent one year in Wisconsin and then moved to Arkansas." Jackson Parks married Sarah Jane Dodd, 15 January 1850, in Clark County, Arkansas. She was born 25 December 1829 in Davidson County, Tennessee. He applied for pension on 28 January 1887, he was a resident of Caddo Gap, Montgomery County, Arkansas. He died 23 March 1893, and Sarah Jane Parks applied for pension from Hopper, Montgomery County. Sarah Jane Parks died intestate on 6 December 1893, Jackie Parks named as administratrix of her estate.

PARRISH,CHARLES L.-Old war pension application, O.W.Wid.Cert.#1534, File #6848. He enlisted into service at Clinton, Arkansas in Captain Lloyd Magruder's Company H, 12th Regiment of Arkansas Volunteers, Mexican War. He died of disease in Cuanavaca, Mexico, on 15 April 1848. Charles Parrish married Kaziah Lunsford, 10 June 1841, in Tippah County, Mississippi. Kaziah Parrish, was inscribed on Arkansas pension rolls on 30 May 1848. She married Samuel Floyd, either 2 September 1849 or 30 September 1850 in Hot Springs County, Arkansas. He died in Hot Springs County on 15 May 1858.

PARRISH,SAMUEL A.-Mexican War Pension Application dated 1887, Arkansas. Service in Company E, 1st Regiment, Tennessee Mounted Volunteers. Mex.Sur.App.#5053, Cert.#16752. (not abstracted)

PARRISH,WALTER M.-Mexican War Pension Application dated 1887, Arkansas. Service in Santa Fe Battalion, Missouri Mounted Volunteers. Mex.Sur.App.#5021, Cert.#6146, Mex.Wid.App.#8767, Cert.#9286. (not abstracted)

PARSONS,PLEASANT K.-Mexican War Pension Application dated 1887, Arkansas. Service in Captain Murray's Company, 2nd Regiment, Tennessee Volunteers. Mex.Sur.App.#12678, Cert.#17182. (not abstracted)

PATTON,JAMES-War of 1812 pension application W.O.#25548, W.C.#13085. B.L.W.#25352-80-50 and #46024-80-55. Service in Captain Benjamin Hewitt's Company of Tennessee Militia. He enlisted in Shelbyville, Tennessee in November 1812. James Patton married Sarah Conley (also stated as McConally) 19 November 1818 in Bedford County, Tennessee. He died in Bedford County, on 28 February 1836. His widow remained in Bedford County until 1847, when she moved to Benton County, Arkansas. In 1851 in Benton County, Arkansas, Ezekiel Dickson, Joseph McKissick, and David McKissick, stated that they had served in the army with James Patton, and that they had all been neighbors, both in Tennessee and Arkansas.

PATTON THOMAS STARR-Mexican War Pension Application dated 1887, Arkansas. Widow, Sarah. Service in Company E, 2nd Regiment, Mississippi Infantry. Mex.Sur.App.#5059, Cert.#9423, Mex.Wid.- App.#16160, no cert.#. (not abstracted)

PAXTON,DAVID-War of 1812 pension application W.O.#6866, W.C.#8227. B.L.W.#44756-120-55.Service in Captain James Paxton's Company of Virginia Militia. He enlisted in Rockbridge County, Virginia. He married Lucy S. Edwards, 17 November 1818, in Woodford County, Kentucky, marriage record enclosed. David Paxton died 1 September 1851 in Washington County, Arkansas. Widow, Lucy, applied for pension in Webster County, Louisana on 29 August 1871, she was age 69. In April 1878, she was living in Bradley County, Arkansas, at which time her signature was witnessed by William E. Paxton, no relationship stated.
1850 Federal Census, Hempstead County, Arkansas, Ozan Township, page 221, family #164: David C. Paxton 66 Va.; Lucy 48 Ken.

PEARMAN,SAMUEL-War of 1812 pension application W.O.#16985 W.C.- #12054. B.L.W.#25265-80-50 and #45407-80-55. He enlisted in Captain John Smith's Company of Kentucky Militia on 15 November 1814 and served at the Battle of New Orleans. Samuel Pearman and Jane Field were married in Bullett County, Kentucky on 18 March 1818. He died in Meade County, Kentucky on 16 September 1835. Widow, Jane, applied for pension on 1 April 1878 in Arkansas County, Arkansas, she was age 81. In that application, she submitted the Family Record from the pages of her Bible, to wit; "Samuel Pearman was born June 22, 1781; Jane Field was born October 14, 1797; Charles Henry Pearman, son of Samuel and Jane Pearman, was born 14 February 1820; J.T. Pearman, son of Samuel and Jane

Pearman, was born 16 July 1821; Granville L. Pearman, son of Samuel and Jane Pearman, was born 22 April 1824; Lucy J. Pearman, daughter of Samuel and Jane Pearman, was born 30 August 1826; George W. Pearman, son of Samuel and Jane Pearman, was born 16 November 1828; Cerenna(?) A. Pearman, daughter of Samuel and Jane Pearman, was born 22 March 1831; Ann Mariah Pearman, daughter of Samuel and Jane Pearman, was born 26 July 1833; Samuel Pearman, son of Samuel and Jane Pearman, was born 2 September 1835; Samuel Pearman departed this life 16 September 1835, age 49; Lucy Pearman departed this life 10 April 1857". George W. Pearman stated that his mother was living with him, his brothers Charles W. and John T. Pearman were dead, that his brother Granville was living in Hendersonville, Kentucky and that Samuel and the surviving sisters were living in Arkansas County near the Town of De Witt.

PEAY,JOHN C.-Mexican War Pension Application dated 1887, Arkansas. Served as 2nd Lieutenant in Pike's Company, 1st Regiment, Arkansas Mounted Volunteers. Widow, Margaret. Mex.Sur.App.#7256, file #3207, Mex.Wid.App.#14830, File #11688. (not abstracted)

PECK,RUFUS A.-Mexican War Pension Application dated 1887, Arkansas. Service in Company G, Indiana Mounted Rifles. Widow, Lydia. Mex.-Sur.App.#9796, Cert.#4837, Mex.Wid.App.#13882, Cert.#10703. Remarks: Inv.Cert.#922694, late war, Co.E, 53rd Ind. O.W.Inv.#26334. (not abstracted)

PENDERGRASS,JOHN J.-Mexican War Pension Application dated 1887, Arkansas. Mex.Sur.App.#9801, Cert.#6623. Remarks: O.W.Inv.Rej.-#17020. John Pendergrass was born 23 September 1825 at Woodville, Marshall County, Alabama. He enlisted in service in Marshall County, in James M. Gee's Independent Company, Alabama Volunteers. He first applied for pension in 1853, while residing in Huntsville, Marshall County, Alabama, stating, "on the 10th or 15th of July 1847, he received a wound, while on the march and in the line of duty, while he was between the mouth of the Rio Grande and Matamoras, from the accidental discharge of his carbine or gun, which discharged it's contents through the ball of his right foot, by which he lost altogether the middle toe on that foot." Affidavit in 1854, by James Gee, in which he stated that he was a resident of the State of Arkansas, but had formerly resided in Marshall County, Alabama. John Pendergrass left Marshall County, Alabama in 1858, moved to Franklin County, Arkansas. In 1907, he stated that his wife was not living, that he had 9 living children, the youngest was 35 years old. Affidavit by W.H.Fletcher, of Chismville, Logan County, Arkansas in 1887, "About the last of May 1847, at Guntersville, Marshall County, Alabama, I volunteered in a company commanded by Captain James M.Gee, and went to Mobile, Alabama, where, in June, I was mustered into service as a soldier of the U.S. in the War with Mexico. From Mobile we went to Matamoras, Mexico and served until July 1848, guarding trains and other services. I know that John Pendergrass was a member of the same company and was confined in the hospital until discharged in April 1848. I know that, in July 1847, the said John J.Pendergrass received an accidental gun shot wound, while on duty near Matamoras and that he had the middle toe on the right foot amputated on account of said wound and I know that he was confined to the hospital with yellow fever."

PENDERGRASS,MATTHEW-Mexican War Pension Application dated 1887, Arkansas. Mex.Wid.App.#3521, Cert.#1824. He served in Captain James M. Gee's Independent Company, Alabama Volunteers. He enlisted in Guntersville, Marshall County, Alabama in June 1847. He married Catherine Phillips, 4 January 1848, at Roman's Landing, Alabama. She was born 27 July 1832 in Carroll County, Georgia. She had a brother named Clifton B. Phillips, who was residing in Franklin County, Arkansas in 1887. Matthew Pendergrass died 20 November

1863 in Waldron, Scott County, Arkansas. Catherine Pendergrass applied for pension 21 May 1887 in Ozark, Franklin County, Arkansas. Her doctor stated that she was disabled by having "both bones of the left leg fractured, the ankle joint crushed and left wrist dislocated by some unruly cattle." Affidavits from John Pendergrass and Clifton B. Phillips.
1850 Federal Census, Marshall County, Alabama, page 208, family #3: Willis Pendergrass 28 Ky.; Nancy 31 Geo.; Mary A. 7 Ala.; Susannah 4 Ala.; William 2 Ala.; John G. 9/12 Ala.; family #4: Alexander 25 Ky.; Susannah 22 Geo.; John 9/12 Ala.; family #13 Joseph Pendergrass 41 N.C.; Cynthia 40 Ga.; Susannah White 23 Tenn.; Caleb Pendergrass 17 Ala.; Louise 15 Ala.; Lucinda 13 Ala.; Philip 11 Ala.; Nathan 9 Ala.; Moses 6 Ala.; Amanda 4 Ala.; Jehu 2 Ala.; Mary 10/12 Ala.; page 210, family #32: Henry Pendergrass 22 Ky.; Elizabeth 22 Geo.; James 5 Ala.; Mary 1 Ala.; page 212, family #73: Matthew Pendergrass 22 Ala.; Katherine 19 Geo.; William 7/12 Ala.; page 214: Hannah Pendergrass 49 N.C. listed with Bohannan Family; page 231, family #328: Landon Pendergrass 27 Ky.; Malinda 24 Ala.; Anna 19 Tenn.; page 233: Calvin Pendergrass 24 Ala.; Jane 26 Tenn.; Martha 27 Ala.; Elizabeth 21 Ala.; Mary 17 Ala.; Margaret 15 Ala.; Benjamin 10 Ala.; page 267, family #55: Atha Pendergrass 49 Tenn.; Betsey 43 Tenn.; Alfred 22 Ala.; Sarah 15 Ala.; Pleasant 11 Ala.; Abram 7 Ala.; Nancy 4 Ala.; Henry Joseph Cobbs 3 Ala.; Louisa Phillips 34 Ala.; Mary 3 Ala.; Atha L. 2 Ala.; page 268, John Pendergrass, age 28 bn Ala. listed with family of Joseph Southerland: page 269: John P. Pendergrass 25 unknown; Mary 17 Ala.; Harriet 4/12 Ala.

PENTER,JAMES-Old War pension application. Service in 1st Regiment of Arkansas Cavalry, Mexican War. O.W. Inv. Cert. #4888, File #45894, O.W.Wid. Cert. #7425, File #27741, O.W. Wid. App. #R27741. (not abstracted)

PERCIFIELD,MARLIN-Mexican War Pension Application dated 1887, Arkansas. Widow, Mary A. Mex.Sur.App.#19631, Cert.#16855, Mex.Wid. App.#18114, Cert.#14399. (not abstracted)

PERRIN,WILLIAM W.-Mexican War Pension Application dated 1887, Arkansas. Service in Company B, 2nd Regiment Kentucky Volunteers. Widow, Lydia C. Mex.Sur.App.#5080, Cert.#3483, Mex.Wid.App.#15009, Cert.#12027. (not abstracted)

PERRY,JAMES-Mexican War Pension Application dated 1887, Arkansas. Service in Company C, 2nd Regiment, Mississippi Infantry. Widow, Frances S. Mex.Sur.App.#5136, Cert.#8299, Mex.Wid.App.#14649, Cert. #11432. (not abstracted)

PERRY,JOHN G.-Mexican War Pension Application dated 1887, Arkansas. Served as Sergeant in Captain George Washington Patrick's Company, Yell's Regiment, Arkansas Volunteers. He enlisted at Washington, Arkansas in June 1846 and was discharged in June 1847 in Camargo, Mexico. He was married to Mary L. Madden, 9 October 1849, in Pope (now Johnson) County, Arkansas. John G. Perry applied for pension on 12 March 1887, age 62, resident of Cabin Creek, Johnson County, Arkansas. John G. Connally and Richard M. Lee stated, "we knew applicant before his enlistment, and we served in the same company at Buena Vista, Mexico, at the same time." John Perry died 8 April 1887 in Lamar, Johnson County, and Mary Perry applied for pension there on 3 May 1890. In 1896, she signed her name, "Mary Perry, now of Eureka Springs, Carroll County, Arkansas." She died about 4 February 1896. Mex.Sur.App.#9808, Cert.#19001, Mex.Wid.App.#8354, Cert.#7003.

PERRY,ROBERT P.-Mexican War Pension Application dated 1890, Arkansas. Service in Company H, 13th Regiment, Alabama Volunteers. Widow, Mary. Mex.Wid.App.#9148, Cert.#8128. (not abstracted)

PETTIT,ABRAHAM-War of 1812 pension application S.O.#29841. Father named James Lawrence, stepfather named Pettit. Service in Captain Blackstone's Company of Pennsylvania Militia. Application rejected. (not abstracted)

PETTIT,JOHN WILLIAM ADDISON-War of 1812 pension application W.O.#26541, W.C.#24253. B.L.W.#6048-80-50 and #8703-80-55. Service in Captain Adam Heath's Company of Georgia Militia. He was born in Wrightsboro, Georgia ca 1797, enlisted into service in Warren County, Georgia on 26 September 1814, and was discharged 2 March 1815. He was married first to Jane Wylie, who died in 1846 in Memphis, Tennessee. He then married Maria Louisa James, 23 September 1846 in Memphis. He died 24 August 1863 in Germantown, Shelby County, Tennessee. Maria Louisa Pettit applied for pension 8 June 1878, at which time she was age 50, a resident of Hot Springs, Garland County, Arkansas, living with her two daughters, Ophelia Connally and Laura Baxter.

PETTUS,HENRY-War of 1812 pension application S.O.#12325, S.C.#22002. B.L.W.#56825-120-55. He was born 3 June 1790 in Prince William County, Virginia. He married Mary Barnes, 18 December 1838, in Lewisburg, Mecklinburg County, North Carolina. In November 1850, he was a resident of Greene County, Missouri, and in 1855, he applied for Bounty Land from Sugar Creek, Benton County, Arkansas. His pension application was executed at Roller's Ridge, Benton County, Arkansas in 1871. This file contains excellent letters, written by Henry Pettus to the pension board, regarding his military service. In 1873, he wrote, "I enlisted in Richmond, Virginia, in August 1812, in Captain Anderson Miller's Company, 19th Virginia Militia. William Wert, who was a private at the time, made up a company of Flying Artillery, which I attached myself to. We were drilled apart from the Regiment. In the winter of 1814, Wert's Company was broken up and I attached myself to Captain A. Turner's Company in the 19th Virginia Regiment commanded by J.Ambler. Well, in August the whole Regiment was ordered into the service of the U.S.A., by Mr. Robert Stanard, Esqr., under rigid martial law. We were ordered some 40 miles below Richmond into camp, where we remained some five weeks. On the march back to Richmond, Captain Wert got news that his wife was at the point of death, he left. We were ordered to take the guns and caissons back to the penitentiary. We did so and were discharged." In 1875, he wrote, "I have written to my son in Richmond, for information, but he cannot find anyone living, who was in the War of 1812. I have a daughter, only 12 years old, dependent on me. During the war of 1861, the Jayhawkers robbed me of nearly all I have. I joined Captain E.Burtram's Company in 1865, by order of Colonel Harrison, we then put a check to their robbing business."
1850 Federal Census, Greene County, Missouri, Campbell Township, page 253, family #132: James H. Pettus 50 Virginia; Mary 27 Va.; Georgianna 10 Va.; William 8 Va.; Mary 2 Tenn.; Andrew Barnes 19 Va.

PHELAN/PHELEN,THOMAS-Revolutionary War Pension Application #R8168, dated 13 April 1837, Washington County, Arkansas. He was born 28 October 1752, place not stated, but was residing in Euwchland (?) Township, Chester County, Pennsylvania in the Summer of 1776, when called into service. He was serving in Washington's Regiment at the Battle of Long Island, when he was stricken with "bloody Flux". He was hospitalized in New York for the remainder of his tour of duty. In 1777, he moved his family to Georgia in St. Paul's Parish near Columbia County. He served in several skirmishes with Tories and several engagements with the Indians. In 1778 he recieved a head wound in a skirmish with Tories. His application for pension was rejected, however, on 14 December 1852, Jeremiah Phelan, aged 75, applied for arrears in pension, stated that he was the son of Thomas Phelan, who died 28 August 1838, that his mother, named Mary, died 14 December 1830. He further stated that his father and mother were married 6 June 1774.

PHILLIPS,GEORGE W.-Mexican War Pension Application dated 1888, Arkansas. Service in Captain Hacker's Company, 2nd Regiment, Illinois Volunteers. Widow, Matilda. Mex.Wid.App.#6202, Cert.#4874. (not abstracted)

PHILLIPS,PARKER-War of 1812 pension application W.O.#11412, W.C.#8750. Service in Captain William Evans' Company of Mississippi Militia. He enlisted in Madison County, Territory of Mississippi. He was married to Elizabeth Hamner in Alabama. She died about 1826, and he remained in Alabama until 1829, when he moved to West Tennessee. He moved to Hot Springs County, Territory of Arkansas in 1830. He married Drusilla Nichols there on 1 October 1847. He served as Judge of the Probate Court for many years before his death on 17 August 1877.
1850 Federal Census, Hot Springs County, Arkansas, Fenton Township, page 280, family #111: Parker Phillips 52 Va.; Drusilla 44 Ky.; Nathan Lloyd 23 Tenn.; John Rye 12 Va.; Saline Township, page 275, family #41: Zack Phillips 40 Va.; Melinda 29 Ala.; Joseph 10 Ark.; Amanda 7 Ark.; Sarah 5 Ark.; Frances 2 Ark.; William P. 5/12 Ark.

PHILLPOT/PHILPOT,WARREN-Revolutionary War Pension Application #S31907, dated 12 December 1833, Washington County, Territory of Arkansas. He was born 28 August 1756 in Charles County, Maryland. He was residing in Frederick County, Maryland in June or July of 1776, when he enlisted in the United States Cavalry under command of Colonel Griffen. He served in that company at the Battle of White Plains. He moved to Bedford County, Virginia in 1778 and served in Captain John Jacob Sly's Company. In 1779, he moved to Guilford County, North Carolina, and served in Colonel Preston's Regiment at the Battle of Whitney's Mill near Guilford. In 1784 he moved to Franklin County, Georgia, in 1801, to Pendleton District, South Carolina and in 1830, he moved to Washington County, Territory of Arkansas.
Washington County, Arkansas Will Records, Vols. A & B; page 29, memo on will of Warren Philpot; signed 21 March 1838, probated 21 July 1845. Legacies to: wife, Martha; daughter, Elizabeth Franklin; grandson, James S. Franklin.

PHIPPS,DAVID-Mexican War Pension Application dated 1887, Arkansas. Service in Captain McAdams' Company, 3rd Regiment, Illinois Volunteers. Widow, Mary Ann. Mex.Wid.App.#1685, Cert.#7036. (not abstracted)

PICKETT,JOHN S.-Mexican War Pension Application dated 1887, Arkansas. Service in Company I, 3rd Regiment, U.S.Dragoons. Widow, Martha W. Mex.Wid.App.#1688, Cert.#1449. (not abstracted)

PILLOW,GIDEON J.-Mexican War Pension Application dated 1887, Arkansas. Served as Brigadier General. Widow, Mary E. Mex.Wid.App. #5553, Cert.#3103. O.W.Rej.#19846. (not abstracted)

PIPER,JAMES S.-Mexican War Pension Application dated 1887, Arkansas. Served as Captain of Company D, Watson's Battalion, Maryland and D.C. Volunteers. Mex.Sur.App.#5191, Cert.#3328, Mex.Wid.App. #7640, Cert.#6075. (not abstracted)

PISTOLE,CHARLES-Revolutionary War Pension Application #W26894, dated 12 September 1832, Maury County, Tennessee. He was born in 1757 in Dinwiddie County, Virginia, his father removed from Dinwiddie to Pittsylvania County, Virginia while Charles was still a child. Charles Pistole enlisted in January 1781, in Captain William Dick's Company of Virginia Volunteers, "to prevent

the British from crossing the Dan River into Virginia." He served
at the Battle of Guilford Court House. After the battle, he
was with Captain Morton, who escorted the prisoners fron Guilford
to Manchester Barracks. Charles Pistole served under command
of Captain Christopher Shelton and Captain Lavender Shelton
in General Green's Regiment of Virginia State Troops at the
Siege of Ninety-Six. Charles Pistole died in Independence County,
Arkansas on 6 September 1839. His widow, Elizabeth, applied
for pension, and because of special Congressional Legislation
was granted pension until her death on 29 September 1854 in
Independence County. Family data mentioned; Charles Pistole
Junior, seventh child of Charles and Elizabeth Pistole, born
9 January 1799. David Pistole, oldest son of Charles and Elizabeth
Pistole, was born in 1785 (he stated that his parents had been
married "shortly after the peace with Great Britain"; Winna
Deaton, daughter of Charles and Elizabeth Pistole, was born
6 July 1806 (in May 1855, Winna stated that she was the only
surviving child of Charles and Elizabeth).
Independence County, Arkansas Marriage Records; page 53, Thomas
Southerland and Susannah Pistole, 8 February 1838.

PLEDGER,JAMES-War of 1812 pension application W.O.#37522, W.C.
#29884. Volunteered into service in Captain Charles Carter's
Company of Georgia Militia, in Elberton, Georgia, and was discharged
at Milledgeville, Georgia. Served in the war with the Creek
Indians. He was married to Polly Ford in Elbert County, Georgia
4 August 1814 by Reverend Murrell(?) Pledger. James Pledger
applied for bounty land in 1851 in Gordon County, Georgia. He
died in Yell County, Arkansas on 4 September 1866. Polly Pledger
moved to Washington County, Arkansas in April 1879, but returned
to Danville, Yell County in September 1879, where she was residing
when she applied for pension. Affidavit dated 14 April 1880,
Danville, Yell County, Arkansas, "Katy Dickens, a person of
color, swears that she is about 71 years of age, that she was
born a slave and when about five years of age was bought by
one Isaac Ford, of Elbert County, in the State of Georgia, father
of Polly Pledger, widow of James Pledger. After the death of
Isaac Ford, she went to live with James and Polly Pledger, with
whom she has remained until the end of the late war". Affidavit
dated 16 February 1881, James Sullivant and James D. McBride
stated that "James and Polly Pledger suffered a great deal on
account of their well known Union principals, and were robbed
of most of their personal property by the Rebels". Affidavit
dated 15 March 1881, by Thomas Boles, Receiver of the United
States Land Office at Dardenelle, Yell County, "during the late
war, I raised a Company for the Union Army, was mustered into
the United States Army in the 3rd Regiment of Ark. Cav. Vols. and
was Captain of E Company. James D. McBride was a member of my
Company". In 1880, Polly Pledger removed the Family Record pages
from her Bible, to submit with her application, she stated that
the record is in the handwriting of her deceased husband, James
Pledger. She also stated at that time that her three oldest
children were dead. FAMILY RECORD: "James Pledger was bornd
January the 21st day 1788; Polly Ford was bornd December the
3 day 1795; we was married August the 4th day 1814; Isaac Pledger
was bornd the 17th day of June in the year of our Lord 1815
and was Baptised by Joseph Tarply; James Asbury Pledger was
bornd July the 7th day in the year of our Lord 1817, Baptised
by D__? P. Jones; Nancy Pledger was borned August the 22 day
1819 baptised by Joseph Tarply; Asa Pledger was bornd October
19 day 1821; Eliza Evaline Pledger was bornd December the 17th
day 1841 (sic); Thomas Henry Pledger was bornd August the 27
day in the year of our Lord 1824; Betsey D__? Pledger was bornd
October the 16 in the year of our Lord 1826; Martha Pledger
was bornd December the 22nd day in the year of our Lord 1828;
Melese Pledger was bornd January the 5th day in the year of
our Lord 1831; Simmeon Pledger was bornd February the 7 1833;

Mary Pledger deceased on the 28 August 1837; also Mary Pledger was bornd March the 9th day in the year of our Lord 1835 (this entry crossed out)". Asa Pledger stated that he was born in Elbert County, Georgia. (Possibly related; Thomas Pledger, War of 1812 pension application S.O.#25507, S.C.#15903, W.O.#40571, W.C.#31658. Widow Lucinda.)
Independence County, Arkansas Marriage Records; page 22, John Pledger and Sarah Hulsey, 12 July 1832.
1850 Federal Census, Gordon County, Georgia, page 52, family #592: James Pledger 60 S.C.; Mary 55 Geo.; Melissa 20 Geo.; Simeon 18 Geo.; Lucy A. 8 Geo.; Martha Chastain 22 Geo.; James Chastain 6 Geo.; Abner A. Chastain 6 Geo.; Mary F. Chastain 2 Geo.; family #593: James H. Pledger 30 Geo.; E.A. 28 Geo.; Mary 10 Geo.; Virgil 8 Geo.; Martha 6 Geo.; Melissa 4 Geo. family #594: Thomas H. Pledger 25 Geo.; Mary A. 22 Geo. Evaline 6 Geo.; Nancy 4 Geo.; Eliza 2 Geo.; Simon 1 Geo.

POE,MONROE G.-Mexican War Pension Application dated 1893, Arkansas. Service in Company E, 14th Regiment, U.S.Infantry. Mex.Sur.App. #24223, Cert.#20087, Mex.Wid.App.#15131, Cert.#11852. (not abstracted)

POOL,GEORGE W.-Mexican War Pension Application dated 1887, Arkansas. Service in Company E, Gray's Battalion, Arkansas Mounted Volunteers. Widow, Catherine. Mex.Wid.App.#5309, Cert.#5666. Remarks: Late War Wid.Orig. #299574, Company C, 1st Ark.Inf. George Pool, 2nd Lt. (not abstracted)

POOLE,OLIVER-Mexican War Pension Application dated 1887, Arkansas. Service in Captain Ford's Company, 3rd Regiment, U.S.Dragoons. Mex. Sur.App.#16249, Cert.#11294. (not abstracted)

POPLIN,MADISON L.-Old War pension application O.W. Wid. Cert. #1864, file #29658, O.W. Minors Cert. #1796, File #10909. Service in Arkansas Mounted Volunteers, Mexican War. Widow Elizabeth. (not abstracted)

PORTER,WILLIAM H.-Mexican War Pension Application. Mex.Sur.App.#5240, Cert.#3208, Mex.Wid.App.#18774, Cert.#14966, Cont.Wid.App.#18141. Widow, Martha E. Cont.Wid., Tabitha E. Remarks: See Mex.Cont.Wid. Orig.#18141 and Old War Wid. (not abstracted)

PORTIS,WILLIAM F.-Mexican War Pension Application, dated 1887, Arkansas. Served in Company K, 1st Regiment, Tennessee Volunteers. Mex.Sur.App.#5239, Cert.#7922. (not abstracted)

POULK,WILLIAM LANE-Mexican War Pension Application, dated 1887, Arkansas. Served as 1st Lieutenant in Company F, 1st Regiment, Louisana Volunteers. Mex.Sur.App.#9874, Cert.#4848. (not abstracted)

POWELL,FREDERICK C.-Mexican War Pension Application dated 1886, Arkansas. Widow, Martha J. Served in Company I, 13th Regiment, U.S.Infantry. Mex.Wid.App.#1718, Cert.#1069.(not abstracted)

PRATER,JOHN D.-Old War Pension Application dated 1884, Arkansas. He served in Captain Allen's Company, 1st Georgia Mounted Volunteers, in the Creek Indian War, 1836. O.W.Inv.App.#23011, Cert. #480160, File #48942, Ind.Wid.#5187, Mex.Sur.#17480. He was born 18 February 1811, at Kings Salt Works, Washington County, Virginia. He married Jane Harris in Upson County, Georgia on 3 February 1836. John Prater was injured when his horse kicked him in the knee, (Prater was a blacksmith) while on duty in the Chickahassee Swamp. This family had lived in Magnolia, Columbia County, Arkansas, "30 years or more" in 1886. In his application for pension, he submitted affidavits from; Osburn Turner, who stated that he had been with the same regiment that John Prater had been with, and that he (Turner) had served as servant to General Turner; Sam Jefferson and Eli Trammell, who stated that they had been close friends and neighbors to the Praters in Georgia and Arkansas; Green Hancock, who stated that he had been close friends "all of my life" and from Nancy Pace, who stated that she had attended the wedding of John and Jane Prater. This pension was granted by special Congressional Act dated 21 April 1890. John Prater died in Columbia County on 19 September 1897.

PREWITT,FRANCIS M.-Mexican War Pension Application dated 1889, Arkansas. Served in Captain Arnold's Company, 1st Regiment, Texas Riflemen. Mex.Sur.App.#22253, Cert.#18842. (not abstracted)

PRIDE,BURTON-Revolutionary War Pension Application #W10930. B.L.W. #43521-160-55. He was born in 1758 in Pennsylvania, and moved to Orange County, North Carolina when he was five years old. He enlisted in 1776 in Caswell County, North Carolina in Captain Hendley's Company, Colonel Habersham's Regiment of Georgia Militia for a 12 month tour of duty. He served a six month duty in Colonel Locke's North Carolina Regiment in 1778. He married, 5 October 1820, in Madison County, Alabama to Elizabeth Millwee, nee Houston, widow of John Millwee. Burton Pride died on 25 May 1835, and his widow moved to Sevier County, Arkansas, where she applied for pension 27 January 1855, at age 67. Henry C. Pride was witness to her signature, relationship not stated. Elizabeth Pride stated that she had no family records, as her Bible had gotten wet in the White River, on the move from Alabama to Arkansas, destroying the records.

PRIDE,HENRY C.-Mexican War Pension Application dated 1887, Arkansas. Mex.Sur.App.#9892, Cert.#3838, Mex.Wid.App.#16640, Cert.#13253. He enlisted at Washington, Arkansas, in June 1846, in Captain Edward Hunter's Company, Colonel Archibald Yell's 1st Regiment, Arkansas Cavalry. He was discharged in June 1847 in Camargo, Mexico. He was married to Harriett Locke, who died 19 July 1857, and was buried "in the Millwee Cemetery, near Walnut Springs, laid to rest in the grove." Henry Pride and Mary E. Smith were married, 13 June 1858, in Sevier County, Arkansas. She was born 24 December 1834 in Bedford County, Tennessee. Henry C. Pride died on 12 April 1902.
1850 Federal Census, Sevier County, Arkansas, Clear Creek Township, page 197, family #156: John Milwee 30 S.C.; Elizabeth Pride 63 S.C.; Savina Halhooks 18 Ark.; Golden Hopper 35 unknown.; Jefferson Township, page 206, family #279: Isaac N. Jackson 34 Mo.; Elizabeth 18 Ala.; Laura 1 Ark.; Henry C. Pride 27 Ala.; Harriett 18 Ala.; James Barnett 14 Ala.

PROCTOR,JAMES S.-Mexican War Pension Application dated 1887, Arkansas. Served in Captain Henry's Company of North Carolina Volunteers. Widow, Susan M. Mex.Wid.App.#3286, Cert.#4057. (not abstracted)

PUCKETT,THOMAS-Old war pension application O.W. Wid. App. #17237, O.W. Wid. Cert. #1569, file #28447, O.W. Minors Cert. #1570, File #7355. He served in Captain George Patrick's Company, 1st Regiment of Arkansas Mounted Volunteers. Surgeon's certificate enclosed, states that Thomas Puckett died of remittent fever on 9 May 1847, while on duty in Mexico. Widow, Ann Toliver, applied for pension on 5 December 1849, Franklin County, Arkansas. She stated that she had married Thomas Puckett on 11 October 1836. They had five children, to wit; Edward F. Puckett, John W. Puckett, Calvin S. Puckett, Hester Ann Puckett and Thomas Puckett; all under age at the time of Thomas Puckett's death. She married John H. Toliver on 30 August 1849. On 16 July 1850 the Franklin County Probate Court appointed Dotsen Belt, guardian of the five minor children.

PULLEY,DANIEL–Mexican War Pension Application dated 1887, Arkansas. He served in Company B, 1st Regiment, Illinois Infantry. Mex.Sur. App.#9907, Cert.#4151. (not abstracted)

PUTMAN,DANIEL–Revolutionary War Pension Application #W26751, dated 21 March 1845, Washington County, Arkansas. He entered service in Colonel Thomas Brandon's South Carolina Militia about the time of the Siege of Ninety-Six. Prudence stated that she and Daniel Putman were married by Publication on 5 January 1786, and that Daniel died 19 July 1816. She then married Landon Key who died 24 August 1821. Affidavit dated 21 March 1845, by Ralph Skelton, age 58 of Washington County, Arkansas, contains this narrative, "about the year 1793, my father, William Skelton, who lived in the State of Georgia, not many miles from the Savanna River, sold a certain mare to Daniel Putman, who lived in South Carolina and near the River aforesaid. My father went in the close of summer to deliver said mare to Daniel Putman at the river. This affiant went home with said Daniel Putman, being a relative, and stayed all night. The colt being just taken from the mare caused the mare to create much ado and squealing, which rendered this affiant very unhappy" The Bible Record of Daniel and Prudence Putman is included in this application, to wit; "A list of the Burth (sic) of our Children and ourselves; Daniel Putman was born January 1, 1764, Prudence Putman was born April the 16th day 1770, Hazeal Putman was born May the 7th day 1787, Lavinia Putman was born November the 7th day 1789, Reading Putman was born April the 20th day 1792, Elijah Putman was born May the 18th day 1794, William Putman was born March the 15th day 1796, Thomas Putman was born July the 30th day 1798, Ezekiel Putman was born January the 13th day 1805 and died at the age of fourteen months"

PUTMAN,DANIEL–Mexican War Pension Application dated 1887, Arkansas. Served in Engart's Company, Arkansas Mounted Volunteers. Widow, Rachel E. Mex.Wid.App.#1734, Cert.#206. (not abstracted)

PUTMAN,JEHU–War of 1812 Pension Application S.O.#5253, S.C.#3374. B.L.W.#29304-80-50 and #19940-80-55. He served in Captain Alexander Morehead's Company of South Carolina Militia. (not abstracted)

PUTMAN,REDING–This application is listed in the War of 1812 index. O.W.Wid.App.Rej.#17241, O.W.Sur.Cert.#1819, O.W.Sur.File #25375, W.O.#41974. The 3rd auditor's report shows that he served from 18 September 1811 to 19 November 1811 in Captain William Hargrove's Company of Indiana Militia. His widow stated that he also served at the Battle of Tippecanoe in the War of 1812. He was wounded on 14 May 1832, while serving as Sergeant in Captain David Barnes' Company, Major Isaiah Stillman's Battalion of Illinois Militia during the Black Hawk War. They were engaged in the Battle of Sycamore Creek with the Sac and Fox Indians, when he was struck by a musket ball, which shattered his left arm and lodged in the left breast. He applied for pension on 19 June 1834 in Fulton County, Illinois. He applied to have his pension transferred to Fayetteville, Washington County, Arkansas on 25 October 1837, stating that his reasons for the move were,"1st, he believed his family would be healthier in Arkansas, 2nd, the length of winters in Illinois were uncomfortable and unfriendly to man and beast, 3rd, the shortness of summers in Illinois and uncertainty of the crops." Reding Putman had been married to Stacy __? in 1812, who died in 1827. He was married to Phoebe Stelle, (this name also spelled Still and Steel) in Fulton County, Illinois on 2 March 1829. She had been married to Alexander Stelle in 1813, and he died in 1826.In 1834, he stated that his family consisted of himself, his wife and 12 children. He died near Fayetteville, Washington County on 9 September 1865, "in the 74th year of his life." Phoebe Putman applied for pension on 15 April 1867, in Washington County,

at which time she stated that their home had been robbed in November 1864, by Confederate Soldiers, and the pension certificate had been destroyed by the plunderers. This file contains affidavits from Dr.Reding Putman, son of Reding Putman, and from John Rizley, who had been friends with them in Illinois and had moved to Arkansas with them. Affidavit from Irena Thomas, who had been friends with Phoebe Putman and her first husband Alexander Stelle, in Preble County, Ohio in 1826. Searing Stelle, who was with Phoebe and Alexander Stelle in Ohio. John Pearson, who stated that he had been close friends with Reding Putman and his first wife, Stacy in Fulton County, Illinois in 1829.
1850 Federal Census, Washington County, Arkansas, West Fork Township, page 380, family #83: D.L.Putman 32 Ill.; Rachel 31 Tenn.; Francis 7 Ark.; Rebecca 4 Ark.; William 1 Ark. Prairie Township, page 385, family #50: Redding Putman 58 S.C.; Phoebe 62 N.C.; Redding 20 Ill. page 400, family #245: William Putman 50 S.C.; Alley 48 Ky.; Solomon 20 Ill.; George 14 Ill.; Joseph 12 Ill.; Prudence 9 Ark.

QUERTERMANS,DAVID P.-Old War Pension Application dated 1872, Arkansas. Served in Company C, 1st Regiment of Kentucky Volunteers, Mexican War. O.W.Inv.App.#R77256. (not abstracted no pension granted)

QUINTAN,SAMUEL-Revolutionary War Pension Application #S32461, dated 13 August 1847, Polk County, Arkansas, Samuel Quintan Senior, "resided in what is now Union District, South Carolina, at the time of the Revolutionary War". He enlisted in Captain John Mapp's Company of Colonel Fair's Regiment of South Carolina Militia, served at the Battle of the Enoree, near Musgrove's Mill and at the Battle of King's Mountain. In 1848, he was age 86, and stated that he had remained in Union District, South Carolina for some years after the war, and had then moved to Rutherford County, North Carolina for about two years. He had lived in Cass and Cobb Counties, Georgia before moving to Arkansas circa 1838. He had lived in Benton County, Arkansas before moving to Polk County. He was "keeping house" for himself and his aged wife in 1848.
1850 Federal Census, Polk County, Arkansas, page 237, family #159: James Quinton 45 S.C.; Nancy 26 Tenn.; Mary A. Tucker 24 Geo.; Thomas Quinton 16 Geo.; Nathaniel 14 Geo.; William 9 Ark.; Henry 7 Ark. Samuel 5 Ark.; Jackson Louther 21 Ind. page 237, family #160: Samuel Quinton 88 S.C.; Jane 69 S.C.; Lurena Tucker 2 Ark.; family #161: William Quinton 43 43 S.C.; Eliza 40 Geo.; Joel 18 Geo.; Elizabeth 16 Geo.; Hester A. 14 Geo.; James 12 Ark.; Nancy 10 Ark.; Samuel 8 Ark.; Eda 6 Ark.; John 3 Ark.; Samuel 23 Geo. family #163: David Quinton 20 Geo.; Albany 28 N.C.; Mary 32 Tenn.; John 15 Geo.; Family #164: Jane Quinton 33 Tenn.; Joel 13 Ark.; Hardin 10 Ark.; Lucinda 2 Ark.; Nathaniel Quinton 33 S.C.; Minerva 29 Geo.; Rachel 10 Ark.; Henry 8 Ark.; James 5 Texas; Elizabeth 2 Tex. family #167: Samuel Quinton 47 N.C.; Lydia 40 Geo.; William Newberg 45 Tenn.; William Woods 3 Ark.

RACE,WILLIAM H-Old War pension application. Service in 2nd Regiment, Army Artillery. Widow, Mary L.A. Old War Inv. Cert.#44759, Widow's Cert.#26538. (not abstracted)

RAGAN,ISAAC A.-Mexican War Pension Application, dated 1881, Arkansas. Served in Company A, 4th Regiment, Tennessee Volunteers. Mex.Sur.App.#5338, Cert.#8886. (not abstracted)

RAGSDALE,HEZAKIAH-Mexican War Pension Application, dated 1887, Arkansas. He served in Comapny A, 1st Regiment, Tennessee Volunteers. Mex.Sur.App.#15334, Cert.#3212. Remarks: Civil War Inv.Cert. #359106, Widow's Cert.#401352; Service in Companies A and F, 1st Regiment, Indiana Cavalry. (not abstracted)

RAINEY/RANEY,JOHN-Revolutionary War Pension Application #S32462. He was born 6 March 1757 in "Jersey State". He was residing in Surry County, North Carolina when he joined Obial Cobb's Company against the Cherokee Indians. He moved to Guilford County, North Carolina, where he enlisted in Captain Moasbey's Company. They were marched to Camden County, South Carolina, where they joined Colonel Sumpter on the Wateree River and were at General Gate's defeat. He served in a Company of Light Horse under command of Captain James Robertson in Colonel John Luttrell's Brigade. He served as a Ranger for two months, during which time they were defeated at the Trading Ford on the Yadkin River. After the war he lived in Hawkins, Overton and White Counties, Tennessee. On 11 June 1845, John Raney applied to have his pension transferred to Independence County, Arkansas, where he had moved "to be with and near his relatives and children, who reside in the State of Arkansas in the County aforesaid".

RAMAY,JONATHAN-Mexican War Pension Application, dated 1887, Arkansas. Served in Company B, 1st Kentucky Mounted Rifles. O.W.Inv.App.#R20966, Mex.Sur.App.#5347, Cert#3212. Special Act Pension. (not abstracted)

RAMSEY,ALLINSON-Old War Pension Application, dated 1883, Arkansas. Served in Campbell's Alabama Infantry, Florida War. O.W.Inv.App. #R23701, Ind.War Sur.#4474. (not abstracted)

RAMSEY,ISAAC-Mexican War Pension Application dated 1887, Arkansas. Served as Corporal in Company B, Arkansas Mounted Volunteers. Mex.-Sur.App.#9921, Cert.#4479, Mex.Wid.App.#11581, Cert.#9620. (not abstracted)

RAMSEY,JOHN-War of 1812 Pension Application, W.O.#21707, W.C. #18083. Service in Captain James Love's Company, Kentucky Militia. The Bounty Land applications and the original discharge certificate are not in this file, though there are references to both. John Ramsey and Rachel Sneed were married in Lawrence County, Arkansas on 19 September 1820, by Reverend George Gill. Interior Department records show that John Ramsey received B.L.Warrant #27914, but not where he applied. He died in Carroll County, Arkansas on 23 March 1856. Rachel Ramsey applied for pension 30 April 1878, from Carroll County, with affidavits from W.R.Sneed and Thomas W. Fancher, both of Osage, Carroll County.

RANTON,WILLIAM JOHN-Mexican War Pension Application dated 1888, Arkansas. Served in Captain Goulding's Company, Calhoun's Battalion, Georgia Mounted Volunteers. Widow, Keziah. Mex.Wid.App.#6854, Cert.#5462. (not abstracted)

RAPER,JOHN L.,alias John L.Lewis-Mexican War Pension Application dated 1887, Arkansas. Served in Company B, 3rd Regiment, Indiana Volunteers. Widow, Louisa J.Lewis. Mex.Sur.App.#24300, Cert.#20485, Mex.Wid.App.#16681, Cert.#14820. (not abstracted)

RATLIFF,ZACHEOUS-Mexican War Pension Application dated 1887, Arkansas. Served in Captain Ficklin's Company, Arkansas Volunteers. Mex.Sur.App.#9936, Cert.#14678. (not abstracted)

RAWLINGS,LEWIS J.-Mexican War Pension Application dated 1887, Arkansas. Service in Captain Newman's Company, 1st Regiment Tennessee Volunteers. Mex.Sur.App.#9942, Cert.#4478, Mex.Wid.App. #13865, Cert.#11345. (not abstracted)

RAY,JACOB-Old war pension application O.W. Wid. Cert. #1064, file #29680, O.W. Minors Cert. #4565, file #11109. Service in Arkansas Mounted Volunteers, Mexican War. Widow Abigail. (not abstracted)

RAY,JAMES-Mexican War Pension Application dated 1887, Arkansas. Served in Captain Thomas' Company, 5th Regiment, Tennessee Volunteers. Widow, Lucy. Mex.Sur.App.#15559, Cert.#11048, Mex.Wid.App.-#9817, Cert.#7462. (not abstracted)

RAY,WILLIAM-Mexican War Pension Application dated 1887, Arkansas. Served in Captain Preston's Company, Yell's Regiment, Arkansas Mounted Volunteers. Widow, Emeline. Mex.Wid.App.#5458, Cert.#3239. (not abstracted)

REA,JOSEPH-War of 1812 pension application W.O.#5954, W.C.#3806. Service in Captain John Quarles Company of Tennessee Militia. He was at the Battle of Horseshoe with the Creek Indians. Joseph Rea married Sarah Robertson, 24 November 1814, in Giles County, Tennessee. He died 6 May 1855 in Searcy County, Arkansas. Sarah Rea applied for pension 14 July 1871 in Richland Township, Searcy County, Arkansas, she was age 75. (not abstracted)

REDWINE,DANIEL-War of 1812 pension application S.O.#23930, S.C.-#15151. He volunteered into service in February 1814 at Salisbury, North Carolina. He served in Captain John Garrettson's Company of North Carolina Militia at the Battle of Horseshoe with the Creek Indians, and was stationed at Fort Jackson, Alabama. He married Nancy Handcock 14 November 1813 in Montgomery County, North Carolina. Soldier's application for pension dated 26 August 1871, Wiles Cove, Searcy County, Arkansas, Daniel Redwine age 78.

REED,DAVID-Mexican War Pension Application dated 1887, Arkansas. Served in Company I, 3rd Regiment, Missouri Mounted Volunteers. Mex.Sur.App.#5392, Cert.#2698. Special Act Pension. (not abstracted)

REED,JAMES-Mexican War Pension Application dated 1887, Arkansas. Served in 3rd Regiment of Illinois Infantry. Widow, Louisa Frances. Mex.Wid.App.#1767, Cert.#1671. Remarks: XC2646888, late war W.O.#505700, Co.F, 60th Ill.Inf. (not abstracted)

REED,JOHN G.-Mexican War Pension Application. Service in Company A, 4th Regiment, Tennessee Infantry. Widow, Mary J. Mex.Sur.App. #12697, Cert.#8543, Mex.Wid.App.#18751, Cert.#15116. (not abstracted)

REEDER,BLUFORD-Mexican War Pension Application dated 1887, Arkansas. Service in Captain John Fitch's Company D, Gray's Battalion, Arkansas Volunteers. B.L.W.#14196-160-47. Mex.Sur.App.#12229, Cert.#4936. Soldier died 1 December 1897. (not abstracted)

REEDER,MICAJAH-Revolutionary War Pension Application #R8678, dated 13 December 1833, Washington County, Territory of Arkansas. He was born in Loudon County, Virginia in 1758. He was residing in Newberry County, South Carolina when he entered service under command of Captain Jeremy Williams. His application for pension was rejected because of length of service. He moved from Newberry County, South Carolina to Livingston County, Kentucky, and from there to Clark County, Territory of Arkansas and finally to Washington County.

REEDER,THOMAS A.-Old War Pension Application, dated 1853, Arkansas. He served as 1st Lieutenant in the Arkansas Mounted Volunteers. O.W.Inv.Cert.#7769, File #25388. (not abstracted)

REESE,BENJAMIN-Mexican War Pension Application dated 1887, Arkansas. Service in Company A, 3rd Regiment, Illinois Volunteers in the Mexican War, Company E, 11th Regiment, Illinois Infantry and Company H, 8th Regiment, Illinois Infantry in the Civil War. B.L.W. #9481-160-47. Mex.Sur.App.#15004, Cert.#11447, Mex.Wid.App.#12462, Cert.#10634. Remarks: Army I.O.#574269, L.W.C. 187342 ca 169138. Soldier died 6 November 1894. (not abstracted)

REESE,GEORGE W.-Mexican War Pension Application dated 1887, Arkansas. Served in Captain Buchanan's Company, 1st Regiment, Tennessee Volunteers. Mex.Sur.App.#11981, Cert.#6155. (not abstracted)

REEVE,CHARLES-Mexican War Pension Application dated 1887, Arkansas. Served on U.S.S.Dale. Widow, Mary E. Mex.Sur,App.#9953, Cert.#4733, Mex.Wid.App.#6341, Cert.#5369. (not abstracted)

REEVES,DAVID-War of 1812 pension application W.O.#36497, W.C.#27206. He was born in Guilford County, North Carolina circa 1786. He was drafted 25 December 1812 into Captain David E. Trigg's Company, Colonel Patrick Jack's Regiment of 8th U.S. Infantry. He married first Frances Hodgon, who died 10 August 1852. He then married Lucy Ann Johnson, 19 March 1854, in Columbia County, Arkansas. She was the widow of Jonathan Johnson, who died 16 September 1845, in Graves County, Kentucky.

REEVES,JEREMIAH-War of 1812 pension application W.O.#41338, W.C.#32234. He was born in Virginia circa 1796, and was residing in Wilson County, Tennessee when he was drafted into service in October or November 1814. He served in Captain Black's Company of Tennessee Militia. He married Elizabeth Handy in Smith County, Tennessee on 9 November 1820. She was the widow of Isham Handy, who had died in 1815. Jeremiah Reeves died in Madison County, Arkansas on 28 March 1861. Elizabeth Reeves applied for pension in Madison County on 4 June 1881. She stated that they had lived in Wilson County, Tennessee from 1815 to 1827, in Cannon County, Tennessee from 1827 to 1850 and had moved to Madison County, Arkansas in 1850. Elizabeth Reeves died 18 January 1884 in Drake's Creek, Madison County, Arkansas, at the home of her son-in-law, James Powell. Her attending physician was her grandson, Dr. G.N. Powell.

REEVES,SAMUEL-Mexican War Pension Application dated 1888, Arkansas. Service in Company G, 2nd Regiment, Illinois Infantry. Widow, Eliza. Mex.Wid.App.#6763, Cert.#5204. (not abstracted)

REID,JOHN-Revolutionary War Pension Application #W26946, dated 8 May 1844, Fayette County, Tennessee, Keziah Reid age 76. This application contains several letters addressed to John Reid, Caswell County, North Carolina "to be left at the Guilford County Court House" containing reports of Congressional Actions and fears of upcoming trouble with Indians. A must for descendents of this man. In her pension application Keziah Reid stated that John Reid had been residing in Washington County, Virginia, "on the waters of the Holston River" when he had enlisted into service. He served as Adjutant in Colonel John Montgomery's Regiment, known as the "Illinois Regiment", and later was appointed Quartermaster of the Regiment. He served as aide to Colonel Campbell at King's Mountain and was at the Battle of Guilford Court House. This application contains a petition from John Reid to the Virginia General Assembly for benefits of his service. He had neglected to have his name placed on the muster rolls and had never received payment for his service. John and Keziah Reid were married in Caswell County, 22 March 1784. He died 23 June 1826 in Fayette County, Tennessee. She moved to Tulip, Dallas County, Arkansas about 1846, and was residing with her daughter, Mrs. Clarissa Smith. Keziah Reid died 9 August 1858 leaving two children, and eight grandchildren, by a deceased son.

REMSHARD/RENSHAW,GEORGE-Mexican War Pension Application dated 1892, Arkansas. Served as Corporal in Company K, 3rd Regiment, U.S.Artillery. Mex.Sur.App.#24086, Cert.#20008, Mex.Wid.App.#18930, Cert.#15442. (not abstracted)

RENFRO,CARROLL-Old War Pension Application, special act dated 1890, Arkansas. O.W.Inv.Cert.#524393, file #49049, Ind.Wid.App. #10490, Ind.Wid.Cert.#7626. Served in Alabama Volunteers, Creek Indian War. (not abstracted)

RENFRO,WILLIAM P.-Old War Pension Application, special act. Served in Alabama Volunteers, Creek Indian War. Widow Nancy. O.W.Wid.Cert. #7906, file #29873. (not abstracted)

RENFROE/RENFROW,GEORGE WASHINGTON-War of 1812 pension application W.O.#10387, W.C.#10437. Service in Captain George Butler's Company, 18th Regiment of U.S. Infantry and in Captain Drayton's Company, 60th Regiment of U.S. Infantry. He enlisted in August 1812 in Union District, South Carolina and was stationed at Sullivan's Island, near Charleston, South Carolina. He married Mary Barron 17 March 1813 in Union District, South Carolina. They had a son, named James, born 3 February 1814, who died in March 1816. Their son Jesse Renfroe was born 27 October 1816 in Union District, South Carolina. George W. Renfroe died in Crawford County, Arkansas on 7 March 1864. His widow, Mary, applied for pension on 30 August 1873, her age 76, and she was a resident of Narrows, Crawford County, Arkansas.

REYNOLDS,ROBERT-Mexican War Pension Application dated 1897, Arkansas.Service in Company F, 1st Regiment, Alabama Volunteers. Mex.Sur.App.#5440, Cert.#12619, Mex.Wid.App.#14216, Cert.#11184. (not abstracted)

REYNOLDS,THOMAS-Mexican War Pension Application dated 1890, Arkansas. Served as 2nd Lieutenant, Company G, 4th Regiment, Indiana Volunteers. Mex.Sur.App.#5445, Cert.#9552, Mex.Wid.App. #9387, Cert.#7641. (not abstracted)

RHODES,JOHN G-Mexican War Pension Application dated 1887, Arkansas. Service in Company K, 1st Regiment, Georgia Volunteers. Mex.Sur.App. #14130, Cert.#10363, Mex.Wid.App.#15125, Cert.#12269. (not abstracted)

RHYNE,JOHN-Mexican War Pension Application dated 1894, Arkansas. Served in Company I, 2nd Regiment, Mississippi Volunteer Infantry. Mex.Sur.App.#5457, Cert.#2386, Mex.Wid.App.#13286, Cert.#9422. (not abstracted)

RICHARDS,REUBEN C.-Mexican War Pension Application dated 1888, Arkansas. Served as blacksmith, QM Dept. U.S.A. Widow, Martha. Mex.Wid.App.#6444, no Cert.#. (not abstracted)

RICHARDS,WILLIAM-Mexican War Pension Application dated 1887, Arkansas. Served in United States Mounted Riflemen. Widow, H.T.C. Mex.Wid.App.#1798. Remarks: Dup.Mex.Wid.O.#9882. (not abstracted)

RICHARDSON,HARVEY P.-Mexican War Pension Application dated 1888, Arkansas. Served in Company D, 1st Regiment, Tennessee Volunteers. Mex.Wid.App.#7078, Cert.#6420. (not abstracted)

RICHARDSON,JAMES-Mexican War Pension Application dated 1887, Arkansas. Service in Company K, 3rd Regiment, Kentucky Volunteers. Widow, Mary Ann. Mex.Wid.App.#1803, Cert.#1639. Remarks: O.W.Wid. Pending. (not abstracted)

RICHARDSON,R.V.-Mexican War Pension Application dated 1887, Arkansas. Served as Insp. General, Tennessee. Widow, Mary. Mex. Wid.App.#1804, no cert.# (not abstracted)

RICHEY,WILLIAM B.-Mexican War Pension Application dated 1889, Arkansas. Service in Company D, 1st Regiment, Kentucky Mounted Volunteers. Mex.Wid.App.#8307, Cert.#7834. (not abstracted)

RIDGEWAY,JAMES C.-Mexican War Pension Application dated 1891, Arkansas. Served as Corporal in Company C, 1st Regiment, Alabama Volunteers. Widow, Catherine. Mex.Wid.App.#9991, Cert.#8230. (not abstracted)

RIDGEWAY,HORATIO G.-Mexican War Pension Application dated 1889, Arkansas. Service in Company F, 13th Regiment, U.S.Infantry. Mex. Sur.App.#21533, Cert.#18212. (not abstracted)

RIEFF,AMERICUS V.-Mexican War Pension Application. Served in Engart's Company of Arkansas Mounted Volunteers. Widow, Mary. Mex.Sur.App.#24005, Cert.#19956, Mex.Wid.App.#20219, Cert.#16026. (not abstracted)

RIEFF,JOHN H.-Mexican War Pension Application dated 1887, Arkansas. Served in Engart's Arkansas Mounted Volunteers. Mex.Sur.App.#5520, Cert.#13270. (not abstracted)

RIGGS,CYRUS-Mexican War Pension Application dated 1887, Arkansas. Served in Captain Patrick's Company, 1st Regiment, Arkansas Cavalry. Mex.Sur.App.#5524, Cert.#2957. Remarks: Reb.Inv.Cert.-#703408, Co.G, 2nd Ark.Vols.

RIGGS,REUBEN-Old War Pension Application, special act, 1897, Arkansas. Served in the Alabama Mounted Volunteers. O.W.Cert. #808355, file #49164. (not abstracted)

RITCHEY,PETER-Revolutionary War Pension Application #S32478, dated 6 October 1832, Jackson County, Tennessee. He was born about the year 1760 in Mecklinburg County, North Carolina. He volunteered into service in Captain John Berringer's Company, General Rutherford's Regiment, and stated that he had served as a spy at Ninety-Six. He served a tour of duty against the Cherokee Indians in Captain John Fifer's Company. He was under command of Captain Beavers at General Gates' defeat. His home was burned by Tories, and his Family Bible was destroyed. After the war he moved to Washington County, Virginia, and from there he moved to Jackson County, Tennessee. On 10 June 1839, he applied to have his pension transferred to the Arkansas agency, as he had moved to Sevier County, Arkansas "because his son, James Ritchie, with whom he resides, made the move to Arkansas, and the father being old and infirm, accompanied him".

RIVERCOMB,GEORGE-Mexican War Pension Application dated 1887, Arkansas. Served in Company B, 1st Regiment, Mississippi Rifles. Widow, Mary J. Mex.Wid.App.#1817, Cert.#1629. (not abstracted)

ROACH,WILLIAM D.-Mexican War Pension Application dated 1893, Arkansas. Service in Company G, 1st Regiment, Tennessee Volunteers. Mex.Sur.App.#8901, Mex.Wid.App.#11283, Cert.#8531. (not abstracted)

ROANE,EWING H.-Mexican War Pension Application dated 1887, Arkansas. Served as Major and Surgeon. Widow, Elizabeth. Mex.Wid.App.#5, Cert.#5. (not abstracted)

ROANE,JOHN SELDON-Mexican War Pension Application dated 1887, Arkansas. Service as Captain and as Colonel of Arkansas Mounted Volunteers. Widow's App.#6, Cert.#4. (not abstracted)

ROBERSON,JAMES-War of 1812 pension application S.O.#29480, S.C.#21312, W.O.#43072, W.C.#33574. He was born ca 1796 in Virginia. Enlisted into service in Captain James Fisher's Company of Virginia Militia, in Brunswick County, Virginia on 31 July 1814. He was stationed at Fort Powhatan until his discharge on 10 February 1815. He was residing in Three Forks, Union County, Arkansas about 1843. His first wife, Betsy M. King died in Union County in 1866. He married Mary Coleman 3 August 1866. She was the

widow of Robert Coleman, whom she had married 23 December 1854. He
had died 27 May 1859. James Roberson died in Union County, Arkansas
on 29 July 1883. His widow applied for pension 31 August 1883,
her age 52.

ROBERTS,ANDREW J.-Mexican War Pension Application. Service in
Captain McGee's Company, Alabama Volunteers. Mex.Sur.App.#5535,
Mex.Wid.App.#10135, Cert.#9408. (not abstracted)

ROBERTS,JAMES-Mexican War Pension Application dated 1890, Arkansas.
Served in Captain Foulk's Company, 3rd Regiment, Tennessee Volunteers. Widow, Irene. Appl.#9269, no Cert.#. (not abstracted)

ROBINSON,DAVID-Mexican War Pension Application dated 1887, Arkansas.
Served in Company E, Gray's Battalion, Arkansas Volunteers. Widow,
Lavinia J. Mex.Sur.App.#15814, Cert.#11170, Mex.Wid.App.#15104,
Cert.#13139. (not abstracted)

ROBINSON,JAMES-Mexican War Pension Application dated 1887, Arkansas.
Served in Company A, 3rd Regiment, U.S.Dragoons. Mex.Sur.App.#16251,
Cert.#11319, Mex.Wid.App.#16829. (not abstracted)

ROBINSON,JOHN-Revolutionary War Pension Application #S32492,
dated 14 January 1833, Jackson County, Territory of Arkansas. He
was born in Pennsylvania on 8 December 1755. He was residing
in Cumberland County, Pennsylvania, when he entered service
in 1774. He enlisted in a company of Militia under command of
his father, Captain George Robinson. In 1776, he served in Captain
Thomas Clark's Company, Colonel Frederick Watt's Regiment. He
remained in Pennsylvania until 1783, when he moved to Kentucky,
where he remained about twenty years. He lived in Illinois for
awhile and then in 1811 he moved to New Madrid, Territory of
Missouri. He was a victim of the New Madrid earthquake in the
year 1811. After that he moved back to Illinois, then to Tennessee,
where he remained until 1832, when he moved to the Territory
of Arkansas. Affidavits given by James Robinson and William
Robinson, relationship not shown.

ROBINSON,JOHN R.-Mexican War Pension Application dated 1887,
Arkansas. Application rejected, no certificate granted. Alleged
service in Captain Walker's Company of Illinois Volunteers. Widow,
Sarah J. Mex.Wid.App.#4155.

ROBINSON,WILLIAM-War of 1812 pension application W.O.#34025,
W.C.#24240. He was born circa 1792, in Grainger County, Tennessee. He
entered service 13 November 1814 in Grainger County, in Captain
Joseph Rich's Company of Tennessee Militia. His first wife,
not identified, died about 1845 and his second wife, also not
identified, died in February 1849. He lived in Grainger County
until 1833, when he moved to Madison County, Territory of Arkansas.
He married Nancy Carter in Madison County, on 24 May 1849. She
was the widow of George Carter, who died in 1847. William Robinson
died in Madison County, Arkansas on 21 March 1863. Nancy Robinson
applied for pension on 9 November 1878, she was age 68, and
a resident of Madison County. Affidavits by Miles E. Robinson,
age 62, and Stokley D. Robinson, age 70, in 1878.

ROBISON/ROBINSON,JOHN-Revolutionary War Pension Application
#W24798. Soldiers application dated 23 September 1833, McNairy
County, Tennessee. He entered service in 1780 in Mecklinburg
County, North Carolina in Captain Alexander's Company of North
Carolina Militia. In 1781 he served in Colonel Wade Hampton's
Regiment of Mounted Dragoons. They were marched into South Carolina,
taking Tory Prisoners on the Congoree and Edest Rivers, and
capturing enemy boats on the Cooper River. When General Sumpter
was wounded, John Robison, was assigned as guard to accompany
him to his family in Charlottesville. John Robison was discharged

at Buck's Island. He remained in Mecklinburg County, North Carolina until 1802, when he moved to McNairy County, Tennessee. In the Fall of 1836, he moved with his son, John B. Robinson to Benton County, Arkansas, where he died 7 September 1842. His widow, Abigail Robinson, applied for pension 4 December 1844, Benton County, Arkansas, submitting the Family Bible Record," John Robison born 7th day of March 1759; Abigail Moore born 30th October 1766(?); John and Abigail Robison was married 3rd day of February 1784 by the Reverend Thomas McCall (compiler's note, they were married by publication in the Church in North Carolina); Jane H. Robison born May 16, 1787; Moses M. Robison born 20th January 1789; Mary S. Robison born December 17th 1791; Robert A. Robison born January 13th 1794; Margaret Robison born 11th December 1796; Harriet A. Robison born 11th January 1799; John B. Robison born 15th September 1801; Adeline A. Robison born 22nd February 1804; Mary S. Robison born 28 February 1806; James A. Robison born September 5th 1808; William Robison born July 17th 1812."

Benton County, Arkansas, Will Book A, page 63 thru 66. "I, John Robinson, of the County of Benton, State of Arkansas; I have heretofore advanced to my beloved sons as much as my situation would justify, therefore, I now bequeath to each of them, Moses Moore Robinson, Robert Anzi Robinson, John Brown Robinson and James Asbert Robinson, one dollar each. To my beloved wife, Abigail Robinson, I bequeath the house in which we live. After the death of my wife, all of the property which she may die possessed of shall be equally divided among my beloved daughters, to wit; Jane M. Morrison, Margaret McKissick, Ann Harriett Lowe, Adeline Patton, and Polly Scott Dickson. I hereby nominate my friend James McKissick, my son-in-law, William Washington Dickson and my grandson John Robert Morrison, executors of this will". Signed 16 June 1840, recorded 31 December 1842.

ROBISON,LEGRAND S.-Mexican War Pension Application dated 1887, Arkansas. Served in Captain Tipton's Company, 1st Regiment, North Carolina Volunteers. Widow, L.B. Mex.Sur.App.#11998, Cert.#10120, Mex.Wid.App.#11734. (not abstracted)

ROBISON,WILLIAM-Old War pension application O.W.Wid.Cert.#4711, file#24815. Service in Arkansas Cavalry, Mexican War. Widow, Lively H. (not abstracted)

ROGERS,JOHN-War of 1812 pension application S.O.#10766, S.C.#6714, W.O.#12221, W.C.#23567. He enlisted into service in Captain Nehemiah Garrison's Company of Georgia Militia, at Fort Hawkins in November 1814, served in the Creek Indian War and was discharged at Fort Hawkins in April 1815. He stated that he served as a substitute for Abraham Pettijohn. He married Amy G. Adams 18 July 1817, in Jackson County, Georgia. He applied for bounty land in 1854 in Crawford County, Arkansas, where he was still residing in 1871, when he applied for pension. He stated at that time that he had three sons who served in the Union Army during the Civil War. John Rogers died in Crawford County, Arkansas on 17 November 1875, his widow applied for pension there on 3 March 1877. Amy Rogers submitted the family record, which she stated was written by her husband in the year 1851, to wit, "MARRIAGES; John Rogers and Amy G. Adams was married July the 18, 1814 Jackson County, State of Georgia by William Montgomery; BIRTHS: John Rogers was born December 16th 1796; Amy G. Adams was born June 13th 1799; Nancy M. Rogers was born August 25th 1816; Enoch S. Rogers was born September 10th 1822; Jane C. Rogers was born September the 22nd 1819; Green W. Rogers was born July 2nd 1826; Lovesey A. Rogers was born August 16th 1829; Lucinda E.Rogers was born December the 30th 1824; Martha E. Rogers was born December the 18, 1831; William L. Rogers was born February the 9, 1834; John C. Rogers was born January 30, 1836; Amy S. Rogers was born October 14, 1841; James C.C. Rogers was born December

17, 1845; DEATHS: Amy S. Rogers died July the 15, 1841; Wm. L. Rogers died September 6, 1852; Enoch S. Rogers died May the 4, 1860; Martha E. Wells died September the 22, 1865; John Rogers died November the 17, 1875".

ROHER,SAMUEL-Mexican War Pension Application dated 1887, Arkansas. Served in Company C, 1st Regiment, Ohio Volunteers. Mex.Sur.App.-#14039, Cert.#13024. (not abstracted)

ROLLINS,GEORGE-Mexican War Pension Application dated 1900, Arkansas. Served in Company F, 5th Regiment, Tennessee Volunteers. Widow, Evaline. Mex.Wid.App.#15709, Cert.#12262. Remarks: O.W.Wid.Pending, O.W.Inv.File #244. (not abstracted)

ROSE,GEORGE-Mexican War Pension Application dated 1887, Arkansas. Served in Captain Pike's Company, 1st Regiment, Arkansas Mounted Volunteers. Widow, Victoria. Mex.Sur.App.#20565, Cert.#17258, Mex.Wid.App.#17142, Cert.#14329. (not abstracted)

ROSE,JAMES-Old War Pension Application, dated 1887, Arkansas. Served in Dunn's Company of Illinois Mounted Volunteers, 1832. O.W.Inv.App. #23590, Ind.War Wid.App.#4943, Cert.#4610.

ROSS,JOHN M.-Mexican War Pension Application dated 1889, Arkansas. Served in Company E, Briscoe's Battalion, Louisiana Mounted Volunteers. Widow, Jane E. Mex.Wid.App.#8617, Cert.#6938. (not abstracted)

ROSS,WESLEY W.-Mexican War Pension Application dated 1888, Arkansas. Served in Captain Ficklin's Company, Gray's Battalion, Arkansas Volunteers. Mex.Sur.App.#18893, Cert.#15025. (not abstracted)

ROTH,JOSEPH A.J.-Mexican War Pension Application dated 1888, Arkansas. Served in Company B, St.Louis Legion, 1st Regiment, Missouri Mounted Volunteers. Widow, Lucinda. Mex.Sur.App.#19886, Cert.#16695, Mex.Wid.App.#15613, Cert.#12680. Remarks: O.W.Minors Pending. (not abstracted)

ROWBOTHAM,BUCKLEY H.-Mexican War Pension Application dated 1887, Arkansas. Served in Captain Collin's Company, Gray's Battalion, Arkansas Volunteers. Mex.Sur.App.#11198, Cert.#14989, Mex.Wid.App. #6855, Cert.#5350. (not abstracted)

ROWLAND,SAMUEL S.-Mexican War Pension Application dated 1887, Arkansas. Served in Company B, 1st Regiment, Arkansas Mounted Volunteers. Widow, Delilah. Mex.Wid.App.#1854, Cert.#3594. (not abstracted)

ROYAL,JOHN-Revolutionary Pension Application #R9054, dated 7 April 1834, Pulaski County, Territory of Arkansas, his age 74. He was born in King William County, Virginia, while he was still young, his parents moved to Pittsylvania County, Virginia. He was residing in Henry County, Virginia, when he enlisted in a Company of Rangers under command of Captain William Allcorn in 1781. He was engaged against Tories in Henry County, Virginia, and in North Carolina, he also served at the Siege of York. After the war he moved to Lincoln County, Kentucky, where he lived about 18 years, then moved to Jackson County, Tennessee for about 27 years. He moved to Pulaski County, Arkansas Territory about 1830. His application was rejected because of his length of service.
Pulaski County, Arkansas Will Book A, page 48, Will of John Royal, signed 18 September 1835, "To my grandson, James Busby (?) a yoke of oxen, cow and calf, and four young sows. The balance of my property to remain as my own during the natural life of myself and my wife, Elizabeth. I appoint my son-in-law, Abraham Stacey, my sole executor, to take care of my property, my land,

my wife and myself while we live; after our death, the property to be his own for compensation for his trouble". Witnesses; John Covey, Milton Williams and William Royal.

RUBOTTOM,WILLIAM P.-Mexican War Pension Application. Served in Company E, 2nd Regimant, Indiana Volunteers. Widow, Rowena. Mex.Sur.App.#10063, Cert.#11902, dated 1887, Texas; Mex.Wid.App.-#17974, Cert.#14184, dated 1905, Arkansas. (not abstracted)

RUNDLEMAN/RANDLEMAN,MARTIN-Revolutionary War Pension Application #S31946, dated 30 September 1832 St. Clair, Illinois. He was born 25 December 1761 in Rowan County, North Carolina, where he was residing at the time of his enlistment in 1779 in Colonel Locke's Regiment of North Carolina Militia. In 1780, he served under command of Captain John Randleman at the Battle of Camden. In 1837, he moved to Arkansas "so that he and his wife might have the assistance and society of their daughter and her husband, David Reece, and also to be near two sons who had moved to the S.W. part of Missouri. (possibly Michael and Martin Jr. Rundleman who lived in Polk County, Missouri).

RUSCO,JOHN W.-Mexican War Pension Application dated 1887, Arkansas. Served in Company B, 5th Regiment, Tennessee Volunteers. Widow, Malinda. Mex.Wid.App.#4157, Cert.#5906. Remarks: O.W.Wid. Pending, O.W.Inv.Rej.#17368. (not abstracted)

RUSS,WILLIAM-Mexican War Pension Application dated 1888, Arkansas. Served in Company F, 3rd Regiment, Louisiana Volunteers. Widow, Sarah. Mex.Sur.App.#18747, Cert.#14828, Mex.Wid.App.#15111, Cert.#12296. (not abstracted)

RUSSELL,JAMES, alias James H. Hawkins-Mexican War Pension Application. Served in Captain Loftland's Company, 3rd Regiment, Missouri Volunteers. Mex.Sur.App.#25041, no certificate #. Remarks: Late War Wid.O.#735743, Late War Inv.Cert.#948365; Mo.Vols. (not abstracted)

RUSSELL,LEWIS-Old War pension application dated 1880 Arkansas. O.W.Wid.Cert.#1689, file #29673, O.W.Min.Cert.#1689, file #7158. Service in Company C, Arkansas Volunteers, Mexican War. Widow, Mary P. Barker. (not abstracted)

RUTHERFORD,JOSEPH-War of 1812 pension application W.O.#23233, W.C.#21866. Entered service in Captain James Penny's Company of Tennessee Militia, at Greenville, Tennessee on 22 October 1813, discharged in January 1814. Married Mariah Hayes, 26 February 1834, at East Tennessee, Jefferson County, Tennessee. He died near Boonesboro, Washington County, Arkansas on 2 January 1866. She applied for pension in 1878, stating that they had lived near Boonesboro "for 30 years or more". Mariah Rutherford died in Boonesboro, Arkansas on 12 April 1885.

RUTHERFORD,JOSEPH R.-Mexican War Pension Application dated 1887, Arkansas. Served in Company B, 14th Regiment, U.S.Infantry. Mex. Sur.App.#11233, Cert.#12776, Mex.Wid.App.#18543, Cert.#14609. (not abstracted)

RYAN,JOHN-Mexican War Pension Application dated 1887, Arkansas. Served in Company A, 6th Regiment, U.S.Infantry. Mex.Sur.App. #5582, Cert.#2958. (not abstracted)

SAGE,PINK H.-War of 1812 pension application S.O.#23165, S.C.#18723, W.O.#32435, W.C.#24296. Service in Captain Bernard Peyton's Company, 20th Regiment of U.S. Infantry, from 8 September 1812 to 15 March 1815. He married Elizabeth Smith in Bedford County, Tennessee, 28 December 1820. She was born 17 January 1800. They moved from Tennessee to Illinois and in 1878, she stated that they had lived together in Arkansas for 43 years. Pinkney H. Sage died in Carroll County, Arkansas 21 October 1875. She applied for pension in 1878, in Randolph County, Arkansas. She moved to Pierce City, Lawrence County, Missouri, where she had a daughter and son-in-law, Mr. and Mrs. John H. Keech.

ST.JOHN,ARTHUR-Mexican War Pension Application. Served in Company F, 1st Regiment, Mississippi Volunteers. Widow, Caroline E. Mex. Sur.App.#6211, Cert.#6432, dated 1887, Mississippi; Mex.Wid.App.-#17347, Cert.#14308, dated 1903, Arkansas. Remarks: Rebellion Widow Cert.#452499, as widow of Thomas B. McGohan, Company A, 5th Regiment, Ohio Volunteer Cavalry. (not abstracted)

ST.JOHN,WILLIAM-War Of 1812 Pension Application, W.O.#34800, W.C.#21352. Served in Captain Barksdale's Company of Virginia Militia. Widow, Mary L. (not abstracted)

SAMPLE,BENJAMIN-Mexican War Pension Application dated 1887, Arkansas. Served in Company I, 5th Regiment, Indiana Volunteer Infantry. Mex.Sur.App.#5603, Cert.#2169, Mex.Wid.App.#17388. (not abstracted)

SAMPLE,WILLIAM R.-Mexican War Pension Application dated, 1887, Arkansas. Served in Captain Moon's Company, 1st Regiment, Alabama Volunteers. Widow, Mary E. Mex.Wid.App.#5162, Cert.#4188. Remarks: O.W.Inv. pending. (not abstracted)

SANDERS,ROBERT H.-Mexican War Pension Application dated 1887, Arkansas. Served in Captain Willis' Company, 2nd Regiment, Mississippi Volunteers. Mex.Sur.App.#16671, Cert.#11677. (not abstracted)

SANDERS,SAMUEL B.-Mexican War Pension Application dated 1887, Arkansas. Served in Captain Ficklin's Company C, Gray's Battalion, Arkansas Volunteers. Widow, Malinda. Mex.Sur.App.#10075, Cert.#12407, Mex.Wid.App.#16264, Cert.#14464. (not abstracted)

SANDERS,SAMUEL J.-Mexican War Pension Application. Served in Captain Armstrong's Company C, Santa Fe Battalion, Missouri Mounted Volunteers. Widow, Sarah. Mex.Sur.App.#10082, Cert.#14836, dated 1887 Missouri, Mex.Wid.App.#15311, Cert.#11906, dated 1899, Arkansas. (not abstracted)

SARASIN,FERDINAND A.-Mexican War Pension Application dated 1887, Arkansas. Served in Captain Danley's Company B, 1st Regiment, Arkansas Mounted Volunteers. Widow, Mattie. Mex.Sur.App.#5624, Cert.#2709, Mex.Wid.App.#10015, Cert.#7707. Remarks: by transfer #515302. (not abstracted)

SAUNDERS,ELISHA-War of 1812 pension application S.O.#28273, S.C.#20217, W.O.#39016, W.C.#29693. Enlisted into service in Captain Otto Cantrell's Company of Tennessee Militia, in Rutherford County, Tennessee on 24 September 1813, discharged 21 December 1813. He served in General Andrew Jackson's Brigade at the Battles of Tulloshatchee and Talladega. He married Zilla Dickinson 26 March 1818 in Rutherford County, Tennessee. They remained in Rutherford County, until 1839, when they moved to Hempstead County, Arkansas. Survivor's application dated 6 October 1872, Washington, Hempstead County, Elisha Sanders, age 78. He died on 8 August 1876. She applied for pension 6 December 1879, age 80. Affidavit of John S. Cannon of Hempstead County, age 68 in 1879, stated that he had been close friend of Elisha and Zilla Sanders for 60 years.

SAUNDERS,RICHARD M.-Old war pension application O.W.Min.Cert.#4373, file #11378. Service in Arkansas Cavalry, Mexican War. Minors, Maria D. and Jesse Saunders. (not abstracted)

SCOTT,WILLIAM-Mexican War Pension Application dated 1887, Arkansas. Served in Company I, 14th Regiment, U.S.Infantry. Widow, Sallie. Mex.Sur.App.#20459, Cert.#17259, Mex.Wid.App.#13371, Cert.#11260. (not abstracted)

SCOTT,WILLIAM-Mexican War Pension Application dated 1888, Arkansas. Served as Teamster, Q.M. Department. Widow, Sallie. Mex.Sur.App.-#20928, no Cert.#, Mex.Wid.App.#10439, no Cert.#. (not abstracted)

SCOTT,WILLIAM F.-Mexican War Pension Application dated 1887, Arkansas. Served in Captain Pelham's Company, Gray's Battalion, Arkansas Volunteers. Widow, Mahelda. Mex.Wid.App.#3113, Cert.#4605. (not abstracted)

SCREWS,GEORGE W.-Mexican War Pension Application dated 1887, Arkansas. Served in Company D, 1st Regiment, Arkansas Cavalry. Mex.Sur.App.#14445, Cert.#10534. (not abstracted)

SCRITCHFIELD,ALFRED-War of 1812 pension application S.O.#5431, S.C.#4388, W.O.#8940. Service in Captain James Stewart's Company of Tennessee Militia. (not abstracted)

SCRITCHFIELD,JESSE-War of 1812 pension application S.O.#5430, S.C.#4389. Service in Captain James Stewart's Company of Tennessee of Tennessee Militia. (not abstracted).

SEAGRAVES,WILLIAM-Mexican War Pension Application dated 1890, Arkansas. Served in Company B, 2nd Regiment, U.S.Dragoons. Widow, Annie. Mex.Sur.App.#22772, Cert.#19085, Mex.Wid.App.#11065, no Cert.#. Remarks: O.W.Inv.Pending. (not abstracted)

SEAHORN/SEHORN,HUGH-War of 1812 pension application W.O.#29031, W.C.#29501. He was born 19 January 1793. Enlisted into service in Jefferson County, Tennessee on 20 September 1814 in Captain Reuben Tipton's Company of East Tennessee Mounted Gunmen. Discharged 1 May 1815. He married Tabitha Ann Owens in Dandridge, Jefferson County, Tennessee, 16 December 1817. She was born 16 March 1799. They remained in Dandridge, Tennessee about 2 Years, then moved to Montgomery, Alabama for about 16 years. They lived in Union County, Arkansas about 8 years and in Hempstead County about 2 years. They moved to Ft. Smith, Sebastian County, Arkansas ca 1869. They had eleven children, the first born in 1819 and the last born in 1839. In 1879, Nicholas Sehorn, son of Hugh and Tabitha Sehorn, was living in Sebastian County, Arkansas, he stated "I was born in August 1825, my mother had 11 children, all of whom except myself and a sister are dead. My sister resided the last we heard in Louisana, we lost track of her during the war."

SEALS,WILLIAM-Mexican War Pension Application dated 1887, Arkansas. Served in Company F, 1st Regiment, Tennessee Cavalry. Widow, Elizabeth. Mex.Wid.App.#1909, Cert.#602. Remarks: O.W.Inv.Rej.-#17724. (not abstracted)

SEARCY,JOHN-Mexican War Pension Application dated 1894, Arkansas. Served in Company F, 1st Regiment, Kentucky Cavalry. Mex.Sur.App.-#24525, Cert.#20501. Remarks: Late War Cert.#370613. (not abstracted)

SELF,LEVI-War of 1812 pension application W.O.#39613, W.C.#32696. He served in Captain Miles Varnum's Company of Tennessee Militia from 13 November 1814 to 13 May 1815. He married first; Sarah Felton, who died in 1821; second, Elizabeth Thrash; third, Mary Douthet, 1 December 1858 at Buffalo Creek, Newton County, Arkansas. She was married first to Lewis Bowen, who died in Hickman County, Tennessee; second to Jonathan Douthard (Douthet?). Residents of Newton County, who stated that they had attended the wedding of Levi and Mary Self; William F. McPherson, Elizabeth Casey,

Robert Boen, Ambrose R. McPherson and Thomas Houston.

SELF,NOBLE J.-Mexican War Pension Application dated 1889, Arkansas. Served in Company C, 12th Regiment, U.S.Infantry. Mex.Sur.App.#22172, Cert.#18639. (not abstracted)

SELF,WILLIAM-Mexican War Pension Application dated 1887, Arkansas. Served in Captain Meare's Independent Company and in Company H, 1st Regiment, Arkansas Mounted Volunteers. Mex.Sur.App.#5747, Cert.#8990. Remarks: Old War Inv. Rej.#21631. (not abstracted)

SERLES,JAMES-Mexican War Pension Application. Served in Captain McMurray's Company C, 1st Regiment, Tennessee Volunteers. Mex.-Sur.App.#10155, Cert.#12448, Mex.Wid.App.#15563, Cert.#12268. (not abstracted)

SEWELL,JAMES-Mexican War Pension Application dated 1887, Arkansas. Served in Company H, 1st Regiment, Arkansas Mounted Volunteers. Widow, Elizabeth. Mex.Sur.App.#14208, Cert.#19211, Mex.Wid.App.-#13311, Cert.#10226. (not abstracted)

SHACKELFORD,SATTERWHITE-War of 1812 pension application W.O.#14379, W.C.#11622. Enlisted into service in Portsmouth, Virginia on 7 July 1812 in Lieutenant Swift's Company of U.S. Marine Corps. Transferred to a Company commanded by Captain William S. White, where he served as Sergeant on board the Frigate "Constellation". he remained in active service aboard the Constellation for a period of 5 1/2 years. He was discharged 25 January 1818 in Washington, D.C. "Marriage Bond dated 19 February 1818, Norfolk County, Virginia, entered into by Satterwhite Shackelford and David Brown; the object of said bond being the intended marriage of Satterwhite Shackelford and Miss Courtney Brown". They remained in Portsmouth, Virginia 13 years, then moved to Pontotoc, Mississippi for 20 years. He died in Pontotoc on 18 August 1855. Courtney Ann Shackelford lived with her son, Josephus Shackelford, in Moulton, Lawrence County, Alabama from 1856 to 1867, when they moved to Forrest City, St. Francis County, Arkansas. Her son, Satterwhite Shackelford, was born in Portsmouth, Virginia on 15 April 1832, in 1878 he was living in Lawrence County, Alabama. Josephus Shackelford was born in Portsmouth, Virginia on 6 February 1830, he stated that "she gave three sons to her Country in the Mexican war."

SHANKS,PENDLETON P.-Mexican War Pension Application dated 1887, Arkansas. Served in Company D, 5th Regiment, Louisiana Volunteers. Widow, Nancy Jane. Mex.Sur.App.#16768, Cert.#14466, Mex.Wid.App.-#6208, Cert.#4352. (not abstracted)

SHANNON,AARON-Mexican War Pension Application dated 1887, Arkansas. Served in Company G, 1st Regiment, Arkansas Mounted Volunteers. Widow, Sarah A. Mex.Sur.App.#5757, Cert.#13898, Mex.Wid.App.#15841, Cert.#12217. (not abstracted)

SHATSWELL,THOMAS-Mexican War Pension Application dated 1888, Arkansas. Served in Company F, 1st Regiment, U.S.Dragoons. (1835-1838) Widow, Elizabeth. Mex.Wid.App.#5970. Remarks: Ind.Wid.O.#3967, Ind.Wid.Cert.#7358. (not abstracted)

SHAVER,JACOB-War of 1812 pension application S.O.#23966, S.C.#20678. B.L.W.#20878-80-50, and #9568-80-55. Served as Corporal in Captain Mathew Neal's Company of Tennessee Militia, from 13 November 1814 to 13 May 1815. He was drafted in Sumner County, Tennessee. He married Thirza Moss, in February 1820, in Randolph County, Arkansas. His Bounty Land Application in January 1851, was executed in Ozark, Franklin County, Arkansas, his age 58. Jacob Shaver died 19 August 1884, in Ozark, Arkansas.

SHAVER,JOHN S.-Mexican War Pension Application dated 1890, Arkansas. Served as Captain of Company D, (1847-1848) 5th Regiment, Tennessee Volunteers. Widow, Mary M. Bounty Land Warrant #16232-160-50. Mex.Wid.App.#9357, Cert.#7539. Remarks: Soldier died 30 April 1862, widow died 3 April 1913. (not abstracted)

SHELL,ALBERT-Mexican War Pension Application dated 1887, Arkansas. Served in Company D, 1st Regiment, Arkansas Mounted Volunteers. Mex. Wid.App.#1937, Cert.#1693. (not abstracted)

SHELL,WILLIAM-Mexican War Pension Application dated 1887, Arkansas. Served in Company D, 1st Regiment, Arkansas Cavalry. Mex.Sur.App. #10186, Cert.#4206. (not abstracted)

SHELTON,JAMES-War of 1812 Pension Application, S.O.#23969, S.C.-#20768, W.O.#43992, W.C.#34594. Service in Captain Adam Vickery's Company, Kentucky Militia from 10 November 1814 to 10 May 1815. James Shelton and Bashabilee Eason were married in September 1838, in DeKalb County, Alabama. He applied for pension on 25 January 1873 in Van Buren County, Arkansas, his age 73. He stated that he had participated at the Battle of New Orleans. He died in Clinton, Arkansas on 19 November 1881. Bashabilee Shelton applied for pension on 3 October 1885, she was age 65 and a resident of Clinton, Van Buren County, Arkansas. She stated that her husband had previously been married, but she could not give the name of the first wife. Affidavits from John Bradley, age 55, Hartwell Greeson, age 67, and James K. Marshall, age 63, all of Van Buren County, and long time friends, who stated that James Shelton had never mentioned his previous wife to them. Bashabilee Shelton stated that they had lived in DeKalb County, Alabama until 1842 when they moved to Conway County, Arkansas. They moved to Van Buren County ca 1844. She died in Van Buren County on 4 October 1895.

SHELTON,JOHN-Mexican War Pension Application dated 1887, Arkansas. Served in Captain Coxey's Company, D Battalion, Mississippi Volunteer Rifles. Widow, Sarah. Mex.Sur.App.#5823, Cert.#4202, Mex.Wid.App.#14428, Cert.#11494. Remarks: O.W.Inv.Rej.#19900. (not abstracted)

SHERROD,ARTHUR-War of 1812 Pension Application, S.O.#21872, S.C.#13963, W.O.#29611, W.C.#21558. Served in Captain Minor Sturgis' Company, 24th Regiment, U.S.Infantry. Enlisted at Franklin, Williamson County, Tennessee on 18 September 1813. His first service was at Newport, Kentucky, guarding prisoners taken by Commodore Perry on Lake Erie, he also served in the Battle of Machinaw, after which he was transferred to Captain Ben Johnson's Company of the 2nd Rifle Regiment. He was married to Susan Ewing, 23 July 1816 in Hickman County, Tennessee. This file does not give any information about Susan Sherrod. Arthur Sherrod moved to Benton County, Arkansas about 1862, where he married Elizabeth McCall (nee Hedges). She had previously been married to James McCall. Arthur Sherrod died in Benton County on 2 January 1873.

SHERROD,WILLIAM-War of 1812 pension application S.O.#15860, S.C.#17341, W.O.#41183, W.C.#32085. Service in Captain Minor Sturgis' Company of U.S. Infantry and in Captain Johnson's Company, 2nd Regiment of U.S. Rifleman, from 26 October 1813 to 31 March 1814. William Sherrod applied for pension on 9 May 1871 in Washington County, Arkansas, where he died on 6 January 1881. Charlotte Sherrod applied for pension, and submitted, "A true copy of the family record of William and Charlotte Sherrod; William Sherrod was born April the 1st 1788; Charlotte Sherrod was born November the 1st 1791; William Sherrod and Charlotte Miller were married October the 17th 1816; (in Murray or Maury County, Tennessee ?) Mary Sherrod was born March the 2nd 1818; Elizabeth Sherrod was born April the 26th 1819; Martha Sherrod was born

May the 18th 1820; Sterling B. Sherrod was born June the 29th
1822; James T. Sherrod was born February the 26th 1823; Emily
Sherrod was born October the 13th 1824; Charlotte Sherrod was
born March the 31st 1826; William V. Sherrod was born April
8th 1828; Nancy Sherrod was born January the 29th 1830; Alva
E. Sherrod was born January the 16th 1832; John F. Sherrod was
born July the 1st 1833; Arthur W. Sherrod was born October the
8th 1835." Affidavits from Mary McCuistian and Charlotte Williams,
daughters of William and Charlotte Sherrod.

SHINN,JACOB L.-Mexican War Pension Application dated 1888, Arkansas.
Served in Captain Taylor's Company A, 1st Regiment, Arkansas
Mounted Volunteers. Widow, Martha. Mex.Sur.App.#20534, Cert.#17202,
Mex.Wid.App.#15337, Cert.#12102. (not abstracted)

SHOEMAKER,SETH W.-Mexican War Pension Application dated 1887,
Arkansas. Served in Company K, 2nd Regiment, Ohio Infantry.
Mex.Sur.App.#10204, Cert.#6672. Remarks: O.W.Sur.Rej. #17819.
(not abstracted)

SIDES,HILLIARD J.-Mexican War Pension Application dated 1887,
Arkansas. Served in Company C, 14th Regiment, U.S.Infantry.
Mex.Sur.App.#5869, Cert.#2161. (not abstracted)

SIMMONS,JOHN P.-Mexican War Pension Application. Served in Captain
Dill's Company H, 5th Regiment, Tennessee Volunteers. Widow,
Mary M. Mex.Sur.App.#5893, Cert.#9558 dated 1887, Arkansas. Mex.Wid.
App.#16448, dated 1901, Missouri. (not abstracted)

SIMON,LUDWIG, alias Lewis Simon-Mexican War Pension Application.
Service in Battery O, 4th Regiment, U.S.Artillery. Widow, Mary.
Mex.Sur.App.#5895, Cert.#13033 dated 1887, Arkansas. Mex.Wid.App.
#11834, Cert.#9051 dated 1894, Oklahoma. Remarks: Late War Wid.
O.#567252; Co. F, 8yh Regt., Ohio Inf. (not abstracted)

SIMS,WILLIAM-Mexican War Pension Application dated 1892, Arkansas.
Served in Company E, 3rd Regiment, Kentucky Infantry. Widow,
Mary Jane. Mex.Wid.App.#10740, Cert.#9487. (not abstracted)

SISCO,HOUSTON-Mexican War Pension Application dated 1887, Arkansas.
Served in Company C, Arkansas Mounted Volunteers. Mex.Sur.App.#10223,
Cert.#4528. (not abstracted)

SKELTON,RALPH-War of 1812 pension application W.O.#33782, W.C.-
#26403. Service in Captain Joseph Montgomery's Company, Colonel
Robert Evan's Regiment of Indiana Militia. He was drafted at
Vincennes, Territory of Indiana, on 20 August 1812, for service
against the Shawnee Indians. He married Casaniah Conner in the
year 1825 in Hempstead County, Arkansas. His Bounty Land Application
dated 2 November 1852, Washington County, Arkansas, Ralph Skelton,
age 65, "B.L.W.#84069-40-50, was laid on the following lands,
by his son Robert Skelton, to wit, SE 1/4 SE 1/4 of section
22 township 15 range 30 west." B.L.W.#38875-120-55, "he sold
to David S. Robinson, who located it in the County of Washington,
in township 15, range 30." Ralph Skelton died at Washington,
Arkansas in March 1861. Casaniah Skelton died 16 November 1900.
Affidavits from Alfred W. and Isaac Conner of Fayetteville,
Washington County, Arkansas.

SLOAN,RANKIN-Mexican War Pension Application dated 1887, Arkansas.
Served in Company C, Anderson's Battalion, Mississippi Rifles. Widow,
Sarah. Mex.Wid.App.#1988, Cert.#3002. (not abstracted)

SMALLWOOD,DANIEL S.-Mexican War Pension Application dated 1887,
Arkansas. Served in Lieutenant Clutter's Detachment, 8th Regiment,
U.S.Infantry. Mex.Sur.App.#15752, Cert.#10962. Remarks: Reb.Wid.O.
#839701, Cos. D and G, 60th Regt. Ohio Inf. (not abstracted)

SMITH,AARON-Revolutionary War Pension Application #R9681, dated 7 April 1818, Anderson County, Tennessee. He apparently entered service in the Continental Line of North Carolina on 6 June 1781. He stated that he was shot through both thighs at the Battle of Eutaw Springs. In April 1822, he was residing in Greene County, Illinois. Aaron Smith died in Washington County, Arkansas on 1 March 1840. His widow, Agnes, applied for pension, submitting the following family record; "Aaron Smith and Agnes Spradlin were married 4 March 1784 in Burks County, North Carolina; George Taylor and Rhoda Smith were married 13 Feb 1813; Aaron Smith was born 5 April 1765; Agnes Spradlin was born 19 Oct 1758; Rhoda Smith was born 4 June 1798".

SMITH,ABRAHAM-War of 1812 pension application W.O.#34036, W.C.-#27208. Served as Scout in Captain Grief Johnson's Company of Mississippi Militia. He volunteered in Madison County, Mississippi Territory, which is now Alabama. He married Nancy Ragsdale on 28 December 1815 in Madison County, Mississippi Territory. Joshua Smith Senior, age 82 in 1879, resident of Navarro County, Texas, stated that he had attended the wedding of Abraham and Nancy. Abraham Smith died in Dorsey County, Arkansas on 17 August 1864. Nancy Smith applied for pension 4 October 1878, she was age 82 and a resident of Toledo, Dorsey County, Arkansas. Her son, Nathan Smith and her grandson, George H. Tisdale served as witnesses.

SMITH,ADAM-War Of 1812 Pension Application, W.O.#5791, W.C.#24422. B.L.W.#8148-80-55. Served in Captain Thomas Anderson's Company of Georgia Militia, from 21 November 1814 to 6 May 1815. Adam Smith and Mary Baugh were married in Franklin County, Georgia on 5 January 1816. He died in Hawkins County, Tennessee on 20 February 1842. Mary Smith applied for pension from Cass County, Missouri on 14 July 1871, she was age 76. She did not respond to the questionaire sent to her by the pension agengy, so the application was rejected. She applied again on 21 March 1879, she was a resident of Mountain View, Stone County, Arkansas.

SMITH,BIRD-War of 1812 pension application S.O.#24290, S.C. #15223, W.O.#34507, W.C.#25066. He enlisted into service in Captain Daniel Newman's Company of Tennessee Militia in White County, Tennessee, but was reassigned to Brigadier General Bird Smith's (his father) staff, in which capacity he served at the Battle of New Orleans. He married first Susan Garner, who died about 1826. He married Frances K. Thweatt on 12 February 1828 in Haywood County, Tennessee. She was born 14 November 1811 in Rutherford County, North Carolina, the daughter of Thomas and Elizabeth Thweatt. She had sister named Lutitia, born in 1817. Lutitia Thweatt married Simon Spight on 4 November 1834, and was a resident of Tippah County, Mississippi in 1879. Bird and Frances Smith had children; Thomas T. Smith born 8 October 1830 in Haywood County, Tennessee, residing in Columbia County, Arkansas in 1879; Bird Smith, born 15 February 1833 in Haywood County, Tennessee; residing in Waxahachie, Texas in 1879 ; Guy Smith; and Susan Smith. Bird and Frances Smith lived in Tippah County, Mississippi about 1839 and moved to Magnolia, Columbia County, Arkansas about 1870. In September 1871, Bird Smith applied for pension, he was age 75 and a resident of Columbia County. He died there on 17 October 1878, and Frances Smith applied for pension on 16 January 1879. Affidavit of former slave, Green Smith, stating that he was born about 1833, that he and his mother, Sophia Smith were given to Frances Smith by her father, Thomas Thweatt.

SMITH,CLAIBORNE-Mexican War Pension Application dated 1887, Arkansas. Served in Company A, Gray's Battalion, Arkansas Volunteers. Widow, Amanda. Mex.Sur.App.#16934, Cert.#12427, Mex.Wid.App. #18412, Cert.#14778. (not abstracted)

SMITH,GEORGE SENIOR-Revolutionary War Pension Application #S31969, dated 7 February 1833, Bedford County, Tennessee, George Smith age 69 years and 14 days. He was born 24 December 1763, in Roan(?), (the County name in this application appears to be Roan, therefore that is the name I have used) County, North Carolina. He was drafted into service in Roan County in August of 1779, under command of Captain Peter Heddrick and Lieutenant Caleb Kimble. He was engaged in battle on the Peedee River against Tories, led by a man named Kimbro. After several skirmishes with Tories on the Deep River and the Yadkin River, he was discharged from service in November 1779. In 1781 he served under Command of Mirick Davis as guard for transferring prisoners taken at Tarlton's defeat. He re-entered service in September 1781, in Captain Frederick Smith's Company, and was in the Gum Swamp and Raft Swamp then to Wilmington, North Carolina, "chasing Tories" when news of peace arrived. He remained in Roan County for many years, then moved to Bedford County, Tennessee, where "I have resided many years". Affidavit by Benjamin Lentz, who was in service with George Smith. Application dated 3 June 1842, for transfer of pension to Arkansas "because he is a widower of advanced age, and is living with his children in Sevier County, Arkansas."

SMITH,GEORGE W.-Mexican War Pension Application dated 1888, Arkansas. Served in Company C, 12th Regiment, U.S.Infantry. Widow, Mary A.C. Mex.Sur.App.#20737, Cert.#17452, Mex.Wid.App.#18994, Cert.#15063. (not abstracted)

SMITH,HENRY C.-Mexican War Pension Application dated 1893, Arkansas. Service in Company C, 2nd Regiment, Illinois Infantry. Mex.Sur.-App.#24210, Cert.#20170. Remarks: O.W.Inv.file #35349. (not abstracted)

SMITH,JOHN-Old war pension application O.W.Wid.Cert.#1717, file #11475. Served as Captain in Alabama Volunteers, Florida Seminole Indian War. Widow, Rebecca. (not abstracted)

SMITH,JOSEPH-Old War pension application O.W.Wid.Cert.#2046, file #28592, O.W.Min.Cert. #4012, file #8739. Service in Company C, 12th Regiment Res. Inf. Widow, Maria L. Minor, Mary Smith. (not abstracted)

SMITH,MATTHEW J.-Mexican War Pension Application dated 1888, Arkansas. Served in Company E, Georgia Volunteers. Mex.Sur.App. #18426, Cert.#14302. (not abstracted)

SMITH,THOMAS N.-Mexican War Pension Application dated 1887, Arkansas. Service in Company K, 1st Regiment, Tennessee Volunteers. Widow, Josephine E. Mex.Sur.App.#10270, Cert.#5446, Mex.Wid.App. #6894, Cert.#5418. Remarks: O.W.Inv.Cert.#6691, file #451. (not abstracted)

SMITH,WILLIAM-Mexican War Pension Application dated 1887, Arkansas. Service in Captain Frierson's Company, 1st Regiment, Tennessee Volunteers. Mex.Sur.App.#10273, Cert.#4878. (not abstracted)

SNIDER,JACOB-Mexican War Pension Application dated 1887, Arkansas. Widow, Johana E.W. Mex.Wid.App.#2032, Cert.#2178. (not abstracted)

SNOW,WILLIAM-Mexican War Pension Application dated 1887, Arkansas. Served in Company I, 1st Regiment, Tennessee Volunteer Cavalry. Widow, Martha A. Mex.Wid.App.#2033, Cert.#211. (not abstracted)

SORRELLS,THEODORIC F.-Mexican War Pension Application dated 1887, Arkansas. Served as Sergeant in Captain Green's Company, 1st Regiment, Texas Mounted Volunteers. Mex.Sur.App.#10287, Cert.#9970, Mex.Wid.App.#16097, Cert.#12661. (not abstracted)

SOUTHARD,JAMES M.-Mexican War Pension Application dated 1888, Arkansas. Service in Captain Vaughn's Company, 5th Regiment, Tennessee Volunteers. Widow, Rachel A. Mex.Wid.App.#7017, Cert. #5558. (not abstracted)

SOUTHERN,WILLIAM-Mexican War Pension Application dated 1887, Arkansas. Served in Captain Blanchard's Company, 7th Regiment, U.S.Volunteers. Mex.Sur.App.#13732, Cert.#12623. (not abstracted)

SPILLERS,JOHN-Old war pension application O.W.Wid.Cert.#1185, file #29129, O.W.Min.Cert.#11515,file #11515. Widow, Elizabeth Severs. Minors, James and Mary Spillers. (not abstracted)

SPLAWN,RICHARD-War of 1812 pension application W.O.#7307, W.C.#3134. Service in Captain Ried's Company of Georgia Militia from 21 November 1814 to 28 March 1815. Richard Splawn married Elizabeth Hathorne, 11 November 1813, in Jones County, Georgia. He died in Pike County, Alabama in 1837. Widow's pension application dated 4 October 1871, Ouachita Township, Bradley County, Arkansas, Elizabeth Splawn age 76.

STACEY,CHARLES-Mexican War Pension Application dated 1887, Arkansas. Served in Captain Hall's Company, 2nd Regiment, Texas Mounted Volunteers. Widow, Armenia. Mex.Wid.App.#2050, Cert.#3895. (not abstracted)

STAMPLEY,WILLIAM JOHN-Mexican War Pension Application dated 1887, Arkansas. Served in Company F, 3rd Regiment, Louisiana Volunteers. Widow, Elizabeth. Mex.Sur.App.#12797, Cert.#8168, Mex.Wid.App.#11481. (not abstracted)

STANFILL,ERVIN-Mexican War Pension Application dated 1887, Arkansas. Service in Captain Truitt's Company, Hay's Regiment, Texas Mounted Volunteers. Mex.Sur.App.#6115, Cert.#11928. (not abstracted)

STANLEY,WILSON M.-Mexican War Pension. Widow, Anna C. Service in Company E, 3rd Regiment, Ohio Volunteer Infantry. Mex.Sur.App. #6142, dated New Mexico; Mex.Wid.App.#17307, Cert.#13453, dated 1903 Arkansas. Remarks: Reb. Inv. Cert.#319507, Captain in Company K, 32nd Regiment, Ohio Volunteer Infantry. (not abstracted)

STARNES,JOHN-Mexican War Pension Application. Widow, Cassandra E. Service in Company C, 2nd Regiment, Mississippi Volunteers. Mex. Sur.App.#21391, Cert.#18281 dated 1889, Mississippi; Mex.Wid.App.-#17344 dated 1903, Arkansas. (not abstracted)

STARNES,NICHOLAS-Revolutionary War Pension Application #W26445. He was born 6 November 1756 in Cecil County, Maryland and when he was one year old, was taken to Fairfax County, Virginia by his parents, where they remained until he was sixteen years old, when they moved to Craven District, South Carolina. At the beginning of the Revolutionary War, he moved to Washington County, Virginia, where he volunteered in September 1775 in Colonel William Campbell's Regiment. His first call to duty was under command of Colonel Arthur Campbell against Tories. He served in that capacity for several tours of duty. He served in Colonel Campbell's Regiment at King's Mountain. In 1780 and 1781, he served against the Cherokee Indians, and was promoted to Sergeant. Nicholas Starnes married Barbary Winters 10 October 1816 in Rhea County, Tennessee, marriage record enclosed. They remained in Tennessee until 1829, when they moved to Jefferson County, Alabama. He died in Talledega, Alabama on 22 May 1835. His widow, Barbara Starnes married John Hibben in Conway County, Arkansas on 25 January 1847. He died 27 October 1856 in Scott County, Arkansas. She applied for bounty land on the War of 1812 service of John Hibbin. She applied for pension in 1858 on the Revolutionary War service of Nicholas Starnes, she was age 67 and a resident of Sebastian County, Arkansas. The only mention of children, Nancy Bradshaw, daughter of Nicholas and Barbara Starnes.

START,BENJAMIN-War of 1812 pension application S.O.#23216, S.C.#16868, W.O.#30724, W.C.#25935. Service in Captain Joseph Scott's Company of Tennessee Militia from 12 September 1814 to 3 May 1815. He was born either January or July 26, 1792 in Virginia. He was a carpenter by trade. Benjamin Start married Martha B. Cates 13 September 1813, she died 7 September 1867. He married Rebecca Bryant 10 April 1868 in Pike County, Arkansas. Soldier's pension application dated 12 August 1871, Star of the West, Pike County, Arkansas, Benjamin Start age 79. He died 14 August 1877 at White Township, and Rebecca Start died 3 October 1898.

STATHAM,GEORGE S.-Mexican War Pension Application dated 1887, Arkansas. Served in Company C, 12th Regiment, U.S.Infantry. Mex. Sur.App.#17014, Cert.#13897. Remarks: Reb.Inv.Cert.#487942, W.O.#964543, Cert.#746455, Company H, 2nd Regiment, Arkansas Cavalry. (not abstracted)

STEELE,AARON-War of 1812 pension application W.O.#15169, W.C.#10748. Service in Captain McKnight's Company of Tennessee Militia. He was born in South Carolina, entered service at Fayetteville, Lincoln County, Tennessee in October 1813, served at the Battle of Talladega, and was discharged in Huntsville, Alabama 1 January 1814. Aaron Steele married Nancy M. Davis, 16 March 1819, at her parent's home in Moorsville, Maury County, Tennessee. He died at his home 16 August 1854 in Marshall County, Tennessee, (They were living in Maury County and the new County formed around them). Widow's pension application dated 3 April 1878, Evening Shade, Sharp County, Arkansas, Nancy Steele, age 75. She sent into the pension agency the two pieces of paper that her husband had used to keep the family record, to wit, "Aaron Steele was born February 12th 1794; was married March 16th 1819; Nancy M. Davis was born October 6th 1802; Hannah Evaline Steele was born September 5th 1821; Mary Elizabeth Caroline Steele was born March 28th 1824; Esther Love Steele was born August 2nd 1826; Abner Alexander Steele was born December 27th 1828; Robert McNutt Steele was born July 8th 1831; Betsey (also referred to as Elizabeth) Did__? Steele was born October 14th 1833; Nancy Jane Steele was born February 21st 1836; Martha Lucy Louiza Steele was born November 2nd 1839; William Davis Anderson Steele was born November 11th 1841; Francis (this name appears as Frances at one place) Lamira Steele was born the 7th day of July AD 1848." In August 1870, Nancy Steele stated that all of these children were alive except William D.A. Steele, who died in the year 1851. Affidavit dated 19 August 1870, Marshall County, Tennessee, "Rachel R. Dillehay, age 72, residing seven miles west of Lewisburg, Marshall County, Tennessee, says that her name, before her marriage to Levi Dillehay, was Rachel Steele, and that she is a sister of Aaron Steele." Affidavits from Robert Wiley and William L. Leonard, both of Sharp County, Arkansas in 1872, that they have been friends of Aaron and Nancy Steele for 35 years.

STEELE,ANDREW-War of 1812 pension application S.O.#30351, S.C.-#21750. Service in Captain James Reed's Company of Tennessee Militia, from 28 January 1814 to 25 April 1814. He was married to Elizabeth Blair, 11 September 1812, in North Carolina. He applied for pension on 15 December 1875, he was age 85 and a resident of Cassville, Newton County, Arkansas. He died 20 December 1879. His pension certificate is contained in this file, which was returned to the agency by his son, James M. Steele.

STEELMAN,JAMES-Mexican War Pension Application dated 1888, Arkansas. Widow, Catherine. Service in Captain Ross's Company, Bell's Regiment, Texas Mounted Volunteers. Mex.Sur.App.#19120, Cert.#15992, Mex.Wid.App.#7282, Cert.#5757. (not abstracted)

STEPHENS,JAMES N.-Mexican War Pension Application dated 1889, Arkansas. Service in Captain Key's Company, A Battalion, Mississippi Volunteers. Mex.Sur.App.#21732, Cert.#18392. (not abstracted)

STEPHENS,JOHN MONROE-Mexican War Pension Application dated 1887, Arkansas. Widow, Mandy. Service as Corporal, Company G, 3rd Regiment, Tennessee Volunteers. Mex.Sur.App.#10335, Cert.#11841, Mex.Wid.App.#15408, Cert.#13293. (not abstracted)

STEVENS,SETH-Mexican War Pension Application dated 1887, Arkansas. Served in Company G, 2nd Regiment, U.S.Dragoons. Mex.Sur.App.#15972, Cert.#11347. (not abstracted)

STEVENSON,JAMES T.-Mexican War Pension Application dated 1887, Arkansas. Widow, Elizabeth. Service as Sergeant in Company E, 1st Regiment, Arkansas Mounted Volunteers. Mex.Sur.App.#6176, Cert.#8610, Mex.Wid.App.#12420, Cert.#9429. (not abstracted)

STEWART,BENJAMIN D.-Mexican War Pension Application dated 1887, Arkansas. Widow, Sarah J. Service in Company F, Arkansas Volunteer Cavalry. Mex.Sur.App.#6147, Cert.#1591, Mex.Wid.App.#10342, Cert.#9116. (not abstracted)

STEWART,BENJAMIN F.-Mexican War Pension Application dated 1887, Arkansas. Widow, Mary Virginia. Service as 1st Lieutenant, Company I, 1st Regiment, Kentucky Volunteers. Mex.Wid.App.#2575, Cert.#470. (not abstracted)

STEWART,JOHN-Mexican War Pension Application. Widow, Unica. Service in Captain Hughsmith's Company, Texas Mounted Volunteers. Mex.Sur. App.#6168, Cert.#16405, dated 1887 Arkansas. Mex.Wid.App.#16479, dated 1902 Missouri. (not abstracted)

STEWART,SAMUEL-Mexican War Pension Application dated 1887, Arkansas. Widow, Ann E. Service in Company B, 5th Regiment, Tennessee Volunteers. Mex.Sur.App.#6185, Cert.#1764, Mex.Wid.App.#16285, Cert.#12602. (not abstracted)

STEWART,SAMUEL-Mexican War Pension Application dated 1887, Arkansas. Widow, Elizabeth. Service in Company A, Gray's Battalion, Arkansas Volunteers. Mex.Sur.App.#6184, Cert.#16353, Mex.Wid.App.#10551, Cert.#8946. (not abstracted)

STEWART,WILLIAM M.-Mexican War Pension Application dated 1887, Arkansas. Service in Company A, 1st Regiment, Tennessee Volunteers. Mex.Sur.App.#6191, Cert.#1759. (not abstracted)

STIFFT,MICHAEL, (name also Sztyfft)-Mexican War Pension Application dated 1887, Arkansas. Service in Captain Harding's Company, U.S.Ordinance Departmant. Mex.Sur.App.#15105, Cert.#10680. (not abstracted)

STINNETT,WILEY-Mexican War Pension Application dated 1887, Arkansas. Widow, Matilda Susan. Service in Company F, Yell's Regiment, Arkansas Mounted Volunteers. Mex.Sur.App.#17078, Cert.#11942, Mex.Wid.App.#16674, Cert.#13046. (not abstracted)

STOLSWORTH,JOHN-Mexican War Pension Application dated 1887, Arkansas. Served in Company E, 16th Regiment, U.S.Infantry. Mex.Sur.App.#12817, Cert.#10123. (not abstracted)

STONE,CALEB H.-Mexican War Pension Application dated 1891, Arkansas. Served in Company G, 4th Regiment, Indiana Volunteers. Mex.Sur.App. #23269, Cert.#19314. Remarks: soldier died 8 December 1916 in Camden, Arkansas. (not abstracted)

STONE, JOHN T.-Mexican War Pension Application dated 1887, Arkansas. Widow, America. Served in Company E, 4th Regiment, Kentucky Volunteers. Mex.Sur.App.#11354, Cert.#7637, Mex.Wid.App.#11681, Cert.#9079. (not abstracted)

STONE,NICHOLAS C.-War of 1812 pension application W.O.#10119, W.C.#5332. Service in Captain Crunk's Company of Tennessee Militia. He served from 13 November 1814 to 13 May 1815, and was at the Battle of New Orleans. Nicholas Stone married Celia Evans, 10 September 1813, in Robertson County, Tennessee. He died in Carroll County, Tennessee on 12 August 1835. Widow's pension application dated 29 April 1873, Eagle Creek, Bradley County, Arkansas, Celia Stone age 79. The only family data contained in this file is nearly illegible, "Evans Stone, the son of Nicholas and Sealy Stone his wife, was born July 28th 1814; Mary __? Stone, the daughter of Nicholas and Sealy Stone his wife, was born October 16th 18__?" Celia Stone died 17 August 1884.

STONE,WALTER C.-Mexican War Pension Application dated 1887, Arkansas. Widow, Elizabeth. Service in Company C, 3rd Regiment, U.S.Dragoons. Mex.Sur.App.#6246, Cert.#2706, Mex.Wid.App.#16845, Cert.#13816. (not abstracted)

STORY,MELVIN-Mexican War Pension Application dated 1887, Arkansas. Widow, Mary C. Service in Company B, Gray's Battalion, Arkansas Volunteers. Mex.Sur.App.#6237, Cert.#16635, Mex.Wid.#19784, Cert.#15728. (not abstracted)

STOTTS, JOHN-Mexican War Pension Application dated 1887, Arkansas. Served in Company B, 3rd Regiment, Tennessee Volunteers. Widow, Rachel. Mex.Wid.App.#2093, Cert.#4941. (not abstracted)

STOUT,JAMES-Mexican War Pension Application dated 1887, Arkansas. Service in Company A, Arkansas Volunteer Cavalry. Mex.Sur.App. #10359, Cert.#4511. Remarks: Late War Original #1078978; Company C, 4th Regiment, Arkansas Cavalry. (not abstracted)

STOVALL,WILLIAM-War of 1812 pension application S.O.#30162, S.C.#21671. B.L.W.#45306-80-50. Service in Captain William Holman's Company of Virginia Militia, form 28 August 1814 to 19 February 1815. He was drafted in Goochland County, Virginia, and was stationed near the city of Richmond. He married Judith Babb, 24 December 1818, in Powhatan County, Virginia. He applied for pension 25 April 1875, Cabot Station, Lonoke County, Arkansas, his age 81. He died 30 April 1887 in Lonoke County, at the home of his son, R.A.Stovall.

STRANGE,THOMAS-Mexican War Pension Application. Widow, Nancy E. Service in Company I, 4th Regiment, Kentucky Volunteers. Mex.Sur.App.#21173, Cert.#17920, dated 1889, Kansas; Mex.Wid.App. #16974, Cert.#13224, dated 1903, Arkansas. (not abstracted)

STROCK,DANIEL H.-Mexican War Pension Application dated 1887, Arkansas. Service in Company B, 2nd Regiment, Tennessee Volunteers. Mex.Sur.App.#15341, Cert.#10867. Remarks: Soldier died 22 June 1914. (not abstracted)

STUBBLEFIELD,ABSOLOM-Mexican War Pension Application dated 1892, Arkansas. Widow, Fanny. Service in Captain Caviman's Company of Arkansas Volunteers. Mex.Wid.App.#10859, no cert. number. (not abstracted)

SULLIVAN,EUGENE-Old war pension application; Inv. Cert. #8898, file #25452, Mex.Wid. #12543. Service as 2nd Lieutenant in Tennessee Volunteers, Mexican War. (not abstracted)

SUMMERS,CALVIN-Mexican War Pension Application dated 1884, Arkansas. Service in Company A, Gray's Battalion, Arkansas Volunteers. Widow, Lucinda H. Mex.Sur.App.#6287, Cert.#14885, Mex.Wid.App.#14672, Cert.#11592. (not abstracted)

SURRITTE,JAMES H.-Mexican War Pension Application dated 1892, Arkansas. Served in Captain Angney's Company, Missouri Volunteers. Mex.Sur.App.#23784, Cert.#19936. (not abstracted)

SUTHERLAND/SOUTHERLAND,DANIEL-Revolutionary War Pension Application #S32545, dated 13 May 1833, Bledsoe County, Tennessee. He was born in March 1753 in Hanover County, North Carolina. He first entered service in Rowan County, North Carolina in Captain William Knox's Company, Colonel Martin's Regiment. He stated that his Ensign was Abel Armstrong and that his Lieutenant was Richard Grimes. His first assignment was guarding Tories who had been taken prisoner in a battle that had taken place between Cross Creek and Wilmington. His second tour of duty, he served in Captain Samuel Reed's Company, Colonel Frank Locke commander in General Rutherford's Regiment, in a skirmish against the Cherokee Indians. After that tour of duty he moved to Wilkes County, North Carolina, where he was again called into service and continued to serve against the Cherokees and the Tories. After the war he remained in Wilkes County for about 23 or 24 years, then spent about a year in Cumberland County, Kentucky. From there he moved to Bledsoe County, Tennessee, where he had lived about 25 years in 1833. On 27 May 1837, he applied to have his pension transferred to the Arkansas agency, as he had moved to Madison County because "his daughter, who intermarried with John Holman, and was residing in Madison County, Arkansas, the affiant is old and infirm and that he wished to live with his son-in-law and daughter the remainder of his life".

SUTTON,ASBURY-Mexican War Pension Application dated 1887, Arkansas. Widow, Elizabeth. He served as Corporal in Company I, 5th Regiment, Tennessee Infantry. Mex.Sur.App.#12821, Cert.#10213, Mex.Wid.App. #13571, Cert.#10953. (not abstracted)

SWEET,JOHN-Mexican War Pension Application dated 1887, Arkansas. Widow,·Susan. He served in Captain Foster's Company E, Seymour's Battalion, Georgia Volunteers. Mex.Sur.App.#6315, Cert.#1964, Mex.Wid.App.#9771, Cert.#8081. (not abstracted)

SWEETEN,SAMUEL M.-Mexican War Pension Application dated 1888, Arkansas. Served in Captain Jackson's Company, 2nd Regiment, Mississippi Volunteers. Mex.Sur.App.#18975, Cert.#15117. (not abstracted)

SWIFT,CROMWELL-Mexican War Pension Application dated 1887, Arkansas. Widow, Ann. Service in Captain Holmes' Company, 7th Regiment, U.S.Infantry. Mex.Wid.App.#2114, Cert.#2099. (not abstracted)

SYBERG,ARNOLD-Mexican War Pension Application dated 1887, Arkansas. Served as Captain, Company I, 11th Regiment, U.S.Infantry. Mex.Sur. App.#14358, Cert.#12167. (not abstracted)

TAPP,WILLIAM-War of 1812 Pension Application. S.O.#29507, S.O. #21336, W.O.#34803, W.C.#24913. Service in Captain Edward Clement's Company, South Carolina Militia from 1 October 1814 to 7 March 1815. He enlisted at Spartanburg District, South Carolina. Moved to Arkansas from Alabama about the year 1860. He married Sarah Carter, 22 May 1872, in Van Buren County, Arkansas. She had been married to William Carter in 1862, he died "during the

War of the Rebellion." William Tapp applied for pension on 9 January 1874, his age 77, he was residing in Riggsville, Stone County, Arkansas. He died 24 June 1877.

TAYLOR,JAMES H.-Mexican War Pension Application. Served in Captain Campbell's Company, 3rd Regiment, Illinois Volunteers. Widow, Mary E. Mex.Sur.App.#12091, Cert.#6456, dated 1887, Illinois; Mex.Wid.App.#9746, Cert.#7980, dated 1891, Arkansas. (not abstracted)

TAYLOR,WILLIAM-Mexican War Pension Application dated 1887, Arkansas. Service in Company D, 1st Regiment, Illinois Volunteers. Mex.Sur. App.#16602, Cert.#12237. Remarks: O.W.Inv.Rej.#149903. (not abstracted)

TEAGUE,LOGAN-Mexican War Pension Application dated 1887, Arkansas. Service in Captain Ranney's Company, 3rd Regiment, Missouri Volunteers. Mex.Sur.App.#15566, Cert.#16381, Mex.Wid.App.#10749. (not abstracted)

TEMPLE,RODERICK-War of 1812 pension application W.O.#35631, W.C.#26143. Service in Captain Giddin's Company of Tennessee Militia, from 28 January 1814 to 18 May 1814. He married Mary Lee, 2 October 1817, in Williamson County, Tennessee (certified copy of marriage license enclosed in file). In 1843, Roderick and Mary Temple moved from Williamson County to Davidson County, Tennessee. He died there in October 1849. Mary Temple applied for pension on 24 December 1878, she was about 79 years old, and a resident of Crawford County, Arkansas. She stated that her oldest child was born in 1818. Affidavits from Frances M. Temple age 49 and William Temple, both of Crawford County, and children of Roderick and Mary Temple.

TERRELL,THOMAS POE-War of 1812 pension application W.O.#20591, W.C.#10998. Service in Captain William Welsh's Company of South Carolina Militia, from 15 October 1814 to 12 March 1815. He was born ca 1795, in Chesterfield District, South Carolina, where he volunteered into service. He married Ann Jackson, 4 September 1824, in Chesterfield District, where they continued to reside on a farm until 1833, when they moved to Sumter County, Alabama. In 1844, they moved to Union County, Arkansas, and finally to Ashley County, Arkansas in 1858. Thomas Terrell died at Marie Saline, Arkansas, on 28 January 1866. Ann Terrell applied for pension on 6 April 1878, at which time she stated that she was age 70, "October last". Margaret Jane Boyett, born 27 December 1825, oldest child of Ann and Thomas Terrell, stated that she had no brother or sister, living in the State of Arkansas, and that she was married in the year 1841.

TERRY,REUBEN-Mexican War Pension Application dated 1887, Arkansas. Widow, Fannie J. He served as Sergeant in Company D, 3rd Regiment, Indiana Volunteer Infantry. Mex.Sur.App.#12096, Cert.#4882, Mex.Wid.App.#18423, Cert.#14452. (not abstracted)

TETRICK,ABRAHAM-War of 1812 pension application W.O.#33966, W.C.#21193. B.L.W.#23146-160-50. Service in Captain Shortz's Company of Illinois Rangers from 16 May 1814 to 16 May 1815. He enlisted in St.Clair County, Illinois. Abraham Tetrick and Ann Huffman were married in St.Clair County, on 29 May 1817. They lived in St.Clair, Fayette and Shelby Counties, Illinois. Soldier died in Shelby County on 12 October 1838. Ann Tetrick applied for Bounty Land in Shelby County on 18 February 1853, and applied for pension on 7 September 1878, a resident of Dora, Labette County, Kansas. Affidavits form Daniel Huffman age 56 and John H. Huffman age 46, both residents of Shelby County, Illinois in 1852, who stated that they had attended the wedding of Abraham and Ann Tetrick. Abraham Tetrick, age 45, resident of Gorham, Kansas and Peter Tetrick, age 39, resident of Dora, Kansas in

1878, both identified as sons of Abraham and Ann Tetrick. On 12 December 1892 at Siloam Springs, Benton County, Arkansas, Mrs. Ann Tetrick applied for a new pension certificate, to replace the one she had lost, stated that she was residing in Benton County, with her daughter.

THOMAS,BARNARD-Mexican War Pension Application dated 1887, Arkansas. Service in Company B, Santa Fe Battalion, Missouri Mounted Volunteers. Widow, Sarah E. Mex.Sur.App.#10430, Cert.#3884, Mex.Wid.App. #14751, Cert.#11666. (not abstracted)

THOMAS,FRANCIS M.-Mexican War Pension Application dated 1889, Arkansas. Served in Company C, 3rd Regiment, U.S.Dragoons. Mex. Sur.App.#21882, Cert.#18399. (not abstracted)

THOMAS,WILLIAM S.-Mexican War Pension Application dated 1887, Arkansas. Service in Company K, 2nd Regiment, New York Volunteers. Mex.Sur.App.#10439, no cert.#. Remarks: O.W.Inv. file #26794. (not abstracted)

THOMASON,ELISHA-Mexican War Pension Application dated 1889, Arkansas. Widow, Martha. He served in Company A, 5th Regiment, Tennessee Volunteers. Mex.Wid.App.#7576, Cert.#6123. (not abstracted)

THOMASON,JOHN J.-Mexican War Pension Application dated 1888, Arkansas. Widow, Elizabeth. Mex.Wid.App.#5899, Cert.#3608. (not abstracted)

THOMPSON,BLAGBWIN-War of 1812 Pension Application. W.O.#8311, W.C.#6314. Service in Captain James Tunnell's Company, Tennessee Militia. Married Lucretia Lawson, June 1809, in Campbell County, Tennessee. Soldier died in Benton County, Arkansas on 4 October 1861. Widow's pension application dated 23 February 1872, Huntsville, Madison County, Arkansas, Lucretia Thompson age 80. Affidavit dated 12 February 1873, Madison County, Arkansas, "We, Zachariah Lewallen and Nancy Lewallen, of the County of Madison, State of Arkansas, say we were well acquainted with Blagburn (sic) and Lucretia Thompson from about the year AD 1838, up to about the year AD 1855 in Campbell County, Tennessee, and that, of their children whom we have known was A.G.Thompson, Harmon Thompson, B.M.Thompson, Milly Thompson, Annie Thompson, Sarah Thompson, Lucretia Thompson, Nancy Thompson and Martha Thompson. Blagburn and Lucretia Thompson left Campbell County, Tennessee about the year AD 1855, and we find the widow, Lucretia Thompson, in the County of Madison, State of Arkansas. Zachariah Lewallen's age is 51 years old the 26th day of April AD 1873, and Nancy Lewallen's age is 55 years old the 18th day of February AD 1873." Lucretia Thompson stated in 1873 that the following persons had attended her wedding; Randolph Lawson, Susan Lawson, Merilley Phillips, May Prewitt, Elisha Lawson, James English and John and Sarah Jeffries, all of whom were deceased in 1873 except Sarah Jeffries.

THOMPSON,JAMES ALLEN-War of 1812 pension application Sur. Cert. #17732, W.C.#24907. Service in Captain Benjamin Cleveland's Company of Georgia Militia from 24 August 1813 to 3 March 1814. The index to this pension contains the following notation; "this woman also applied for pension on account of the services of her former husband, Redbird Tiger, Private in Co. B. Indian Home Guard, Civil War. (W.O.#110629) which claim is consolidated with the claim of Mary J. Woodall, the minor child of said Redbird Tiger. All of these papers in admitted files under Minor's Original #274560". This file would be in the General Pension files, which I have not abstracted. James Thompson's pension application filed 8 April 1872, he was age 72, and a resident of The Delaware District, Cherokee Nation (P.O. Maysville, Benton County, Arkansas)he stated that he had enlisted into service in Franklin County,

Georgia. He married Patsy Lynch, 2 December 1817 in the Cherokee Nation. She died 13 September 1861. He married Ann Tyger 8 October 1867. She was the widow of Redbird Tiger. James Thompson died 8 January 1875 and Ann Thompson applied for pension 6 May 1878, her age 50, and she was a resident of Delaware District, Cherokee Nation. She died ca 1895.

THOMPSON,PETER G.-Mexican War Pension Application datted 1887, Arkansas. Service in D Battalion, Georgia Infantry. Widow, Catherine. Mex.Sur.App.#13093, Cert.#7387, Mex.Wid.App.#19584. (not abstracted)

THORN,MICHAEL-War of 1812 pension application S.O.#25478, S.C.#20814, W.O.#42323, W.C.#32772. "The Adjutant General's Office at Washington, D.C, reports the following on Michael Thorn, he enlisted the eighth day of January 1812, to serve five years, and was assigned to the 7th Regiment of U.S.Infantry. He served in Lieutenant Brontin's Company and was present at New Orleans April 30th 1814; roll dated December 5th 1814 reports him in hospital; Order Book of Lt. Brontin's Company reports him discharged December 20th 1815, without claim to bounty or land. He is also reported as serving in the 1st Regiment, U.S.Infantry, Captain William O. Butler's Company, and absent on furlough from 31 August to 31 December 1815; roll dated at New Orleans 29 February 1816 reports him "deserted the 1st Regt. U.S.Infantry, whilst on furlough." Much of this file is concerned with this man trying to straighten out the confusion in his records. He smashed a leg while loading artillery aboard a schooner at New Orleans. He was hospitalized, and then given a furlough. While home on furlough, (in Monongalia, Virginia now West Virginia) his father (Thomas Thorn) petitioned for a discharge for his injured son. The discharge was received, without any benefit of bounty. Colonel Baldwin tried to have the discharge corrected, and sent the discharge to Washington D.C. where it apparently was misplaced. Michael Thorn applied for pension 9 November 1871 at Berryville, Carroll County, Arkansas. He had never received bounty land, but did finally persuade the Interior Department to review his records. The examiner petitioned the Adjutant General's Office to correct the records, to which the Adjutant General's Office replied, "Respectfully returned to the Commissioner of Pensions; the records of this office cannot be changed at this late day to show that the within named man was not a deserter!" Michael Thorn was married to Susan Knotts, 23 December 1815, in Monongalia County, Virginia. She died in 1865 and he married Elizabeth Gibson, 21 May 1872, in Carroll County, Arkansas. (Carroll Co. Marriage Book A, page 62) She was the widow of William E. Gibson, who was killed on the last day of January 1864. Michael Thorn had enlisted into service at Natchez, served at The Battle of New Orleans, and died 3 June 1882 in Carroll County, Arkansas.

TILLMAN,JOHN-Mexican War Pension Application dated 1888, Arkansas. Widow, Susan A. Service in Company B, 1st Regiment, Alabama Volunteers. Mex.Wid.App.#6324, Cert.#5456. Remarks: Rebellion, Company D, 3rd Regt. Arkansas Cavalry. Wid.Orig.#855286. (not abstracted)

TIMS,JOHN-Mexican War Pension Application dated 1887, Arkansas. Widow, Elizabeth J. Service in Company F, 3rd Regiment, Illinois Infantry. Mex.Sur.App.#15432, Cert.#11100, Mex.Wid.App.#19960, Cert.#15900. Remarks: O.W.Inv.Rej.#20739. (not abstracted)

TOLLETT,HENRY-War of 1812 pension application S.O.#16234, S.C.#17340, W.O.#13118, W.C.#10330. B.L.W.#43515-80-50. Service in Captain Miles Vernon's Company of Tennessee Militia. He enlisted at Pikeville, Rhea County, Tennessee. He married Eliza Brown 15 January 1819 in Bledsoe County, Tenn. Bounty Land application dated 2 March 1852, Washington County, Arkansas, Henry Tollett's

age about 56. Miles Vernon, of Laclede County, Missouri, affirmed
the claim for bounty land. Henry Tollett died 13 August 1871
in Washington County, Ark., and Eliza Tollett applied for pension.
She died 15 October 1885; the family data contained in this
file; Eliza E. Easley, age 44 in 1887, granddaughter of Eliza
Tollett; Mrs. James Morton, daughter of Eliza Tollett. Henrietta
Barringer stated that her husband was grandson of Eliza Tollett.

TOMBLESTON,WILLIAM H.-Mexican War Pension Application dated
1887, Arkansas. Widow, Mary A. Service in Captain West's Company
B, Gray's Battalion, Arkansas Volunteers. Mex.Sur.App.#12847,
Cert.#14273, Mex.Wid.App.#8107, Cert.#6408. (not abstracted)

TONEY,WILLIAM F.-Mexican War Pension Application dated 1887,
Arkansas. Service in Company F, 1st Regiment, Tennessee Cavalry.
Mex.Sur.App.#6485, Cert.#9569. (not abstracted)

TOOLEY,ANDERSON M.-Mexican War Pension Application dated 1887,
Arkansas. Service in Company D, 1st Regiment, Arkansas Mounted
Infantry. Mex.Sur.App.#17019, Cert.#13647. (not abstracted)

TRAMMEL,GEORGE S.-Mexican War Pension Application dated 1887,
Arkansas. Widow, Mary E. Served in Captain Engart's Independent
Company, Arkansas Volunteers. Mex.Wid.App.#2182, Cert.#2985. (not
abstracted)

TRIMBLE,JOHN N.-Mexican War Pension Application dated 1888,
Arkansas. Widow, Amanda. Service in Company D, Arkansas Mounted
Volunteers. Mex.Sur.App.#19024, Cert.#15166, Mex.Wid.App.#20344,
Cert.#16222. Remarks: XC 2664289; soldier died 23 March 1915
at Harrison, Arkansas. (not abstracted)

TRITT,CLARK-Mexican War Pension dated 1887, Arkansas. Service
in Company D, 3rd Regiment, Missouri Mounted Volunteers. Widow,
Sarah. Mex.Sur.App.#10486, Cert.#5963, Mex.Wid.App.#17915,
Cert.#14126. Remarks: W.O.#91692, Wm. Raney, A 4 Ark.Inf. Rebellion
F 12 Kan.Vol.Inv.Orig.#924491. (not abstracted)

TROLINGER,WILLIAM P.-Mexican War Pension Application dated 1887,
Arkansas. Service in Company K, 1st Regiment, Tennessee Volunteers.
Mex.Sur.App.#6516, Cert.#1856. (not abstracted)

TSCHIEMER,JACOB-Mexican War Pension Application dated 1887,
Arkansas. Service in Company E, 1st Regiment, Arkansas Cavalry.
Widow, Harriett. Mex.Sur.App.#6538, Cert.#8388, Mex.Wid.App.#11963,
Cert.#9321. (not abstracted)

TUBBS,JOHN L.-Old War pension application dated 1851, Arkansas. O.W.
Inv.Cert.#7567, file #25463. Service in Company C, 12th Regiment
of U.S.Infantry, Mexican War. (not abstracted)

TUCKER,JONAS-War of 1812 pension application W.O.#24004, W.C.#28622.
Service in Captain Joel Barnard's Company of Massachusetts Militia.
He was married first to Abigail Harper, who died in Salon, Ohio
on 4 April 1854. He married Mary Harper 24 September 1856 in
Cuyahoga County, Ohio, certificate enclosed. She was the widow
of Cotton Harper, who died at Orange County, Ohio 10 March 1855.
Jonas Tucker died at Byron, Michigan on 7 February 1862. The
widow's pension was being paid at the Arkansas Pension agency
from the year 1880, her address being Hico, Arkansas. In the
year 1886, the Special Examination Division of the Department
of Interior, Pension Office, addressed the Postmasters at Bentonville
and Hico, Arkansas, seeking knowledge of this lady. No further
word was received, so she was dropped from the pension roll.
This file does not give any information on her removal to the
State of Arkansas.

TUGGLE,WASHINGTON-Old War Pension Application. Service in Arkansas Cavalry, Mexican War. Widow, Eliza. O.W.Wid.Cert.#4712, File #22468. (not abstracted)

TURNER,JOHN THOMAS-Mexican War Pension Application dated 1887, Arkansas. Service in Company H, 5th Regiment, U.S.Infantry. Mex. Sur.App.#10512, Cert.#12123. Remarks: Mex.Sur.O.#11281 duplicate of #10512. (not abstracted)

TURNER,JOHN M.-Mexican War Pension Application dated 1887, Arkansas. Served as Corporal in Company C, Arkansas Mounted Infantry. Widow, Arabel. Mex.Sur.App.#6551, Cert.#1966, Mex.Wid.App.#15477, Cert. #12079. B.L.W.#9703-160-47. Remarks: Soldier died 12 January 1900 at Lamar, Arkansas. (not abstracted)

TURNER,WILLIAM-Old War Pension Application dated 1852, Arkansas. Served in Arkansas Militia, Mexican War. O.W.Inv.Cert.#7303, File #25893. (not abstracted)

UMSTATTD,ARCHIBALD F.-Mexican War Pension Application dated 1887, Arkansas. Service in Company G, 4th Regiment, Indiana Infantry. Mex.Sur.App.#14466, Cert.#10461. (not abstracted)

UNDERWOOD,ELDRIDGE-Mexican War Pension Application dated 1887, Arkansas. Service in Company D, 4th Regiment, Tennessee Volunteers. Mex.Sur.App.#22090, Cert.#18537. (not abstracted)

VADEN,GEORGE W.-Mexican War Pension Application dated 1887, Arkansas. Service in Company G, 1st Regiment, Tennessee Volunteers. Mex.Sur.App.#6581, Cert.#1251. (not abstracted)

VANCE,DAVID-Revolutionary War Pension Application #S32031 dated 8 January 1833, Independence County, Arkansas Territory. David Vance was born 25 August 1757 in Winchester, Virginia. He first entered service as a drafted soldier of the militia in February 1778, under command of Captain William Dobson in Salisbury, Rowan County, North Carolina. He was marched from Hanging Rock to Charleston, to Cowpens and then to Black Swamp. After this tour of duty, he returned to his home in Guilford County, N.C., where he was taken prisoner. He was in jail for four weeks before he was given parole. He "hid out" until after the Battle of Guilford. After that time he served as a scout in a company of lighthorse under command of Colonel Lee. After the war he moved to South Carolina, where he remained for 18 years before moving to Tennessee. He remained in Tenn. about 10 years. He lived in Missouri about 8 years before moving to Arkansas Territory.

VANDERBILT,AARON D.-War of 1812 pension application S.O.#26928, S.C.#18855, W.O.#36288, W.C.#27006. B.L.W.#49597-40-50 and #96213-120-55. Service in Captain Homer Whitmore's Company of New York Militia from 2 September 1814 to 3 December 1814. He served at Harlem Heights, where he assisted in "throwing up breastworks and making entrenchments, thus fortifying the heights." He was then assigned to guard duty, "watching for the British, who laid off in the East River in their ships of war." Aaron Vanderbilt was born in New Jersey ca 1796, and was a blacksmith by occupation. He married Elizabeth Littlefield, 29 June 1823, in Shelby County, Alabama. The ceremony was performed by her brother, Nathaniel Littlefield. Elizabeth was born in November 1805. Soldier's pension application dated 24 February 1872, Rondo, Lafayette County, Arkansas, he was age 78. He died in Miller County, Arkansas on 3 January 1879. Elizabeth Vanderbilt applied for pension 26 April 1879, she was 74 years old and a resident of Texarkana, Miller County. Affidavit dated 1879, Miller County,"I, Absalom Vanderbilt, am forty five years old. I am the fourth child of Aaron and Elizabeth Vanderbilt. I was born in Shelby County, Alabama. We lived in Alabama until 1844, when we moved to the State of Mississippi. We moved to Bradley County, Arkansas in 1847, where we lived until 1855, when we moved to Miller County, Arkansas." This file also contains an affidavit from Aaron D. Vanderbilt, born ca 1830, sixth child of Aaron and Elizabeth. Mrs. Vanderbilt also referred to a daughter, residing in Bowie County, Texas in 1879. In January 1869, the U.S.Land Office at Washington, Arkansas, wrote to the Commissioner of Pensions at Washington, D.C., "The enclosed B.L.W.#96213, act of 3 March 1855, issued to Aaron Vanderbilt 16 October 1860 and assigned to Edwin Culley 19 January 1861, was attempted by Mr.Culley to be located on U.S.Land on the 26th November 1861, during the Rebellion and has been mutilated by the State Officers by crossing it with black lines and crossing out the commissioner's name, and Mr.Culley now requests me to enclose it to you and ask you to issue a duplicate."

VANLANDINGHAM,JOHN-War of 1812 pension application S.O.#10332, S.C.#4495. He served from 24 November 1814 to about 23 November 1819. He was appointed Corporal 26 June 1815, transferred to the 4th Regiment, U.S.Infantry. He was transferred to the 7th U.S.Infantry 13 December 1815, sent on Command to the Creek Nation 21 January 1816; he was promoted to Sergeant 18 December 1816, served in Captain William Taylor's Company, Captain Richard H. Bell's Company, Captain A.L.Langham's Company and Captain George Birch's Company. He married Lucy ? 11 April 1820. In 1871, he was a resident of Boone County, Arkansas (P.O. Yellville, Marion County). In 1883, he was age 93 and a resident of Marshall Prairie, Newton County, Arkansas.

VANSANT,ELIJAH L.(name also Vinsant)-Mexican War Pension Application dated 1887, Arkansas. Widow, Sarah. Service in Captain Gutherie's Company A, Tennessee Volunteers. Mex.Wid.App.#2225, Cert.#2811. Remarks: Late War, Co.A, 1st Ark.Cav. Wid.O.#610387. (not abstracted)

VAN ZANT,JAMES-Revolutionary War Pension Application #S32034, dated 20 November 1832, Lawrence County, Territory of Arkansas. He was born in 1756 in Pennsylvania. He entered service in July 1775 in Bedford County, Pennsylvania in Captain Robert Cluggage's Company, Pennsylvania Regiment under command of Colonel Thompson and Colonel Edward Hands. He served at the Siege of Boston, then was stationed at Graves End on Long Island. He was discharged after the arrival of the British Fleet. He again volunteered in the Spring of 1778 at Frankstown in Bedford County, Pa., and served in Captain Henry Black's Company, then served another six month tour of duty in 1779. After the war he moved to Kentucky, from there to Indiana and from Indiana he moved to Lawrence County, Territory of Arkansas.
Lawrence County, Arkansas, Probate Book B, page 221, "James Van Zandt, late of said County, is dead without having made Last Will and Testament, and Martin Van Zandt of said County having duly qualified according to law as administrator to said James Van Zandt, deceased, ___ to perform all and singular the duties of administrator, according to law" recorded "14th day of February AD 1834 and of the American Independence the 58th year".

VAUGHN,JOSEPH-Mexican War Pension Application dated 1887, Arkansas. Served in Company G, 13th Regiment, U.S.Infantry. Mex.Sur.App.#16939, Cert.#12131. (not abstracted)

VAUGHN,RANDOLPH/RANDALL-Old war pension application O.W.Wid. Cert.-#984, file #29145, O.W.Min. Cert.#3899, file #11693. Service in Company C, 12th Regiment, U.S.Infantry; Mexican War. Widow, Matilda. (not abstracted)

VENABLE,WILLIAM-Revolutionary War Pension Application #W7366, dated 8 October 1832, Bond County, Illinois. He was born in Prince Edward County, Virginia in February 1755. He volunteered into service in Spartenburg, South Carolina in Captain Lewis Musick's Company, Colonel John Earl's Regiment of South Carolina Militia. He served against the Cherokee Indians in the years 1778,79 and 80. His Captain Musick was killed in a skirmish with Cherokees at a place called "Hight's Old Place" in Rutherford County, North Carolina. Captain Musick was replaced by Captain Edward Hampton, who was also killed in a later skirmish. In January of 1781, William Venable enlisted into a company of Lighthorse in Captain George Taylor's Company, Colonel "Billy" Washington's Regiment. In the Battle of Cowpens, William Venable was wounded in the right leg by a musket ball and received two sword cuts on the head, but continued in battle. After the war, he remained in South Carolina about 20 years before moving to Tennessee and Kentucky for 20 years. He spent about 3 years in North Carolina and then moved to Illinois about the year 1829. William Venable died 12 April 1836, and his widow, Sarah, applied for pension in Franklin County, Arkansas on 3 July 1854. She stated that she had married in South Carolina in January 1792.

VERDIN,JAMES-Mexican War Pension Application dated 1887, Arkansas. Widow, Lucinda. Service in Captain Taylor's Company, Archibald Yell's Regiment, Arkansas Mounted Volunteers. Mex.Wid.App.#2221, Cert.#1844. (not abstracted)

VESS,WILLIAM W.-Mexican War Pension Application dated 1887, Arkansas. Widow, Amanda J. Service in Captain Freeman's Company, 4th Regiment, Tennessee Volunteers. Mex.Sur.App.#6620, Cert.#14403, Mex.Wid.App.#15853. Remarks: O.W.Inv.Rej.#20115, Rebellion K25. (not abstracted)

VINCENT,ALLEN L.-Mexican War Pension Application dated 1888, Arkansas. Service in Captain Arnold's Company, Johnston's Texas Rifle Volunteers. Mex.Sur.App.#19123, Cert.#17019. (not abstracted)

VINSON,WILLIAM-Mexican War Pension Application dated 1887, Arkansas. Service in Company C, Gray's Battalion, Arkansas Volunteers. Mex.Sur.App.#10547, Cert.#15543. (not abstracted)

VODING,ELIJAH-Mexican War Pension Application dated 1888, Arkansas. Widow, Jane. Service in Company C, Willock's Battalion, Missouri Mounted Volunteers. Mex.Wid.App.#6138, Cert.#4323. (not abstracted)

VOSE,HENRY T.-Mexican War Pension Application dated 1888, Arkansas. Served in Captain Crowninshield's Company, Massachusetts Volunteers. Mex.Sur.App.#18905, Cert.#15675. Remarks: O.W.Inv. pending. (not abstracted)

WADKINS,CARMON-Mexican War Pension Application dated 1887, Arkansas. Service in Company G, 2nd Regiment, Tennessee Volunteers. Mex.Sur. App.#13098, Cert.#9358. Remarks: O.W.Inv.file #25475. Rebellion Cert.#690805, Co.M, 3rd Ark.Vol.Cav. (not abstracted)

WAKEFIELD,WILLIAM-Old war pension application O.W.Wid. Cert.#1878, file #11717. Service in 12th Regiment of U.S.Infantry; Mexican War. Widow, Anney. (not abstracted)

WALDEN,TERRY-War of 1812 pension application S.O.#6129, S.C.#24428. Service in Captain William Payne's Company of Virginia Militia. (not abstracted)

WALDROP,JOSEPH R.-Mexican War Pension Application dated 1887, Arkansas. Widow, Isabella. Service in Captain William's Company, Palmetto's Regiment, South Carolina Volunteers. Mex.Sur.App.#6668, Cert.#9279, Mex.Wid.App.#9435, Cert.#7459. (not abstracted)

WALKER,JESSE C.-Mexican War Pension Application dated 1887, Arkansas. Widow, Mary. Service in Company I, 1st Regiment, Indiana Volunteers. Mex.Sur.App.#6679, Cert.#1406, Mex.Wid.App.#12800, Cert.#9911. (not abstracted)

WALKER,JOHN 2nd-Mexican War Pension Application. Widow, Allie F.Carter. Service in Company H, 2nd Regiment, Illinois Volunteers. Mex.Sur.App.#20816, Cert.#17787, dated 1888, Arkansas; Mex.Wid.App. #18714, Cert.#14959, dated 1907, California. Remarks: O.W.Inv.Rej. #24168. Soldier died 20 April 1907.

WALKER,WILLIAM-Mexican War Pension Application dated 1887, Arkansas. Widow, Dorinda. Service in Company C, 1st Regiment, Georgia Volunteers. Mex.Wid.App.#4163, Cert.#3968. (not abstracted)

WALKER,WILLIAM T.-Old war pension application O.W.Wid. Cert. #3392, file #14112. Service as Sergeant in 12th Regiment of U.S.Infantry; Mexican War. Widow, Margaret. (not abstracted)

WALLACE,EDWARD F.-Mexican War Pension application dated 1887, Arkansas. Service in Company K, 1st Regiment, Louisiana Volunteers. Mex.Sur.App.#15347, Cert.#10893. (not abstracted)

WALLACE,JOSEPH B.-Mexican War Pension Application dated 1889, Arkansas. Widow, Elizabeth. Service in Captain Crump's Company, Bell's Regiment, Texas Volunteers. Mex.Sur.App.#22365, Cert.#18930, Mex.Wid.App.#17747, Cert.#14790. (not abstracted)

WALLER,CHARLES R.-Mexican War Pension Application dated 1892, Arkansas. Widow, Mary E. Served as Corporal in Captain Curtis' Company, Raiford's Battalion, Alabama Volunteers. Mex.Sur.App. #10787, Cert.#9041. (not abstracted)

WALLER,THOMAS-Mexican War Pension Application dated 1887, Arkansas. Widow, Jane. Service in Captain Moss' Company, 1st Regiment, Missouri Mounted Volunteers. Mex.Sur.App.#18907, Cert.#15865, Mex.Wid.App.#11145, Cert.#8760. (not abstracted)

WALLIS,WILLIAM-Mexican War Pension Application dated 1887, Arkansas. Widow, Jemima. Service in Captain Coleman's Company, 1st Regiment, Alabama Volunteers. Mex.Wid.App.#4198, Cert.#2582. (not abstracted)

WALTON,ALFRED M.-Mexican War Pension Application dated 1889, Arkansas. Widow, Kizirah. Service in Company G, 1st Regiment, Arkansas Volunteer Cavalry. Mex.Wid.App.#3623, Cert.#2266. (not abstracted)

WAMAC/WAMACK,JOHNSON-Revolutionary War Pension Application #S32577, dated 30 October 1837, Madison County, Arkansas. He was born 2 January 1762 in Goochland County, Virginia. He entered into service in a company of horsemen or mounted gunmen in the Volunteer Militia under the command of Captain Jonathan Kemp near Pleasant Gardens on the Catawba River in Burke County, North Carolina, on 20 June 1780. His company was fired upon by Ferguson's Regiment in the Broad River area of Ferguson County, N.C. They retreated to the Watauga River, where they were joined by Colonel Campbell's Virginia Regiment. In the ensuing battle they had one man killed (Peter Branks), but they captured several Tories and a British Dragoon. They received substantial reinforcements, and marched in pursuit of Ferguson's Army. His unit served at King's Mountain, but Wamac was on a special assignment at the time. He was discharged from that tour of duty in October 1780. He rejoined the Militia in April 1781 under command of Captain Joshua Inman. His company was in General Greene's Regiment at the Siege of Ninety-Six, from there they marched to Augusta, Georgia to assist in the taking of Burntfoot's Fort and Fort Grayson. Wamac was discharged at Augusta, Georgia on 25 June 1781, but reenlisted in July

1781 at "Spirit Creek Bridge" in Georgia. He was sent on a scouting mission and received a wound in his right side. He was taken to the Widow Alday's, near Waynesborough, where he was met by Major Boykin. In the ensuing battle, the Tories were repulsed, after which, Wamac was placed in a hospital. He was discharged from service 25 October 1781. After the war he lived in Pendleton District, South Carolina, also in the State of Tennessee, county not named and in Lawrence, Crawford, Washington and Madison Counties, Arkansas.

WARD,LAFAYETTE-Mexican War Pension Application dated 1890, Arkansas. Served in Company C, 2nd Regiment, Kentucky Volunteers. Mex.Sur. App.#22783, Cert.#19131. (not abstracted)

WARD,WILLIAM-Mexican War Pension Application dated 1887, Arkansas. Widow, Marilda. Service in Company B, 1st Regiment, Alabama Volunteers. Mex.Sur.App.#10596, Cert.#6706, Mex.Wid.App.#8085, Cert.#6872. Remarks: Old War Inv. Pending. (not abstracted)

WARDLOW,WILLIAM-Mexican War Pension Application dated 1888, Arkansas. Widow, Elizabeth. Service in Captain Travis' Company, 4th Regiment, Tennessee Volunteers. Mex.Sur.App.#19124, Cert. #15516, Mex.Wid.App.#8568, Cert.#6957. Remarks: Old War Inv. Pending. (not abstracted)

WATKINS,GREEN B.-Mexican War Pension Application dated 1887, Arkansas. Widow, Nancy. Service in Captain Ligon's Company, Alabama Volunteers. Mex.Wid.App.#2260, Cert.#5773. Remarks: late war wid.orig.#312244. (not abstracted)

WATSON,ARTHUR P.-War of 1812 pension application S.O.#30058, S.C.#21608, W.O.#34040, W.C.#31633. Service in Captain Gabriel Gunn's Company of Georgia Militia from 23 August 1813 to 11 March 1814. His pension application dated January 1875, Buchanan, Ouachita County, Arkansas. He stated that he had enlisted in Monticello, Georgia, and was discharged at Fort Hawkins, Georgia. He was married to Jane Duke in Jasper County, Georgia on 1 March 1815. She died in 1867(?), and he married Nicey E. Jones 20 December 1869. Arthur Watson died 22 September 1877 in Ouchita County, Arkansas. Widow, Nicey, died 18 December 1904 in Bienville Parish, Louisana.

WATSON,JAMES-Mexican War Pension Application dated 1887, Arkansas. Widow, Delia E. Service in Company E, 1st Regiment, Tennessee Volunteers. Mex.Wid.App.#3184, Cert.#741. (not abstracted)

WATSON,JOHN W.-Mexican War Pension Application dated 1887, Arkansas. Widow, Caroline. Service in Company B, 1st Regiment, North Carolina Volunteers. Mex.Sur.App.#13517, Cert.#7650, Mex.Wid.App.#14539, Cert.#11708. (not abstracted)

WATSON,JOSEPH S.-Old war pension application dated 1855, Arkansas. O.W.Inv.Cert.#8362, file #6338. Service in Company C, 12th Regiment of U.S.Infantry; Mexican War. (not abstracted)

WATSON,WILLIAM-Mexican War Pension Application dated 1887, Arkansas. Served in Captain Walker's Company, Texas Rangers. Mex.Sur.App.-#17250. Remarks: Old war pending and Indian War #2719, Cert.#1477. (not abstracted)

WAYMOCK,CAGE-Mexican War Pension Application dated 1887, Arkansas. Served in 4th Regiment, U.S.Infantry. Mex.Sur.App.#17631, Cert.-#13178. (not abstracted)

WEAR,LAVATER-Mexican War Pension Application dated 1887, Arkansas. Service in Company I, 5th Regiment, Tennessee Volunteers. Mex.Sur. App.#10619, Cert.#5222. Remarks: O.W.Inv.file #48570. (not abstr)

WEAVER,BENJAMIN-War of 1812 pension application W.O.#10809, W.C.#6154. B.L.W.#88978-120-55. Served as Lieutenant in Captain R.M.Ratton's Company of Tennessee Militia. He was married to Polly Broyles in White County, Tennessee on 16 February 1812 by Benjamin Weaver, uncle of Benjamin Weaver. Soldier died in Washington County, Arkansas, in 1854, and Polly Weaver applied for pension there on 17 April 1874, her age 80. In December 1885, the Postmaster at Cincinnati, Arkansas stated that Polly Weaver had been dead some two or more years at Viney Grove. Washington County, Arkansas, Will Book A, page 138, signed 19 July 1854, recorded 10 August 1854, Will of Benjamin Weaver "Entire estate to my wife, Polly".

WEAVERS,SAMUEL-Mexican War Pension Application dated 1887, Arkansas. Served in Company F, 1st Regiment, Alabama Volunteers. Mex.Sur.App. #13289, Cert.#5968. (not abstracted)

WEBB,ISAIAH-War of 1812 Pension Application, S.O.#9676, S.C.#12084. B.L.W.#6888-160-50. He enlisted in Fayetteville, Tennessee and served from 15 September 1814 to 10 April 1815 in Captain Joseph Kincaid's Company of Tennessee Militia. He served from 1 February 1818 to 30 June 1818 in Captain Hugh Kirk's Company of Tennessee Mounted Gunmen in the Seminole Indian War. Isaiah Webb married Frances May, 1 December 1818, in Rutherford County, Tennessee. His bounty land application dated 2 December 1850 was executed in Bedford County, Tennessee, at which time Benjamin Webb and Samuel Webb, also of Bedford County, gave affidavits. Isaiah Webb applied for pension in April 1871, Pea Ridge, Benton County, Arkansas.

WEBB,JAMES-War of 1812 pension application W.O.#11022, W.C.#6482. B.L.W.#81711-40-50 and #89203-120-55. Service in Captain Richard Benson's Company of Tennessee Militia, from 28 January 1814 to 23 May 1814. He was drafted at Sperryfield, Robinson County, Tennessee. James Webb and Elizabeth Fitts were married 18 July 1814 in Robinson County, Tennessee. He died in Union County, Arkansas on 18 March 1848. Elizabeth Webb applied for bounty land in Union County, in 1855, at which time Winston and Jesse Bruce, also of Union County, stated that they had been close personal friends of the Webbs for twenty years or more. In 1874, Elizabeth Webb applied for pension, her age 75, she was residing in Hillsboro, Union County. She submitted a very mutilated page from her Bible, the only legible entrys, to wit, "James Webb and Elizabeth Fitts was married in the year of our Lord 1814 July 18th; George W. Cravin and Agness M. Webb was married the 14th of August 1848; Francis A.Johnson and Emmarinda Webb was married January 2th 1838; James S.Webb was born in the __? (year) of our __? 1767; Elizabeth Webb was born December the 22, 1800; Daniel L.Webb born January the 18th 1818; Emoundy Webb __ born August __? 1820; Jane (could be James) K.Webb was born August 20, 1824; Rebecca Webb was born May 15th 1833; Jackson Webb was born in the year of our Lord 1815 August the __?; James Webb was borned September 7th 1795 and died the 18th of March 1848." Elizabeth Webb died in Union County on 22 March 1885.

WEBB,JOEL H.-Mexican War Pension Application dated 1888, Arkansas. Widow, Margaret E. Service in Enyart's Independent Company, Arkansas Mounted Volunteers. Mex.Wid.App.#6810, Cert.#5687. (not abstracted)

WEBB,THOMAS J.-Mexican War Pension Application dated 1887, Arkansas. Served in Company D, 1st Regiment, Arkansas Mounted Volunteers. Mex. Sur.App.#6798, Cert.#7131. (not abstracted)

WEEMS,DANIEL-Mexican War Pension Application dated 1887, Arkansas. Served in Company F, 2nd Regiment, Mississippi Rifles. Mex.Sur. App.#15205, Cert.#10797. Remarks: soldier died 16 Sept. 1916, Lebanon, Ark. (not abstracted)

WEIRICK,FREDERIC-War of 1812 pension application W.O.#37258, W.C.#32626. Served as 1st Lieutenant in Captain Henry Hunter's Company, Tennessee Militia from 20 September 1814 to 3 May 1815. He married Phebe __?, who died in Meigs County, Tennessee in the year 1840. He then married Sarah Rodgers, 5 October 1841, in Meigs County. She was the widow of Andrew Rodgers, who died in Tennessee, 5 September 1836. Frederic and Sarah Weirick remained in Meigs County, until 1846, when they moved to Carroll County, Arkansas. In an affidavit, dated 3 July 1879, Carroll County, James M. Hague, age 77, resident of Berryville, stated that he had known Sarah and Frederic Weirick for forty years, that he was a Justice of the Peace in and for Meigs County, Tennessee, and as such had married Sarah and Frederic Weirick, that he had resided near the Weiricks both in Tennessee and Arkansas. Benjamin Frederic Weirick, born 24 August 1842, identified as son of Sarah and Frederic, also, Sarah J.Ledbetter, age 32 in 1879, identified as granddaughter.

WELDON,JOHN-Revolutionary War Pension Application #S32053, dated 1 July 1833, Independence County, Territory of Arkansas. He was born 17 August 1759 in Halifax County, Virginia. He was residing in St. Mark's Parish, Craven County, South Carolina, in 1774, when he enlisted in Captain Robert Ellison's Company of Cavalry under Regimental Commanders, Colonel John Winn and Colonel Richardson. He served several tours of duty against Tories and Indians. In March 1778, in a skirmish at Orangeburg, his arm was so badly injured that he was temporarily unfit for duty, so he returned to his home in Craven County, and sent his brother, Samuel Weldon, as his substitute. John Weldon was commissioned First Lieutenant in 1779 by John Rutledge, Governor of South Carolina. Lieutenant John Weldon was serving under command of Colonel Joseph Brown, whose Regiment was marching on Charleston, when they were met by Governor John Rutledge and informed that the City of Charleston had fallen to Clinton and Cornwallis. The troops were dispatched, and Weldon was sent home. He was taken prisoner by a band of Tories. After his release, he reentered service and continued throughout the war. John Weldon remained in Craven County (that part that is now in Fairfield District), South Carolina until 1788, when he moved to Wilkes County, Georgia. In 1796 he moved to Christian County, Kentucky, where he was living on 16 March 1804, when his house burned. He moved to Johnson County, Illinois in 1814, and finally to Arkansas Territory in 1818. He died 31 March 1835, and in 1837 his widow, Nancy Weldon applied for pension.
Independence County, Arkansas Marriage Records; Book 1, page 62, 1 July 1839, Lurinda Weldon and Riley Clark. page 36, 13 October 1836, Nancy Weldon and James Cato. page 11, 9 February 1830, Zelpha Weldon and Josh Barnett.
Independence County, Arkansas, Probate records, Will Record A, page 23, "The last will and testament of John Weldon, I do this day bequeath to my wife, Nancy Weldon, all the estate both real and personal belonging to me after the discharge of all the just demands against said estate during her life. I do also nominate Samuel L. Weldon and James L(?). Weldon, executors of this my last will and testament" signed 29 March 1835, recorded 4 April 1836.

WELLS,ALFRED-Mexican War Pension Application dated 1888, Arkansas. Widow, Mary Ann. Service in Company G, 3rd Regiment, Kentucky Volunteers. Mex.Sur.App.#20751, Cert.#17384, Mex.Wid.App.#12644, Cert.#13038. (not abstracted)

WELLS,DAVID-Mexican War Pension Application dated 1887, Arkansas. Served in Company I, 12th Regiment, U.S.Infantry. Mex.Sur.App.#14303, Cert.#18209. (not abstracted)

WELLS,HUGH S.-Mexican War Pension Application dated 1889, Arkansas. Widow, Paulina. Service in Company I, 12th Regiment, U.S.Infantry. Mex.Wid.App.#8173, Cert.#6497. (not abstracted)

WELLS,JAMES B.-Mexican War Pension Application. Widow, Catherine. He served as 2nd Lieutenant in Company E, Seymour's Battalion, Georgia Volunteers. Mex.Sur.App.#14471, Cert.#10488, dated 1887 Mississippi; Mex.Wid.App.#14076, Cert.#11152, dated 1897 Arkansas. Remarks: O.W.Inv.Rej.#20502. (not abstracted)

WELLS,JAMES I.-Mexican War Pension Application dated 1888, Arkansas. Widow, Bettie. Service in Company H, 13th Regiment, U.S.Infantry. Mex.Sur.App.#19495, Cert.#16227, Mex.Wid.App.#12366, Cert.#10306. (not abstracted)

WELLS,JOHN S.-Mexican War Pension Application dated 1887, Arkansas. Widow, Mary. Service in Company D, 1st Regiment, Virginia Volunteers. Mex.Sur.App.#15759, Cert.#12134, Mex.Wid.App.#17780. (not abstracted)

WEMPLE,JOHN-Mexican War Pension Application dated 1887, Arkansas. Served in Company K, 5th Regiment, Louisiana Infantry. Mex.Sur. App.#12147, Cert.#4902. (not abstracted)

WEST,DAVID-War of 1812 pension application S.O.#28137, S.C.#20208, W.O.#39875, W.C.#31177. B.L.W.#19063-80-50 and #36777-80-55. He was mustered into service at Nashville, Tennessee on 10 December 1812 as Private in Captain Absalom Bledsoe's Company, Colonel Hall's Regiment, Andrew Jackson's Brigade. He stated,"Early in the Spring 1813, orders came to General Jackson, as we were informed, to disband his troops, this order he refused to obey, but marched us back to Nashville, through the Indian Country (Choctaws and Chickasaws) in the now State of Mississippi, by what was afterwards known as the old Natchez Trail. We were marched through the Creek Indian Nation to the Coosa River, at Ten Islands, where we built Fort Strother and in a few days fought and whipped the Creek Indians on the opposite side of the river, Colonel Coffee in command. At a place called Tallahatchie, a few days afterward, there came a runner (a friendly Creek) from Talledega, some thirty miles south of Fort Strother, who stated that some 3 or 4 hundred of them were in a fortified camp or fort, that they were surrounded by hostile Creeks. The following night we waded the Coosa, and put the hostile Indians to flight." David West and Millet (Milly) Payne were married 11 November 1816 in Robertson County, Tennessee. In 1839, they moved to Pope County, Arkansas, where Milly West died on 4 August the same year. He married Lucinda Latimore, 11 May 1841, in Pope County, at the home of William Hamilton. During the Mexican War, David West served as Captain of Company B, Gray's Battalion of Arkansas Volunteers. He died at his home in Dover, Pope County on 13 May 1880. Lucinda West applied for pension in 1880, at which time she stated that she was born 17 September 1821. Phebe J.James, daughter of Milly and David West was born 17 February 1823, and David P.West, born 30 June 1831, son of David and Milly, were both residing in Pope County in 1881. David Matlock, age 78, resident of Crawford County in 1872, served in the same regiment with David West in the War of 1812.
1850 Federal Census, Pope County, Arkansas, page 240, family #10: David West 56 N.C; Lucinda 30 Tenn; David P. 18 Tenn.; Victoria 13 Tenn.; Treferia 5 Ark.; Andrew N. 3 Ark.; Alexander 1 Ark.

WHEELER,ALEXANDER-Mexican War Pension Application dated 1887, Arkansas. Widow, Sybalina. He served in Captain West's Company B, Gray's Battalion, Arkansas Volunteers. Mex.Sur.App.#6874, Cert.#1711, Mex.Wid.App.#15177, Cert.#11706. (not abstracted)

WHITELEY,SAMUEL-War of 1812 Pension Application, W.O.#37893, W.C.#28910. Served in Captain J.H.Campbell's Company, 24th Regiment, U.S.Infantry and in the 7th Regiment, U.S.Infantry. He married Lucy Maynard, no further information on her. He married Luvana Kerby, 18 November 1860, at Dry Fork, Carroll County, Arkansas, the ceremony was performed by his brother, Isaac Whiteley. Luvana (name spelled Lurana and Luvana in this application) was the widow of Reuben Kerby, who died 24 February 1859. Luvana and Reuben Kerby had four children, among whom was James M.Kerby. Isaac Whiteley stated in 1879, "Samuel Whiteley died or was killed on or about the 4th day of October 1864 at his residence in Newton County State of Arkansas." Luvana was living with her son, James Kerby and his wife Martha, in Dry Fork, Carroll County in 1875, when she applied for pension. She died at their home 21 October 1885.

WHITTEN,LEVI C.-Mexican War Pension Application dated 1895, Arkansas. Widow, Sarah L. Holmes. He served in Company K, 1st Regiment, U.S.Dragoons. B.L.W.#71959-160-47. Mex.Wid.App.#12939. Remarks: O.W.Inv.Rej.#21407, Cert.#274376, file #48075; O.W.Wid. Rej.#25532. Soldier died 7 September 1895, Washington County, Arkansas. (not abstracted)

WHITTHORNE,SAMUEL H.-Mexican War Pension Application dated 1888, Arkansas. Widow, Margaret. Service in Captain Frierson's Company, 1st Regiment, Tennessee Volunteers. Mex.Sur.App.#19747, Cert.#16508, Mex.Wid.App.#15395, Cert.#12013. (not abstracted)

WHITTINGTON,ISAAC-Mexican War Pension Application dated 1889, Arkansas. Service in Captain Mercer's Company, 6th Regiment, Louisiana Volunteers. Mex.Sur.App.#21687, Cert.#18348. (not abstracted)

WHYTE,JAMES E.-Mexican War Pension Application dated 1888, Arkansas. Mexican Widow Application #5694, Certificate #3283. (not abstracted)

WILBANKS,JOHN-Mexican War Pension Application dated 1887, Arkansas. Service in Company D, 3rd Regiment, Illinois Volunteers. Mex.Sur.-App.#13955, Cert.#10333. (not abstracted)

WILBORN,FRANCIS M.-Mexican War Pension Application dated 1887, Arkansas. Widow, Sarah. He served in Company B, 16th Regiment, U.S.Infantry. Mex.Sur.App.#11300, Cert.#6229, Mex.Wid.App.#9715, Cert.#8010. (not abstracted)

WILCOX,NATHAN B.-Mexican War Pension Application dated 1887, Arkansas. Widow, Samantha. Service in Enyart's Company, 1st Regiment, Arkansas Volunteers. Mex.Wid.App.#2356, Cert.#6172. B.L.W.#51949-160-47. Remarks: O.W.Inv.file #24878, O.W.Wid.Rej. Soldier died 30 April 1873. (not abstracted)

WILES,GEORGE-War of 1812 pension application S.O.#23450, S.C.#20592. Service in Captain Richard Moore's Company of Missouri Militia. He enlisted in July 1814, and assisted in the building of a fort at Iowa Town on the Illinois River in what is now the State of Illinois. He was discharged at Camp Russell, Illinois in November 1814. He was married to Mary Ann (Polly) Miller in Missouri in November 1841(?). His pension application, dated 1871, Waldron, Scott County, Arkansas, he was age 77. His original pension certificate is enclosed in this file. In 1912, Mrs. Elizabeth Wiles, widow of Jake Wiles, applied for reembursement of funds for care, doctor's bills and funeral expenses she had incurred in behalf of her father-in-law. She stated that she had cared for him from the year 1873 until his death in 1880 in Blackfork, Scott County, Arkansas.

WILKINS,BERRYMAN-Mexican War Pension Application dated 1887, Arkansas. Widow, Elizabeth. Service in Company D, 1st Regiment, Virginia Volunteers. Mex.Sur.App.#7054, Cert.#1720, Mex.Wid.App. #13499, Cert.#10659. (not abstracted)

WILLIAMS,HARLEY-Mexican War Pension Application dated 1887, Arkansas. Widow, Amanda. Service in Company G, 5th Regiment, Tennessee Volunteers. Mex.Wid.App.#4385, Cert.#2516. (not abstracted)

WILLIAMS,JACOB-Mexican War Pension Application dated 1887, Arkansas. Widow, Amanda. Service in Company I, 1st Regiment, Arkansas Volunteers. Mex.Sur.App.#10692, Cert.#5967, Mex.Wid.App.#16511, Cert.#13359. Remarks: O.W.Inv. file #25493. (not abstracted)

WILLIAMS,JAMES-Revolutionary War Pension Application #S32607. He stated that he was born in Sullivan (?) County, Virginia in 1763, where he was living when he entered service in 1778. In 1778, he served in Colonel William Campbell's Regiment for three months, and served in Captain Henry Turner's Company in Colonel Sevier's Regiment for three months. During the years 1779 and 1780, he served five tours of three months each, in Captain Chile's Company, Colonel Sevier's Regiment, during which time he was in a battle at Boyd's Creek. In 1780, he was commissioned Captain of a Company of Rangers. During the War of 1812, James Williams served under Shelby in Canada. On 7 June 1832 he was residing in Cumberland County, Kentucky, where he applied for and was granted pension. His pension was transferred from Cumberland Co., Ky. to Hempstead County, Arkansas on 4 September 1837. Two of his children were residing in Hempstead County, Ark.: John W. Williams and Kesiah Perdue. James Williams died 2 May 1851 in Hempstead County and is buried there.
1850 Federal Census Record: Red Land Township, Hempstead County, Arkansas, family #69: John W. Williams 60 Tenn., Catherine 46 Va., Susan Shock 16 Ark., Josephine Davis 6 Ark., James Williams 87 S.Car., George Harrison 56 Ala., John Murphy 36 Va., William Elliot 45 Maine, Margaret Williams 8 Ark.

WILLIAMS,JAMES-War of 1812 pension application W.O.#24929, W.C.-#23531. He served as Sergeant in Captain John Kennedy's Company of Tennessee Militia. Married Sarah ___? 4 July 1812 or 1815 in Howard County, Missouri. James Williams died in Newton County, Missouri on 14 February 1841, his widow, Sarah was administrator of his estate. Sarah Williams died in Newton County, Arkansas on 8/9 June 1887. Phalby Dotson, age 53 in 1879, resident of Christian County, Missouri, daughter of James and Sarah Williams stated that she had a sister and a brother older than she. The brother had been dead for many years, the sister was last seen in Arkansas, but they had lost track of each other during the "late war".

WILLIAMS,JAMES C.-Mexican War Pension Application dated 1887, Arkansas. Widow, Sarah. Served as Corporal in Company F, 1st Regiment, Tennessee Infantry. Mex.Sur.App.#10711, Cert.#13946, Mex.Wid.App.#19927, Cert.#15810. (not abstracted)

WILLIAMS,JAMES F.-Mexican War Pension Application dated 1887, Arkansas. Served in Captain Lilley's Company, 4th Regiment, Ohio Infantry. Mex.Sur.App.#14067, Cert.#20017. Remarks: late war cert.#273136, Iowa Volunteers. (not abstracted)

WILLIAMS,JAMES H.-Mexican War Pension Application dated 1887, Arkansas. Service in South Carolina Volunteers. Mex.Sur.App. #16678, Cert.#16697. (not abstracted)

WILLIAMS JAMES M.-Mexican War Pension Application dated 1887, Arkansas. Service in Company E, 1st Regiment, Mississippi Volunteers. Mex.Sur.App.#7124, Cert.#1725. (not abstracted)

WILLIAMS,MILTON-Mexican War Pension Application dated 1887, Arkansas. Service in Company A, 3rd Regiment, Kentucky Infantry. B.L.W.#31783-160-47. Mex.Sur.App.#10719, Cert.#7406. (not abstracted)

WILLIAMS,PHILIP-Mexican War Pension Application dated 1887, Arkansas. Widow, Nancy. Service in Company F, 12th Regiment, Tennessee Volunteers. Mex.Sur.App.#17491, Cert.#13368, Mex.Wid. App.#9684, Cert.#7768. (not abstracted)

WILLIAMS,PLEASANT-Old war pension application dated 1851, Arkansas. O.W.Wid. Cert.#1814, file #29170, O.W.Min.Cert.#4173, file #11813. Service in Company C, Arkansas Mounted Volunteers, Mexican War. Widow, Eliza J. Bartlett. (not abstracted)

WILLIAMS,SAMUEL-Mexican War Pension Application dated 1887, Arkansas. Widow, Parilee. He served in Company A, Coffee's Regiment, Alabama Volunteers. Mex.Sur.App.#17278, Cert.#12432 (also listed as #11432) Mex.Wid.App.#11344, Cert.#8875. (not abstracted)

WILLIAMS,THOMAS-War of 1812 pension application S.O.#24749, S.C.#16683, W.O.#23418, W.C.#25713. Served in Captain William Edward's Company, General Andrew Jackson's Brigade from 24 September 1813 to 9 January 1814. He was at the Battle of New Orleans. He received a discharge certificate, which was left at his father's home in Sumner County, Tennessee. He married Martha Crawley in February 1816 in Hopkins County, Kentucky. She died "sometime during the Civil War", and he married Ruth R. Jones in October 1866 in Izard County, Arkansas. She was the widow of James Jones who died in 1858. Thomas Williams applied for pension 11 November 1871 in La Crosse, Izard County, Arkansas, his age 76. He died 5 March 1876 in Evening Shade, Sharp County, Ark. and his widow applied for pension there on 23 May 1878.

WILLIAMS,WILLIAM-Mexican War Pension Application dated 1887, Arkansas. Service in Captain Collin's Company, Gray's Battalion, Arkansas Volunteers. Mex.Sur.App.#10721, Cert.#9942. (not abstracted)

WILLIAMS,WILLIAM A.-Mexican War Pension Application dated 1887, Arkansas. Service in Captain Williams' Independent Company, Kentucky Volunteers. Mex.Sur.App.#7145, Cert.#3105. Remarks: Soldier died 22 January 1920, Kenna, New Mexico. (not abstracted)

WILLIAMSON,JOHN-Mexican War Pension Application dated 1887, Arkansas. Service in Company G, 7th Regiment, U.S.Infantry. Mex.Sur. App.#7156, Cert.#1987. (not abstracted)

WILLIS,EDWARD H.-Old war pension application O.W.Wid.Cert.#1558, file #28646, O.W.Min.Cert.#4006, file #9006. Service in Company C, 12th Regiment of U.S.Infantry, Mexican War. Widow, Elizabeth Morrison. (not abstracted)

WILMOTH,WILLIAM-Mexican War Pension Application dated 1887, Arkansas. Widow, Mary. Service in Company H, Yell's Regiment, Arkansas Mounted Volunteers. Mex.Wid.App.#2355, Cert.#5309. (not abstracted)

WILSON,GEORGE A.-Mexican War Pension Application dated 1888, Arkansas. Widow, Castila. Service in Battalion B, Mississippi Riflemen. Mex.Wid.App.#6176, Cert.#5235. (not abstracted)

WILSON,HUGH G.-Mexican War Pension Application dated 1888, Arkansas. Served as Sergeant in Company A, Gray's Battalion, Arkansas Volunteers. Mex.Sur.App.#20787, Cert.#18092. (not abstracted)

WILSON,LEWIS-Mexican War Pension Application. Widow, Mary L. He served in Company H, 3rd Regiment, Kentucky Volunteers. Mex.Sur.App. #21322, Cert.#18494, dated 1889 Arkansas; Mex.Wid.App.#19408, Cert.#15329 dated 1909 Washington. (not abstracted)

WILSON,SAMUEL W.-Mexican War Pension Application dated 1887, Arkansas. Served in Company D, 1st Regiment, Arkansas Mounted Volunteers. Mex.Sur.App.#7102, Cert.#1686. (not abstracted)

WINGFIELD,CHARLES B.-Mexican War Pension Application. Widow, Matilda C. Service in Company A, 1st Regiment, U.S.Dragoons. Mex.Wid.App.#18992, Cert.#15167. Remarks: O.W.Inv.File #3608. (not abstracted)

WINLAND,JOHN H.(alias John Madden)-Mexican War Pension Application dated 1896, Arkansas. Service in Missouri Cavalry. Mex.Sur.App.- #24816. Remarks: late war Inv. O.#981195. E, 49th Mo.Cav. (not abstracted)

WINNINGHAM,ANDREW-Mexican War Pension Application dated 1887, Arkansas. Service in Captain McConnell's Company, 1st Regiment, Illinois Volunteers. Mex.Sur.App.#14871, Cert.#12082. Remarks: MI #529485, Co.A, 10th Ill.Vols. (not abstracted)

WITT,DAVID-Mexican War Pension Application dated 1887, Arkansas. Widow, Charlotte M. Service in Company E, 5th Regiment, Tennessee Volunteers. Mex.Sur.App.#12169, Cert.#5221, Mex.Wid.App.#15665, Cert.#12592. (not abstracted)

WOLF,ENOCH O.-Mexican War Pension Application dated 1888, Arkansas. Widow, Elizabeth. Served in Captain Desha's Company D, Yell's Regiment, Arkansas Mounted Volunteers. Mex.Sur.App.#20217, Cert.- #16884, Mex.Wid.App.#19685, Cert.#15618. (not abstracted)

WOLFF,OSCAR P.-Mexican War Pension Application dated 1888, Arkansas. Widow, Cornelia. Service in Company A, 3rd Regiment, U.S.Dragoons. Mex.Wid.App.#6248, Cert.#4965. (not abstracted)

WOOD,ENOCH-Mexican War Pension Application dated 1889, Arkansas. Served in Captain Manson's Company, 5th Regiment, Indiana Volunteers. Mex.Sur.App.#21733, Cert.#18401. Remarks: Rebellion Wid.Orig. #742519, Companies I and B, 32nd Ind.Vol.Inf. (not abstracted)

WOOD,GEORGE-Mexican War Pension Application dated 1888, Arkansas. Service in Captain Ramsey's Company, 1st Regiment, Ohio Volunteers. Mex.Sur.App.#18675, Cert.#14796. (not abstracted)

WOOD,THOMAS H.-Mexican War Pension Application dated 1887, Arkansas. Widow, Oma. Mex.Sur.App.#7201, Cert.#13651, Mex.Wid.App.#12673, Cert.#11069. (not abstracted)

WOOD,WILLIAM-Mexican War Pension Application dated 1887, Arkansas. Service in Company G, 5th Regiment, Tennessee Volunteers. Mex.- Sur.App.#14676, Cert.#10616. (not abstracted)

WOODRUFF,ALDEN W.-Mexican War Pension Application dated 1887, Arkansas. Served as 2nd Lieutenant, 1st Regiment, Arkansas Mounted Volunteers and in Company E, 12th Regiment, U.S.Infantry. Mex.Sur. App.#7206, Cert.#19246. (not abstracted)

WOODRUFF,WILLIAM-War of 1812 pension application S.O.#30689, S.C.#22412, W.O.#43899, W.C.#34312. He was a few months over eighteen years, when he enlisted into service in Captain Lawrence Brown's Company, New York Militia. He enlisted at Brooklyn, New York on 2 September 1814, and was discharged on 2 December 1814. He was a native of Suffolk County, Long Island, but after the war, he moved to Nashville, Tennessee. In the Autumn of

1819, William Woodruff moved to Little Rock, Pulaski County, Territory of Arkansas, where he married Jane Eliza Mills, 14 November 1827. In 1885, John Logan, age 76, stated, "I came to Little Rock in the year 1820, I have known Mrs. William Woodruff since her early childhood. She was married at the home of her uncle, Isaac Watkins, I was a member of Isaac Watkins' family." Alden Woodruff, born 27 August 1828, son of William and Jane Woodruff, submitted the Bible record of Mrs. Hannah Woodruff, mother of William Woodruff, "as afar as relates to the marriage of my Father and Mother." William E. Woodruff Sr. died in Little Rock on 19 June 1885; Jane E. Woodruff died 27 February 1887, both are buried in the family plot at Mount Holly Cemetery. A copy of the "Last Will and Testament of William E. Woodruff, Senior," is enclosed in this file, to wit, "I, bequeath all my estate both real and personal to my son, William E. Woodruff Jr., for the payment of my just debts; the residue he is to hold, use and manage according to his best judgement, and apply the profit or income to and for the support of my beloved wife, Jane Eliza Woodruff and such of our unmarried children who continue to live with her. After her decease he is to divide what may be left among all of my children. He, William E. Woodruff Jr. to be executor of this will." signed 8 September 1867.
1850 Federal Census, Pulaski County, Arkansas, page 344, family #416: William E. Woodruff age 54 printer and editor N.Y.; Jane E. 41 Ky.; Homer 13 Ark.; Mary E. 11 Ark.; Eveline 9 Ark.; Frances 7 Ark.; Geogena 5 Ark.; Lizzie 3 Ark.; Chester H. 5/12 Ark.; William Davis 22 Pa.; Virgil Lewis 16 Pa.; Sobra Hudgens 16 Pa.; H.M.Hudgens 14 Pa.

WOODS,BENJAMIN-War of 1812 Pension Application, W.O.#10556, W.C.#6158. He enlisted into service in White County, Tennessee on 4 October 1813, into Captain James Cole's Company, Tennessee Militia, discharged on 17 January 1814. He was married to Milly Jackson in Raliegh, Wake County, North Carolina on 18 September 1812. Benjamin Woods died 1 March 1865, at Blue Mountain, Stone County, Arkansas, and Milly Woods applied for pension there on 8 December 1873. She stated that, "while living with said soldier as his wife, she had the following children: Charloty Woods was born on the 10th day of May AD 1815; Mary Woods was born on the 10th day of May AD 1817; Sarah Woods was born on the 15th day of June AD 1819; Elizabeth Woods (twin) was born on the 15th day of June AD 1819; Delila Woods was born on the 19th day of August AD 1821; China (?) Woods was born on the 25th day of July AD 1823; Isam Woods was born on the 12th day of August AD 1825; Faney Woods (twin) was born on the 12th day of August AD 1825; Albert Woods was born on the 7th day of September AD 1827; Calvin Woods was born on the 18th day of December AD 1829; Silvester Woods was born on the 12th day of April AD 1831; Tiresa Woods was born on the 10th day of May AD 1833; Jane Woods was born on the 6th day of June AD 1835; Nancy Woods was born on the 13th day of December AD 1838; Miley (could be Wiley) Woods was born on the 1st day of November AD 1841; William Woods was born on the 8th day of July AD 1843; that all of the above named children are now (1874) dead, except William Woods, the youngest who is now 31 years of age." Ellen Cooper, age 76, resident of Stone County, stated that she had been a close friend of Benjamin and Milley Woods since the year 1814.

WOODS,OBADIAH-Revolutionary War Pension Application #S32613, dated 29 August 1832, Anderson County, Tennessee, Obadiah Woods age 73. He was living in Wake County, North Carolina, when he was drafted into service in Colonel John Humphrey's Regiment, in which service he was at General Horatio Gate's defeat at the Battle of Camden in August 1780. In the Battle of Eutaw Springs, Obadiah Woods served in Captain Martin Lane's Company, Colonel Farmer's Regiment. On 27 September 1837, Obadiah Woods applied to have his pension transferred to Marion County, Arkansas,

where he had moved to be near three of his children, who lived
in Arkansas and another who resided in a neighboring county
in Missouri. Two of his sons were named: George Woods and William
Woods. Obadiah Woods died in Marion County, Ark. on 10 August
1845, leaving no surviving wife or children except James Woods
of Benton County, Territory of Oregon.

WOODY,JOHN-War of 1812 pension application S.O.#20453, S.C.#14893.
Application for pension made in Bellefonte, Boone County, Arkansas
in June 1871. He was born ca 1792 in Virginia, married Nancy
Beerer (?) in Lincoln County, Tennessee on 22 June 1810. He
served as 3rd Lieutenant in Captain John Doke's Company, Williamson's
2nd Regiment, Coffey's Brigade at the Battles of Pensacola and
New Orleans.
1850 Federal Census Records, Benton County, Arkansas, page 45: M.
Woody 30 Tenn., Eliza 30 S.C., Sarah 4 Ark., John Woody 58 Va.,
Nancy 59 N.C., Reuben B. 21 Ark., James M. 17 Ark.

WOOTEN,JOHN R.-Mexican War Pension Application dated 1887, Arkansas.
Widow, Ann. Service in Company I, 5th Regiment, Tennessee Volunteers. Mex.Sur.App.#6933, Cert.#1885, Mex.Wid.App.#10779, Cert.-
#8164. Remarks: O.W.Inv.Rej.#19229. (not abstracted)

WORTHEN,JOHN-War of 1812 pension application W.O.#20190, W.C.#14644.
He served as Sergeant in Captain William Russell's Company of
Tennessee Militia. Enlisted in Franklin County, Tennessee on
9 November 1814, discharged in November 1815. He lived in Fayette
County, Tenn., Shelby County, Alabama, Atalla County, Mississippi
and in Jefferson, Saline and Grant Counties, Arkansas. He was
married to Julia Veazey in Saline County, Ark., on 27 June 1868. She
was the widow of Elzy Veazey, who died 11 August 1864. John
Worthen died 2 October 1876 in Grant County, Arkansas. Widow,
Julia, applied for pension 1 May 1878 in Sheridan, Grant County,
she was aged 55.

WREN/RENN,JAMES-War of 1812 pension application S.O.#29216,
S.C.#21132. Served as 2nd Sergeant in Captain James Martin's
Company, Colonel James A. Pearson,s 7th Regiment of North Carolina
Militia from 1 February 1814 to 4 September 1814. He enlisted
in Rutherford County, North Carolina, assisted in the building
of Fort Jackson, Alabama, and was discharged at Salisbury, North
Carolina. His original discharge certificate dated 4 September
1814, signed by Colonel Pearson enclosed in this file. James
Wren married Elizabeth Hightower in Warren County, Kentucky
on 17 August 1817. He applied for Bounty Land in Izard County,
Arkansas on 1 March 1851, at which time he was age 59. He died
28 April 1889, and his "aged Mother" applied for arrears in
his pension.
1850 Federal Census, Izard County, Arkansas, Rocky Bayou Township,
page 13, family #175: James Wren 58 N.C.; Elizabeth 56 S.C.;
Shadrack 25 Ky.; Mary Ann 21 Ky.; James 9 Ark.; J.W.Hightower
35 Ky.

WRIGHT,CLARK-War of 1812 pension application S.O.#30039, S.C.#21604,
W.O.#40843, W.C.#31735. Served in Captain Huckaburley's Company
of Georgia Militia from 21 November 1814 to 8 March 1815. Enlisted
in Sandersville, Georgia. He married Annie Davis 28 December
1837 in Buncomb County, North Carolina. His application for
pension dated 15 December 1874, Oak Grove, Carroll County, Arkansas.
He died 9 July 1879 in Boone County, Ark., and his widow applied
for pension there on 19 February 1881. She stated that she had
raised five children, the oldest of whom was age 42 and the
youngest was age 30. Daughter Jane Wright, age 38 and daughter
Martha E. White, age 42, both of Boone County. Anna Wright died
13 September 1885.

WRIGHT,JAMES-War of 1812 pension application W.O.#40104, W.C.#32616. B.L.W.#72949-120-55. Service in Captain J.B.Bosier's Company of Tennessee/Missouri (?) Militia from 21 April 1815 to 4 June 1815. He married Rebecca Ward 12 March 1827 in Hempstead County, Territory of Arkansas. He died in Sevier County, Arkansas on 1 October 1869. Widow, Rebecca, applied for pension on 2 July 1880 in Ben Lamond, Sevier County, Arkansas, her age 68. Her application was rejected for the reason that the soldier's service was not rendered in, but after the War of 1812, for which he had received Bounty Land. In 1882, the case was reopened, submitted to the Congress of the United States and on 15 July 1882 the following Special Act was approved, "Be it enacted by the Senate and House of Representatives of the United States of America in Congress assembled, that the Secretary of the Interior be, and he is hereby authorized and directed to put the name of Rebecca Wright, widow of James Wright, who was a private in Captain Bosier's Company, War of Eighteen Hundred and Twelve, on the Pension Rolls, subject to the provisions and limitations of the Pension Laws."

WRIGHT,JAMES C.-Mexican War Pension Application dated 1887, Arkansas. Widow, Susan. Service in Captain Travis' Company, 4th Regiment, Tennessee Volunteers. Mex.Sur.App.#6954, Cert.#13028, Mex.Wid.App.#16669. (not abstracted)

WRIGHT,JOHN G.-Mexican War Pension Application dated 1893, Arkansas. Widow, Julia. Service in Company H, 4th Regiment, Illinois Volunteers. Mex.Wid.App.#11621, Cert.#9077. (not abstracted)

WRIGHT,JOHN I.-Mexican War Pension Application dated 1887, Arkansas. Widow, Frances. Service in Company F, 2nd Regiment, Tennessee Volunteers. Mex.Wid.App.#4990, Cert.#2763. (not abstracted)

WYATT,WILLIAM A.-Mexican War Pension Application dated 1891, Arkansas. Widow, Sarah. Service in Company E, Gray's Battalion, Arkansas Volunteers. Mex.Sur.App.#23331, Cert.#25453. Mex.Wid.App. #20377. Remarks: XC2900734; soldier died 9 March 1916, St.Joe, Ark. (not abstracted)

YATES,ENGLISH L.-Mexican War Pension Application dated 1889, Arkansas. Widow, Sarah. Service in Captain Patrick's Company, Yell's Regiment, Arkansas Mounted Volunteers. Mex.Wid.App.#7962, Cert.#6533. (not abstracted)

YATES,GABRIEL S.-Mexican War Pension Application dated 1888, Arkansas. Widow, Sarah Ann. Service in Captain West's Company, Gray's Battalion, Arkansas Volunteers. Mex.Wid.App.#6972, Cert.- #6383. (not abstracted)

YATES/YEATES,NICHOLAS-War of 1812 pension application S.O.#12796, S.C.#10364. B.L.W.#53993-80-50 and #13105-80-55. Service in Captain Jacob Hoyle's Company, Colonel Samuel Daugherty's Regiment of Tennessee Militia. He enlisted at Fort Strother, Greene County, Tennessee on 10 January 1814. He was in General Andrew Jackson's Brigade at the Battle of Horseshoe, with the Creek Indians. He was discharged 23 May 1814. He married Elizabeth Hayes in Greene County, Tennessee in 1810. He was in Washington County, Arkansas by 1853, and in 1871, he applied for pension in Washington County, at which time his age was 80.

YATES,WHITSEL-Mexican War Pension Application dated 1890, Arkansas. Widow, Susan. Service in Company E, Gray's Battalion, Arkansas Volunteers. Mex.Wid.App.#9511, Cert.#15679. (not abstracted)

YEAKLEY,SAMUEL-Mexican War Pension Application dated 1889, Arkansas. Widow, Barsheba. Service as 2nd Lieutenant in Company B, 4th Regiment, Indiana Volunteers. Also served in Company F, 40th

Regiment, Indiana Infantry 1862-63, and in 45th Company, 2nd Battalion, VRC (?) 1863-64. Mex.Sur.App.#22284, Cert.#18723, Mex.Wid.App.#13766, Cert.#10673. B.L.W.#66008-160-47. Remarks: Soldier died 20 October 1896, Choctaw, Arkansas. I.O.#201919. (not abstracted)

YOCUM,GEORGE T.-Mexican War Pension Application dated 1888, Arkansas. Widow, Malinda. Service in Company E, 12th Regiment, U.S.Infantry. Mex.Sur.App.#18869, Cert.#15680, Mex.Wid.App.#14650, Cert.#11563. (not abstracted)

YORK,RICHARD-Mexican War Pension Application dated 1887, Arkansas. Service in Company H, Arkansas Mounted Volunteers. Mex.Sur.App.#7223, Cert.#8836. (not abstracted)

YOUNG,ARCHIBALD-War of 1812 pension application W.O.#40972, W.C.#31489. Service in Captain Adam Dale's Company of Mounted Volunteers, Andrew Jackson's Regiment, Tennessee Militia from 23 December 1813 to 8 February 1814. He enlisted into service in Wilson County, Tennessee, and served at the Battle of Emuckfaw. Archibald Young and Mary Barrett were married 24 February 1826 in Warren County, Tennessee. He died in Yellville, Marion County, Arkansas on 1 June 1870. She applied for pension on 24 February 1881, her age 72. Affidavit dated 4 March 1881, Marion County, Arkansas, "John Estes, age 77 and Charlotte Estes, age 72, his wife, state that they are well acquainted with Archibald and Mary Young, both in Warren County, Tennessee and in Marion County, Arkansas. They lived within two miles of him in Warren County, Tennessee when he was married. John and Charlotte Estes left Tennessee and came to Marion County, Arkansas about the year 1848, and Archibald Young and Mary, his wife, came here and settled in the same neighborhood, two or three years later. John Estes further stated that his father, Gallent Estes, was a member of the same command with Archibald Young in the War of 1812. When he was a small boy, in Wilson County, Tennessee, John Estes remembers seeing Archibald Young with Robert Knight and Henry Lewis come by the house of his father, Gallent Estes, on their way to join their command, and that his father went with them and was later killed in the Battle of Emuckfaw, and he has often heard Archibald Young state that he had helped carry Estes off the field and bury him."

YOUNG,DAVID-Mexican War Pension Application dated 1887, Arkansas. Service in Captain Bennett's Company, 1st Regiment, Tennessee Infantry. Mex.Sur.App.#7231, Cert.#9757. (not abstracted)

YOUNG,NATHAN M.-War of 1812 pension application S.O.#14734, S.C.#16646, W.O.#24070, W.C.#27761. Service in Captain Thomas Sterrett's Company of Louisiana Militia, from 20 November 1814 to 20 May 1815. He enlisted at Bowling Green, Kentucky, was stationed at New Orleans, and served in that battle. He married Susan Cunningham, who died in Blount County, Tennessee. He married Mahala Kune, 2 September 1845, at Spring Place, DeKalb County, Georgia. They were in Mississippi for awhile and moved to Fayetteville, Washington County, Arkansas in 1858, where Nathan Young died on 17 March 1878. In 1879, Jason Barnes, age 52, Washington County, stated that his wife, to whom he was married in Blount County, Tennessee, was the daughter of Nathan Young and his first wife, Susan.

ZORN,PHILIP-Mexican War Pension Application dated 1887, Arkansas. Service in Company E, Alabama Battery. Mex.Sur.App.#9081, Cert.-#3425. (not abstracted)

Rendezvous at Little Rock, Arkansas on 9 August 1836, stationed at Fort Gibson.

Name	Residence
Akin, Samuel; Pvt.	residence-Clinton, Van Buren County
Beason, Thomas; Corp.	" Lewisburg, Conway "
Benson, Jethro; Pvt.	" Conway "
Bentley, Oliver; Sgt.	" Conway "
Butler, John; Pvt.	" Conway "
Butram, Hamilton; Pvt.	" Conway "
Butler, John; Pvt.	" Conway "
Campbell, John; Pvt.	" Point Remove, Conway County
Carlisle, Stephen; Pvt.	" Cadron, Conway County
Cato, Hile; Pvt.	" Clinton, Van Buren County
Cook, David L.; Pvt.	" Lewisburg, Conway County
Couch, John; Bugler	" Clinton, Van Buren County
Crane, Joel; Pvt.	" Conway County
Curzine, Able; Pvt.	" Clinton, Van Buren County
Curzine, Reuben G. Pvt.	" " " "
Cutter, William C.; Pvt.	" Cadron, Conway County
Doyle, Thomas; Pvt.	" Conway County
Dunn, B.H.; Pvt.	" Little Rock, Pulaski
Ellis, James; Corp.	" Point Remove, Conway "
Ellis, William; Sgt.	" " " "
Evans, Leroy; Pvt.	" Lewisburg, Conway County
Flanikin, Isaac; Pvt.	" " " "
Frazier, William; Pvt.	" Hardin, Conway County
Gilmore, William; Pvt.	" Lewisburg, " "
Greer, Amos; Pvt.	" Welborn, " "
Greer, James M.; Pvt.	" Hardin, " "
Harris, Silas A.; Pvt.	" Welborn, " "
Harris, William; Pvt.	" Point Remove, Conway
Harrison, William; Pvt.	" Cadron, Conway County
Hogan, Samuel; Pvt.	" Lewisburg, Conway County
Holsomback, Abraham; Pvt.	" Hardin, Conway County
Joslin, William; Pvt.	" Clinton, Van Buren County
Kuykendall, Adam; Pvt.	" Hardin, Conway County
Kuykendall, Peter; 2nd. Lt.	" Conway County
Lee, Adam; Pvt.	" Lewisburg, Conway County
Lee, Martin; Pvt.	" Cadron, Conway County
Lewis, Joshua; Corp.	" Point Remove, Conway
Lusk, Preston; Pvt.	" Clinton, Van Buren County
McCoy, Harmon; Pvt.	" Cadron, Conway County
McCoy, Jesse; Pvt.	" " " "
McFarlane, Alexander; 1st.Lt.	" Conway County
McMullen, Thomas; Pvt.	" Hardin, Conway County
Maddox, John; Pvt.	" Clinton, Van Buren County
Martin, William; Pvt.	" Fayetteville, Washington
Mathers, Thomas; Capt.	" Conway County
Morrison, James; Pvt.	" Clinton, Van Buren County
Mushback, George; Pvt.	" Fulton, Hempstead County
Nance, Ezekiel; Pvt.	" Washington, Hempstead
Nevill, Patrick; Pvt.	" Hardin, Conway County
Peel, Richard; Pvt.	" Clinton, Van Buren County
Rogers, Joseph; Pvt.	" Lewisburg, Conway County
Sledge, Thomas; Pvt.	" Hardin, Conway County
Spears, Thomas; Pvt.	" Cadron, " "
Stratton, John W.; Pvt.	" Clinton, Van Buren County
Tucker, James; Pvt.	" Lewisburg, Conway County
Turley, Thomas; Pvt.	" Clinton, Van Buren County
Tweedy, Jackson; Sgt.	" Lewisburg, Conway County
Twitty, Allen; Pvt.	" Little Rock, Pulaski
Vane, Cyrus; Pvt.	" Welborn, Conway County
Vane, Willis; Pvt.	" " " "
Watson, Thomas; Pvt.	" Lewisburg, Conway County

```
Watson, William F.; Pvt.    Residence    Lewisburg, Conway County
Webster, John; Pvt.             "         "         "       "
Whitson, Jesse; Pvt.        Residence    Lewisburg, Conway County
Willis, Richard; Pvt.           "         "         "       "
```

DEATHS:
Goldsmith, A.J.; Pvt. Resident of Little Rock; died at Fort
        Gibson, 27 November 1836.
Harris, Timothy; Pvt. Resident of Conway County; died at Fort
        Gibson, 29 November 1836.

MUSTER ROLL
CAPTAIN ROBERT BRAZIL'S COMPANY B
1ST REGIMENT MOUNTED GUNMEN
ARKANSAS VOLUNTEERS
COLONEL LABAN HOWELL, COMMANDER

Rendezvous at Little Rock, Arkansas on 12 August 1836, stationed
at Fort Gibson.

```
Alby, Peter; Pvt.               Residence- Union, Saline County
Alford, John H.; Sgt.              "       Saline,   "      "
Bankston, Abner; Pvt.              "       Brazil,   "      "
Bankston, Alford; Pvt.            "         "        "      "
Bland, William; Pvt.              "                Conway County
Bode, William; Pvt.               "       Saline, Saline County
Brazil, John; Pvt.                "       Owen, Saline County
Brazil, Richard, Jr.; Pvt.        "       Union, Saline County
Brazil, Richard, Sr.; Pvt.        "         "      "      "
Brazil, Robert; Capt.             "       Owen,    "      "
Clanton, Stephen; Pvt.            "       Saline,  "      "
Collier, Stephen; Sgt.            "       Union,   "      "
Conn, Thomas; Pvt.                "       Saline,  "      "
Davidson, Alexander; Corp.        "       Dyer,    "      "
Davidson, George; Corp.           "         "      "      "
Davidson, Miner; Pvt.             "         "      "      "
Dodd, James; Pvt.                 "       Brazil   "      "
Dodd, Zachariah; Pvt.             "       Saline,  "      "
Dyer, Charles; Pvt.               "       Dyer,    "      "
Dyer, Given; Pvt.                 "         "      "      "
Dyer, John; Corp.                 "       Dyer,    "      "
Fowler, Wiley B; Pvt.             "       Union,   "      "
Goff, Henry H.; Pvt.              "       Saline,  "      "
Hence, William; Pvt.              "         "      "      "
Henderson, Alford; Pvt.           "         "      "      "
Henderson, Jethro P.; Pvt.        "         "      "      "
Henderson, Samuel T.; Pvt.        "         "      "      "
Hutchinson, William M.; Sgt.      "       Union,   "      "
James, Jesse; Corp.               "       Brazil,  "      "
Jones, Izra; Pvt.                 "         "      "      "
Joyner, Johnson; 2nd Lt.          "       Owen,    "      "
Kendall, Andrew; Pvt.             "       Dyer,    "      "
Kendall, Epaproditus; Pvt.        "         "      "      "
McClenon, Thomas; Pvt.            "       Union,   "      "
Mark, Lebias; Pvt.                "       Fenter, Hot Springs
Mills, John L.; Pvt.              "       Antoine, Clark County
Nelson, Elijah; Pvt.              "       Brazil, Saline County
O'Kelly, David; Pvt.              "       Fourche,  "      "
Powel, Jesse; Pvt.                "       Brazil,   "      "
Price, Moses; Sgt.                "       Saline,   "      "
Ramey, William; Pvt.              "       Union,    "      "
Sanders, Daniel; Pvt.             "       Fourche,  "      "
Sanders, Hansford; Pvt.           "                Sevier County
Shobuck, William; Pvt.            "       Saline, Saline County
Spencer, Jesse; 1st Lt.           "       Dyer,    "      "
Terry, William; Pvt.              "       Saline,  "      "
Wallace, Jonathan; Pvt.           "       Brazil,  "      "
```

```
                      MUSTER ROLL
          CAPTAIN JOHN R.H. SCOTT'S COMPANY C
             1ST REGIMENT MOUNTED GUNMEN
                  ARKANSAS VOLUNTEERS
          COLONEL LABAN HOWELL, COMMANDER
```

Rendezvous at Little Rock, Arkansas on 18 August 1836, stationed at Fort Gibson.

Aikman, Alexander; Pvt.	Residence-Petit Jean, Pope County
Aikman, Pleasant; Pvt.	" " "
Aikman, William; Pvt.	" " "
Allen, Elleazer H.; Pvt.	" Scotio, "
Andrews, Thomas H.; Pvt.	" Scotio, "
Bowles, Robert D.; Pvt.	" Spadra, Johnson County
Brewster, Perry; Pvt.	" Scotio, Pope County
Brigance, Alexander; Pvt.	" " "
Brown, John; Musc.	" " "
Bryant, George; Pvt.	" Dardenelle, Pope County
Bryant, William; Pvt.	" " "
Byrd, Andrew; Pvt.	" Scotio, Pope County
Carr, George W.; Pvt.	" Dwight, Pope County
Conley, Isaac C.; Pvt.	" Dardenelle, Pope County
Cox, Batton W.; Pvt.	" Little Piney, Johnson
Crowson, Jacob; Pvt.	" Petit Jean, Pope County
Dolton, Samuel M.; Pvt.	" Scotio, Pope County
Doyle, John; Pvt.	" Illinois Creek, Pope
Doyle, William; Pvt.	" " " "
Ewing, Anthony B.; Pvt.	" " " "
Ewing, John; Pvt.	" " " "
Fort, Jackson; Pvt.	" Dardenelle, Pope County
Garner, George W.; Pvt.	" Little Piney, Johnson
Hays, Samuel M.; 1st Lt.	" Scotio, Pope County
Hill, John G.; Sgt.	" Spadra, Johnson County
Howell, James; Sgt.	" Scotio, Pope County
Howell, Thomas; Pvt.	" " "
Hubble, Joel C.; Pvt.	" Petit Jean, Pope County
Hudgens, Thomas; Pvt.	" Scotio, Pope County
Hufstedler, Martin; Pvt.	" " "
Hughes, Joseph; Pvt.	" Petit Jean, Pope County
Humphreys, David; Pvt.	" Scotio, Pope County
Humphreys, Joseph; Pvt.	" Dardenelle, Pope County
James, Able; Pvt.	" Kiamiche, Choctaw Nation
Jamison, Robert W.; 2nd Lt.	" Morrison Bluff, Johnson
Johnson, Burk; Corp.;	" Scotio, Pope County
Laramore, Shelton; Pvt.	" Sevier County
Lee, John; Pvt.	" Spadra Bluff, Johnson
Lewis, Reuben W.; Pvt.	" Kiamiche, Choctaw Nation
Logan, William A.; Sgt.	" Scotio, Pope County
Maddin, John; Pvt.	" Big Piney, Pope County
Maddux, John; Pvt.	" Fort Towson
Morse, Thomas; Pvt.	" Dardenelle, Pope County
Oliver, William; Pvt.	" Scotio, Pope County
Owens, William; Pvt.	" Fort Towson
Parks, Willis E.; Pvt.	" Petit Jean, Pope County
Perro, Joseph; Pvt.	" Dardenelle, Pope County
Poplin, Israel M.; Corp.	" " "
Price, John; Pvt.	" Scotio, Pope County
Price, Willis A.; Pvt.	" " " "
Reasoner, William; Pvt.	" " " "
Ross, Robert B.; Pvt.	" " " "
Rushing, Burrel; Pvt.	" " " "
Rushing, David; Pvt.	" " " "
Rushing, Edmont; Pvt.	" " " "
Scott, John R.H.; Capt.	" "
Stith, Learner B.; Corp.	" Dardenelle, Pope County
Tate, George W.; Corp.	" Scotio, Pope County
Taylor, Thomas; Pvt.	" Big Piney, Pope County

Vanduyne, John; Pvt.	Residence	Petit Jean, Pope County
Weaver, John; Pvt.	"	Fort Towson
Williams, Owen; Pvt.	Residence-	Scotio, Pope County
Williams, Zachariah; Pvt.	"	Sevier County
Wood, Moses; Pvt.	"	Scotio, Pope County

MUSTER ROLL
CAPTAIN SAMUEL MOORE'S COMPANY D
1ST REGIMENT MOUNTED GUNMEN
ARKANSAS VOLUNTEERS
COLONEL LABAN HOWELL, COMMANDER

Rendezvous at Little Rock, Arkansas on 31 August 1836, stationed
at Fort Gibson.

Ashbrooks, Aaron; Sgt.	Residence-	Fort Towson
Babb, Benjamin; Pvt.	"	Hempstead County
Baldwin, Wilkie D.; Sgt.	"	" "
Basey, Jonas; Pvt.	"	Fort Towson
Bassett, Thomas; Pvt.	"	Clark County
Benedict, Jacob; Pvt.	"	Washington, Hempstead
Bloodworth, John; Corp.	"	Sevier County
Boren, Israel; Pvt.	"	Fort Towson
Boren, James; Pvt.	"	Hempstead County
Burk, Samuel; Pvt.	"	Sevier County
Burlison, James A.; Pvt.	"	Washington, Hempstead
Burrow, John; Bugler	"	Fort Towson
Carneyham, Thomas; Pvt.	"	Sevier County
Chamblis, Ansel; Pvt.	"	Washington, Hempstead
Click, Calvin M.; Pvt.	"	Hempstead County
Cook, Thomas; Pvt.	"	Miller County
Cross, Robert; 2nd Lt.	"	Ozan, Hempstead
Davis, Robert L.; 1st Lt.	"	Washington, Hempstead
Dollarhide, James; Pvt.	"	Sevier County
Dowdy, Thomas; Pvt.	"	Fort Towson
Draper, Henderson, Pvt.	"	Hempstead County
Flanikin, Joshua; Pvt.	"	Fort Towson
Hanger, Peter; Pvt.	"	Washington, Hempstead
Holbrooks, John M; Pvt.	"	Fort Towson
Holt (Hott ?) William; Pvt.	"	Washington, Hempstead
Hopson, Abram; Sgt.	"	Hempstead County
Hopson, William; Corp.	"	" "
Irwin, William; Pvt.	"	Washington, Hempstead
Johnson, Jacob; Pvt.	"	Ozan, Hempstead County
Johnson, Samuel; Pvt.	"	" " "
Lawrence, David; Pvt.	"	Washington, Hempstead
McClinton, Harvey; Pvt.	"	Fort Towson
Moore, Samuel; Capt.	"	Washington, Hempstead
Peacock, Stephen; Pvt.	"	Hempstead County
Props, Lewis C.; Sgt.	"	" "
Sanders, Leonidus; Pvt.	"	Fort Towson
Shook, David; Pvt.	"	" "
Smith, Abram; Pvt.	"	Washington, Hempstead
Smith, John H.; Pvt.	"	" "
Snider, John; Pvt.	"	Fort Towson
Teal, Charles; Pvt.	"	" "
Tollett, Daniel; Pvt.	"	Washington, Hempstead
Tooley, William; Pvt.	"	" "
Tyree, Stephen; Corp.	"	Hempstead County
Walden, Elisha; Pvt.	"	Fort Towson
Ward, Michael; Pvt.	"	Hempstead County
Williams, Henry; Pvt.	"	Fort Towson
Wilson, Berry; Corp.	"	Hempstead County
Young, Jackson; Pvt.	"	Fort Towson

MUSTER ROLL
CAPTAIN JOHN R. CUMMINS' COMPANY E
1ST REGIMENT MOUNTED GUNMEN
ARKANSAS VOLUNTEERS
COLONEL LABAN HOWELL, COMMANDER

Rendezvous at Little Rock, Arkansas on 13 August 1836, stationed at Fort Gibson.

Angling, James A.; Pvt.	Residence-	Saline County
Angling, William; Pvt.	"	" "
Badgett, William; Pvt.	"	Pulaski "
Berry, Frederick; Corp.	"	Pulaski "
Bishop, Jared; Pvt.	"	" "
Bissell, Jeremiah; Pvt.	"	" "
Blackborn, Samuel D.; Pvt.	"	" "
Blackborn, Sidney; Pvt.	"	" "
Brown, James W.; 1st Lt.	"	Saline "
Bullock, Luther Z.; Sgt.	"	Pulaski "
Childress,Robertson, Pvt.	"	" "
Clift, Halwin; Sgt.	"	Hot Springs County
Clift, Harlon; Bugler	"	" " "
Clingman, Arthur A.; Pvt.	"	Clark County
Cocke, John H.; Pvt.	"	Pulaski County
Collins, Alexander; Pvt.	"	Pulaski County
Coosa, John; Pvt.	"	Hot Springs
Culbreth, Laughlin; Pvt.	"	Pulaski County
Cummins, John R.; Capt.	"	Little Rock, Pulaski
Cummins, Joseph; Pvt.	"	Pulaski County
Desha, Marcus B.; Pvt.	"	Arkansas County
Desrouseaux, Joseph; Pvt.	"	" "
Dodd, James; Pvt.	"	Pulaski County
Farris, Isham; Pvt.	"	Clark County
Farris, John; Pvt.	"	" "
Ford, Hayle; Pvt.	"	Pulaski County
Ford, Levi; Pvt.	"	" "
Freeman, Lewis; Pvt.	"	Sevier County
Garrett, Wiley; Pvt.	"	Pulaski County
Gordon, Charles; Pvt.	"	Clark County
Guice, John; Pvt.	"	" "
Hodge, Amos; Pvt.	"	" "
Hodge, Calloway; Pvt.	"	Pulaski County
Hogan, John D.; Pvt.	"	" "
Humphrey, William H.; Pvt.	"	" "
Imbean, Paul; Pvt.	"	" "
Janes, William; Corp.	"	Clark County
Johnston, Oliver C.; Pvt.	"	Pulaski County
Jones, Hardy; Pvt.	"	" "
Jones, Isaac; Pvt.	"	" "
Lefore, Peter E.; Pvt.	"	" "
Lewis, Washington; Pvt.	"	" "
McDaniel, A.B.; Pvt.	"	Clark County
Marcus, Ezekiel; Sgt.	"	Pulaski County
Mitten, John; Pvt.	"	Hot Springs County
Moore, John; Pvt.	"	Clark County
Moore, Walker; Pvt.	"	" "
Mosley, Fielden G.; 2nd Lt.	"	" "
Murphy, George W.; Pvt.	"	Saline County
Nixson, Samuel; Sgt.	"	" "
Oliver, John; Pvt.	"	Pulaski County
Perkins, James; Pvt.	"	Hempstead County
Rea, William; Pvt.	"	Pulaski County
Reed, Washington; Pvt.	"	Jefferson County
Richardson, John M.; Pvt.	"	Pulaski County
Richardson, Lewis; Pvt.	"	" "
Sanders, Cornelius; Pvt.	"	Jefferson County
Sawyers, Robert; Pvt.	"	Hempstead County
Scarborough, John; Pvt.	"	Miller County

```
Secrest, Andrew J.; Pvt.        Residence Pulaski County
Smiley, John; Pvt.                 "      Hot Springs County
Smith, Madison; Corp.           Residence- Pulaski County
Spence, John; Pvt.                 "       "       "
Spencer, John; Pvt.                "       "       "
Stanley, Ephraim; Pvt.             "      Clark County
Sweckendoeff, Arthur; Pvt.         "      Pulaski County
Sweekard, Benjamin; Pvt.           "       "       "
Taylor, William; Pvt.              "      Clark County
Tuder, Jared; Pvt.                 "      Saline County
Tyree, William; Corp.              "      Hot Springs County
Ward, Martin; Pvt.                 "       "     "     "
Ward, Noah A.; Pvt.                "      Clark County
West, Benjamin; Pvt.               "      Pulaski County
Wingfield, Thomas; Pvt.            "      Clark County
```

DEATHS:
Laird, James; Pvt. Saline Co; died 22 October 1836.
McHenry, Henry; Pvt. Pulaski Co; died 13 December 1836.
Smith, Mathison; Corp. Pulaski Co; died 24 December 1836.
White, William W.; 2nd Lt. Pulaski Co; died 29 Sept 1836
Wingfield, William R.; Pvt. Clark Co; died 9 Sept 1836.

MUSTER ROLL
CAPTAIN CHARLES PETTIGREW'S COMPANY F
1ST REGIMENT MOUNTED GUNMEN
ARKANSAS VOLUNTEERS
COLONEL LABAN HOWELL, COMMANDER

```
Alexander, Daniel; Pvt.         Residence- Sevier County
Anderson, Jackson; Sgt.            "       "       "
Bledsoe, William; Pvt.             "       "       "
Bradshaw, Shared; Pvt.             "       "       "
Buchanan, David; Pvt.              "       "       "
Carlton, Hiram; Pvt.               "       "       "
Carter, James W.; Pvt.             "       "       "
Chambles, Solomon; Pvt.            "       "       "
Cooper, Jesse; Pvt.                "       "       "
Cooper, William; Pvt.              "       "       "
Cottrell, Washington; Pvt.         "      Hot Springs County
Cox, Jesse; Pvt.                   "       "     "     "
Crisup, William; Corp.             "      Sevier County
Dollarhide, Andrew; Pvt.           "       "      "
Edom, Thomas; Pvt.                 "       "      "
Ewing, John; Pvt.                  "      Hot Springs County
Flanaghan, Felix; Pvt.             "      Sevier County
Gear, John; Pvt.                   "      Sevier County
Griffin, James E.; Bugler          "      Hempstead County
Griffith, George; Pvt.             "      Sevier County
Halbrooks, Burton; Corp.           "       "      "
Hampton, Amos; Pvt.                "       "      "
Haskins, John; Pvt.                "       "      "
Hays, John; Pvt.                   "       "      "
Hogan, Davis; Pvt.                 "       "      "
Hogan, Walter; Pvt.                "       "      "
Holbert, Euel; Pvt.                "       "      "
Holeman, William; Pvt.             "       "      "
Hooper, Elias C.; Corp.            "       "      "
Humphreys, Spencer; Pvt.           "       "      "
Hunter, Edward; Sgt.               "       "      "
James, Abraham; Pvt.               "       "      "
James, Gideon; Pvt.                "       "      "
Lackey, Henry T.; Pvt.             "       "      "
Ladd, Amos; Pvt.                   "       "      "
Ladd, William; Pvt.                "       "      "
Leaper, John; Pvt.                 "       "      "
Leonard, Samuel; Pvt.              "      Miller County
Lewis, John; Pvt.                  "      Sevier County
Lewis, Thomas B.; Pvt.             "       "      "
```

```
Little, Andrew; Pvt.            Residence  Sevier County
Lynch, John; Pvt.                  "          "      "
McCombe, John; Pvt.             Residence  Hempstead County
McCowen, Macolm; Corp.          Residence- Sevier County
McCown, Francis; Pvt.              "         "       "
McCown, John; Pvt.                 "       Miller County
McCown, William; Pvt.              "       Sevier County
McFall, James; Pvt.                "         "       "
Pearce, Irvin; Pvt.                "         "       "
Pearce, John; Pvt.                 "         "       "
Perryman, Jackson; Pvt.            "         "       "
Pettigrew, Charles; Capt.          "         "       "
Robinson, Absalom; Pvt.            "         "       "
Rulong, Morris; Sgt.               "         "       "
Sanders, David; Pvt.               "         "       "
Shelton, William; Pvt.             "         "       "
Slaven, Robert; Pvt.               "         "       "
Smith, Canon; Pvt.                 "         "       "
Smithwick, Jordon; Pvt.            "         "       "
            (died while in service)
Sparks, Willis; Pvt.               "         "       "
Spence, Arthur; Sgt.               "         "       "
Staats, Nicholas; Pvt.             "         "       "
Stewart, Edward; Pvt.              "         "       "
Tidwell, William; Pvt.             "       Hot Springs County
Walker, Robert W.; 1st Lt.         "       Sevier County
Whitehead, Richard; 2nd Lt.        "         "       "
Williams, Harmon; Pvt.             "         "       "
Wilson, William; Pvt.              "         "       "
Woods, Pataman; Pvt.               "         "       "
```

MUSTER ROLL
CAPTAIN BIRD M. SIMPSON'S COMPANY G
5TH REGIMENT MOUNTED GUNMEN
ARKANSAS VOLUNTEERS

Rendezvous at Little Rock, Arkansas on 5 September 1836, stationed at Fort Gibson.

```
Allen, Benjamin; Pvt.           Residence- Randolph County
Bettis, Uriah; Pvt.                "         "       "
Biggs, Calvin; Pvt.                "       Independence "
Blount, Caswell; Pvt.              "       Randolph County
Boyde, William H.; Pvt.            "         "       "
Boyde, William L.; Pvt.            "         "       "
Bradford, James H.; Pvt.           "         "       "
Bridges, Bain F.; Pvt.             "         "       "
Brown, Samuel; Pvt.                "       Arkansas    "
Copeland, Anthony; Pvt./Sgt.       "       Randolph County
Copeland, David; Pvt.              "         "       "
Essary, John; Pvt.                 "         "       "
Essary, Thomas; Pvt.               "         "       "
Foster, John W.; Pvt.              "       Independence "
Gray, Daniel; Pvt.                 "       Randolph County
Hicks, Benjamin F.; Pvt.           "         "       "
Houston, James; 2nd Lt.            "         "       "
Houston, John; Pvt.                "         "       "
Hubble, Jonathan; Pvt.             "         "       "
Kavanaugh, John; Pvt.              "         "       "
Kincheloe, Thomas C.; Pvt.         "         "       "
Lisenby, Richard; Pvt.             "       Little Rock
Louallan, William; Pvt.            "       Randolph County
McCain, William; Pvt.              "       Randolph County
McWilliams, Nelson; Pvt.           "         "       "
McWilliams, William; Pvt.          "         "       "
Mackintire, Richard; Pvt.          "       Little Rock
Mansker, William H.; Corp.         "       Green County
```

```
Mills, John; Bugler              Residence  Randolph County
Minyard, William; Pvt.              "        Independence "
Mitchel, William; Sgt.           Residence- Randolph County
Moore, Alexander; Pvt.              "          "        "
Moore, Hiram; Pvt.                  "          "        "
Morgan, Blake; Sgt.                 "          "        "
Morgan, William; Corp.              "          "        "
Pyburn, John; Pvt.                  "          "        "
Pyburn, William, dropped from rolls, member of legislature
Ritchey, James; Sgt.             Residence  Randolph County
Roark, Larkin; Pvt.                 "        Independence
Robinson, David; Pvt.               "        Randolph County
Shaver, William G.; Pvt.            "          "        "
Simpson, Bird M.; Capt.             "          "        "
Smith, Jacob; Pvt.                  "          "        "
Smith, James; Corp.                 "          "        "
Story, Larkin; Pvt.                 "          "        "
Stubblefield, Absalom; Pvt.         "          "        "
Stubblefield, William; 1st Lt.      "          "        "
Swan, Simon; Pvt.                   "        Fort Towson
Talbert, Benjamin; Pvt.             "        Little Rock
Tyler, William, H.; Pvt.            "        Randolph County
Watson, Jacob; Corp.                "          "        "
White, Howel; Pvt.                  "          "        "
White, William A.; Pvt.             "          "        "
Wilson, William; Pvt.               "          "        "
Winniham, Jesse; Sgt.               "          "        "
Wood, Curtis; Pvt.                  "          "        "
```

DEATHS:
Evans, Jabee; Randolph Co.; died 19 Dec 1836.
Mansker, George W.; Randolph Co.; died 14 Nov 1836.
Mansker, William L.; Randolph Co.; died 11 Dec 1836.
Philips, Madison; Randolph Co.; died 18 Dec 1836.

MUSTER ROLL
CAPTAIN MARCUS W. REINHARDT'S COMPANY H
1ST BATTALION, 2ND REGIMENT
ARKANSAS MOUNTED GUNMEN

Rendezvous at Little Rock, Arkansas on 24 November 1836, stationed
at Fort Gibson.

```
Bailey, Samuel; Pvt.          Residence-Batesville, Independence
Button, Ossa; Corp.;             "      Fort Gibson
Carpenter, Thomas; Pvt.          "      Batesville, Independence
Cavin, Alexander; Corp.          "      Independence County
Conner, John; Pvt.               "         "          "
Cornwell, Alexander; Pvt.        "      Batesville, Independence
Coughran, James; Pvt.            "      Independence County
Davis, Benjamin; Pvt.            "         "          "
Davis, James; Pvt.               "         "          "
Davlin, Thomas; 1st Lt.          "      Batesville, Independence
Dillingham, James; Pvt.          "         "           "
Dillingham, John; Pvt.           "         "           "
Dillingham, Joshua; Pvt.         "         "           "
Dillingham, William; Pvt.        "         "           "
Dove, David; Pvt.                "         "           "
Dunham, Dennis; Pvt.             "      Little Rock, Pulaski
Dunn, James; Pvt.                "        "     "     "
Finley, John; Sgt.               "      Independence County
Foster, William; Sgt.            "         "          "
Gest, John; Pvt.                 "      Batesville, Independence
Gest, William; Pvt.              "         "           "
Gibbins, Milton; Pvt.            "      Independence County
Gill, William; Pvt.              "         "          "
Hall, James G.; Pvt.             "      Batesville, Independence
```

```
Hawkins, Benjamin; 2nd Lt.    Residence Independence County
Hawkins, Buchannon; Pvt.          "         "         "
Hazell, Richard; Pvt.         Residence-Independence County
Heffner, Frederick; Pvt.          "         "         "
Hess, James; Pvt.                 "         "         "
Hess, John; Pvt.                  "         "         "
Hess, Riley; Pvt.                 "         "         "
Johnson, Overton; Pvt.            "         "         "
Johnson, Warren; Sgt.             "         "         "
Landers, John; Pvt.               "         "         "
Lofton, John D.; Corp.            "         "         "
Moser, Frederick; Pvt.            "         "         "
Moser, Peter; Pvt.                "         "         "
Owings, Perry; Pvt.               "         "         "
Penter, Samuel; Pvt.              "         "         "
Penter, William; Pvt.             "         "         "
Pitman, Samuel; Pvt.              "         "         "
Rawlings, Thomas; Corp.           "         "         "
Reinhardt, Marcus; Capt.          "         "         "
Sherrill, Alanson P.; 1st Lt.     "         "         "
Smalley, Joseph; Farrier          "         "         "
Spencer, Samuel; Pvt.             "         "         "
Weaver, John; Pvt.                "    Little Rock, Pulaski
Wilson, Jerome; Pvt.              "    Independence County
Wycough, Nicholas; Sgt.           "         "         "
```

DEATHS:
Dulaney, John; Indept. Co. died 8 Dec 1836 near Dardenelle.
Gest, Isaac; Indept. Co. died 29 Dec 1836 at Ft. Gibson.
Morse, James; Indept. Co. died 4 Dec. 1836 near Plummerville.

MUSTER ROLL
CAPTAIN WILLIS PHILLIPS' COMPANY I
1ST REGIMENT MOUNTED GUNMEN
ARKANSAS VOLUNTEERS
COLONEL LABAN HOWELL, COMMANDER

Mustered 31 October 1836, stationed at Fort Gibson.

```
Barnet, William H.; Pvt.      Residence-Lawrence County
Bellough, Elijah; Pvt.            "         "         "
Bevey, Bird; Pvt.                 "         "         "
Brandon, Christopher; Pvt.        "         "         "
Brandon, James A.; Pvt.           "         "         "
Brinelly, Henry; Pvt.             "         "         "
Buster, James; Pvt.               "         "         "
Cofford, Elijah; Pvt.             "         "         "
Cozeah, George W.; Pvt.           "         "         "
Duprey, Alfred; Pvt.              "         "         "
Duprey, M.E.; Pvt.                "         "         "
Eliot, Michael; Pvt.              "         "         "
Fargison, Hiram; Pvt.             "         "         "
Finley, Joseph; Pvt.              "         "         "
Galasso, William B.; Pvt.         "         "         "
Hales, James; Pvt.                "         "         "
Hardin, Andrew; 1st Lt.           "         "         "
Hillhouse, Aaron; Corp.           "         "         "
Huddleston, Pinkney; Pvt.         "         "         "
Hudson, Wade H.; Pvt.             "         "         "
James, Henry F.; Pvt.             "         "         "
Jeffers, Leroy; Pvt.              "         "         "
Johnston, Avery; Sgt.             "         "         "
Johnston, William; Sgt.           "         "         "
Kellette, Alfred; Pvt.            "    Saline County
Kellette, John; Pvt.              "         "    "
Kellette, Joseph; Pvt.            "         "    "
Lasewell, Joseph; Pvt.            "    Lawrence County
Ledford, James; Pvt.              "         "         "
Loyde, James C.; Sgt.             "         "         "
```

```
McKnight, James; Pvt.          Residence Lawrence County
Marshall, James; Corp.            "        "        "
Martin, Henry; Pvt.            Residence-Lawrence County
Moore, Robert J.; Corp.        Residence-Lawrence County
Murry, James; Pvt.                "        "        "
Norris, John; Pvt.                "        "        "
Perkins, Joshua; Pvt.             "        "        "
Phillips, Willis; Capt.           "        "        "
Ragsdell, Benjamin; Pvt.          "        "        "
Ragsdell, William; Pvt.           "        "        "
Reynolds, Hamilton; Pvt.          "        "        "
Richardson, Drewery; Pvt.         "        "        "
Ross, Obadiah; Pvt.               "        "        "
Sharp, John; Pvt.                 "        "        "
Sharp, William; Pvt.              "        "        "
Shaw, John; Pvt.                  "        "        "
Simmons, Charles E.; Pvt.         "        "        "
Smith, John; Pvt.                 "        "        "
Smithee, Ruffin; Pvt.             "        "        "
Stone, Westly; Pvt.               "        "        "
Stuart, Samuel; Pvt.              "        "        "
Tucker, Henry G.; Pvt.            "        "        "
Tucker, John; Pvt.                "        "        "
Tucker, William H.; Pvt.          "        "        "
Ware, Thomas; Sgt.                "        "        "
Watts, John; Pvt.                 "        "        "
Wayland, James; 2nd Lt.           "        "        "
West, William; Pvt.               "        "        "
Williams, John; Pvt.              "        "        "
Williams, Nathaniel; Pvt.         "        "        "
Willmoth, Joseph B.; Bugler       "        "        "
Wilmoth, James; Pvt.              "        "        "
```

MUSTER ROLL
CAPTAIN BENAIH BATEMAN'S COMPANY
ARKANSAS MOUNTED VOLUNTEERS

Mustered the eighth day of October 1836 into the service of the United States, under requisition of Brevet Brigadier General M. Arbuckle, commanding the Southwestern Frontier. Stationed at Fort Gibson.

```
Bateman, Benaih; Capt.         Residence-Independence County
Bateman, Jonathan; Pvt.           "        "        "
Beard, David; Pvt.                "        "        "
Beard, Thompson; Pvt.             "        "        "
Bingham, George W.; Pvt.          "     Litchfield, Jackson
Bond, Elisha B.; Pvt.             "     Independence County
Burns, Stephen; Pvt.              "        "        "
Caldwell, Andrew; Pvt.            "        "        "
Casson, Wyatt; Pvt.               "        "        "
Chapman, William B.; Pvt.         "        "        "
Costellow, William; Pvt.          "        "        "
Crawley, Landy W.; Pvt.           "     Fayetteville, Washington
Dillard, Thomas; Pvt.             "     Independence County
Dutton, Moses; Pvt.               "     Fayetteville, Washington
Everit, John; Pvt.                "     Independence County
Everit, William; Pvt.             "        "        "
Gibbins, Auston A.; Pvt.          "        "        "
Gibson, Isom; Pvt.                "     Fayetteville, Washington
Gibson, William; Corp.            "     Independence County
Golding, John; Pvt.               "     Independence County
Halcomb, Claiborne; Pvt.          "        "        "
Hale, McKindry; Pvt.              "        "        "
Hulsey, John; Sgt.                "        "        "
Hulsey, William; Pvt.             "     Blackriver, Independence
Iview, Vardemur; Pvt.             "     War Eagle, Washington
Johnson, Samuel; Pvt.             "     Independence County
```

Kendrick, George; Pvt.	Residence-Independence County	
Kennedy, William E.; Pvt.	"	" "
Kenyon, Napoleon; Pvt.	"	" "
Kenyon, Simson; Pvt.	"	" "
Kirk, George; Pvt.	"	" "
Larrabee, Lewis; Pvt.	"	Litchfield, Jackson
McDanniel, Thomas H.; Pvt.	"	Independence County
McKinney, Charles F.; Pvt.	"	" "
McKinney, Thomas G.; Pvt.	"	" "
Mahan, Alfred; Pvt.	"	" "
Meeks, Eliphes (?); Pvt.	"	" "
Minyard, James; Pvt.	"	" "
Minyard, Levi; Pvt.	"	" "
Morrison, Stephen; Pvt.	"	" "
Palmer, David M.; Corp.	"	" "
Palmer, William; Pvt.	"	" "
Perry, James; Pvt.	"	" "
Pickett, James A.; Pvt.	"	Fayetteville, Washington
Polston, John; Pvt.	"	Independence County
Pool, Washington; Corp.	"	" "
Porter, William; Sgt.	"	" "
Powers, Simeon; Pvt.	"	" "
Reaves, Elias; Pvt.	"	" "
Reaves, William; 1st Lt.	"	" "
Robinson, Elisha; Pvt.	"	" "
Robinson, Jeremiah; Pvt.	"	Fayetteville, Washington
Robinson, John; Sgt.	"	Independence County
Rollins, Armstead; Pvt.	"	" "
Rust, James W.; Pvt.	"	" "
Smith, Lewis H.; Pvt.	"	" "
Steel, Isaac; Corp.	"	" "
Tourney, Pleasant; 2nd Lt.	"	" "
Tuttle, Moses; Pvt.	"	" "
Waldon, William; Pvt.	"	" "
Watson, Benjamin; Sgt.	"	" "
Watson, George F.; Pvt.	"	" "
Webel, Philip; Pvt.	"	Fayetteville, Washington
Wood, Francis; Pvt.	"	Jackson, Lawrence
Young, Joseph; Pvt.	"	Independence County
Young, William H.; Pvt.	"	" "

MUSTER ROLL
CAPTAIN BENNETT G. CLARK'S COMPANY A
1ST BATTALION, 2nd REGIMENT
ARKANSAS MOUNTED GUNMEN

Enrolled 27 September 1836 at Fort Coffee, commanded by Major
Osimous Evans, stationed at Fort Gibson. (All of the Townships
listed below are in Washington County, unless otherwise stated)

Arrington, Ethelbert; Pvt.	Residence-	Fayetteville
Baity (Baily ?), Alexander; Pvt.	"	Illinois
Boatwright, Calvin; Pvt.	"	Cane Hill
Browning, A.W.; Pvt.	"	Fayetteville
Bunker, Joseph; Bugler	"	Fayetteville
Campbell, Thomas M.; Pvt.	"	"
Clark, Bennett G.; Capt.	"	"
Clary, Gilliton; Pvt.	"	Cane Hill
Coldwell, James; Bugler	"	Osage
Coldwell, Thomas; Corp.	"	Fayetteville
Collins, Lewis; Pvt.	"	Cane Hill
Cozine, William; Pvt.	"	Fayetteville
Craig, James; Pvt.	"	"
Cuthbirth, Willis; Pvt.	"	Illinois
Dagley, William B.; 1st Lt.	"	Cane Hill
Davidson, A.R.; Pvt.	"	Illinois
Devenport, William; Pvt.	"	Fayetteville
Edmiston, Harvey; Sgt.	"	Cane Hill
Edmiston, James; Pvt.	"	Cane Hill

```
Edmiston, Moses; Corp.              Residence- Prairie
Fellows, Cyrus A.; Pvt.                 "       Fayetteville
Forkner, Greenberry; Pvt.               "            "
Freyschlag, Edward; 2nd Lt.             "            "
Givans, Alexander; Sgt.                 "       Cane Hill
Grager, George; Corp.                    "       Mountain
Hardesty, L.E.; Sgt.                    "       Cane Hill
Hewitt, Jackson; Pvt.                   "       Illinois
Hubbard, Andrew; Pvt.                   "       Osage
Hubbard, Benjamin; Pvt.                 "       Osage
Johnson, H.A.; Pvt.                     "       Fayetteville
Johnson, John; Pvt.                     "       Cane Hill
Johnson, William C.; Pvt.               "       Fayetteville
Jones, John B.; Pvt.                    "            "
Kincheloe, George W.; Pvt.              "            "
McKinney, W.B.; Pvt.                    "       Madison County
Martin, James; Pvt.                     "       Fayetteville
Martin, Tilman; Pvt.                    "            "
Mayfield, William; Pvt.                 "            "
Miller, John; Pvt.                      "            "
Miller, Joseph; Pvt.                    "            "
Neal, Joab; Pvt.                        "            "
Padgett, Franklin; Pvt.                 "       Cane Hill
Pierson, John; Pvt.                     "       Fayetteville
Pogue, John; Pvt.                       "            "
Price, Isaac; Pvt.                      "            "
Risley, John; Pvt.                      "            "
Robinson, Elbert; Pvt.                  "            "
Robinson, Jackson; Pvt.                 "       Cane Hill
Rose, Thomas; Pvt.                      "        "    "
Scantlin, Walter; Pvt.                  "       Sugar
Scrimshire, James W.; Pvt.              "       Cane Hill
Sharp, Adam; Pvt.                       "       Fayetteville
Sherry, Green W.; Pvt.                  "            "
Spencer, George W.; Sgt.                "       Cane Hill
Standifer, Samuel; Pvt.                 "       Fayetteville
Summers, Ewing; Pvt.                    "       Illinois
Thomason, William; Pvt.                 "            "
Trusdale, James L.; Pvt.                "       Cane Hill
Wagner, Bazil; Pvt.                     "       Illinois
Williams, William; Pvt.                 "       Fayetteville
Wilson, Stockley D.; Pvt.               "            "
Yates, James; Sgt.                      "       Mountain
Yates, Richard; Pvt.                    "            "
Yeary, John; Cornet                     "       Illinois
```

DEATHS:
Davidson, A.M.; Pvt. resident of Cane Hill, died 22 Jan 1837.
Kincaid, John L.; Pvt. "   of Fayetteville, died 21 Feb 1837.
McKinney, Giles; Pvt.   " not stated, died 6 Nov 1836.

MUSTER ROLL
CAPTAIN THADIUS C. WILSON'S COMPANY C
1ST BATTALION, 2ND REGIMENT
ARKANSAS MOUNTED VOLUNTEERS

Mustered into service 26 November 1836 at Fort Gibson, commanded
by Major Onesimus Evans. (All of the townships listed below
are in Washington County, unless otherwise specified)

```
Barlow, John H.; Pvt.              Residence-Vineyard
Billingsley, Robert; Pvt.               "       Osage, Benton
Brotherton, B.B.; Corp.                 "       Vineyard
Chandler, Enoch; Pvt.                   "       Illinois
Chandler, Preston; Pvt.                 "       Vineyard
Cooper, William; Pvt.                   "       Crawford County
Coultor, Hudson; Pvt.                   "       Cane Hill
Coultor, I.M.; Pvt.                     "        "    "
```

```
Coultor, Pleasant M.; Pvt.          Residence-Cane Hill
Davis, Thomas; Pvt.                    "      Osage, Benton
Dennis, Benjamin; Pvt.                 "      Vineyard
Dennis, Green; Pvt.                    "         "
Dill, Archibald; Sgt.                  "      Cane Hill
Dillingham, Archibald; Pvt.            "      Vineyard
Dillingham, Joshua; Pvt.               "         "
Dolton, Joseph N.; Pvt.                "      Illinois
Finley, Robert; Pvt.                   "      Fayetteville
Garrett, John; Pvt.                    "      Vineyard
Gillett, James; 1st Lt.                "      Fayetteville
Gray, Charles B.; Corp.                "      Vineyard
Hays, William N.; Sgt.                 "      Fayetteville
Hodge, William; Sgt.                   "         "
Hughes, Silas N.; Pvt.                 "      Vineyard
Hunt, William; Bugler                  "      Fayetteville
Irby, Dillen H.; Pvt.                  "         "
Kincheloe, John; Pvt.                  "         "
Kirby, William S.; Corp.               "      Cane Hill
Leonard, John G.; Bugler               "      Vineyard
McInturff, John; Pvt.                  "         "
Marrs, James; Pvt.                     "      Fayetteville
Marrs, James F.; Pvt.                  "      Vineyard
Marrs, Jeremiah; Pvt.                  "      Fayetteville
Marrs, John; Pvt.                      "      Vineyard
Marrs, William; Pvt.                   "         "
Matlock, William; Pvt.                 "      Fayetteville
Miller, Richard I.; Pvt.               "      Crawford County
Miller, William M.C.H.; Pvt.           "      Fayetteville
Moore, Garrison M.; Pvt.               "      Cane Hill
Moore, Thomas; Pvt.                    "      Cane Hill
Musgrove, John; Pvt.                   "      Vineyard
Nidiver, Daniel; Pvt.                  "      Crawford County
O'Bryant, Hugh; Pvt.                   "      Vineyard
O'Bryant, Jacob; Pvt.                  "         "
Payne, Ammon; Pvt.                     "      Crawford County
Payne, Claiborne; Sgt.                 "         "       "
Payne, Hiram; Pvt.                     "         "       "
Poore, William P.; Pvt.                "      Cane Hill
Price, William D.; Pvt.                "      Richland
Richmond, Alexander; Pvt.              "      Vineyard
Richmond, Asbury; Pvt.                 "         "
Robinson, William Jr.; Pvt.            "      illegible
Robinson, William Sr.; Pvt.            "      illegible
Shores, Willard R.; 2nd Lt.            "      Vineyard
Slate, Reuben; Pvt.                    "         "
Smith, Burton; Cornet                  "         "
Stover, Enoch; Pvt.                    "      illegible
Strot (?), Peter B.; Pvt.              "      Vineyard
Sweeney, B.J.; Pvt.                    "      illegible
Taylor, Henry; Pvt.                    "      Illinois
Titsworth, Benjamin; Pvt.              "      Richland
Trent, John; Pvt.                      "      Fayetteville
West, John B.; Pvt.                    "      Vineyard
Williams, Alexander; Pvt.              "      Crawford County
Williams, James; Pvt.                  "         "       "
Wilson, Thadius; Capt.                 "      Vineyard
Wilson, William J.; Corp.              "      Fayetteville
Wood, John; Pvt.                       "      Vineyard
```

Returns of the 1st Regiment, Arkansas Mounted Volunteers, under
Command of Colonel Archibald Yell, for the months of July and
August 1846; "The Regiment took up the line of march on the
7th of July at Washington, Arkansas, the place of rendezvous
and reached Camp Crockett near San Antonia de Bexar, Texas on
the 28th August 1846, a distance of 580 miles, and joined General
Wool and am now under his Command and subject to his orders."
Signed, A.Yell

Returns of the 1st Regiment, Arkansas Mounted Volunteers, at
Buena Vista, Mexico, 24 February 1847, "In obedience to an order
of this date, I have the honor to report the following individuals
of the Arkansas Regiment Volunteers as having been killed, wounded
or missing from the battle of 23 instant"

KILLED

Higgins, Green H.
Hogan, David
Landers, Richard
Martin, George W.
Pelham, John
Penter, Harrison
Phipps, William
Porter, Andrew

Ray, Jacob
Robinson,William
Rowland,Thomas C.
Stewart, Darwin
Teague, Andrew
Tomberlin, Wilson
Williams, Pleasant
Wynn, Harmond
Yell, Archibald

WOUNDED

Adams, John
Allen, James F.
Arnold, Ralph
Beckwith, Lawrence
Biggerstaff, John
Bogard, ? (Sgt)
Brown, Franklin
Gipson, William
Graham, Moses
Hamilton, H.L.
Harris, Alfred
Johnson, Isaac
Jones, Osere (?)
Kelly, Moses
Latham, George
Lewallen, John

Logan, David
McCool, Elias
McGruder, Lloyd
Nicholson, Benjamin
Penter, Joseph
Poplin, M.L.
Ray, Jacob
Reeder, Thompson
Ross, Benjamin
Searcy, William
Sullivan, Christopher
Taylor, Claiborne
Turner, William
Turouski, L.A.
Williams, Jacob
Wilmoth, Jackson

MISSING

Green, Joseph
Little, Lafayette

Norwood, George
Parker, Meredith

OFFICERS and FIELD STAFF

Borland, Solan; Major, elected from Captain in his own Company
        4 July 1846, Washington, Ark.
Calvert, William; 2nd Lieutenant
Carr, Hiram; 2nd Lieutenant
Causin, William H; 2nd Lieutenant
Cochran, Addison; 2nd Lieutenant
Danley, Christopher C; Captain, Company B
Dickson, Thomas M; Q.M.Sergeant, by order of Colonel Yell.
Dillard, John J; Captain, Company F
Dollarhide, J.S; 1st Lieutenant
Douglas, J.C; 2nd Lieutenant
English, William K; Captain, Company I, sick at Washington,
        Ark. 17 July, rejoined Regt. at the Colorado

Foster, George S; 1st Lieutenant
Gilbert, E.H; 2nd Lieutenant
Glenn, John W.; surgeon, appointed from citizen by President,
            joined Regiment at San Antonio de Bexar.
Hamilton, Isaac; 1st Lieutenant, elected from Pvt. on 4 July
Houston, Josiah; appointed Sgt. Major from Pvt. in Company B
Hunter, Edward; Captain, Company G
LeRoy, James; Musician, appointed from Private in Company B
McClain, William A; 2nd Lieutenant
McCown, R; 2nd Lieutenant
Meares, Gaston; Adjutant, later Captain at Buena Vista
Moffett, James S; Captain, Company A.
Patrick, George Washington; Captain, Company C; sick at Washington,
            Ark. 17 July, rejoined Regt. at Camp Santa Anna
Patrick, John W; 1st Lieutenant
Peay, John C; 2nd Lieutenant
Peyton, Craven; surgeon, by order of Brigadier General Wool.
Pike, Albert; Captain, Company E
Poe, Lewis S; 1st Lieutenant, Acting Commissary
Porter, Andrew; Captain, Company D, Killed at Buena Vista 23
            February 1847.
Preston, John Jr.; Captain, Company K
Preston, William G; Captain, Company H
Reeder, Thomas A; 1st Lieutenant, wounded at Buena Vista
Reynolds, Hamilton; 1st Lieutenant
Roane, Ewing H. Surgeon, appointed by President, joined Regiment
            at Patos, Mexico 20 Dec. 1846.
Roane, John Seldon; Lieutenant Colonel, elected from Captain
            in his own Company 4 July 1846; elected Colonel
            of Regiment after death of Colonel Yell.
Sagely, R; 2nd Lieutenant
Scott, Walter F; 2nd Lieutenant
Searcy, Jesse; 2nd Lieutenant
Searcy, Richard; 2nd Lieutenant
Stewart, A.L; 2nd Lieutenant
Stewart, G.C; 2nd Lieutenant
Stewart, Joseph; 2nd Lieutenant
Taylor, Hiram; 1st Lieutenant, later Captain of Moffett's Company
Thompson, Davis; 2nd Lieutenant, Acting Assistant Q.M.
Tomlinson, John W; 2nd Lieutenant
Tomlinson, Thomas C; 1st Lieutenant
Trousdale, Cincinattus; appointed Q.M. Sergeant 5 July 1846
Wilhoff, Leonard; 2nd Lieutenant
Yell, Archibald; Colonel of Regiment, elected from Private in
            Captain Borland's Company, at Washington, Arkansas,
            on 4 July 1846, killed at Buena Vista 23 February
            1847.

MUSTER ROLL
CAPTAIN JAMES MOFFETT'S COMPANY A
YELL'S REGIMENT
Enrolled at Washington, Arkansas
1 July 1846

Allen, James F; Pvt.
Aylor, John W.; Bugler
Barkley, Lowry; Pvt. disability Disc. 27 May 1847
Beeson, James W; Pvt. disability Dis. 20 Sept at San Antonio
Beeson, Marcus; Pvt.
Brett, Jefferson; Pvt. enlisted at Walnut Hills, Ark.
Bruce, Andrew; Pvt.
Brown, Simeon; Pvt. sick at San Antonio 23 Oct 1846, Left Saltillo,
            Mexico for camp on 21 Jan. 1847, not heard
            from again, supposed killed by Mexicans.
Bunch, James A; Pvt.
Burlison, Joseph; Pvt. enlisted at Camp Crockett, disability
            disc. 27 May 1847

171

Cochran, Addison; Pvt. also 2nd Lt.
Carlton, William; Pvt.
Cellog, Stephen; Pvt.
Chambers, Bennett; Pvt.
Copland, James C; Pvt.
Dow, Calendar; Pvt. died at San Antonio, Texas 29 October 1846
Edmiston, Andrew W; Pvt.
Edmiston, Bapoleon B; Pvt.
Empson, James A; Pvt. died near Greenwood, Louisiana 30 July
Eubanks, Nelson K; Farrier
Franklin, Marcus; Pvt. disability disc. 23 Sept 1846, San Antonio
Garner, James L; Pvt. Horse stolen at San Antonio, remounted
        himself next day
Graham, Moses; Pvt.
Hamilton, Hugh L; 1st Sergeant
Hamilton, Robert L; Corporal
Hand, Joseph; Pvt.
Harkey, Silas M; Pvt. died at San Antonio 3 November 1846
Harkins, Philantus; Pvt.
Howard, Ervin; Pvt.
Holleger, George W; Pvt. sick at San Antonio 26 October 1846
Howell, Asa B; Pvt.
Hughes, Starling; Pvt.
Johnson, Isaac; Pvt.
Johnson Isaac H; Pvt. Horse stolen at San Antonio, disability
        disc. 27 May 1847.
Jordan, John M; Pvt. enlisted at Trinity River, Texas, disability
        disc. 2 June 1847
Kiser, James F; Pvt. enlisted at Trinity River, Texas, sick
        at Rio Grande 8 Nov.1846
Linsley/Linzey, William; Pvt. disability disc. 23 Sept 1846
Logan, David; Pvt.
Logan, James B; Pvt. died at Saltillo, Mexico, 30 Dec 1846
Logan, Thomas; Bugler
Louallen, John A; Pvt.
Louthers, Napoleon; Pvt.
Lowrey, Buckley; Pvt.
Macomb, Levi; Sgt. enlisted 30 June 1846
Macon, John; Pvt.
Macon, Levi; 1st Sergeant
Madax, Simeon; Pvt.
Maddox, Harvey; Pvt.
Mason, Samuel; Corporal
Moffett, James A; Captain, died at San Antonio de Bexar, Texas
        8 November 1846
Moffett, William; Pvt. died at camp near Aqua Nueva, Mexico
        23 December 1846
McAlister, Joseph; Pvt.
McAlister, William; Pvt.
McCune, William; Pvt. sick at San Antonio 23 Oct 1846
McNairy, John; Pvt. died at Patos, Mexico 2 Jan 1847
Murdock, James; Pvt.
Norwood, George; Pvt. killed at Buena Vista 23 Feb 1847
Parker, Henry; Pvt. disability disc 23 Sept 1846
Parker, Merdal (?); Pvt.
Petray, Jonah A; Pvt.
Petray, William S; Pvt.
Poplin, Madison; Corporal, died of wounds received at Buena
        Vista, 23 March 1847
Reasoner, William; Pvt.
Reed, Leonard; Pvt. died at San Antonio 28 Oct 1846
Ross, Alfred; Pvt. died at San Antonio 14 Nov 1846
Rushing, Dennis; 1st Sergeant
Rushing, William R; 1st Sergeant
Rye, Madison; Pvt. died at Trinity River, Texas 12 Aug 1846
Rye, Solomon; Pvt. died in 1846 ?

CAPTAIN MOFFETT'S COMPANY A
Continued

Scott, Walter H.; 2nd Lt.
Shinn, Jacob; Corp.
Shinn, Silas M.; Pvt. sick at San Antonio 23 Oct 1846
Smith, James H.; Pvt.
Stout, James; Pvt.
Taylor, Hiram W; 1st Lieutenant, elected Captain after death
          of James Moffett.
Teague, Andrew; Pvt. killed at Buena Vista 23 Feb 1847
Trousdale, Cincinnattus; Pvt. elected to 1st Lieutenant
Underwood, Anderson; Pvt.
Verdun, James; Pvt.
Walker, Andrew; Pvt.
Whitlock, Alexander; Pvt.
Williams, Martin; Pvt. enlisted at Camp Crockett, Texas 22 Aug
Wilson, Moses; Pvt.
Wood, William; Pvt.
Yarbrough, Willis; Pvt.

MUSTER ROLL
CAPTAIN CHRISTOPHER C. DANLEY'S COMPANY B
YELL'S REGIMENT
Enrolled at Washington, Arkansas
30 June 1846

This Company mustered at Monclova, Mexico on 31 October 1846;
Patos, Mexico on 31 December 1846; Aqua Nueva on 28 February
1847; Camargo, Mexico on 20 June 1847.

Beard, Isaac N; Pvt.
Bilby, Oliver P.H; Pvt. Bugler, captured by enemy at Incarnacian
          23 Jan 1847
Borland, Solon; Captain, elected Major and transferred 4 July,
          captured at Incarnation
Bostrick, John; deserted at San Antonio 25 Sept. 1846
Blakeney, Benjamin; Pvt. disability disc. at Camargo, Mexico
Brower, Jeremiah E; Pvt. captured by enemy at Incarnacion
Buhoup, Jonathan W; Corporal
Bybee, Adam; Pvt.
Carr, Hiram; Pvt.
Cloos, John A; Pvt.
Colquitt, Samuel H; Pvt. murdered by Mexican near Camp Taylor
          at Aqua Nueva
Colthorp, James; Pvt. died at Camp near Parras, Mexico 14 Dec
Cook, Walker; Pvt.
Cox, Robert M; Pvt.
Danley, Benjamin F; Sergeant, disability discharge at Camargo,
          Mexico
Danley, Christopher C; 1st Lieutenant, elected Captain 6 July
          1846, captured by the enemy at Incarnacion
          23 January 1847
Danley, Joshua M; Pvt. disability disc. at Camargo, Mexico
Dawson, Henry; Corporal, Disab. Disc. at Camargo, Mexico
Deihl, Christian; Bugler
Denton, Thomas J; Pvt.
Denton, William; Pvt. died at Camp near Parras, Mexico on 10
          December 1846
Dowd, Horatio; Pvt.
Dunahoo, William; Pvt.
Fraley, John L; Pvt. Disability disc. San Antonio 2 Sept 1846
Field, John W; Pvt. deserted at San Antonio 25 Sept 1846
Fingerbender, Charles; Pvt. died at Patos, Mexico 27 Jan 1847
Foster, John E; Pvt.
Gaines, Nathaniel; 1st Sergeant
Giles, Josiah; 2nd Lieutenant
Gollier, Benjamin; Pvt.
Griggs, Samuel P; Pvt.

Hamilton, Isaac; Pvt. elected 1st Lt. 6 July 1846
Hare, Ethan; Pvt. died at camp near Patos 29 Dec 1846
Henry, John; Corp.
Hodges, Isham; Pvt. disab. disc. at Camargo
Hogan, Almarine; Pvt.
Hogan, Woodson; Pvt.
Hughes, Benjamin T; Pvt.
Humphries, John B; Pvt.
Isbell, William; Pvt.
Jeffries, Samuel; Corporal
Kelley, Thomas J; Pvt.
Kirkpatrick, Wesley; Pvt.
Lavers, George; Pvt.
Leeper, Greenup; Pvt.
LeRoy, James H; Bugler
Love, James A; Pvt.
Lucas, William; Pvt.
McNabb, Wiley B; Sergeant
Magness, John; Pvt.
Martin, Ezekiel; Pvt. captured by enemy at Incarnacion
Mooney, Charles S; Pvt. enlisted at Camp Crockett, captured
     by enemy at Incarnacion 23 January 1847
Morris, David; Pvt. died at Saltillo, Mexico 26 Jan 1846
Morrison, Daniel; Pvt. disab. disc. at Camargo, Mexico
Osborne, Andrew J; Pvt.
Osborne, John; Pvt.
Peake, Alfred B; Pvt.
Pelham, John B. Jr; Pvt.
Purtle, John; Pvt. died at Rio Grande River
Purtle, William R; Pvt. died at Camp near Monclova, Mexico
     9 November 1846
Ramsey, Isaac; Pvt.
Roberts, Joel; Pvt.
Roberts, William; Pvt.
Rowland, James; Pvt.
Rowland, Josima; Pvt.
Rowland, Samuel S; Pvt.
Rowland, Thomas; Pvt.
Russell, William; Pvt. captured by enemy at Incarnacion
Russell, Willis; Pvt. disab. disc. at Camargo, Mexico
Sarasen, Ferdinand; Pvt. disab. disc. at Camargo, Mexico
Smith, James; Pvt.
Sneed, James; Pvt.
Turner, William; Sergeant
Turouski, Louis; Pvt. wounded at Buena Vista, disab.disc. at
     Camargo, Mexico
Van Meter, Ebenezer; Pvt. died at San Antonio 9 Sept 1846
Walker, Green; Pvt.
Weems, Zare; Pvt. disab. disc. at Camargo, Mexico
Whitten, Count Pulaski; Pvt. captured by enemy at Incarnacion
Williams, Lewis; Pvt. captured by enemy at Incarnacion 23 Jan
Yell, Archibald; elected Colonel of Regiment at Washington,
     Arkansas 4 July 1846, transferred.

MUSTER ROLL
CAPTAIN GEORGE WASHINGTON PATRICK'S COMPANY C
YELL'S REGIMENT
Enrolled at Washington, Arkansas
30 June 1846

"This Company mustered at San Antonio, Texas on 31 August 1846; at Patos, Mexico on 31 December 1846; at Aqua Nueva, Mexico on 28 February 1847; at Camargo, Mexico on 20 June 1847."

Adams, John D; Sergeant
Adams, William N; Corporal
Aden, Washington; Pvt. disab. disc. 27 May 1847
Arnold, Ralph; Pvt.
Arbaugh, William; Pvt. age 25, left Camp at Patos, Mexico, presumed
            murdered 12 January 1847
Ashworth, Benjamin; Pvt.
Awalt, William; Pvt.
Baskins, James C; Pvt.
Bickerstaff, John; Pvt.
Black, James; Pvt.
Braley, Austin P; Pvt. age 21, died at San Antonio 29 Oct 1846
Brodie, John A; Pvt. age 29, died at Saltillo, Mexico 21 Jan
            1847
Cameron, Philip; Pvt.
Carpenter, Moses W; Pvt. disab. disc. at San Antonio 15 Sept
Coleman, James; Pvt.
Connelly, John G; Pvt.
Campbell, Allen; Pvt.
Davis, Alexander; Pvt.
Fagan, James F; Pvt.
Feltner, Lewis; Pvt.
Freight, John D; Pvt.disab. disc. San Antonio 24 Sept 1846
Frost, Robert H; Farrier
Gentry, John; Pvt. disab. bisc. 27 May 1847
Gentry, William H; Pvt.
Gipson, Allen; Corporal
Gipson, William; Pvt.
Goldsworthy, Job; Pvt.
Haigler, John W; Pvt, age 40, enrolled at Shreveport, La, 26
            July 1846, died at Monclova, Mexico 9 Dec 1846
Hamm, James; Pvt. disab. disc. San Antonio 24 Sept 1846
Hickey, John R; Pvt.
Hill, John F; Pvt.
Hodges, Pleasant; Pvt. disab. disc. San Antonio 15 Sept 1846
Hogan, David; Pvt. age 30, killed in battle, Buena Vista, 23
            February 1847
Houston, John; Pvt. appointed Serg. Major of Regiment 1 Mar
            1847, transferred
Jackson, Mark; Pvt.
James, George; Pvt.
Karnes, James W; Pvt. disab. disc. 20 Mar 1847
King, Thomas; Pvt.
Lee, Richard M; Pvt.
Logan, James; Sergeant
Logan, Pleasant D; Pvt.
McClain, William A; 2nd Lieutenant
Magill, Joel; Pvt.
Manasco, Josiah; Pvt.
Martin, James; Pvt. discharged 27 May 1847
Matheny, John; Pvt. discharged 27 May 1847
May, William B; Pvt.
Merryman, Doctor A.;
Merryman, Reuben; Pvt.
Nesbitt, John C; Pvt. disab. disc. San Antonio 15 Sept 1846
Nesbitt, Robert; Pvt.
Newton, Jesse; Bugler
Overton, Addison; Pvt.
Patrick, George L; Pvt.
Patrick, George W; Captain

CAPTAIN PATRICK'S COMPANY C
Continued

Patrick, John; 1st Lieutenant
Parker, George W; Pvt.
Perry, John G; Pvt.
Pryor, William P; Sergeant, age 24, died at Aqua Nueva, Mexico
                15 February 1847
Puckett, Thomas; Pvt. age 28, died at La Encantada, Mexico
                9 May 1847
Riggs, Cyrus; Pvt.
Riggs, John; Pvt.
Roland, John F; Pvt.
Russell, Lewis; Pvt. age 28, died at Camp Crockett 6 Oct 1846
Shropshire, Hutson; 1st Lieutenant
Shropshire, Joel W; Pvt.
Sickle, Joseph; Pvt.
Siscoe, Houston; Pvt.
Stewart, Samuel B; Pvt.
Stuart, Joseph; 2nd Lieutenant
Tatum, Thomas; Pvt. age 24, died at San Antonio 2 Nov 1846
Turner, John M; Corporal
Ward, Jesse; Pvt.
White, John F; Bugler
White, William; Pvt. age 18, died at Patos, Mex. 8 Jan 1847
Williams, ? ; Pvt. age 33 killed at Buena Vista
Williams, Pleasant; Corporal
Willis, John; Pvt. deserted at Washington, Ark. 8 July 1846
Yates, English S; Pvt.

MUSTER ROLL
CAPTAIN ANDREW R. PORTER'S COMPANY D
YELL'S REGIMENT
Enrolled at Washington, Arkansas
3 July 1846

This Company mustered at San Antonio, Texas on 31 August 1846;
at Monclova, Mexico on 31 October 1846; at Patos, Mexico on
31 December 1846.

Adams, Robert; Pvt. age 20, captured at Incarnacion
Batiman, William H; Sergeant
Bennett, Calvin H; Pvt.
Bogard, Zachariah D; Sergeant
Bowen, Norman C; Pvt.
Brown, John; Pvt.
Boyd, Micajah; Sergeant
Cason, James; Pvt.
Cason, Simeon; Sgt. age 23, captured at Incarnacion
Chandler, Marcus; Corporal
Chandler, Samuel; Pvt.
Chrisman, Martin; Corporal
Clark, Hiram; Pvt. age 21, died at Saltillo 4 Feb 1847
Clark, John; Pvt.
Crooks, James W; Pvt. captured at Incarnation
Desha, Franklin; 1st Lieutenant, elected Captain of Company
                after death of Captain Porter
Edwards, William; Pvt. captured at Incarnation
Finley, Robert; Pvt. enlisted at Camp Crockett
Foster, Jacob; Pvt.
Freeas, Theobald; Pvt.
Garrison, William; Bugler
Golden, Isaac; Pvt.
Golden, Richard; Pvt.
Golden, William; Pvt. died at San Antonio 27 Nov 1846
Hardin, Jonathan; Pvt. died at San Antonio 7 Oct 1846
Hardy, Ransom H; Pvt. disab. disc. 25 Sept 1846
Henson, Albert; Pvt.

176

Hess, Solomon; Pvt.
Higgins, Green H; Pvt. age 19, killed at Buena Vista
Hogan, Eli; Pvt. age 22, died at Saltillo 23 Jan 1847
Holland, James C; Pvt. discharged at Camargo, Mexico
Holland, Reuben; Pvt.
Holland, William; Pvt.
Hughes, William C; Pvt.
Johnson, William; Pvt.
Jones, William D; Corporal
Jordan, Edward; Bugler
Ledford, Thomas; Pvt. died at San Antonio 27 Nov 1846
Magness, John; Pvt. age 24 captured at Incarnacion
Magruder, Lloyd; Pvt. discharged at Camargo
Matthews, James; Corporal, disab. disc. 25 Sept 1846
Morgan, Thomas; Pvt.
Mosier, Henry; Pvt.
Morris, William; Pvt.
Nelson, Moses; Pvt. age 20, captured at Incarnacion
Odom, John; Pvt. discharged at Camargo, Mexico
Osteen, James; Pvt.
Parker, James; Pvt.
Penter, Harrison; Pvt.
Penter, James; Pvt. wounded at Buena Vista
Phipps, William; Pvt. age 32, killed at Buena Vista
Porter, Andrew R; Captain, killed at Buena Vista
Rainey, George; Pvt.
Ramsey,George; Pvt. captured at Incarnation
Richmond, James; Farrier, age 34, captured at Incarnacion
Saunders, Richard M; Pvt. later Corporal, age 40, killed at
                    Buena Vista
Screw, George; Pvt.
Searcy, Jesse; 2nd Lieutenant
Searcy, Richard; Pvt. later 2nd Lieutenant
Searcy, William B; Pvt.
Shell, Albert; Pvt.
Shell, William; Pvt.
Sherrill, Jesse; Pvt.
Smalley, Winfield; Pvt.
Smith, Lewallen; Pvt.
Stephens, Hartwell; Pvt. disab. disc. 2 Sept 1846
Taylor, Claiborne; Pvt. wounded at Buena Vista, died 29 Mar
Tooley, Anderson; Pvt.
Trimble, John M; Pvt.
Tuggle, Washington; Pvt. age 25, captured at Incarnacion
Waggoner, Francis; Pvt. died near Parras, Mex. 17 Dec 1846
Waggoner, John L; Pvt.
Waggoner, Robert M; Pvt. died near Parras, Mex. 14 Dec 1846
Weaver, Golbert; Pvt. died near Rio Grande River 10 Oct 1846
White, Jackson; Pvt. discharged at Camargo, Mex.
Wilson, Jesse; Pvt. died at Saltillo 25 May 1847
Wilson, Samuel; Pvt.
Wolf, Enoch; Pvt.

MUSTER ROLL
CAPTAIN ALBERT PIKE'S COMPANY E
YELL'S REGIMENT
ARKANSAS MOUNTED VOLUNTEERS
Enrolled at Washington, Arkansas
30 June 1846

This company mustered 31 August 1846 at San Antonio, Texas;
31 October 1846 at Monclova, Mexico; 31 December 1846 at Haciende
de Patos, Mexico; 28 February 1847 at Saltillo, Mexico; 7 June
1847 at Monterey, Mexico.

Adamson, William; Pvt.
Anson, Hiram; Pvt. disab. disc. 25 Sept. 1846 at San Antonio
Bales, Stephen; Pvt.
Barnes, William K.; Pvt. disab. disc. 10 Sept. 1846 at San Antonio
Blunden, Willaim N.; Bugler
Bolton, Franklin; Pvt.
Borden, John B.; Pvt.
Brock, A. Hamilton; Pvt.
Brock, James; Pvt.
Brookin, Samuel; Pvt.
Brownlee, Thomas; Pvt.
Butler, Sterling G.; Pvt.
Byrd, William; Corp. disab. disc. 25 Sept. 1846 at San Antonio
Causin, William H.; 2nd Lt.
Cellars, C. Andrew; Pvt.
Collins, Hugh; Pvt.
Collins, Joseph A.; Pvt.
Crease, Henry; Corp.
Crouch, Augustus; Bugler
Dismukes, Elisha E.; Pvt
Duff, Richard L.; Pvt.
Eagle, George A.; Pvt.
Eagle, Joseph; Pvt. age 25, died 6 Oct. 1846 at San Antonio
Erwin, Edwin L.; Pvt.
Farrelly, Robert C.; Pvt.
Freyschlag, Herman; Pvt.
Furr, Daniel O.; Pvt
Garner, Joseph N.; Pvt.
Glascow, William; Pvt. disab. disc. 25 Sept. 1846 at San Antonio
Goodresson, John; Pvt.
Gray, Henry C.; Pvt. age 18 died 22 Jan. 1847 at Saltillo
Gray, Jacob S.; Pvt. disab. disc. 25 Sept. 1846 at San Antonio
Gray, William C.; Pvt.
Hammond, Elijah; Pvt.
Hammond, William H.; Pvt.
Harnegan, Enos; Pvt.
Harns, George F.; Pvt.
Harris, George F.; Pvt. disab. disc. 18 Nov. 1846 at Monclova
Hendricks, James H.; Pvt.
Hicks, William F.; Corp.
Hinkston, John M.; Pvt. disab. disc. 25 Sept. 1846 at San Antonio
Hinkston, Sampson G.; Pvt. disab. disc. 26 Sept. 1846   "   "
Hogan, John; Pvt.
Johnson, Isaac; Pvt. wounded at Buena Vista
Jones, James; Pvt. disab. disc. 25 Spet 1846 at San Antonio
Jones, Jesse; Pvt.
Knapp, George; Pvt. discharged 23 Dec 1847
McVicar, James; Pvt. appointed Master Sergeant by Col. Yell,
                transferred 17 Dec 1846
Morrison, George L.; Pvt.
Mosely, John; Pvt. age 24 died 5 Dec 1847 at Monclova
Musser, George; Pvt.
Newman, Milton P.; Pvt.
Newman, William C.; Pvt. age 23 died 24 Nov 1846, San Antonio
Pate, Edward; Pvt.
Patterson, William; Pvt. age 19 died 18 Jan 1847 at Saltillo
Peay, John C.; 2nd Lt.
Pike, Albert; Capt.

178

CAPTAIN PIKE'S COMPANY E
Continued

Poe, William; Pvt. deserted 5 Oct. 1846 at San Antonio
Pscheimer, Jacob; Pvt.
Pursley (Pasley ?) David; Pvt. age 44 died 27 Feb 1847 Saltillo
Reed, James; Pvt.
Reynolds, Hamilton; 1st Lt.
Rose, George; Pvt.
Schlatter, Adam; Pvt.
Schneider, Joseph; Farrier
Schweitzer, Jacob; Pvt. disab. disc. 13 Sept 1846 San Antonio
Sitzes, Lawson; Pvt.
Smith, Elias; Pvt.
Smith, Woods; Pvt. disab. disc. 25 Sept 1846 at San Antonio
Stephenson, James T.; Sgt.
Stephenson, John C.; Sgt.
Sullivan, Christopher; Sgt. wounded at Saltillo 23 Feb 1847
Terry, John; Pvt.
Tharpe, John D.; Pvt.
Toler, William; Corp.
Ussery, Morgan; Pvt.
White, Newton; Pvt. age 18 died 13 Feb. 1847 Los Polonius
Whitely, Lambert A.; Sgt.
Wolfe, Charles; Pvt.
Woodruff, Alden; Pvt. appointed 2nd Lt. 12th Regt. U.S.Army

MUSTER ROLL
CAPTAIN JOHN J. DILLARD'S COMPANY F
YELL'S REGIMENT
ARKANSAS MOUNTED VOLUNTEERS
Enrolled Van Buren County
26 June 1846

This company mustered 31 August 1846 at San Antonio, Texas;
31 October 1846 at Monclova, Mexico; 31 December 1846 at Monclova,
Mexico; 28 February 1847 at Camargo, Mexico.

Aikins, David; Pvt. discharged at Camargo, Mexico
Allen, William; Pvt.
Bell, Gideon R.; Bugler
Boyd, Andrew; Pvt.
Boyd, James; Pvt.
Bone, James; Pvt. died at Presidio 28 Oct 1846
Caddean, Elexander; Pvt.
Campbell, Joseph F.; Pvt. died at Saltillo, 24 March 1847
Capps, William; Pvt.
Chew, Alexander B.; Pvt. discharged at Camargo, Mexico
Compton, Joseph B.; Pvt. discharged at Camargo
Criner, George; Pvt.
Dale, Aaron; Pvt.
Davis, James W.B.; Sgt.
Dillard, John; elected Captain and mustered as such
Duty, William; Pvt. discharged at Camargo
Estes, James J.; Pvt. age 30 died 3 Jan 1847 at Monclova
Fears, Ebenezer; Pvt. age 32 died 14 Jan 1847 at La Encantada
Finley, John; Pvt. captured at Incarnacion
Fogarty, Owen; Pvt.
Forrester, Rufus; Pvt. died 20 Nov 1846 at Monclova
Foster, Riley; Pvt.
Hagood, James A.; Pvt. discharged at Camargo
Hardin, Howell; Pvt. age 18 died 27 Jan 1847 at La Encantada
Harris, James; Pvt. died 8 Dec 1846 at Monclova
Hart, David; Pvt. discharged at Camargo
Haynes, John L.; Pvt.
Holman, William L.; Pvt. captured at Incarnacion

179

Houck, Felix; Pvt.
Houck, William A.; Pvt
Ingraham, Alexander C.; Pvt.
Johnson, Samuel; Pvt.
Kelly, Moses; Pvt.
Larimore, James; Pvt.
Larimore, Thomas; Pvt. disab. disc. 23 Sept. 1846
Lassiter, John W.; Pvt.
Latham, George; Sgt.
Lewis, David E.; Pvt.
Little, James; Pvt.
McFarlane, William R.; Pvt.
Marshall, Andrew L.; Pvt. captured at Incarnacion
Moore, Lewis; Pvt. discharged at Camargo
Nesbitt, James C.; Pvt. died 16 Dec 1846 at Monclova
Nicholason, Benjamin F.; Pvt. discharged at Camargo
Parker, Micajah H.; Bugler discharged at Camargo
Patty, Isaac; Pvt.
Perkins, Thomas; Pvt. disab. disc. 23 Sept 1846
Peyton, George W.; Pvt.
Pope, Burton; Pvt. died no date given
Porter, George; 1st Lt.
Price, John; Corp.
Price, George B.; Pvt. disab. disc. 23 Sept 1846
Price, Reece; Pvt. discharged at Camargo
Quesenbury, William; Pvt.
Roane, John Seldon; Capt., elected Lt. Col. of Regt., selected
                Colonel of Regt. after death of Col. Yell.
Roberts, James C.; Pvt.
Ross, Benjamin; Sgt.
Rudy, John; Corp. discharged at Camargo
Smart, Alexander; 2nd Lt.
Smart, Darwin; Corp. (see Steward, Darwin)
Smith, Berry; Pvt.
Smith, James H.; Pvt.
Smith, Riley; Pvt. discharged at Camargo
Spratt, John; Sgt.
Steward, Darwin; Corp. age 22, killed at Buena Vista (I suspect
                this is the same man listed as Smart)
Stinnett, Wiley; Pvt.
Story, John; Pvt. diacharged at Camargo
Stuart, Benjamin L.; Farrier
Taylor, Asbury H.; Pvt. age 18 died at Trinity River, Texas
Taylor, Berry H.; Pvt.
Taylor, John W.; Pvt. discharged at Camargo
Thomas, Marcus; Pvt.
Thomas, William C.; Pvt.
Thompson, David; Corp.
Vice, John; Pvt. discharged at Camargo
Waters, James J.; Pvt. died 4 Mar 1847 at Camargo
White, Solomon; Pvt.
Willhoff, Leonard; 2nd Lt.
Worley, Michael A.; Pvt.
Wynn, Harmon 1st; Pvt. age 24 died at Patos 10 Jan 1847
Wynn, Harmon 2nd; Pvt. age 18 killed at Buena Vista

MUSTER ROLL
CAPTAIN EDWARD HUNTER'S COMPANY G
YELL'S REGIMENT
ARKANSAS MOUNTED VOLUNTEERS
Enrolled at Washington, Arkansas
21 June 1846

This company mustered 31 August 1846 at San Antonio, Texas; 31 December 1846 at Patos, Mexico; 28 February 1847 at Aqua Nueva, Mexico; 20 June 1847 at Camargo.

Ashbrook, Aaron; Pvt.
Baker, English; Pvt.
Barnett, Wesley A.; Pvt. age 25 died 8 Sept 1846 at Trinity
        River, Texas.
Beckwith, Lawrence B.; Pvt. wounded at Buena Vista
Bennett, Benjamin; Pvt. joined Meare's Co. 27 May 1847
Bradley, Edward; Pvt.
Brewer, William; Pvt.
Brooks, Robert G.; Sgt.
Call, Francis A.; Pvt. disab. disc. 22 Sept 1846
Cherry, William H.; Pvt. joined Capt. Meare's Co. 27 May 1847
Coughran, Lewis; Pvt.
Crosland, William C.; Corp. age 19 died Camp Yell 13 Sept 1846
Davis, Isham G.; Pvt.
Derrick, Washington; Bugler
Dollarhide, Andrew; Pvt. disab. disc. 18 Sept 1846
Dollarhide, James S.; 1st Lt. disab. disc 20 Sept 1846
Dunlap, Moses W.; Pvt. joined Meare's Co. 27 May 1847
Eastwood, Hiram; Pvt. joined Meare's Co. 27 May 1847
Falkner, George W.; Pvt. age 25 died San Antonio 25 Oct 1846
Gentry, Daniel; Pvt.
Golden, Harper; Pvt.
Gooch, Thomas; Corp. joined Meare's Co. 27 May 1847
Graham, Joseph R.; Pvt.
Greenwood, Bailey; Pvt. age 19 died San Antonio 13 Nov 1846
Greer, Josiah; Pvt. age 18 missing at Buena Vista
Hail, William; Pvt.
Ham, Joseph D.; Pvt.
Hardwick, James H.; Pvt.
Higgins, James D.; Pvt.
Higgins, William S.; pvt.
Holbrook, Benton; Sgt.
Houston, Josiah; Pvt.
Hughes, James; Pvt. age 21 died at Saltillo 2 May 1847
Hull, Joel A.; Bugler
Hull, John W.; Corp.
Hunter, Edward; Capt.
James, Isaac N.; Pvt. age 21 died at Encantada 6 Feb 1847
Little, Josiah F.; Pvt.
Lyons, Charles G.; Sgt. captured at Incarnacion
McAfee, Allen S.; Pvt. joined Meare's Co. 27 May 1847
McComb, Henry; Pvt.
McCown, Roger; 2nd Lt.
McFall, Hiram; Pvt. joined Meare's Co. 27 May 1847
McKean, William K.; Sgt.
Matthews, John; Pvt. joined Meare's Co. 27 May 1847
Mayfield, Samuel M.; Pvt.
Morris, Alfred; Pvt.
Morris, Henry; Pvt. age 19 died San Antonio 1 Nov 1846
Morris, James; Pvt. disab. disc. 18 Sept 1846
Nalls, James; Pvt. age 32 died at Rio Grande River 23 Oct 1846
Nelson, William; Pvt. age 21 died at Patos 18 Dec 1846
Panter, John; Pvt.
Perrin, Robert; Pvt. age 23 died Trinity River 17 Sept 1846
Petters, James E.; Corp.
Pettin, Allen; Pvt.
Phillips, Solomon M.; Pvt.
Posten, William F.; Pvt.

Prater, George C.; Pvt.
Pride, Henry; Pvt.
Sanders, William C.; Pvt.
Self, Cooper; Pvt.
Shannon, Aaron; Pvt.
Skidmore, Gideon; Pvt. age 28 died Camp Crockett 12 Sep 1846
Slaven, Lewis; Pvt. age 20 died Camp Yell 9 Oct 1846
Sloan, William; Pvt. disab. disc 18 Sept 1846
Smith, Jacob; Pvt.
Smoot, Joseph C.; Pvt.
Sorrel, Green; Pvt.
Spence, Jefferson; Pvt. age 30 died Trinity River 13 Sept 1846
Stewart, George C.; 2nd Lt. died at San Antonio 28 Oct 1846
Stinnett, George; Pvt.
Tate, Zachariah; Pvt. age 24 died at Rio Grande 11 Nov 1846
Thompson, Alexander; Farrier
Tollett, Cornelius B.; Pvt. age 27 Died Rio Grande 25 Oct 1846
Underwood, George; Pvt. captured at Incarnacion
Walton, Alfred M.; Pvt.
Willingham, Thomas; Pvt.
Wright, Thomas W.; Pvt. age 18 died Camp Crockett 5 Sept 1846
Wood, James; Pvt.

MUSTER ROLL
CAPTAIN WILLIAM G. PRESTON'S COMPANY H
YELL'S REGIMENT
Enrolled at Washington, Arkansas
30 June 1846

This company mustered 31 August 1846 at San Antonio, Texas;
31 October 1846 at Monclova, Mexico; 31 December 1846 at Patos,
Mexico; 28 February 1847 at Aqua Nueva, Mexico; 20 June 1847
at Camargo, Mexico.

Barney, Oliver; Pvt.
Bowerland, Addison; Pvt.
Brown, Franklin; Pvt. age 19 died of wounds received at Buena
                Vista.
Brown, Henry; Pvt. age 20 died at La Encantada 4 May 1847
Carpenter, Jasper N.; Pvt.
Carpenter, Martin; Pvt.
Carpenter, Oliver; Pvt.
Carpenter, Patterson; Pvt.
Christian, Yancy P.; Pvt. age 27 died at Saltillo 10 Mar 1847
Clay, William R.; Pvt. died at Monclova 19 Nov 1846
Cureton, Jackson; disab. disc. at San Antonio
Curtis, Joel W.; Pvt. captured at Incarnacion
Deggraffinreed, Francis M.; Pvt.
Deggraffinreed, John; Pvt.
Dunn, Frederick; Pvt.
Eppler, Jonathan; Pvt. disab. disc. at San Antonio
Foster, Alvin; Pvt. joined Capt. Meare's Co.
Gage, Martin; Pvt.
Guess, Abram; Sgt.
Hamilton, Francis A.; Bugler
Hamm, Alexander; Pvt.
Hamm, Elisha; Pvt.
Hawkins, John; Pvt.
Hendrix, David; Corp. age 24 died at La Encantada 4 Jun 1847
Hudson, Daniel; Pvt.
Huggins, Richard; Pvt. captured at Incarnacion
Johnston, Russell H.; Pvt.
Kilgin, Patrick O.; Pvt.
Lilly, Joshua; Farrier
McCaslin, James B.; Pvt.

CAPTAIN PRESTON'S COMPANY H
Continued

Martin, Carroll; Pvt.
Martin, George W.; Pvt. age 21 killed at Buena Vista
Martin, Hugh; Pvt.
Maynard, George; Pvt.
Miller, Richard D.; Pvt.
Morrison, Thomas; Pvt.
Morrison, William; Pvt. disab. disc. at San Antonio
Nott, Russell; Pvt. deserted 8 Feb 1847
Pickens, William M.; Pvt.
Pierson, Thomas; Pvt. disab. disc. at San Antonio
Preston, William G.; Capt.
Ray, William; Pvt.
Rector, James P.; Pvt.
Reed, Aaron; Pvt.
Reeves, William M.; Pvt. captured at Incarnacion
Richardson, William J.; Pvt.
Russell, David; Pvt.
Russell, Jonathan; Corp.
Sagely, Redmond B.; 2nd Lt.
Self, William; Pvt. joined Capt. Meare's Co.
Settle, Lafayette W.; Pvt.
Smith, William; Pvt. age 24 died at Saltillo 26 Mar 1847
Sorrel, James J.; disab. disc. at San Antonio
Speegle, William R.; Pvt. captured at Incarnacion
Spencer, Charles; Pvt.
Steel, David R.; Pvt.
Steel, John N.; Pvt. died at San Antonio 20 Oct 1846
Steel, Richard G.; Pvt. captured at Incarnacion
Taylor, James; Bugler disab. disc. at San Antonio
Tennyson, Harrison; Pvt. joined Capt. Meare's Co.
Terry, Aaron C.; Pvt.
Throckmorton, William; Sgt.
Tomberlin, Eleazer; Pvt.
Tomberlin, James; Corp. age 25 killed at Buena Vista
Tomberlin, John W.; 2nd Lt.
Tomberlin, Thomas C.; !st Lt.
Towers, William; Pvt. joined Capt. Meare's Co.
Tucker, Andrew J.; Pvt.
Tucker, Elijah; Pvt. disab. disc. at San Antonio
Webb, Joel; Pvt.
Webb, Thomas; Pvt. captured at Incarnacion
Whited, John K.; Sgt.
Williams, Russell; Pvt. captured at Incarnacion
Wilmouth, Jackson; Pvt.
Wilmouth, William; Corp.
Wright, Andrew; Pvt.
York, Richard; Pvt.

MUSTER ROLL
CAPTAIN WILLIAM K. ENGLISH'S COMPANY I
YELL'S REGIMENT
ARKANSAS MOUNTED VOLUNTEERS
Enrolled at Washington, Arkansas
1 July 1846

This Company mustered 31 August 1846 at San Antonio, Texas;
31 October 1846 at Monclova, Mexico; 31 December 1846 at Monclova,
Mexico; 28 February 1847 at Aqua Nueva, Mexico; 20 June 1847
at Camargo, Mexico.

Adams, James; Pvt.
Allen, Joseph; Bugler, age 24, died at Rio Grande 18 Oct 1846
Allen, Josiah; Pvt.

Anglin, Job S.; Pvt.
Benson, Cullin; Pvt.
Benson, Spencer; Pvt.
Berry, Emanuel; Pvt.
Bland, James; Pvt. age 24 died at Encantada 7 Feb 1847
Bland, Moses; Pvt.
Bond, George A.; Pvt.
Buchan, Abner H.; Pvt. age 22 died at Monclova 17 Dec 1846
Calvert, William; 2nd Lt.
Colbert, Hiram; Corp.
Conway, Thomas; Pvt. later 2nd Lt. in 12th U.S.Infantry
Crane, Stephen; Corp. age 31 disab. disc. 23 Sept 1846
Crawford, James; Pvt.
Crawford, William; Pvt.
Cunningham, Anderson; Pvt.
Dawson, George T.; Pvt.
Douglas, John C.; 2nd Lt.
Dunahoo, Calvin; Farrier
Dunahoo, William; Pvt.
Duvaul, Peter; Pvt.
English, William K.; Capt.
Franklin, Ephriam, Pvt. joined Capt. Meare's Co.
Garrett, Daniel; Pvt.
Gentry, John S.; Pvt.
Gentry, Samuel; Pvt.
Glenn, William; Pvt.
Graves, Thomas; Pvt.
Gunter, Robert H.; Pvt age 26 disab. disc. 23 Sept 1846
Haley, Miles; Pvt.
Hammond, Richard P.; Pvt.
Harrison, William; Pvt.
Henderson, James; Sgt.
Henson, William; Pvt.
Irwin, John; Pvt.
Jeam, James; Pvt.
Jester, Joseph; Pvt. captured at Incarnacion
Jester, Stephen; Pvt. captured at Incarnacion
Jones, Oscar E.; Pvt.
Keltner, William K.; Pvt.
Ketteral, John (also listed as Kitterwell) Corp. age 32 died
              at Saltillo 7 May 1847.
King, Joseph R.; Pvt.
Lindsey, Addison; Pvt. age 21 died at Monclova 20 Jan 1847
Lindsey, Rufus M.; Pvt.
Lunsford, James W.; Pvt.
McCool, Elias; Pvt. wounded at Buena Vista
McKnight, William; Pvt.
Mayfield, William; Bugler
Milliner, David L.; Pvt.
Milliner, Jefferson; Pvt. age 18 died Trinity River 20 Aug 1846
Milliner, John C.; Pvt. age 25 (?) killed at Buena Vista
Mimms, John H.; Pvt. joined Capt. Meare's Co.
Montgomery, William; Pvt.
Morgan, John; Pvt.
Morrow, Asa G.; Sgt. age 25 died at San Antonio
Neil, Burton; Pvt.
Neil, Francis; Pvt.
Nicholas, George W.; Pvt.
Pettitt, Charles S.; Sgt.
Pinkerton, Samuel; Sgt.
Powell, Jesse; Pvt.
Rea, Jacob; Pvt. age 38 killed at Buena Vista
Rector, William G.; Pvt.
Reed, John H.; Pvt.
Reeder, Thomas A.; 1st Lt. wounded at Buena Vista
Richards, Wilson; Pvt. age 38 disab. disc. 13 Sept 1846

CAPTAIN ENGLISH'S COMPANY I
Continued

Robinson, William; Pvt. age 19 killed at Buena Vista
Simmons, James; Pvt.
Smart, Thomas; Pvt. captured at Incarnacion
Spencer, William T.; Pvt. age 18 died at Moncloca 27 Dec 1846
Stacey, Simon; Pvt.
Stinson, Henderson; Pvt. captured at Incarnacion
Such, Patterson; Corp.
Whaland, William; Pvt. age 26 died at Monclova 11 Dec 1846
White, John F.; Pvt.
Williams, Jacob; Pvt. wounded at Buena Vista
Workman, Nathan; Pvt.
Wright, Benjamin F.; Pvt. age 20 disab. disc. 23 Sept 1846

MUSTER ROLL
CAPTAIN JOHN PRESTON JR.'S COMPANY K
YELL'S REGIMENT
ARKANSAS MOUNTED VOLUNTEERS
Enrolled at Washington, Arkansas
10 July 1846

This company mustered 31 August 1846 at San Antonio, Texas;
31 October 1846 at Monclova, Mexico; 31 December 1846 at Patos,
Mexico; 7 June 1847 at Monterey, Mexico.

Allen, James; Pvt.
Alley, Stephen; Pvt.
Barker, Peire; Sgt.
Becker, Frederick; Pvt.
Bevil, Edward H.; Pvt. age 24 died at Patos 27 Dec 1846
Bryant, Alfred; Pvt.
Burge, Nicholas; Pvt.
Clifford, Luke; Pvt.
Cockerell, James; Pvt.
Coree, Samuel; Pvt.
Crawford, Anthony W.; Pvt. deserted at Greenwood, La.
Dailey, Joseph; Pvt.
Dersey, Augustus G.; Pvt.
Dickson, George O.; Pvt. disab. disc. 19 Sept 1846
Dickson, Thomas; Sgt.
Dillingham, Dachel S.; Pvt.
Duty, Thomas; Pvt.
Edwards, William; Pvt.
Edwards, William J.; Pvt. disab. disc. 19 Sept 1846
Elliott, Sanford; Pvt.
Ferebee, Ambrose; Pvt.
Finch, Matthew; Pvt.
Fleenor, John; Pvt.
Foster, Nathan; Pvt. disab. disc. 17 July 1846
Gilbert, Ezekiel H.; 2nd Lt.
Gilbert, John; Pvt.
Gilbert, Phillip A.; Pvt.
Goodman, Solomon K.; Pvt.
Gray, John; Pvt.
Gutherie, Matthew; Pvt.
Hamilton, James; Corp. age 26 died 5 Feb 1847
Harland, James B.; Pvt.
Harris, Ebenezer G.; Bugler
Harris, George W.; Pvt.
Hawkins, John M.; Pvt. age 21 died at Monclova 10 Nov 1846
Head, Robinson; Pvt.

185

Holder, William; Pvt.
Ingraham, James; Pvt. age 21 died at Monclova 1 Dec 1846
James, A. Wade; Pvt.
James, Bartlett R.; Pvt.
Johnson, Richard M.; Pvt.
Johnson, Wilkinson B.; Pvt.
Jones, James M.; Pvt.
Jones, William H.; Pvt.
Kendall, Thomas C.; Pvt.
Latimer, James D.; Pvt.
Laxon, William; Pvt.
Loyd, Lafayette; Pvt. died at Saltillo
Lustee, John; Pvt.
McBroom, John; Pvt.
Manning, Isam; Pvt.
Matlock, Abner; Pvt. age 21 died on march from Monclova to Parras
                25 November 1846
Moore, William E.; Pvt.
Munsey, William D.; Pvt.
Murphy, Dennis; Pvt.
Neal, James H.; Pvt.
Odle, Albert B.; Corp.
Palmer, James B.; Pvt. disab. disc. 19 Sept 1846
Palmer, John C.; Sgt.
Poe, Lewis S.; 1st Lt.
Preston, John Jr.; Capt.
Price, Ransom H.; Pvt.
Rapplee, William; Pvt. disab. disc. 19 Sept 1846
Righter, Nicholas; Corp.
Risinger, Israel P.; Sgt.
Robinett, Moses; Pvt.
Saunders, Archibald; Bugler
Seaborn, Alexander; Pvt.
Semple, George; Pvt.
Simms, Joel D.; Pvt. age 24 died at Rio Grande 14 Nov 1846
Smith, Freeman; Pvt. disab. disc 19 Sept 1846
Snively, William M.; Farrier
Spenser, Joseph; Pvt.
Sullivan, James W.; Corp.
Thompson, Andrew J.; Pvt.
Thompson, Davis; 2nd Lt.
Tomlinson, Lorenzo; Pvt. discharged 28 Feb 1847
Webb, Joseph; Pvt.
Wren, Thomas W.; Pvt. disab. disc. 19 Sept 1846

MUSTER ROLLS
ARKANSAS VOLUNTEERS
MEXICAN WAR

LT. COLONEL WILLIAM GRAY'S BATTALION

GRAY, WILLIAM; Lieutenant Colonel, mustered into service 1 July
1846 at Ft.Smith, Arkansas by Captain Printz. Elected Lt.Colonel
of the Battalion 21 July 1846, at an election held in pursuance
of the orders of the Governor of Arkansas.

MUSTER ROLL
CAPTAIN COLLIN'S COMPANY A
GRAY'S BATTALION
Enrolled at Clarkesville, Arkansas
10 June 1846

Arbaugh, L.W.; Corporal
Armstrong, Jasper N; Pvt.
Armstrong, William; Pvt.
Arnold, William; Pvt.
Baskins, Robert;Pvt.
Bassham, Calvin; Pvt.
Bassham, Oliver; appointed Sgt.Mjr. of the Battn, 22 July 1846
Bayer, William H; Pvt.
Been, John; Pvt.
Belew, Renncy; Pvt.
Belt, William; Pvt.
Browers, Michael; Pvt. died at Ft.Gibson, 10 October 1846
Butts, Henry G; Pvt.
Cargail, William; Pvt. deserted at Ft.Gibson, 23 October 1846
Carlisle, James; Pvt.
Casey, C.C; Pvt. appointed Chief Musician of Battn, 22 July
Clark, B.L; Pvt.
Clay, Henry; Pvt. deserted at Ft.Gibson 1 January 1847
Cloud, Alexander; Pvt.
Cloud, John; Musician, appointed 1st Sgt. 22 July 1846
Cloud, William; Pvt.
Collins, P.B; Sgt, chosen Capt. of Company A, 22 July 1846
Cupp, James M; Pvt. deserted at Ft.Gibson 13 December 1846
Dark, William; Pvt.
Davis, Verminon; Pvt, enrolled 15 July at Ft.Smith, deserted
            at Ft.Gibson 7 Sept. 1846.
Dolay, James; Pvt.
Duncan, William T; Pvt.
Ferguson, James M; Pvt.
Gillam, James T; Sgt.
Gillam, Thomas E; 2nd Lieutenant
Gilleland, James; Pvt.
Gilleland, Reuben; Pvt.
Grace, William; Pvt. deserted at Ft.Gibson 23 October 1846
Greenwood, William P; Pvt.
Grider, William; Pvt.
Hamilton, A.T; Pvt.
Hamilton, George; Pvt.
Hardgraves, James; Sgt.
Hays, Anderson; Corporal
Hays, John; Corporal
Hazell, Aaron; Pvt. died at Ft.Gibson 29 September 1846
Hickenbotham, Pullam; Pvt.
Hiles, David; Pvt.
Hill, Marcus; Pvt.
Hogan, Alston; Pvt. died at Ft.Gibson 9 September 1846
Holt, Willis; Pvt. deserted at Ft.Gibson 23 October 1846
Houston, Isaac; Pvt.
Hylton, William; Pvt.

CAPTAIN COLLIN'S COMPANY A
Continued

James, Joseph; Pvt.
Johnson, Francis H; Pvt. died at Ft.Gibson 16 September 1846
Johnson, Riley; Pvt.
Johnson, Thomas; Musician
Johnson, William; Corporal
Kates, Isaiah; Pvt. deserted at Ft.Gibson 16 September 1846
Lassatter, T.H; Pvt. died at Ft.Gibson 14 September 1846
Marney, Samuel; Pvt.
Matthews, Abraham; Pvt.
Matthews, James A; Pvt.
McFaden, Reuben; Pvt.
McKee, William; Pvt.
Moore, Thomas; Pvt.
Normand, William; Pvt.
Oadham, Robert; Pvt. deserted at Ft.Gibson 23 October 1846
Pierson, John; Pvt.
Prim, John P; Pvt.
Riffe, Christopher; Pvt.
Riley, James; Pvt. deserted at Ft.Gibson 23 October 1846
Ring, Joseph; Pvt.
Rowbotham, B.N; Pvt.
Ryan, John; Pvt.
Smith, Clayburn; Pvt.
Smith, John; Pvt.
Smith, L.W; Pvt.
Stewart, Samuel; Pvt.
Summers, Calvin; Pvt.
Tomlinson, Hiram; Pvt. disab.Disc., Ft.Smith 3 August 1846
Ward, B.M; 1st. Lieutenant
Warren, Needham; Pvt.
Williams, John; Pvt. deserted at Ft.Gibson 23 October 1846
Williams, William; Pvt.
Wilson, H.G; Sergeant
Zachery, Ezeriah; Pvt. died at Ft.Gibson 28 August 1846

"The Company left Ft.Smith August 3rd, arrived at Ft.Gibson
August 7th 1846."

MUSTER ROLL
CAPTAIN DAVID WEST'S COMPANY B
GRAY'S BATTALION
Enrolled at Dover, Pope County, Arkansas
15 June 1846

Note; Because most of this roll is listed by surnames, with
initial, and because of the difficulty in reading initials,
I have omitted most of them, those that are included are simply
guesses.

Anthony, J.R; Pvt.
Agustine, J.W; Pvt
Benefield, Willis; Pvt.
Boon, J.P; Pvt.
Brady, John; Pvt.
Brigance, J.F; Pvt. died at Ft.Smith 10 August 1846
Brusheers, Isaac; Pvt.
Brown, Newton W; 2nd Lieutenant
Brown, ?; Pvt.
Bruton, ?;Pvt.
Chambers, J.C; Pvt. died at Ft.Gibson 8 September 1846
Crouch, Solomon; Pvt.
Crouch, William; Pvt.
Davis, Caleb; Brevet 2nd Lieutenant
Dickson, J.C; Pvt.
Dickson, ? ; Corporal

Dillard, T.G; Pvt. deserted at Ft.Gibson 23 October 1846
Duval, William; Pvt.
Duval, ?; Sgt.
Ellis, Ryan; Pvt. deserted at Ft.Gibson 7 November 1846
Ellis, ?; 1st Sgt.
Eno, Joseph; Musician
Fowler, J.P; Pvt.
Graves, Jacob; Pvt.
Haire, Aaron; Pvt.
Harkey, ?; Corporal
Hifley, James; Pvt.
Hill, Larkin; Pvt.
Hillis, Wiley; Pvt.
Hufstedler, J.P; Pvt.
Hufstedler, W.N; Pvt.
Hulsey, William; Pvt. died at Ft.Gibson 5 September 1846
Johnson, U.M; Pvt. died at Ft. Gibson 1 September 1846
Kiser, Caleb; Pvt. deserted at Ft.Gibson 23 October 1846
Kendrick, J.W; Pvt.
Lane, W.C; Pvt.
Lewis, Joseph; Corporal
Lewis, William; Pvt.
Linum, T.J; Pvt. deserted at Ft.Gibson 5 November 1846
Linton, ?; Pvt.
Maddox, Wesley; Pvt.
Marshall, S.H; Pvt.
Marshall, W.M; Pvt.
McElya, Hiram; Pvt.
Mobley, Clement; Pvt. died at Ft.Gibson 19 September 1846
Neeley, G.A; Pvt.
Nelson, Hugh; Pvt.
Nelson, William; Pvt.
Ogle, Brown; Pvt.
Oliver, J.N; Pvt.
Owens, W.N; Pvt.
Parish, David; Pvt.
Parish, G.I; Pvt.
Park, George; Pvt.
Park, Jonathan; Pvt. died at Ft.Gibson 9 September 1846
Prince, Mark; Pvt.
Reed, Isaac; Pvt. deserted while on furlough at Pope County,
          Arkansas 14 January 1847
Reed, Charles; Pvt.
Rye, J.W; Pvt.
Rye, Stephen; 1st Lieutenant
Severs, ? ; Pvt.
Story, Melvin; Pvt.
Stout, William; Pvt.
Tatom, A.C; Pvt.
Tackett, M.D; Pvt.
Tedford, W.M; Pvt. deserted at Ft.Gibson 23 October 1846
Taylor, Jesse; Pvt. Deserted at Ft.Gibson 20 October 1846
Taylor, Washington; Pvt.
Tomlinson, William; Pvt.
Vick, Alfred; Pvt. died at Ft.Gibson 11 September 1846
Warner, J.W; Pvt.
West, David; Captain
West, ? ; Sgt.
West, T.B; Pvt. died at Ft.Gibson 14 September 1846
Wheeler, Alexander; Pvt.
White, George W; Pvt.
Whittle, John/ James; Pvt. died at Ft.Smith 24 July 1846
Williams, J.L; Pvt.
Williams, W.M; Pvt.
Williamson, ? ; Sgt.
Williamson, ? ; Corporal

Yates, G.S; Pvt.
Yates, Elijah; Pvt.

"The Company left Ft.Smith, August 3rd and arrived at Ft.Gibson
August 7th 1846; they remained in Ft.Gibson through 20 April
1847."

MUSTER ROLL
CAPTAIN JOHN FICKLIN'S COMPANY C
GRAY'S BATTALION
Enrolled at Smithville, Lawrence County, Arkansas
18 June 1846

Alcorn, M.F; Sgt.
Anthony, Joseph; Pvt.
Baldwin, A.J.; Pvt.
Berry, Jasper M; Pvt.
Bridges, John; Sgt.
Blackwell, James; Pvt.
Bush, Benjamin; Corp.
Carr, G.W; Pvt.
Curtis, Madison; Pvt.
Curtis, W.R; Pvt.
Childers, B.M; Pvt.
Chandler, B.F; Pvt.
Davis, J.W; Pvt.
Drake, H.T; Pvt.
Ferguson, Hiram; Corp.
Ficklin, John S; Captain, died at Ft.Smith 17 December 1846
Finley, Edmund; age 21, Pvt. died at Ft.Smith 5 August 1846
Gray, Riley; age 19, Pvt. died 2 January 1847
Gray, William; age 21, Pvt. died at Ft.Smith 21 July 1846
Hammond, William H; Sgt.
Harris, J.B; Pvt.
Harris, William; farrier and blacksmith
Humphreys, William; Pvt.
Imboden, Andrew H; 1st Lt, elected Captain 24 December 1846
                   to fill vacancy of Captain Ficklin.
Johnson, Henry; Pvt.
Johnson, Thomas; Sgt.
Johnson, William F; Pvt.
Lassater, G.W.; age 18 Pvt. died at Ft.Smith 26 July 1846
Lingo, G.W; Bugler, age 21, died in hospital 28 November 1846
Marshall, E.H; Pvt.
Mills, James; Pvt.
Miller, William; Pvt
Mitchell, James A; 2nd Lieutenant
Mitchell, J.C; 1st, age 22
Mitchell, J.C; 2nd, age 18
Moore, Charles; Pvt.
Moore, Marvel K; Pvt.
Morris, M.A; Pvt.
Morris, M.H; Pvt.
Norris, Nicholas; Pvt.
Ogden, Jonathan; age 18, Pvt. died at Ft.Smith 19 July 1846
Ogden, Stephen; Pvt.
Perkins, William; Pvt. age 19, died at Ft.Smith 22 Sept. 1846
Poer, William G; Pvt.
Purtle, G.W; Pvt.
Ragsdale, Calvin; Pvt.
Ratliff, Zacheus; Pvt.
Richardson, E.J; Pvt.
Ritchey, D.S; Pvt.
Ritchey, J.E; Pvt.

CAPTAIN FICKLIN'S COMPANY C
Continued

Ross, William W.; Pvt.
Royls, William; Pvt.
Royster, John; Pvt.
Russell, L.M; Pvt.
Sanders, S.B; Pvt.
Sharp, Levi; Pvt.
Sharp, Solomon; Pvt.
Sharpage, John; Pvt, age 28, died at Ft.Smith 2 August 1846
Sims, Wilburn; Pvt.
Sims, Preston; Pvt.
Smith, Elisha; 1st. age 20, Pvt.,died 1 January 1847
Smith, Elisha 2nd; Pvt.
Tucker, Henry P; Corp.
Tucker, Hy G; 2nd Lieutenant
Tucker, Samuel; Pvt.
Tweedy, R.C; Pvt.
Vance, John; Pvt.
Vinson, Clarendon; Pvt. age 19, died 12 January 1847
Vinson, William; Corporal
Waddle, C.L; Pvt.
Wallace, Mandeville; Pvt.
Williams, Isaac; Bugler
Williams, James O; Pvt.
Winstead, William; Pvt.
Wry, William; Pvt.

"This Company took up it's line of march from Ft.Smith on the
3rd day of August and arrived at Ft.Gibson on the 7th."

MUSTER ROLL
CAPTAIN JOHN H.H. FELCH'S COMPANY D
GRAY'S BATTALION

Acklin, John; Pvt. age 25 disab. disc Feb 1847
Allen, Lawrence; Pvt. age 19
Anderson, Robert; Pvt. age 20
Benge, Presley G.; Pvt. age 27
Birchfield, Elijah; Pvt. age 21 joined 12th U.S.Inf. Apr. 1847
Blackwell, James.; Pvt age 36 died 26 Jan 1847
Blalock, John; Pvt. age 40 died 29 Jan 1847
Blanchard, Ira; Pvt. age 25 died 7 Feb 1847
Bradburry, Samuel; Pvt. age 32
Bradley, William; Sgt. age 39 died date illeg.
Bushnell, Henry C.; Pvt. age 40
Byler, Eldridge; Pvt. age 26
Campbell, Robert; Pvt. age 25 trans. to 12th U.S.Inf. Apr 1847
Chick, Edgar W.; Sgt. age 29
Cobb, John; Pvt. age 39 died 26 Jan 1847
Coleman, John; Pvt. age 29
Connally, Patrick; Pvt. age 31 deserted 25 Mar 1847
Crouch, Israel; Corp. age 21 trans to 12th U.S.Inf Apr 1847
Cunningham, Benjamin; Pvt. age 19
Dobs, John; Pvt. age 19
Dobson, Preston; Pvt. age 33
Doyle, John; deserted 19 July 1847
Easlis, John; Pvt. age 19 died 25 Sept 1846
Felch, John H.; Capt. trans. to 12th U.S.Inf. Apr. 1847
Fesler, Frederick; Pvt. age 28
French, Benjamin; Pvt. age 31
Galliger, Michael; Pvt. age 30
Gillihan, William; Pvt. age 19

Goff, Falcott T.; Pvt. age 36 Disab. disc. Feb 1847
Gould, James E.; Pvt. age 43 died 18 Feb 1847
Gray, Charles; Sgt. age 26 trans. to 12th U.S.Inf. Apr 1847
Hall, John; Pvt. age 26
Harris, Robert; Pvt. age 30
Holybee, Henderson; Pvt. age 20
Hood, Jesse; Pvt. age 26
Hooper, Obadiah; Pvt. age 42
Hudspeth, Charles M.; 1st Lt. elected Capt. 2 April 1847
Hudspeth, William G.; Pvt. age 19 trans. 12th U.S.Inf Ap 1847
Huie, William H.; Pvt. age 22 died 14 Feb 1847
Ingalls, George; Sgt. age 25
Irvine, William; Pvt. age 36 disab. disc. Feb 1847
Jackson, Thomas; Pvt. age 29 trans. to 12th U.S.Inf.Ap 1847
James, John; Pvt. age 30
Johnson, Marcus; Musician age 31
Keeler, David; Sgt. age 26 died date illeg.
Koontz, Henry; deserted 22 July 1846
LaForce, Robert M.; Pvt. age 33
Lamb, William; Pvt. died date illeg
Long, William; Pvt. age 19
McGraw, Thomas; Pvt. age 18
McNett, Adino; Pvt. age 40
Mackmur, John; Pvt. age 31
Martin, Thomas; Pvt. age 33 died 31 Jan 1847
Maulby, William; Pvt. age 18
Metlock, Alfred; Pvt. age 18
Morris, Abraham; Musician age 25
Mott, Russell; Pvt. age 23
Petty, John; Pvt. age 33 died 28 Sept 1846
Peyton, Adam; Pvt. age 19
Pickens, Abraham; Pvt. age 25 died 7 Feb 1847
Pilly, Ransom P.; Pvt. age 28
Pond, George; Pvt. age 25 disab. disc. Feb 1847
Pyron, John; Pvt. age 19 trans. to 12th U.S.Inf. Ap. 1847
Rafield, William (also listed Redfield); Corp. age 25 trans. to
          12th U.S.Inf. Apr. 1847.
Reeder, Ambrose; Pvt. age 18
Reeder, Beuford; Pvt. age 22
Reeder, Warren; Pvt. age 21
Rice, Nathan; Pvt. age 43
Rodgers, Alfred B.; Pvt. age 27
Rodgers, James I.; Pvt. age 25
Rowland, Jefferson; Pvt. age 34 died 13 Feb 1847
Rumley, Charles; 2nd Lt.
Russell, Charles W.; 2nd Lt.
Sanders, James M.; Pvt. age 23 died 9 Feb 1847
Shelby, Samuel; Pvt. age 25 died 12 Sept 1846
Sorrels, Victor; Pvt. age 18
Statem, Benjamin; Pvt. age 28
Statem, George S.; Pvt. age 21
Stemmler, John; Pvt. age 34
Stephens, James B.; Pvt. age 22
Sutton, James; Pvt. age 28 deserted Oct 1846
Sutton, Joshua; Corp. age 24
Todd, William M.; Pvt. age 26 trans to 12th U.S.Inf.
Traylor, Reuben; Pvt. age 42
Tubbs, John L.; Pvt. age 19 trans to 12th U.S.Inf Apr. 1847
Tucker, Thomas M.; Pvt. age 18
Vaughn, Peter; Pvt. age 31 disab. disc. Feb 1847
Ward, Philemon; Pvt. age 19
Wardrup, James; Pvt. age 19
Weathers, George; Pvt. age 24
Wilbourne, Richard; Pvt. age 22
Young, George W.; Corp. age 26 trans. to 12th U.S.Inf. Apr.1847

ARKANSAS MOUNTED VOLUNTEERS
CAPTAIN GASTON MEARE'S INDEPENDENT COMPANY
Enrolled at Buena Vista, Mexico
27 May 1847

Adin, George W.; Pvt. age 21 died at Buena Vista
Atkins, David; Pvt. age 25 died at Saltillo 20 Apr 1848
Baggs, Banurd; Pvt. age 32
Baker, Daniel; Pvt. age 23
Bender, Elias; Corp. age 26
Bennett, Benjamin; Pvt. age 29 deserted
Black, Adam; Pvt. age 23
Bramble, Thomas; Pvt. age 21
Brinker, Clark; Pvt. age 26
Burke, Robert; Pvt. age 33
Burleson, Joseph; Pvt. age 22
Burrows, Francis; Pvt. age 22 died at Buena Vista 31 Jul 1847
Campbell, Thomas; Sgt. age 24
Catron, James M.; Pvt. age 30 deserted
Cherry, William H.; Pvt. age 29
Coyle, Peter; Pvt. age 27
Crane, Nelson; Pvt.
Danker, John; Pvt. age 24 deserted at Buena Vista 22 Jan 1848
Davidson, Thomas H.; Pvt. age 24
Dawson, Henry; Pvt. age 27
Dean, William; Pvt. age 21
Decker, Alonzo; Pvt. age 21
Dewitt, George; Pvt. age 24 murdered at Saltillo 25 Sep. 1847
Dignan, Dominick; Pvt. age 28 deserted Buena Vista 22 Jan 1848
Dunlap, Moses; Pvt. age 30
Duty, William; Corp. age 40
Eastwood, Hiram; Pvt. age 24
Foster, Alvin F.; Pvt. age 34
Franklin, Ephriam; Pvt. age 21
Frymire, Henry; Pvt. age 30 deserted Buena Vista 22 Jan 1848
Galbreth,(also Gilbreath) Victor; Bugler age 32 died Buena Vista
Gillett, Leonard; Pvt. age 25
Gooch, Thomas; Pvt. age 20 deserted Buena Vista 22 Jan 1848
Graves, Jason; Pvt. age 20 died of accidental wounding at Buena
                                Vista 26 June 1847.
Griffin, John W.;Pvt. age 25
Hagewood, James A.; Pvt. age 35
Herrold, Robert; Pvt. age 21
Hines, Edward; Bugler age 20
Hitchcock, Thomas; Pvt. age 36
Hodges, Isham; Pvt. age 35
Hunter, Charles; Pvt. age 26, born in N.Y., enrolled 24 Oct
                        1847 as sub. for Francis Kirtly.
Johnson, Isaac H.; Pvt. age 21
Jordan, John; Pvt. age 21
Kelly, Patrick; Pvt. age 25
Kelly, William; Pvt. age 23 deserted Buena Vista 22 Jan 1848
Kemper, Frederick; Pvt. age 25
Kirkman, Noble; Pvt. age 21
Lacy, John; Pvt. age 30
Lannon, Isaac; Pvt. age 25
Laycock, John M.; Pvt. age 24
Leeper, Greenup; Pvt. age 41
Lockheart, William; Pvt. age 26
Loomas, Ralph; Pvt. age 30
Low, Edgar M.; Pvt. disab. disc. 21 Oct 1847
Lowry, Barkley H.; Pvt. age 33 died at Saltillo 5 Feb 1848
McAffee, Allen L.; 2nd Lt.
McFall, Hiram; Corp. age 37
McFarland, Robert M.; Pvt. age 40 died at Saltillo 13 Jul 1847
McGillicuddy, John; Pvt. age 35 deserted
Marshall, Josiah B.; Pvt. age 38 disab. disc 10 Aug 1847
Martin, James; Pvt. age 21
Mathews, John; Pvt. age 28

Meares, Gaston; Capt.
Melton, Gilford M.; Pvt. age 21
Mimms, John H.; Pvt. age 21
Minturn, John; Pvt. age 25 deserted Buena Vista 22 Jan 1848
Mohan, James; Pvt. deserted at Buena Vista
Moore, Lewis; Pvt. age 35
Morris, Thomas; Pvt. age 40
Morrison, Daniel T.W.; 2nd Lt.
Murray, James; Sgt. age 31
Nettleton, James; Pvt. age 43
Nicholson, Benjamin F.; Pvt. age 22
Nucent, Alexander; Pvt. age 30 died at Saltillo 12 Jan 1848
Odom, John H.; Pvt. age 24
Parker, Micajah H.; Pvt. age 28
Parker, William E.; Pvt. age 21
Patton, Harrison; Pvt. age 21 deserted Buena Vista 22 Jan 1848
Peterman, Charles; Corp. age 31
Price, Reece; Pvt. age 22
Ross, Benjamin F.; 1st Lt.
Russell, Willis; Pvt. age 21
Sarasin, Ferdinand; Pvt. age 27
Self, William; Pvt. age 21
Smithers, George; Pvt. age 35
Sowers, William H.; Pvt. age 27
Spencer, Ephriam; Pvt. age 24
Stewart, Robert M.; Pvt. deserted Oct 1847
Story, John M.; Pvt. age 22
Szmanski, Charles; Pvt. age 30 deserted Buena Vista 22 Jan 1848
Tenneson, Harrison; Farrier age 30
Turouski, Louis A.; Sgt. age 35
Vandergriff, Howard; Sgt. age 21
Vandergriff, James; Pvt. age 21
Weever, Frederick; Pvt. age 22
White, John M.; Pvt. age 35 murdered near Saltillo 17 Jul 1847
Willett, Francis; Pvt. age 36
* two names on this muster are completely illegible

ARKANSAS MOUNTED VOLUNTEERS
CAPTAIN STEPHEN B. ENYART'S INDEPENDENT COMPANY
Enrolled at Fayetteville, Arkansas
9 June 1846

Adams, Erwin; Pvt. age 23
Anderson, David; Pvt. age 19
Armstrong, Jesse; Pvt. age 28
Ballard, James B.; Pvt. age 31
Bates, __? Pvt. age 19
Bates, William; Pvt. age 26
Baylor, Charles G.; Pvt. age 22
Berry, Albert; Sgt. age 21
Berry, James; Pvt. age 19 died no date
Blakemore, Jesse; Pvt. age 24
Boen, David; Pvt. age 24
Boen, William; Pvt. age 19
Borland, Samuel; Pvt. age 19
Brodie, William; Pvt. age 23
Brown, James R.; Pvt. age 19
Cain, __?; Pvt. age 23
Chapman, Wilson; Pvt. age 37
Clark, George; Pvt. age 21
Cline, George M.; Sgt. age 24
Cox, Jesse; Pvt. age 19 deserted
Cox, Nathan; Pvt. age 21 deserted
Crawford, Moses; Pvt. age 21

Crittendon, Moses; Pvt. age 20 deserted
Curtis, __? bush?; Pvt. age 21 died no date
Davis, M.C.B.; Pvt. age 30
Davis, Nicholas; Pvt. age 18
Denny, William; Pvt. age 19 died no date given
Dunham, John; Pvt. age 22 died no date
Dunn, William; Pvt. age 19
Enyart, Stephen (also spelled Engart); Capt.
Ferguson, Thomas; Pvt. age 23
Fisher, John; Pvt. age 23
Fletcher, James W.; Pvt. age 23
Gann, Isaac; Pvt. age 20 deserted
Gardner, George; Pvt. age 18
Givins, James M.; Pvt. age 22
Grubb, Jacob; Pvt. age 27
Hamilton, Ephraim; Pvt. age 10
Hamilton, James; Pvt. age 21
Hammock, __?; Pvt. age 27
Harrel, William; Pvt. age 21
Harris, Brozella F.; Pvt. age 27
Harris, David G.; Pvt. age 41
Harris, William; Pvt. age 25
Hart, Wilson D.; Pvt. age 35
Hays, William N.; Pvt. age 44 died 20 Dec 1847 __? Mexico
Henry, James; Pvt. age 24
Hodges, John; Pvt. age 22 died no date
Hifley (?), James; Pvt. age 26
Hudson, Andrew J.; Corp. age 21
Hudson, Berry; Pvt. age 20
Hughes, James C.; Pvt. age 22
Hukill, James S.; Pvt. age 45
Hulse, William A.; Pvt. age 26
Irby, Benjamin F.; Pvt. age 27
Johns, Thomas; Bugler age 21
Kimbrell, Sol; Corp. age 19
Kulin, Joshua; Pvt. age 18
Ledford, William; Bugler age 28
Lynch, Edward; Pvt. age 18
McElroy, Philip; Pvt. age 26
McPherson, Joseph P.; Corp. age 19
Merrill, Peter; Pvt. age 24
Morris, Abraham; Pvt. age 23
Neal, James P.; 1st Lt.
O'Brion, E. ?; 2nd Lt.
Oldham, David; Pvt. age 25
Oldham, Jesse; Pvt. age 30
Parks, James; Pvt. age 20
Pettigrew, William; Pvt. age 22
Philips, Thomas; Pvt. age 26
Pollock, John; Pvt. age 18 deserted
Reddick, Andrew J.; Pvt. age 19 died no date given
Reuben, Joshua; Pvt. age 18 died no date
Reynolds, Cyrus; Pvt. age 22
Rieff, __?; 2nd Lt.
Rieff, Americus; Pvt. age 18
Rieff, John H.; Pvt. age 19
Rowton, William; Pvt. age 27
Sanders, Arthur; Corp. age 19
Sanders, Elijah; Pvt. age 18
Schmidt, William; Pvt. age 19
Sizemore, Asa; Pvt. age 21 deserted
Skelton, James; Sgt. age 20
Skelton, John; Pvt. age 24
Snider, Henry; Farrier age 28
Stanifer, Thomas; Pvt. age 33
Stanifer, William S.; Pvt. age 21

Taylor, James; Pvt. age 21
Tice, John; Pvt. age 20
Trammel, George; Sgt. age 22
Tunnell, David; Pvt. age 21
Tunnell, Nicholas; Pvt. age 19
Westmorland, Welbern; Pvt. age 18 deserted
Wilcox, James H.; Pvt. age 18
Wilcox, Nathan B.; Pvt. age 38
Williams, John; Pvt. age 31 died 9 Aug 1847 San Antonio
Williams, William J.; Pvt. age 19
Willis, William; Pvt. age 18
Young, James; Pvt. age 26

Catherine,9,72
Charity,52
David,114
F.W.,9
James,8,9
Jason,156
Mary,8,9,109
BARNETT
Jacob,59
James,113
Josh,147
BARR
Elizabeth,7
BARRETT
Mary,156
BARRINGER
Henrietta,140
BARRON
Elizabeth,9
Mary,119
Thomas,9
BARTLETT
Eliza,151
BARTON
Willoughby,101
BASKINS
James C.,28
Louisa Jane,28
BASS
Ezekiel,24
BAUGH
Elizabeth,50,51
Mary,130
BAUGHMAN
Dorathy,9
John,9
BAXTER
Laura,109
BEALL
Eliza,101
BEAN
Fannie,29
Jesse,29
BECK
Sarah,9
Viven,9
BECKMAN
Thomas,34
BECKWITH
Jenetha,9
Laurence,9
BEEBE
Lucy Ann,9
Samuel,9
BEERER
Nancy,154
BELL
Edward,9
John P.,9
Mary,9,77
Richard,142
Robert B.,9
William,9
Zadok,9
BELLOTE
Polly,68
BELLOW
Polly Ann,68
BELOTE
Edmund,9,10
Elizabeth,10
John,10
BELT
Dodsen,113
BENNETT
Amanda,63
Frances,63
BENSON
Benjamin,10
Richard,146

BENTHALL
Rosa,24
BENTLY
Carry,12
BERRINGER
John,120
BERRY
Francis,26,65
John,10
Mary J.,69
Robert,24
Sorena,10
BERRYMAN
William,43
BERTRAND
Mary H.,85
R.C.,85
BETTERTON
Elizabeth,48
Thomas,48
BEVANS/BIVINS
Eliza Jane,10
James Wilson,10
Jason,10
Martha Jane,10
BIGGS
Benjamin,57
BIGHAM
Lydia,60
William,60
BILLINGSLEY
Lucy,70
Susan,56
BILTON
George,3
BIRCH
George,142
BIRD
William C.,10
BIVINS
Ann,11
Dolly,11
Elias,11
John,11
John Jr.,11
Jonas,11
Joseph,11
Marcus L.,11
Margaret,11
Mary Ann,11
Patience,11
Sarah,11
Turner,11
William,11
BLACK
Alexander,11
Emily,11
Henry,142
Jane,11
John,11
Jonathan,11
Margarett,11
Mary,11
Samuel,11
Thomas,11
William,11
BLACKSTOCK
Lavinia,57
BLACKWOOD
Mary,35
BLAIR
Elizabeth,133
Mary,62
BLAIR/BLARE
Elam,54
Elizabeth,54
Hiram,54
Lucinda,54
Martha,54
BLAKE

Isabella,87
BLAKELEY
John,11
Lavinia,11
BLEDSOE
Absalom,148
Ann Caroline,15
BLEVINS
Allen,12
Armstead W.,12
Catherine,12
Elizabeth,12
Emily,12
Hugh Armstrong,11
John C.,12
John M.,53
Martha,12
Sarah,12
BLOUNT
Wiley,89
BOATRIGHT
Cerilda,12
Eliza,12
Emily,12
Fanny,12
Henry,12
Hugh,12
John,12
Lucinda,12
Martha,12
Nancy,12
William,12,75
BOEN
Robert,127
BOLEN
David,42
Sarah,42
BOLES
Thomas,111
BOLINGER
Henry H.,75
Sarah,75
BOND
Clara,78
William,78
BONHAM
Rachel,12
William,12
BONNER
Alfred,12
Aurelia,12
Carry,12
Elizabeth,12
Evaline,12
Florida,12
Harriett,12
John,12
Joseph,12
Lucinda,12
Marina,12
Mary,12
Minerva,12
Thomas L.,12
Williamson,12
BOOKER
Samuel,73
BOONE
Ann,11
George,11
BOOTHE
David S.,55
BORDIN
Charlotte,48
BOREN
Bertha,13
James,12,13
John,13
Ruthy,13
Sarah,13
Stephen,13

Susan,13
BOSWELL
  Anna,13
  Nancy,13
  William,13
BOURLAND
  Eliza,13
  Polly,13
  Slaten,13
BOURN
  Clarinda,13,14
  Dudley,14
  Frank,14
  George,14
  Levi,14
  Margaret,14
  Mary,14
  Medaline,13,14
  Whitfield,13,14
BOWEN
  Charles,14
  George,16
  Lewis,126
  Susan,14
BOWMAN
  Elizabeth,25
BOYD
  Bruce,14
  Martha,14
  William,14
BOYETT
  Margaret,137
BOYLE
  Amanda M.,35
  John M.,35
BRACKEN
  Eugene,4
BRADLEY
  John,128
  Louisa,79
  Mary Jane,30
BRADSHAW
  Nancy,133
BRANDON
  Thomas,114
BRANKS
  Peter,144
BRANUM
  Thomas,62
BRATTON
  William,73
BREEDING
  Abram,68
BRIANT/BRYANT
  Amanda,14
  Elisa,14
  Joseph,14
  Martha,14
  William,14
BRIGHT
  Alfred,15
  Amanda,15
  Charlotte,15
  Dozier,15
  Eliza,15
  Garland,15
  Godfrey,15
  Pennington,15
  Purrington,15
  Roxy,15
  Sarah,15
  William E.,15
BRIGHTWELL
  Margaret,17
BRIGUM
  William,97
BROCK
  Ann Caroline,15
  Ann Frances,15
  Caleb,15

James,15
Lucy,74
Mary Frances,15
William H.,15
BROOKINS
  Vivian,51
BROOKS
  Elizabeth,61
  Martha,11
BROWN
  Andrew,15
  Courtney,127
  David,127
  Eliza,139
  Elizabeth,15
  Hugh,50
  James,15,75
  John,16
  Joseph,16,147
  Judith,16
  Lavinia,11
  Martha,72
  Mary,15
  Polly,15
  Rachel,4
  Stephen,15
  William,15,16
  Zedekiah,16
BROWNE
  Elijah,16
  Jonathan,16
  Malinda,16
BROYLES
  Polly,146
BRUCE
  Eliza,17
  Jesse,146
  Rebecca,17
  Winston,17,146
BRUNDRETT
  James,88
  Minerva,88
BRYAN
  Elizabeth,17
  Mary,17
  Sethy,22
  Tarance,17
  Thomas,17
  Thomasin,17
BRYANT
  Rebecca,133
BUCHANAN
  Andrew,17
  James,17
  Sinai,17
BUCHANNAN
  Edward,36
BULL
  Ambrose,18
  Elizabeth,18
  Henry,18
  James,18
  Malinda,18
  Mary,18
  Nancy,18
  Robert,17,18
  Susan,18
  Susannah,18
  William,18
  William L.,18
BUNCH
  Anna,18
  Bradley,13,18
  Calvin,18
  Charles,18
  Jane,13
  John,18
  Larkin,18
  Nancy,18
  Nathaniel,13,18

Obedience,18
Samuel,26,65,89
Sarah,18
BURFORD
  Edward,19
  Edward W.,18
  Rebecca,19
BURGE
  Mary T.,60
BURGEN
  Nancy,51
BURKEN
  Mary,42
BURKS
  Delila,19
  George F.,19
  Harriet,19
  Mary,19
  Nancy,19
  Permelia,19
  William,19
BURLESON
  James,67
BURNHAM
  Frederick,13
  James,13
  Polly,13
  William,13
BURNS
  Thursea,22
BURRIS
  Mary,30
BURROUGH/BURROWS
  Nancy,19
  William Jr,19
  William Sr,19
BURT
  Andrew,19
  George,19
  Hewitt,19
  Mary,19
  Susan,19
  William,19
BURTON
  Charlotte,20
  James,49
  Nancy,20
  Noel,20
BUSBY
  Celia,20
  James,123
  Mary,20
  Robert,20
BUSSEY
  Harriett,21
BUTLER
  Bailey,97
  George,119
  Isaac,16
  William O.,43
BUXTON
  Catherine,20
  Eliner,20
  Frances,20
  Franky,20
  George,20
  James,20
  John OK,20
  Mary Ann,20
  Mary Jane,20
  Mills Wells,20
  Sary,20
  Thomas,20
  William H.,20
BYRD
  Richard,60
BYRD/BIRD
  Charlotte,20,21
  William,20,21
CABANISS

Elijah,21
Harriett,21
Jesse,21
Joicy,21
CABELL
William H.,22
CAIN
Hannah,21
John,21
CALDWELL
Robert,72
Samuel,50
CALHOUN
John C.,99
Mary J.,99
CALLAHAN
Benjamin,21
Beston,21
Cynthia,21
Dennis,21
George,21
Hannah,21
Jane,21
Josephine,21
Ohier,21
Sarah,21
Sebastian,21
CALLEN
Charles,22
Margaret,22
Sethy,22
CAMERON
Peninah,38
CAMP
Elizabeth,22
Emily,22
George,22
Harris K.,22
Henry C.,22
Thursea,22
Wyly,22
CAMPBELL
Amanda,23
Arthur,63,132
Caty Ann,23
Eliza,23
Elizabeth,23
Isaac B.,23
James,23
John,22,23
Mary,23
Mary E.,22
Mary M.,23
Melvina,23
Nancy,27
Rebecca,23
Sarah Jane,23
Thomas,23
William,66,132,150
CANDLOE
Ezekiel,73
CANNON
James,54
Jane,64
Jemima,24
John,23
John S.,125
Sarah,54
William,23,48
CANTRELL
Jemima,24
CAPPS
Henry,92
Minerva,92
CARDWELL
Delaney,61
Henry C.,61
CARLOCK
Elizabeth,47
CARNETT

Mary,24
William,24
CARPENTER
Elizabeth,65
Sarah,12
CARRIS
Hugh,61
CARROLL
William,12
CARSON
James M.,79
Robert,42
CARTER
Allie,144
Bernard,24
Charles,111
George,121
John,24
Nancy,121
Rosa,24
Sarah,136
William,136
CARUTHERS
John,24,63
Samuel,24
CASE
Putnam,28
CASEY
Elizabeth,126
CASSADAY
John,78
CASSIDY
Isabella,24
Jeremiah,24
CASTNER
Salena,92
Winfield,92
CASWELL
Elizabeth,25
Isham,25
CATES
Martha,133
CATES/KATES
Elizabeth,54
Isaac,54
CATLETT
Margaret,11
CATO
James,147
CHAMBERS
James,62
CHAPMAN
Cynthia,25
Douglass,25
Wilson,25
CHASTAIN
Abner,112
James,112
Lucy,36
Martha,112
Mary,112
Vilet,2
CHEATHAM
Christopher,25
Elizabeth,25
Granville K.,25
Henry,25
Martha,25
Matthew,25
Owen,25
Richardson,25
Salley,25
Virginia,25
William,25
CHILES
John,74,95
CHITWOOD
Daniel,25
Didamer,26
Mary,25

Richard,25
CHRISP
Mary Jeffers,26
William,26
CHRISTOPHER
Martha,56
CLAPTON
Nancy,17
CLARK
Benjamin,26
Frances,67
George Rogers,101
Gilbert,26
Isaac,67
Levy,72
Luman,72
Mary A.,72
Riley,147
Sophia,72
Thomas,121
CLAY
Joseph,24
CLEM
David,26
Jack,26
Mason,26
Phoebe,26
CLEMENT
Edward,136
CLEMMONS
Ann,34
CLEMONS
Charlotte,20
CLEVELAND
Benjamin,138
CLIFFORD
Charles,31
CLINE
Mary,26
Nancy,27
Permelia,26
William,27
William Madison,26
CLINKENBEARD
Jonathan,27
Sarah,27
CLOWER
Catherine,27
Daniel,27
Delilah,27
Elizabeth,27
James L.B.,27
Jonathan,27
Lurana Bush,27
Malinda,27
Mary,27
Miriam,27
Nancy,27
Rebecca,27
CLUGGAGE
Robert,142
CLUTTER
Rebecca,23
COBB
Christian,27
Daniel,27
Elizabeth,27
Fanny,27
Joseph,27
Nancy,27
Obial,116
Samuel,27
William,27
COBBS
Henry J.,108
Mary T.,93
COBLER
Frederick,27
John L.,28
Polly Ann,28

Rachel,28
William,28
COCHRAN
  Harper,28
  Lydia,28
COCHRANE
  Richard E.,28
  Sally,28
COFFEE
  Henry,1
  James G.,28
  John,52
  Louisa Jane,28
  Melvin,28
  Melvina Penelope,28
COKER
  Arminta,48
  Martha,16
  Thomas,61
COLE
  Hiram,29
  James,153
  Mary,29
  Nancy,29
  Thomas,29
COLEMAN
  Frank,30
  Mary,120
  Robert,121
COLLIER
  David,18
COLLINS
  Eli,29
  Fannie,29
  Isaac C.,29
  John,30
  Louisa,29
  Lydia,28
  Malisa,29
  Margaret,29
  Matthew,29
  Robert,90
  Robert J.,29
  Teresa,82
  William R.,29
CONLEY
  Sarah,106
CONNALLY
  John G.,108
  Ophelia,109
CONNER
  Alfred,129
  Casaniah,129
  Isaac,129
  John,94
  Jonathan,29,30
  Mahaley P.,30
  Mary,30
CONWAY
  Charles,74
  Eliza,30
  Henry,30
  James,30
  Jeremiah,30
  Mary Jane,30
  William,30
COOK
  Benjamin,30
  George W.,30
COOKE
  Nancy Ellen,64
COONEY
  Briget,30
  Elizabeth,30
  Joanna,30,31
  Thomas,30
COOPER
  Benjamin,31
  Ellen,153
  Nancy,31

William,22
COPELAND
  Anna,13
CORBELL
  Mary,68
CORBETT
  Eliza,31
  Jesse,31
  John,28
  John R.,31
  Mary,31
  Sarah,31
CORNELIUS
  Sally,64
CORNISH
  Issabella,32
  Jackson,32
  Jane,32
  John H.,32
  John L.,32
  Lydia,32
  Nancy,32
  Rufus,32
  Sarah,31,32
  Thomas,31
  Thomas J.,32
  Wesley,32
  William H.,32
  William Jr.,31
  William Sr.,31,32
CORNWALL
  Josephus,64
COTTRELL
  Elizabeth,51
COUGHRAM
  George,32
COUNTS
  Etilita,42
COVEY
  John,124
COWAN
  Andrew,89
COWEN
  John,54
COX
  Sarah,78
COYER
  Barbery,96
CRABTREE
  Anderson,32,33
  Benjamin,33
  Benjamin F.,32
  David,32
  Elizabeth,32
  Hiram,32
  James E.,32
  John W.,32
  Jonathan,32
  Mary A.M.,32
  Nancy,32
  Sam J.,33
  Samuel,32
  Sarah,32,33
  William A.,33
CRAIG
  John L.,64
  Thomas,41
CRAINE
  Harris,103
  Hasky,103
CRAINE/CRANE
  Clarice,33
  Jasper,33
  Maryann E.,33
  Nancy,33
  Orpha Caroline,33
  Sarah,33
  Thomas,33
  William T.,33
CRAMER

Sarah,82
CRANFORD
  Polly,15
CRAVIN
  Agness,146
  George,146
CRAWFORD
  C.A.,33
  Elizabeth,33,98
  James,98
  Lucinda,98
  William D.,98
CRAWLEY
  Martha,151
CROSSLIN
  Edwin,33,34
  Elizabeth,33,34
  Susan,33
CROSTHWAITE
  Elizabeth,47
CROW
  Benjamin,34
  Elizabeth,34
  Emily,34
  James H.,34
  Matilda,24
  William,34
CROWLEY
  Charles,21
CROWNOVER
  Benjamin,34
  Daniel,34
  Daniel Jr.,34
CRUMP
  Eliza G.,34
  John G.,34
  Sue E.,47
CRYER
  Ailcy,34
  Honor,34
  Morgan,34
  Thomas,34
  William,34
CULLEY
  Edwin,142
CULLOM
  Green,34
CUNNINGHAM
  Susan,156
CURNELL
  Elizabeth,9
CURTIS
  Ann,34
  John D.,34
CYPERT
  Abigail,5
  Isabelle,5
  Mary,4
  Robert,5
DALE
  Adam,156
DALTON
  John,60
DANIELS
  Amanda,35
  Isaac,35
  Jane,21
  Jasper M.,35
  John F.,35
  Joseph,35
  Margaret,35
  Mary,35
  Vica,35
DANLEY
  Amanda M.,35
  Benjamin F.,35
  Christopher,35
  Joshua,35
DAUGHERTY
  Samuel,155

DAUGHTRY
Susan,33
DAVENPORT
Eliza,101
DAVERSON
Sarah,56
DAVIDSON
George,63
DAVIS
Amanda,36
Andrew J.,35
Annie,154
Buckeye John,36
Catherine,35
George,36
Harris,36
John,35,36
John H.,36
John M.V.,35
Jonathan,92
Josephine,150
Julia Ann,92
Martha E.,36
Mary,36
Melinda,36
Mirick,131
Nancy,36,58,133
Nathaniel,36
Rebecca,46,49
Robert,35,59
Sarah J.,35
Susan,64
Thomas,36
William,36,153
DEADMAN
Ellen,12
DEAN
David H.,65
Muhulda,65
Thomas,44
DEANS
Elizabeth,36
Reuben,36
DEATON
Winna,111
DEAVER
Elijah,36
DECKIE
Frances,8
DEESE
Eliza,68
DELANO
Lorenza,77
Minerva,77
DELANY
Thomas,58
DELL/TELL
Adelia,36
Valentine,36
DEMPSEY
John,31
John B.,6,52
DENTON
Charity,36
Elizabeth,32
Jonas,36
DERAINE
Annie E.,37
Charles W.H.,37
Delina L.,37
Henry C.,37
Juliana,37
Virginia M.,37
DESHEAL
Joseph,23
DIAL
Anna,53
Jeremiah,53
Nancy,53
DICK

William,110
DICKENS
Katy,111
DICKINSON
John,21
Zilla,125
DICKSON
Caledonia,87
Ephriam,78
Ezekiel,86,87,106
Isabella,87
James M.,87
Joseph Daniel,87
Joseph McKisick,87
Margaret,87
Margaret Adeline,87
Mary,87
Mary Harris,87
Nancy Eliza,87
Polly S.,122
Robert,87
William W.,122
DICKSON/DIXON
Abram,38
Alisha,38
James,38
Joanna,38
Joseph,38
Peninah,38
Thomas,38
DILLARD
Alexander,37
Alford A.,37
Elizabeth Jane,37
Ida M.,37
James H.,37
Jennie M.,37
Joseph A.,37
Lemuel,77
Melinia,37
Sarah C.,77
Sims,77
William,57
DILLEHAY
Levi,133
Rachel,133
DIXON
David,62
John C.,38
Nancy,30
Sarah,38
DOAK
John,36,98
DOBBINS
Nancy,20
DOBSON
William,141
DODD
Sarah Jane,105
DOKE
John,154
DONALDSON
John,65
DONNELSON
Elizabeth,38
William,38
DOOLEY
Betsey,38
Isaac,38
Julia,38
Linney,38
Mary,17
Mary Jane,38
Polly,38
Samuel,38
William H.,38
DOSHER/DOZIER
Adam,39
Alley,39
Daniel,39

Judith,39
Margaret,39
Nancy,39
Peter,38,39
DOSS
Martha,63
DOTSON
Morton,14
Phalby,150
DOUGAN
Betsey,39
George,39
Hester,39
James,39
Joseph,39
Phinice,39
Pulina,39
Rachel,39
Robert,39
Saley M.,39
Thomas,39
William,39
DOUGHERTY
Hugh,40
Patrick,40
William,40
DOUGLAS
Henry,50
DOUGLASS
John C.,100
DOUTHET
Anderson,97
Effie G.,97
Jonathan,126
Mary,126
DOWNUM
Celia,40
Easter,40
Elijah,40
Elizabeth,40
Esther,40
George,40
Hannah,40
James,40
James L.,40
John,40
Lucinda,40
Lydia,40
Margaret,40
Mary,40
Sidney,40
Speakman,40
Tilday,40
William,40
DRAKE
Jackson,41
James,41
Malissa,41
Margaret,41
Martha,41
Sarah,41
Wesley,41
DRANE/DRAINE
Affa,41
David,41
Elizabeth,41
Emeline,41
George,41
James,41
John,41
Margaret,41
Martha,41
Mary,41
Recca,41
Richard,41
Robert,41
Roxanna,41
Sarah,41
Susan,41
Washington,41

Wesley,41
DU VAL
  Susan,105
DUKE
  Jane,145
DUNCAN
  Joseph,11
  Judith,16
DUNLAP
  Adam,42
  Daniel,42
  Frances,42
  Mary,42
DUNN
  Etilita,42
  Francis,42,75
  Mary W.,42
  Samuel,42
  William J.,42
DYER
  Abram H.,43
  Catherine,43
  Eliza,43
  Elizabeth Jane,43
  Emaline Fletcher,43
  Emeline,43
  George W.,43
  James,43
  Joseph G.,43
  Martha,43
  Mary A.,43
  Nancy,19
  Richard B.,43
  Robert H.,43
  Tellitha,43
  William,43
EAGAN
  Cornelius,43
EARHEART
  Rodney,63
EARL
  John,143
EARNEST
  Andrew,43
  Joseph,43
  Nancy,43
EASLEY
  Eliza,140
EASON
  Bashabilee,128
EASTER
  Eliza,44
  James,44
  John,44
  Joseph,43,44
  Lucretia,44
  Malinda,44
  Margaret,44
  Mary,44
  Peter,44
  Sarah,44
  Solomon,44
  William,44
EATON
  Robert D.,56
EDDLEMAN
  Mary,24
EDERINGTON
  Henry,44
  Martha,44
  Robert,44
  Sarah,44
EDMISTON
  David,71
  Synthia,71
EDWARDS
  Lamech,44
  Lucy,106
  Mary,44
  Nancy,44

William,151
ELDER
  Mary Jeffers,26
ELDRIDGE
  Julia,75
ELKINS
  Catherine,35
ELLINGTON
  George,95
ELLIOT
  Didamer,26
  William,150
ELLIOTT
  George,62
ELLISON
  Burch,44,45
  David,45
  Harriett,45
  Hugh,45
  John J.,44
  Margaret,44,45
  Rebecca,45
  Robert,147
  Rufus,45
  Rufus C.,44
  Sarah,45
ELMORE
  Warner,44
EMPSON
  James A.,45
  Mary,45
ENDSLEY
  Abram,45
  Almeda,45
  Deborah,45
  Elizabeth,45
  Ellender,45
  Ida,45
  James,45
  Jane,45
  John,45
  Martha,45
  Mary,45
  Mary E.,45
  Peasant,45
  Sarah,45
  Susann,45
  Tinsy,45
  William,45
ENGHART
  Stephen,65
ENGLISH
  James,138
ERWIN
  Delina L.,37
  Elizabeth C.,46
  Franklin B.P.,46
  Harriett A.,46
  Henrietta T.,46
  Hettisue,46
  Irene,46
  John D.,46
  Joseph,45,46
  Joseph L.F.,46
  Mary Helen P.,46
  Matilda,46
  Matthew,46
  Michael P.,46
  Nancy A.,46
  Rebecca,46
  Rebecca A.,46
  Thomas J.,46
  William D.,37
  Wilson,46
ESTERLING
  Charlotte,15
ESTES
  Charlotte,156
  Gallent,156
  John,156

EUBANKS
  Catherine,74
  John,74
EVANS
  Anna,46
  Catherine,72
  Celia,135
  Jeff,46
  John,46
  Laura,95
  Lucretia,44
  Martha,54
  Mary,46
  Nancy,46
  Owen,12
  Robert,129
  Sarah,54
  Thomas J.,46
  William,46
EWING
  Susan,128
EZELL
  Asa,47
  Elizabeth,47
  Emily,47
  Mary,47
  Micajah,47
  Nancy,47
  Sarah,47
  Timothy,47
  William,47
FAIR
  William,62
FAIRCHILD
  Benjamin,47
  John,47
  John L.,47
  Joseph,47
  Sarah Ann,47
  William,47
FALKNER
  George,47
  Mary E.,47
  Sarah,47
FANCHER
  Alexander,48
  Arminty,47
  Asenath,47
  Bynum,47
  Celia,47
  Claborn,47
  Elizabeth,47,48
  George M.,48
  Hampton Binum,47
  Henrietta,48
  J.P.,47
  James,47,48
  James P.,13,18
  Jane,48
  Margaret C.,47
  Martha Jane,47
  Richard,47,48
  Sarah M.,47
  Sue E.,47
  Thomas,47
  Thomas W.,116
FARR
  Carolina,48
  David,48
  Elizabeth,48
  James,48
  Jane,48
  John,48
  Mary,48
  Mary Ann,48
  Melissa,48
  Pauline,48
  Sarah,48
  Thomas,48
  William,48

FARRAR/FARROW
  Elizabeth,48
  John H.,48
FARRELL
  William,1
FEARS
  Ebenezer,48
FELLERS
  Julia,90
FELTON
  Sarah,126
FENLEY
  Charlotte,48
  Jane,49
  John,48,49
  Martha,48,49
FERGESON
  Jane,49
  Joseph R.,49
FERGUSON
  James,49
  Mary Ann,49
FERRELL
  Lucy,49
  William,49
FIELD
  Jane,106
FIELDS
  Margaret,41
FIFER
  John,120
FINE
  Alfred,50
  Caladonia,50
  Catherine,49,50
  Cuniller,50
  Elizabeth,50
  Isaac,50
  James,50
  Jane,50
  John,50
  Jonathan,50
  Malonia,50
  Martha,50
  Milly,50
  Peter,50
  Rachel,50
  Sophronia,50
  Spencer,50
  Thomas,50
  Walter,50
  William,49,50
FINKLEY
  Malinda,18
  Thomas,18
FINLEY
  Jane R.,53
FINLY
  Thomas,53
FINNEY
  Lucinda,77
FINTON
  Louretta Jane,7
FISHER
  Anderson,50
  James,120
  Sina,50
FITTS
  Elizabeth,146
FITZGERALD
  William,69
FITZHUGH
  Benjamin S.,50
  Claiborne C.,50
  Eariel,50
  Ezekiel Harrison,50
  Franey Morilda,50
  Franklin,50
  George W.,50
  Jackson,50

  James Earl,50
  John White,50
  Margaret,50
  Mary Ann,50
  Mary Jane,50
  William Eariel,50
FLEMING
  Jane,6
FLETCHER
  Emaline,43
FLINN
  J.A.,57
  Margaret,44
  W.C.,57
FLIPPEN
  Agness,51
  Elizabeth,50,51
  Ellen Jane,51
  Harriett,51
  Letitia,51
  Thomas,51
  Thomas H.,50
  William,51
FLOYD
  Kaziah,106
  Samuel,106
FORD
  Ann,52
  Ann Tucker,51
  Anne,51
  Benjamin,52
  Benjamin F.,51
  Elizabeth,51
  Isaac,111
  James M.,51
  Jenny,52
  Lewis,51
  Lucy,51
  Mary E.,51
  Nancy,51
  Nimrod,51,52
  Polly,111
  Thomas B.,51
FOSTER
  David Henry,52
  Elizabeth,52
  George R.,52
  George Riley,52
  John,59
  John Wethersby,52
  Loving,52
  Margaret,52
  Martha Adeline,52
  Mary,52
  Robert Carroll,52
  Sarah,52
  Susan,52
  Thomas,52
  William,52
FOX
  Ann,52
  Catherine,52
  Cornelius,52
  Eliza,52
  Jacob,52
  Jane,52
  John J.,52
  Margaret,52
  Mary,52
  Nancy,52
  Thomas,52
FRANKLIN
  Ailcy,34
  Charity,52
  Darkie,52
  Eliza,31
  Elizabeth,110
  James,110
  L.O.,52
  Sarah,52

  Thomas,52
FRANKLINE
  Eliza,68
  Nancy,68
  William,68
FRANSICO
  Adelia,70
  Celia,70
  Henry,70
FREEMAN
  Alexander,53
  Anna,53
  Daniel,53
  George W.,53
  Jane,53
  Letha,53
  Matthew,53
  Rucker,53
  Sarah,53
FRESHOUR/FROSHOUR
  Barbary,54
  Dempsey,54
  Henry,53
  Jane R.,53
  Martha,54
  Mary,54
  Mary J.,53
  Nancy,54
FREYSHLAG
  Edward,65
FULKERSON
  James,66
FULTON
  William S.,60
GAFFNEY
  Michael,64
GAGE
  Clara,54
  Eliza,54
  Eliza Jane,54
  Elizabeth,54
  George,54
  James,54
  John,54
  Lucinda,54
  Lydia,54
  Margaret,54
  Marion,54
  Rhoda,54
  Sarah,54
  Stephen,54
  Susan,54
  Tennessee,54
  William,54
GALT
  John,22
GANAWAY
  William,9
GARDNER
  Adeline,68
  Samuel,68
GARLAND
  B.P.,55
  Elizabeth,55
  Martha,55
  Nancy,55
  Patrick,55
  Samuel,55
GARNER
  Nancy,52
  Susa,130
GARRET/GARRIOT
  Catherine,43
  Tellitha,43
GARRETT
  Abraham,55
  Betsey,55
  Frances,55
  John,55
  Josiah,55

Malinda,55
Mary Ann,55
Nicholas,55
Sarah,55
William,27
GARRETTSON
John,117
GARRISON
Allen,55
Charles,55
Frances,55
George,55
Henry,55
Malinda,55
Nehemiah,122
Rebecca,55
Robert,55
Zebulon,55
GARVIN
Asher,56
Benjamin,56
Elizabeth,56
Joseph,56
Thomas,55,56
GATES
Horatio,153
GATLIN
Aaron P.,56
Elizabeth,56
Hannah,56
Jesse,56
Mary,56
GAULT
James,73
GEE
James M.,107
GIBBS
Abigail,26
George,71
GIBSON
Abiram,56
Benjamin,88
Elizabeth,139
Mary,56
William,139
GIDEON
James,67
GILBERT
Jane,64
Obed,64
GILES
James,56
Martha,56
GILL
George,116
GILLEHAN
Clemmons,57
Clemons,56
Nancy,56,57
William,37
GILLIAM
Elizabeth,74
Harris,74
GILLIHAN
Blewford,29
Elizabeth,29
Louisa,29
GILLILLAND
James,50
GILMORE
James,79
GINGLE
Edward,91
GLISSON
Adolphus,58
Adolphus Burton,57
Ameretta,57
Commodore Perry,57
Ethaline,57
Finis Caloway,57

Harvey Henderson,57
Henry Elby,57
Jesse Tilford,57
Lavinia,57,58
Melissy,57
Melvina,58
Sarah,57
Thomas,57,58
GOAD/GOOD
Nancy,58
Reuben,58
GOBBERT
Fayette,84
Mary,84
GOLDIN
Mariah,58
William,58
GOODALL
John D.,37
GORDON
Elizabeth,58
Jane,58
John,58
Martha,58
GOTCHER
Ann,58
Annie,59
James,58
Jesse,58,59
Nathaniel,58,59
GOWER
Ebeline,5
Mary,5
GRAHAM
Archie,72
Betsey Ann,59
Bryant,59
Catherine,10
Charles,10
Elizabeth,41,72
George,59
George Henry,59
Martha Jane,10
Melinda,41
Phillip,10
Robert,72
Sallie Campbell,75
Sarah,41,59
GRANT
John W.,29
GRAVES
Philip,59
GRAY
Ann Tennesse,60
George,52
George W.,60
Jacob,59,60
James A.,60
John,59,60
John C.,60
Mary,60
Mary E.,60
Mary G.,59
Sanford F.,60
Shared,59,60
Thomas J.,60
William F.,60
Wyllard,60
GRAYSON
Permelia,26
GREEN
John,92
William,15,34
GREENLEE
Malinda,16
GREER
John,60
Joshua,60
Malvina,60
Mary,60

GREESON
Hartwell,128
GREGG
Adaline,61
Adolphus,61
Andrew,61
Constantine,61
Ellis,60
Henry,60,61
James,61
Jane,60
John,61
Lafayette,61
Livonia,61
Lydia,60
Marget,61
Mary,61
Nathan,61
Samuel,60,61
Sarah,61
GRESHAM/GRISHAM
Mary,61
Thomas P.,61
William H.,61
GRIFFIN
Rebecca,55
GRIFFITH
Elizabeth,61
Henry W.,61
Nancy Mariah,61
GRIGG
Abraham,90
GRIMMIT
William,61
GROGAN
Thomasin,17
GROSS
Andrew,62
George,62
Jacob,62
Lockey,62
Mary,62
Morrison,62
GRUBB
Ellen,65
GUINN
Lucy,49
GUNN
Gabriel,145
GURLEY
Joel,92
Virginia,92
HABERSHAM
John,30
HADLEY
Martha,2
HAGAN
William,60
HAGERTY
Joshua,48
HAGUE
James,147
HALE
Benjamin,59
HALHOOKS
Savina,113
HALL
Allen,62
Anthony,62
Dorothy,62
Edward,22
Elizabeth,33,62
Esther,62
Hannah,62
Isom R.,10
James,10,62,79
Leonard,33
Martha,62
Mary,20,62
Sampson,62

Sarah,62
HAMILTON
 Alfred,97
 Amanda E.,97
 Elizabeth,62
 Eupha,97
 Euphy,96
 Henry,49
 Hugh L.,97
 James,62,97
 James M.,97
 Joseph P.,62
 Malinda,62
 Martha,97
 Martha Jane,63
 Mary,45,62,63
 Nancy,62,63
 Oliver,97
 Polly,63
 Robert,63,96,97
 Sarah,63
 Susan,97
 Thomas,62,63,97
 William,45,62,75,82,96
  148
 William S.,63
 William T.,97
 Zerrilda,63
HAMMONS
 Samuel,83
HAMPTON
 Edward,143
 Henry,59
 Wade,59,121
HANCOCK
 Elbert,63
 Green,113
 Muranda,63
 Robert,96
HAND
 Rachel,12
HANDCOCK
 Nancy,117
HANDS
 Edward,142
HANDY
 Elizabeth,118
 Isham,118
HANKS
 Elizabeth,37
HANNA
 Andrew Jackson,63
 Arta E.,63
 Elmina,63
 Hiram,63
 Jack,63
 James W.,63
 Jerusha,63
 Martha,63
 Mary,63
 Milton M.,63
 Muranda,63
 Reuben,63
HANNAH
 William,16
HARDIN
 Benjamin,24,63
 Euel,64
 James,63
 Joseph,64
 Margaret,64
 Mark,57
 Martin,57
 Matilda,64
 Mordecai,57
 Nancy,57,64,85
 Nancy Ellen,64
 Susan,64
 Thomas,64
HARDING

Jane,64
John,64
John J.,64
Ophelia,64
HARGRAVES
 William,94
HARGROVE
 William,114
HARKLEROAD
 Daniel,7
 Elizabeth,7
 Frank,7
 Hiram,7
 John,7
HARP
 Alla,64
 Benjamin,64
 D.D.Cavin,64
 Jabal,64
 Martha,64
 Nancy,64
 Nelson,64
 Sehorn,64
 Solomon,64
HARPER
 Abigail,140
 Cotton,140
 Mary,140
 Thomas H.,64
HARRIS
 Charles,64
 Clark M.,55
 Eliza,56
 Elizabeth R.,48
 Emaline,64
 Jane,64,112
 Mary Ann,55
 William,55
HARRISON
 George,150
HART
 Jincy,84
 Martha,14
HARVEY
 Jane,103
 John,70
HASKINS
 Creed,25
HATHAWAY
 Catherine,41
 Jonathan,41
 Mary,41
 Nancy,41
 Phillip,41
HATHORNE
 Elizabeth,132
HAWKINS
 Elizabeth,55,65
 Flora Ridge,65
 James,124
 Jane,65
 John,65
 John L.,55
 Martin L.,65
 Mary,65
 Rhoda,65
 Sarah,65
 Stephen,65
 William,65
HAYDON
 John,95
HAYES
 Elizabeth,155
 Jack,37
 Mariah,124
 Polly,38
HAYS
 Alia,65
 Campbell,65
 Dodson Clayton,65

Ellen,65
Malinda,65
Mary Adeline,65
Miriam A.H.,65
William N.,65
HEARIN
 John,21
HEATH
 Adam,109
HEDDRICK
 Peter,131
HEDGES
 Elizabeth,128
HENDERSON
 David,98
 John J.,98
HENDRICKS
 Bertha,13
 David D.,65
 James R.P.,65
 Muhulda,65
HENRY
 John,7,73
HERRING
 Elmina,63
 James M.,63
 Martha,63
 Stephen,63
HESTER
 Mary,61
HEWITT
 Benjamin,106
 Sylvester,65
HIBBEN
 Barbary,132
 John,132
HICKMAN
 Caleb,66
HICKS
 James,103
HIGGS
 Thomas,66
HIGHLAND
 Harry,8
HIGHTOWER
 Elizabeth,154
 J.W.,154
HILL
 Alexander,4,12
 Anne,66
 Elizabeth,66
 Jenetha,9
 Joel,66
 John P.,66
 Margaret,66
 Mary,66
 Robert,66
 William,66
HOBBS
 Abner,66
 Absalom,66
 Absolom,66
 Elizabeth,66
 Ezekiel,66,67
 Hannah,66
 James,66
 Job,66
 Joel,66
 Merry,66
 Rachel,66
 Ruth,66
 Vinson,66
 William,66
HODGE
 Fleming,60
 John,44,48
HODGON
 Frances,118
HOFFMAN
 Mary J.,53

HOGAN
  Anderson,67
  Anna,67
  Bathsheba,67
  Becky,67
  David,67
  Edward,67
  Elizabeth,67
  Holland,67
  Isaiah,67
  James M.,67
  John,67
  Mary Jane,67
  Polly,67
  Samuel,67
  Sarah S.,67
  William,67
HOGG
  William,31
HOLDER
  James,20
HOLEMAN
  Frances,67
  Jackson,67
  John,67
  Peter,67
HOLIDAY
  Nancy,18
HOLLAND
  Sarah,31
HOLLEDGER
  Margaret,81
  P.C.,81
HOLLIDAY
  Synthia,68
HOLMAN
  John,67,136
  William,135
HOLMES
  Sarah,149
HOOD
  Affa,41
  Benjamin,41
  David,41
  James,41
  John,41
  Martha,41
  Mary,41
  Sarah,41
  Wesley,41
HOPKINS
  Samuel,73
HOPPER
  Golden,113
HORN
  Harmon,67
HORTON
  William,42
HOUSE
  Adeline,68
  Malinda,65
  Mary,68
  Nancy,68
  William H.,68
HOUSTON
  Elizabeth,113
  Thomas,127
HOWE
  Martha P.,55
HOWELL
  Mary,46
HOYLE
  Jacob,155
HUBBARD
  Elizabeth,36
HUDDLESTON
  Benton,68
  David,68
  Lewis,68
  Mariah,68

  Mary,8,68
  Thomas,47
  William,68
  Willis,23
HUDGENS
  H.M.,153
  Sobra,153
HUDSON
  Cuthbert,62
  Eli,69
  Henrietta,69
  Lucretia,69
  Mary J.,69
  Richard,69
  Samuel,56
HUDSON/HUTSON
  Bashaby,68
  Edward,68
  Elender,68
  Henry,68
  Joseph,68
  Mary Ann,68
HUDSPETH
  Martha,44
HUFF
  Mary Ann,50
HUFFMAN
  Ann,137
  Daniel,137
  John,137
HUGGINS
  Andrew,49
  Benjamin,49
  Eliz,49
  Laveza,49
  Martha,48
  Scott,49
  William,49
HUGHES
  George,69
HUKILL
  James,65,69
HULSE
  Abraham,69
  Adelia,70
  Elizabeth,69
  Enoch,69
  Jacob,69
  James P.,69
  John P.,69
  Lucy,70
  Nancy,69
  Polly,69
  William A.,69,70
HULSEY
  Sarah,112
HUMBER
  Charles H.,70,71
  Laura,70,71
HUMPHREY
  Charles,3
  John,153
HUNTER
  Edward,47,113
  Henry,147
  James,20
HURT
  Bird S.,7
HUTT
  William,27
HYLTON
  Elijah,51
  Lucy,51
INGE
  John J.,61
INGLISH
  William,100
INGRAM
  Joshua,90
  Margaret,22

  Mary,88
INMAN
  Joshua,144
IRVINE
  Edward,60
  Mary,7
  William,7
IRWIN
  James,62
ISH
  Columbus,71
  David,71
  Elizabeth,71
  Frances,71
  Jacob,71
  John,71
  Mary,71
  Phebe,71
  Sarah,71
  Synthia,71
  William,71
ISLEY
  George,71
JACK
  Patrick,118
  Samuel,62
JACKSON
  Andrew,8,18,39,43,50,59
    72,93,125,148,151,155
    156
  Ann,137
  Elizabeth,72
  George W.,72
  Henry,72
  Isaac,113
  Jasper,72
  Lewis,72
  Louisa,72
  Lucretia,69
  Madison,72
  Milly,153
  Thomas,72
JACOBS
  Justin,72
  Mary A.,72
JAMES
  Catherine,72
  Daniel W.,72
  Henry W.,72
  Hiram,72
  Lewis,72
  Maria L.,109
  Martha,72
  Phebe,148
JEFFRIES
  John,138
  Sarah,138
JENKINS
  Jesse,73
  Thomas,73
  William,73
JENNINGS
  Benjamin,31
  Jackson,31
  Nancy,31
JESTER
  Joseph,73
JEWELL
  Sarah,21
JOHNSON
  Ben,128
  Benjamin,59,60
  Charles,59
  Emmarinda,146
  Francis,146
  Grief,130
  Isaac,73
  Jonathan,118
  Lucy Ann,118
  Sina,50

William,26
JOHNSTON
  James,73
  Richard,83
  Sarah,73
  William J.,73
JONES
  Gabriel,73
  Hamilton,73
  James,98,151
  John,79
  Marshall,1
  Mary,52,98
  Mary Frances,15
  Nicey,145
  Philip,73
  Ruth,151
JORDAN
  Jeremiah,59
JUDSON
  Ichabod,88
KEENER
  Stacey,74
  Tillman,74
KEITH
  Riley,74
KELL
  James,29
KELLEY
  Mary,87
  Medaline,13
  Moses,13
KELLUM
  Isaac,41
  Jacob,41
KENDRICK
  William,84
KENEDAY
  James,74
  Louisa,74
KENEDY
  Thomas,8
KENNEDY
  Elizabeth,90
  John,150
KENSING
  August,4
KERBY
  James,149
  Luvana,149
  Martha,149
  Reuben,149
KERSEY
  Levi,53
KERSEY/CASEY
  Elizabeth,74
  George,74
  Lucy,74
KEY
  Eliza,19
  Harriet B.,19
  James,19
  Landon,114
  Prudence,114
KILGORE
  James,92
  Melissa F.,92
KIMBALL
  Solomon,74
KIMBLE
  Caleb,131
KINCAID
  Joseph,146
KING
  Betsey,120
  Catherine,74,100
  Emily,12
  Isaac,100
  Isabelle,74
  Sarah,74

William,74
KIRBY
  Christopher,74
  James M.,75
  Joseph,75
KIRK
  Barbary,75
  Henderson,75
  Hugh,146
  Sarah,75
  Thomas,75
  William G.,75
  William Riley,75
KLINE
  Frederick,75
KNIGHT
  Catherine,75
  John,42
  John E.,30
  Robert,156
  Samuel,75
KNOTTS
  Susan,139
KNOX
  Mary,36
  William,136
KUNE
  Mahala,156
LACEY
  Archibald,76
  B.T.,75
  Drury,76
  Fanny,76
  John,76
  Julia,75,76
  Sallie Campbell,75
  Sterling,76
  Susan,76
  Watson,76
  William,75,76
LACK
  Benjamin,76
LAFFERTY
  James R.,76
LAFTWICK
  Jesse,22
LAGRONE
  Martin,48
LAKE
  Samuel,42
LAMBERT
  Matthew,76
LAMPKIN
  Griffin,23
  William,22
LANCASTER
  Nancy L.,51
LANCE
  Sarah,91
LANE
  Lewis,76
  Martin,153
  Samuel,25,68
LANIER
  David,94
LANKESTER
  Anne,51
  Anney,51
  Elizabeth,51
  John,51
  Judith,51
  Martha,51
  Mary,51
  Richard,51
  Robert,51
  Susann,51
  Thomas,51
  William,51
LATIMER
  Charles,76

Jonathan,76
  Mary,76
  Robert,76
  Witheral,76
LATIMORE
  Lucinda,148
LAUDERDALE
  William,46
LAWRENCE
  Asa M.,77
  James,76,77,109
  John W.,77
  Kizziah,76,77
  Lucinda,77
  Margaret,50
  Mary,77
  Nancy Elizabeth,77
  Sarah Jane,77
LAWSON
  Elisha,138
  Lucretia,138
  Randolph,138
  Susan,138
LEA
  Emily,77
  James A.,77
  Minerva,77
LEAKE
  Armstead,77
  Barnet,77
  Eliza,77
  Elizabeth,77
  George,77
  John,77
  Julia,77
  Lemuel,77
  Martha,77
  Mary,77
  Moses,77
  Nancy,77
  Polly,77
  Sarah,77
  Suda,77
  Thomas,77
  Western,77
  Whitfield,77
LEATHERS
  Amanda,95
  Martha,14
  William,95
LEDBETTER
  Sarah,147
LEDYARD
  John B.,59
  Sarah,59
LEE
  Henry,27
  Joseph W.,77
  Mary,137
  Richard,77,108
  Thomas B.,28
LEEPER
  Allice,78
  James,77,78
  Jane,78
  Laura,78
  Lucy,78
  Matthew,78
LEGG
  John M.,78
LEMMONS
  Sarah,78
  William,78
LENTZ
  Benjamin,131
LEONARD
  Clara,78
  John,78
  William,133
LESTER

Nancy,84
LEVERTON
  Alcy,78
  Amanda,78
  Bailey,78
  Elizabeth,78
  George,78
  John,78
  Mary,78
  Sarah,78
  William,78
  Zachary,78
LEVY
  Chapman,20
LEWALLEN
  Daniel,97
  James,97
  John,45,97
  Mary,45,97
  Nancy,138
  Zachariah,138
LEWIS
  Benjamin,77
  Evin,78
  Henry,156
  John L.,116
  Louisa,79,116
  Minnie,79
  Nancy,79
  Rebecca,85
  Richard,21
  Stephen,79
  Thomas,13
  Virgil,153
  William,79
LIGET
  John,79
LILLY
  Elizabeth,66
  Hardy,66
LINDERMAN
  Isaac,79
LINDSEY
  Rufus,80
LINGO
  Alexander,53
  Caroline,53
  Frances,53
  Zachariah,53
LISLE
  Ephriam,96
LISTENBEE
  Benedict,79
  Creicy J.,79
  David,79
  Isiah,79
  James A.,79
  Jane,79
  John,79
  Mary,79
  Robert,79
  William,79
LITTLE
  George,16
  John,16
  Jonas,16
  Joseph,16
  Mary,16
LITTLEFIELD
  Elizabeth,141
  Nathaniel,141
LITTLETON
  Savage,80
LOCK
  Ellen,80
  Fields,80
LOCKE
  Frank,136
  Matthew,63,80
LOGAN

John,153
LONG
  Anna,80
  Franklin,80
  Joseph,62
  William,80
LOPP
  John F.,80
LOUDERBACH
  Mahaley,30
LOUTHER
  Jackson,115
LOVE
  James,116
  James H.,80
  Mary,80
LOVEJOY
  John,61
LOVETT
  Aaron,80
LOW
  Thomas,80
LOWE
  Ann H.,122
LOWERY
  Celia,20
LUCAS
  John,80
  Sarah,80
LUCKETT
  Samuel,80
LUMBLEY
  Mary,81
  Washington,81
  William,81
LUNSFORD
  Kaziah,106
LUTTRELL
  John,116
LYNCH
  Patsy,139
LYON
  Giles,81
LYTLE
  Archibald,47
MABREY
  Sarah,90
  Seaborn W.,90
MACHEN
  John,90
  Leah,90
MADDEN
  John,152
  Mary,108
MADDUX
  Margaret,97
MAGNESS
  John R.,90
  Mary,90
MAGRUDER
  Lloyd,106
MAHAFFEY
  William,90
MALIN
  Mary,2
MALONE
  Moses,90
MANASCO
  Willis,91
MANEES
  James W.,91
MANN
  Isabelle,74
MANNING
  Isam,91
  Samantha,91
MAPLE
  Benjamin,91
  Lucy Ann,91
  Wilson,9,10,31

MAPP
  John,115
MARBURRY
  Sarah,47
MARIAN
  Francis,68
MARSHALL
  James,31,128
  Thomas,39
MARTIN
  Abigail,5
  Carral,91
  Ezekiel,91
  Fanny,92
  Gatey,91
  Hannah,92
  Henry,91
  James,28
  James B.,91
  Jesse,92
  John,91,92
  Joseph,91,92
  Martha,91
  Mary Ann,92
  Michael,92
  Muhulda,65
  Nancy,91,92
  Nathaniel,45
  Owen,91,92
  Polly,92
  Rachel,91
  Rebecca,92
  Sallie,92
  Sarah,91,92
  William,29
MASON
  Samuel,92
  Sarah,92
MASSEY
  Adaline,92
  Christiana,92
  Delilia,92
  Grief J.,92
  Hardin P.,92
  John C.,92
  Julia Ann,92
  Lucinda,92
  Malissa,92
  Maneroy C.,92
  Martha,92
  Mary P.,92
  Salena,92
  Samuel,92
  William,92
MATCHETT
  Joseph,92
MATHENY
  William G.,93
MATHES
  James E.,93
  Mary Ann,93
MATLOCK
  Celia,47
  David,148
  John S.,14
  Mary,14
MATTHEWS
  John,93
  Joseph B.,93
  Mary,93
MAUPIN
  Fleming,93
  John D.,93
  Mary,93
  Thomas,93
MAXEY
  Judith,39
  Nancy,39
  Walter,39
MAXFIELD

Alfred,93
Nancy,93
MAY
Frances,146
Hannah,56
John,28
Leroy,93
Mary,56,93
MAYNARD
Lucy,149
MAYS
Martha Ann,93
Samuel,87
William M.,93
MEADORS
Nancy,93
William J.,93
MEEK
Jacob,46
Samuel S.,46
MEEKS
James,73
MELLON
Lucy,93
Thomas,93
MEMFORD
Serena,77
MENDENHALL
Elizabeth,30
Mary J.,94
William,94
MERCER
Hermon,55
MIDDLETON
Charity,36
MILAM
Amanda,94
Ann,94
Bartley,94
Burris,94
Calvin,94
Cordelia,94
Druciller,94
Edward,94
Elizabeth,94
Frances,94
Henry,94
James B.,94
Jordan,94
Josiah,94
Mary,94
Nancy,94
Rebecca,94
Roda,94
Samuel,94
Sarah,94
Susannah,94
MILBURN
John,103
Sarah,73
MILES
James,24
MILHOLEN
Micha,94
William,94
MILLER
Anderson,109
Charlotte,128
Daniel,94
Ellender,45
Francis,59
Harriett,30
Isaac,94
John,13,47,94
Joseph A.,95
Louisa,95
Mary,94,95
Mary A.,149
Mary Eunice,7
Nicholas,43

Rebecca,95
Virginia,25
William J.,95
MILLINER
David L.,95
MILLS
Eliza J.,153
James,95
Seth,49
MILLWEE
Elizabeth,113
John,113
MILSTEAD
James,95
Sarah,95
MILUM
Dudley,95
MITCHELL
Alfred,95
Amanda,95
David,11,95
George,95
James,95
John,95,103
Margaret,95
Marget,95
Mary,95
Mary Ann,7,95
Nancy,95
Roderick,95
Sarah,95
William,95
Winniford,95
MIZE
Harvie J.,96
MOAD
Alfred,96
MOBLEY
Ann M.,96
Barbery,96
Clement,96
David,96
Elijah,96
Francey,96
Isaiah,96
Jonathan,96
Julia,96
Leanna,96
Margaret,96
Martha,96
Martin,96
Mary,96
Sibella,96
William,96
MOFFIT
Elijah,96
Euphy,96
Euthy,97
Fanny Jane,96
James,96
Mahala,96
Martha S.,96
Robert,96
Thomas,96
MOIER
Dorathy,9
MONK
Menan,97
Sarah,97
MONTAGUE
Daniel,28
MONTGOMERY
Alexander,97
Benjamin,97
Caroline,97
Hamilton,97
James,1
James M.,43
John,79,118
Joseph,129

Lamanda,97
Mary,97
Nancy,97
Penelope,97
Robert,97
Sally,97
Thomas,97
William,122
MOODY
Boran D.,104
Elvira,104
Samuel A.,98
MOONEY
George S.,98
Israel,98
Jane,98
Martha B.,98
MOORE
Allen,98
Darkie,52
James,98
James G.,98
James T.,98
Jane,98
Jane Bell,87
John,17,63,98
Laura,99
Letitia,99
Lucinda,98
Lydia,98
Marget,98
Mary,98,99
Naomi,99
Polly,98
Rebecca,98
Reuben,98
Richard,149
Robert,15,62
Sarah,98
Thompson,98,99
William,98
William C.,99
William E.,99
William H.,10
MOREHEAD
Alexander,114
MORGAN
Benjamin F.,99
Daniel T.,99
James,99
John,66,99
John G.,99
Martha,99
Nancy,99
Rufus,14
Thomas,99
Virginia,99
MORLEY
George,99
Lydia,99
MORPHEW
Silas,99
Sophronia,99
MORRIS
Bradford,100
Joseph W.,99
Lavinia,99
Polly,88
Virginia,99
William,88,99
MORRISON
Elizabeth,151
George S.,100
Jane,122
John,62
John R.,122
Martha,100
Mary,62
Sarah Ann,47
MORROW

210

Asa G.,100
Catherine,100
Francis M.,100
James Asa,100
MORTON
  James,140
  Letitia,87
MOSER
  Emeline S.,100
  Henry,100
MOSS
  Thirza,127
MURPHY
  Anna,100
  Arthur,100
  Bartholomew,100
  Dennis,100
  Elizabeth,100
  John,150
  Susan,100,101
  Thomas,100,101
MURRELL
  Mary,61
  Richard,61
MUSICK
  Lewis,143
MUSSER
  George,82
MYRICK
  Howell,81
  Nancy Ann,101
  William,101
McALLISTER
  Amanda,82
  Andrew,82
  Cassy,81
  Clark,81
  Crawford,81,82
  Eliza,82
  Elizabeth,82
  George,82
  James,82
  John,82
  Joseph,82
  Marinda,82
  Martha,82
  Mary,82
  Polly,81
  Sarah,82
  Sibaline,82
  William C.,81
  Wilson,82
McAVOY
  Mark,82
McBRIDE
  Francis,82
  James D.,111
  Mary G.,59
McBROOM
  John J.,82
McCABE
  Love,82
  Patrick,82
McCAFFRY
  Elizabeth,7
McCALL
  Daniel,82
  Elizabeth,128
  James,128
  John,82
  Thomas,122
McCANN
  Agnes,82
  Catherine,83
  David,82
  Emma,82,83
  Francis,82,83
  Hiram,83
  John,83
  Lucinda,82

Martha,83
Sarah,82,83
Teresa,82
McCARROLL
  Nathaniel,100
  Thomas,49
McCARVER
  Sarah,83
  William,83
McCASLIN
  Amanda,83
  Andrew,83
  John,83
  Nancy,83
  William,83
McCAULEY
  Hannah,21
  Thomas,83
McCAUSLIN/McCASLIN
  Webster,83
McCLELAN
  Jesse C.,83
  Melissa,83
McCLENON
  Sarah,96
McCLINTICK
  Adam,83
McCLUNG
  James,84
  John,83,84
  Nancy,84
McCOMB
  George,62
McCOOL
  Elias,84
McCORKLE
  Elizabeth,2
  Jincy,84
  Joseph,84
  Mary,84
  Stephen,84
  W.H.,84
McCORMICK
  Joseph,84
McCOWAN
  Matthew,93
McCRACKIN
  Frances,88
  Jane,88
  Mary,25
McCRARY
  Jonathan,84
McCREERY
  Decius,84
McCUISTAN
  Mary,129
McCULLOCK
  John,66
McCURRY
  Jane,92
McDANIEL
  Mary,15
McDONALD
  Nancy,53
  Sarah,9
McDOWELL
  Alexander,85
  Edward,85
  Elvira,85
  Ephriam,85
  Harvey,85
  James,85
  John,85
  John L.,84
  Joseph,85
  Mary,85
  Nancy,85
McELROY
  Chapley W.,85
McFARLIN

John,8
McGIMSEY
  Charles,85
McGOHAN
  Caroline,125
  Thomas,125
McGRAW
  James,85
McGREGOR
  George,85
McGREW
  James,85
McGUYRE
  Neeley,85
McINTERF
  Nancy,85
  Thomas,85
McINTOSH
  Sarah,58
  William,30
McKANNEY
  James,89
McKEE
  Andrew M.,85
  Elizabeth,85
McKEEHAN
  Charles C.,85
  Sarah,85
McKENZIE
  Joseph G.,86
McKIMENS
  Amanda,87
  Michael B.,87
McKINNEY
  Archibald,81
McKISICK
  Alexander,87
  Amanda,87
  Daniel,86,87
  David,86
  Eliza Ruth,87
  James,86
  Jane,86
  Jane Bell,87
  Joseph,87
  Letitia,87
  Madeline,87
  Polly Vance,87
  Sarah Louisa,87
  Wilson,87
McKISSICK
  David,106
  James,122
  Joseph,106
  Margaret,122
McKNIGHT
  David,87,88
  Hugh,88
  James,87,88
  Jane,88
  John,88
  Martha,88
  Mary,88
  Minerva,88
  Polly,88
  Thomas,87,88
  William,87,88
McLEAN
  Alexander,88
  Anabella,88
  Elijah,89
  Eliza,88
  Flora,89
  Frances,88
  Giles,89
  Hugh,88
  James,88,89
  John G.,88
  Lauchlin,88,89
  Lavinia,88

Stacey,114
Thomas,114
William,114,115
QUARLES
John,117
QUERTERMANS
David P.,115
QUINTAN
Albany,115
David,115
Eda,115
Eliza,115
Elizabeth,115
Hardin,115
Henry,115
Hester,115
James,115
Jane,115
Joel,115
John,115
Lucinda,115
Lydia,115
Minerva,115
Nancy,115
Nathaniel,115
Rachel,115
Samuel,115
Thomas,115
William,115
RACE
Mary,115
William H.,115
RAFER
Elizabeth,2
RAGAN
Isaac,115
RAGSDALE
Elgathon,94
Elizabeth,94
Hezakiah,115
Nancy,130
RAINEY
John,116
RAMAY
Jonathan,116
RAMSEY
Allinson,116
Isaac,116
John,116
Rachel,116
RANDLEMAN
John,124
RANTON
Keziah,116
William J.,116
RAPER
John L.,116
RATLIFF
Zacheous,116
RAY
Emeline,117
Jacob,116
James,117
Lucy,117
Sarah,18
William,117
REA
Joseph,117
Sarah,117
RECTOR
Frank,71
Laura,71
Nancy,69
REDDING
Elizabeth,73
REDIT
Marina,12
REDWINE
Daniel,117
Nancy,117

REED
David,117
Elizabeth,42
Jacob,19
James,117
Jesse,42
John,17,42,76
John G.,117
Louisa F.,117
Mary,56,117
Polly,42
Samuel,136
Sarah,42
William,42
REEDER
Bluford,117
Micajah,117
Thomas A.,117
REEFE
Polly,13
REESE
Benjamin,117
George W.,118
REEVE
Charles,118
Mary E.,118
REEVES
David,118
Eliza,118
Elizabeth,118
Frances,118
Jeremiah,118
Lucy Ann,118
Samuel,118
REID
John,118
Keziah,118
RENFRO
Carroll,119
Nancy,119
William P.,119
RENFROE
George W.,119
James,119
Jesse,19,119
Mary,119
RENSHAW
George,118
Josiah,45
RENWICK
Leah,90
REYNOLDS
Frances,21
Robert,119
Sarah,57
Thomas,119
RHODES
John G.,119
RHYNE
John,119
RICE
Bashaby,68
RICH
Isaac,37
John W.,37
Joseph,121
William D.F.,37
RICHARDS
Martha,119
Reuben C.,119
William,119
RICHARDSON
Harvey P.,119
Holt,51,73
James,119
Mary,119
Mary Ann,119
R.V.,119
RICHEY
Mary,93

William B.,119
RIDGEWAY
Catherine,120
Horatio G.,120
James C.,120
RIEFF
Americus V.,120
John H.,120
Mary,120
RIGGS
Cyrus,120
Reuben,120
RITCHEY
James,120
Peter,120
RIVERCOMB
George,120
Mary,120
RIZLEY
John,115
ROACH
William,120
ROANE
Elizabeth,120
Ewing H.,120
John Seldon,45,47,96,120
ROARK
John,65
ROBERTS
Andrew J.,121
Christiana,92
Irene,121
James,121
Mary,94
William G.,97
ROBERTSON
Betsey,120
James,116,120,121
Mary,120
Sarah,117
ROBINSON
Abigail,122
Adeline,122
Amanda,95
David,121
George,121
Harriett,122
James,16,121,122
Jane H.,122
John,86,121,122
John R.,121
Lavinia,121
Margaret,122
Mary S.,122
Miles,121
Moses M.,122
Nancy,121
Robert,122
Sarah J.,121
Stokely,121
William,104,121,122
ROBISON
John,121
Legrand,122
Lively,122
William,122
RODGERS
Andrew,147
Sarah,147
ROGERS
Amy,122
Amy S.,123
Enoch,122,123
Green W.,122
James,122
Jane,122
John,122,123
John A.,29
John C.,122
Lovesey,122

215

Martha,6
Nancy,135
Seth,6
Thomas,135
STROCK
Daniel,135
STROTHER
George,48
Mary Ann,48
STUART
James,73
STUBBLEFIELD
Absolom,135
Fanny,135
STURGIS
Minor,128
SULLIVAN
Eugene,136
Isaac,88
Susannah,18
SULLIVANT
James,111
SUMMERS
Calvin,136
Lucinda,136
SUMMERVILLE
Robert,8
SURRITTE
James,136
SUTHERLAND
Daniel,136
SUTTON
Asbury,136
Elizabeth,136
SWEET
John,136
Susan,136
SWEETEN
Samuel,136
SWIFT
Ann,136
Cromwell,136
SWOFFORD
Louisa,74
SYBERG
Arnold,136
SZYFFT
Michael,134
St.JOHN
Arthur,125
Caroline,125
Mary,125
William,125
TAPP
Sarah,136
William,136,137
TARPLY
Joseph,111
TARWATER
Jacob,39
Margaret,39
TATE
Margaret,44
Richard,28
TAYLOR
Francis,49
George,130,143
James H.,137
Mary E.,137
Mary M.,23
Rhoda,130
Samuel,34
William,14,137,142
TEAGUE
Logan,137
TEED
Adelia,70
Anna,70
Arlo,70
Frank,70

Harry,70
Homer,70
Ida,70
Louisa,70
TEMPLE
Frances,137
Mary,137
Roderick,137
William,137
TERRELL
Ann,137
Margaret J.,137
Thomas P.,137
TERRY
Fannie,137
Reuben,137
TETRICK
Abraham,137,138
Ann,137,138
Peter,137
THOMAS
Barnard,138
Francis,138
Hardin,57
Irena,115
John,34,62
Nancy,79
Ruth,66
Sarah,138
William,138
THOMASON
Elisha,138
Elizabeth,138
John J.,138
Martha,138
THOMPSON
A.G.,138
Ann,139
Annie,138
B.M.,138
Blagburn,138
Blagbwin,138
Catherine,139
Harmon,138
James,3,139
James A.,138
Judith,67
Lucretia,138
Martha,138
Milly,138
Nancy,138
Patsy,139
Peter,139
Sarah,138
THORN
Elizabeth,139
Michael,139
Susan,139
Thomas,139
THRASH
Elizabeth,126
THURMAN
Mary,16
THWEATT
Elizabeth,130
Frances,130
Lutitia,130
Thomas,130
TIDWELL
Elenor,2
Peter,2
Polly,2
TIGER
Redbird,138
TILLMAN
John,139
Susan,139
TIMS
Elizabeth,139
John,139

TIPTON
Jonathan,16
Reuben,126
TISDALE
George,130
TOLIVER
Ann,113
John H.,113
TOLLETT
Eliza,139,140
Henry,139,140
TOMBLESTON
Mary,140
William,140
TOMPSON
Nancy,13
TONEY
William,140
TOOLEY
Anderson,140
TOWN
John,75
TRAMMEL
George,140
Mary,140
TRAMMELL
Eli,113
TRAWICK
Lucinda,89
Peter,89
TRIGG
David E.,118
TRIMBLE
Amanda,140
John,53,140
TRITT
Clark,140
Sarah,140
TROLINGER
William,140
TSCHIEMER
Harriett,140
Jacob,140
TUBBS
John,140
TUCKER
Abigail,140
Jonas,140
Mary,140
Mary A.,115
TUGGLE
Eliza,141
Washington,141
TUNNELL
James,138
TURNER
Amanda,35
Arabel,141
Henry,150
John M.,141
John T.,141
Osburn,112
Sorena,10
William,141
TYGER
Ann,139
UMSTATTD
Archibald,141
UNDERWOOD
Eldridge,141
William,74
VADEN
George,141
VAN ZANT
James,142
Martin,142
VANCE
David,141
Enoch,92
James,85

Alexander,81,148
Sybalina,148
WHITBY
  Charles G.,25
  Cynthia,25
  George,25
WHITE
  Aden,78
  Alice,3
  Isaac,45
  James,89
  Jane,60
  Martha,154
  Nellie,68
  Robert,60
  Sally,97
  William,127
WHITELEY
  Isaac,149
  Lucy,149
  Luvana,149
  Samuel,149
WHITELY
  Nancy,18,27
WHITESIDE
  William,24
WHITMORE
  Homer,141
WHITTEN
  Levi C.,149
  Sarah,149
WHITTHORNE
  Margaret,149
  Samuel,149
WHITTINGTON
  Isaac,149
WHYTE
  James E.,149
WILBANKS
  John,149
WILBORN
  Francis,149
  Sarah,149
WILCOX
  Nathan,149
  Samantha,149
WILES
  Elizabeth,149
  George,149
  Jake,149
  Mary A.,149
WILEY
  Robert,133
WILKINS
  Berryman,150
  Elizabeth,150
WILLIAMS
  Amanda,150
  Ann Tucker,51
  Catherine,150
  Charlotte,20,129
  Eliza,151
  Frances,21
  Harley,150
  Henry,21
  Jacob,150
  James,150
  James C.,150
  James F.,150
  James H.,150
  James M.,150
  Jeremy,117
  John,89
  John W.,150
  Jonathan,31
  Joseph,5,74
  Margaret,150
  Martha,151
  Milton,124,151
  Nancy,151

Nancy Mariah,61
Nicie,7
Parilee,151
Phalby,150
Philip,151
Pleasant,151
Robert,51
Ruth,151
Samuel,151
Sarah,3,150
Stafford,61
Thomas,151
William,151
William A.,151
WILLIAMSON
  John,151
  Melissa,97
  Thomas,8,50,62
WILLIS
  Abel,18
  Edward,151
  Elizabeth,151
WILLSON
  John,48
WILMOTH
  Mary,151
  William,151
WILSON
  Alfred M.,65
  Allen,26
  Amanda,14
  Castila,151
  George,151
  Hugh A.,151
  Lewis,152
  Madeline,87
  Mary,152
  Samuel,152
WINGFIELD
  Charles,152
  Matilda,152
WINLAND
  John,152
WINN
  John,96,147
WINNINGHAM
  Andrew,152
WINSELL
  Adam,85
WINSTON
  George,98
WINTERS
  Barbary,132
  Elizabeth,16
  George,34
  William,42
WITCHER
  Jack,3
WITHROW
  James T.,10
WITT
  Charlotte,152
  David,152
WITTY
  Catherine,62
  William,62
WOLF
  Elizabeth,152
  Enoch O.,152
  George,39
WOLFF
  Cornelia,152
  Oscar P.,152
WOOD
  Allen,10,104
  Amanda,90
  Eliza,90
  Enoch,152
  Francis,19
  George,152

Oma,152
Squire,57
Thomas,152
William,57,152
WOODALL
  Mary J.,138
WOODRUFF
  Alden,153
  Alden W.,152
  Chester,153
  Eliza J.,153
  Eveline,153
  Frances,153
  Geogena,153
  Hannah,153
  Homer,153
  Lizzie,153
  Mary,153
  William,152,153
WOODS
  Albert,153
  Benjamin,153
  Calvin,153
  Charlot,153
  China,153
  Delila,153
  Elizabeth,153
  Faney,153
  George,154
  Isam,153
  James,154
  Jane,153
  Mary,153
  Miley,153
  Milly,153
  Nancy,44,153
  Obadiah,153,154
  Sarah,153
  Silvester,153
  Tiresa,153
  Wiley,153
  William,115,153,154
WOODSIDE
  Nancy,43
WOODSON
  Anthony,19
WOODY
  Eliza,154
  James,154
  John,154
  Nancy,154
  Reuben,154
  Sarah,154
WOOTEN
  Ann,154
  John,154
WORD
  James,45
WORTHEN
  John,39,154
  Julia,154
WREN
  Elizabeth,154
  James,154
  Mary Ann,154
  Shadrack,154
WRIGHT
  Annie,154
  Clark,154
  Frances,13,155
  Hannah J.,64
  Jack,3
  James,155
  James C.,155
  Jane,154
  John G.,155
  John I.,155
  Joseph,13
  Julia,155
  Martha,154

www.ingramcontent.com/pod-product-compliance
Lightning Source LLC
Chambersburg PA
CBHW021901020426
42334CB00013B/434